A Voice Without End

Journal of Theological Interpretation Supplements

DARREN SARISKY
Australian Catholic University
Editor-in-Chief

1. Thomas Holsinger-Friesen, *Irenaeus and Genesis: A Study of Competition in Early Christian Hermeneutics*
2. Douglas S. Earl, *Reading Joshua as Christian Scripture*
3. Joshua N. Moon, *Jeremiah's New Covenant: An Augustinian Reading*
4. Csilla Saysell, *"According to the Law": Reading Ezra 9–10 as Christian Scripture*
5. Joshua Marshall Strahan, *The Limits of a Text: Luke 23:34a as a Case Study in Theological Interpretation*
6. Seth B. Tarrer, *Reading with the Faithful: Interpretation of True and False Prophecy in the Book of Jeremiah from Ancient Times to Modern*
7. Zoltán S. Schwáb, *Toward an Interpretation of the Book of Proverbs: Selfishness and Secularity Reconsidered*
8. Steven Joe Koskie, Jr., *Reading the Way to Heaven: A Wesleyan Theological Hermeneutic of Scripture*
9. Hubert James Keener, *A Canonical Exegesis of the Eighth Psalm: Y̱ʜᴡʜ's Maintenance of the Created Order through Divine Intervention*
10. Vincent K. H. Ooi, Scripture and Its Readers: Readings of Israel's Story in Nehemiah 9, Ezekiel 20, and Acts 7
11. Andrea D. Saner, *"Too Much to Grasp": Exodus 3:13–15 and the Reality of God*
12. Jonathan Douglas Hicks, *Trinity, Economy, and Scripture: Recovering Didymus the Blind*
13. Dru Johnson, *Knowledge by Ritual: A Biblical Prolegomenon to Sacramental Theology*
14. Ryan S. Peterson, *The* Imago Dei *as Human Identity: A Theological Interpretation*
15. Ron Haydon, *"Seventy Sevens Are Decreed": A Canonical Approach to Daniel 9:24–27*
16. Kit Barker, *Imprecation as Divine Discourse: Speech Act Theory, Dual Authorship, and Theological Interpretation*
17. Douglas S. Earl, *Reading Old Testament Narrative as Christian Scripture*
18. Matthew T. Bell, *Ruled Reading and Biblical Criticism*
19. Nathan J. Chambers, *Reconsidering Creation Ex Nihilo in Genesis 1*
20. Andrew C. Witt, *A Voice Without End: The Role of David in Psalms 3–14*

A Voice Without End

The Role of David in Psalms 3–14

Andrew C. Witt

EISENBRAUNS | University Park, Pennsylvania

Library of Congress Cataloging-in-Publication Data

Names: Witt, Andrew C., author.

Title: A voice without end : the role of David in Psalms 3–14 / Andrew C. Witt.

Description: University Park, Pennsylvania : Eisenbrauns, [2021] I Includes biblio-graphical references and indexes.

Summary: "Examines the construction of the speaking voice in Psalms 3–14. Demon-strates how the Psalter introduces the figure of David as the primary voice, one speak-ing ideally and representatively in both literal and figural dimensions"—Provided by publisher.

Identifiers: LCCN 2020058289 I ISBN 9781646021116 (paperback)

Subjects: LCSH: Bible. Psalms, III–XIV—Criticism, interpretation, etc. I David, King of Israel.

Classification: LCC BS1430.52 .W58 2021 I DDC 223/.206—dc23

LC record available at https://lccn.loc.gov/2020058289

Eisenbrauns is an imprint of The Pennsylvania State University Press.
The Pennsylvania State University Press is a member of the Association of University Presses. The paper used in this publication meets the minimum requirements of the American National Standard for Information Sciences—Permanence of Paper for Printed Library Materials, ANSI Z39.48-1984.

To Christopher Seitz

~

In memory of Prof. John H. Sailhamer

"Blessed are those who take refuge in him" (Ps 2:12)

Contents

Acknowledgments...viii

Abbreviations.. x

Chapter 1: The Figure of David and a Canonical Approach to Psalms 3–14.......... 1

Chapter 2: The Speaking Persona(e) in the History of Interpretation............... 29

Chapter 3: The Shaping of the Figure of David in the Psalms............................ 79

Chapter 4: The Figure of David in Psalms 3–6 122

Chapter 5: The Figure of David in Psalms 7-14 164

Chapter 6: Conclusions and Implications.. 203

Bibliography... 212

Ancient Sources Index.. 226

Subject Index 235

Acknowledgments

My study of the Old Testament began in a debate with my seminary roommates about an Old Testament Theology class taught by Prof. John H. Sailhamer. A major turning point in my biblical education came when I read his article, "The Messiah and the Hebrew Bible" (*JETS* 44 [2001]: 5–23). Indeed, I often refer to one of its footnotes as "the footnote that changed my life." It reads:

> To say the Pentateuch is about the Messiah is not yet to say it is about Jesus. Those are two separate and equally important questions. We must first ask whether the Pentateuch is about the Messiah and then ask whether Jesus is the Messiah. The Pentateuch (and the rest of the Hebrew Bible) tells us there will be a Messiah. The NT tells us that Jesus is the Messiah spoken of in the Hebrew Bible. It does so by identifying Jesus as the one about whom the Hebrew Bible speaks.

This simple but profound observation about the relationship between the two-testament witness of Scripture to Jesus the Messiah set me on an enduring path of Old Testament study. It is with great fondness that I dedicate this book *in memoriam* to Prof. Sailhamer.

A second—but equally important—person of acknowledgement is my doctoral supervisor, Prof. Christopher R. Seitz. He has modeled for me the high calling of scholarship for the church, and I am thankful for his pastoral sensitivities and patience, giving needed words of encouragement, advice, and direction at the right time. His consistent appeal to consider how the words of Scripture address not only later generations of God's people, but how they have aided them in their own context, will continue to prod me deeper into the providential mysteries of God's two-testament witness. This book is a revised edition of the thesis I completed under his guiding wisdom.

A warm thank you to the editorial team at PSU Press, especially Jen Singletary, for bringing this project to completion. I would be remiss to not mention Jim Eisenbraun, for being willing to take on this project, and my reviewers with *JTI*, who helped immeasurably in the transformation of this book from its original dissertation form.

Special thanks are due to the faculty, staff, and students at Wycliffe College (Toronto), who, though too numerous to name, provided a spiritually rich and academically rigorous study environment. I particularly want to thank the members of my dissertation committee: Professors Glen Taylor, Marion Taylor, Brian Irwin, and Harry Nasuti (of Fordham University). Dr. Nasuti, in particular, for taking on the extra work of plodding through the pages to come, and for his generous words of commendation and criticism. Glen and Marion, your friendship and encouragement over the past years are an important part of what has made Wycliffe a special place for me; thank you. I also want to thank Dr. Rachel Lott for her time in editing my dissertation; Anthony Fredette for help in translating an obscure Latin text; and Dr. Mark Boda, who responded to a paper related to my thesis and provided valuable criticism at an important stage in the writing process. Another round of thanks and acknowledgement are due to my good friend, Dr. Charles Meeks, for his careful read through and edit of this book. I will appear far less foolish because of his helping hand (all remaining errors, of course, are my responsibility).

הודו ליהוה כי־טוב כי לעולם חסדו

Abbreviations

AB	Anchor Bible
AcBib	Academia Biblica
ACW	Ancient Christian Writers
AIL	Ancient Israel and Its Literature
AJSL	*American Journal of Semitic Languages and Literatures*
AnBib	Analecta Biblica
AsTJ	*Asbury Theological Journal*
BCOT	Baker Commentary on the Old Testament
BDB	Brown, Francis, S. R. Driver, and Charles A. Briggs, *The Brown-Driver-Briggs Hebrew and English Lexicon*. Boston: Houghton and Mifflin, 1906.
BETL	Bibliotheca Ephemeridum Theologicarum Lovaniensium
Bib	*Biblica*
BibInt	*Biblical Interpretation*
BibRep	*The Biblical Repository*
BRLJ	The Brill Reference Library of Judaism
BSNA	Biblical Scholarship in North America
BTB	*Biblical Theology Bulletin*
CBQ	*Catholic Biblical Quarterly*
CCSL	Corpus Christianorum: Series Latina
CSCO	Corpus Scriptorum Christianorum Orientalium
CTC	Christian Theology in Context
CWE	Collected Works of Erasmus
CWS	Classics of Western Spirituality
DCH	Clines, David J. A., ed. *Dictionary of Classical Hebrew*. 9 vols. Sheffield: Sheffield Phoenix, 1993–2016.
ET	*Expository Times*
FAT	Forschungen zum Alten Testament
FC	Fathers of the Church
FOTL	Forms of Old Testament Literature
FRLANT	Forschungen zur Religion und Literatur des Alten und Neuen Testaments

GCS	Griechischen christlichen Schriftsteller
GOTR	*Greek Orthodox Theological Review*
HALOT	Hebrew and Aramaic Lexicon of the Old Testament
HBM	Hebrew Bible Monographs
HBT	*Horizons in Biblical Theology*
HerdBS	Herders Biblische Studien
Hermeneia	Hermeneia: A Critical and Historical Commentary on the Bible
HSS	Harvard Semitic Studies
HTR	*Harvard Theological Review*
IBC	Interpretation: Bible Commentary for Teaching and Preaching
ICC	International Critical Commentary
IJST	*International Journal of Systematic Theology*
Int	*Interpretation*
JBL	*Journal of Biblical Literature*
JBMW	*Journal of Biblical Manhood and Womanhood*
JESOT	*Journal of the Evangelical Study of the Old Testament*
JETS	*Journal of the Evangelical Theological Society*
JHS	*Journal of Hebrew Scriptures*
JQR	*Jewish Quarterly Review*
JR	*Journal of Religion*
JSBLE	*Journal of the Society of Biblical Literature and Exegesis*
JSOT	*Journal for the Study of the Old Testament*
JSOTSup	Journal for the Study of the Old Testament Supplement Series
JSS	*Journal of Semitic Studies*
JTI	*Journal of Theological Interpretation*
LHBOTS	Library of Hebrew Bible/Old Testament Studies
LW	Luther's Works
NCBC	New Cambridge Bible Commentary
NEB	Neue Echter Bibel
NechtB	Die Neue Echter Bibel Kommentar sum Alten Testament
NICOT	New International Commentary on the Old Testament
NIVAC	New International Version Application Commentary
NPNF¹	*Nicene & Post-Nicene Fathers*, Series 1
NPNF²	*Nicene & Post-Nicene Fathers*, Series 2
OBO	Orbis Biblicus et Orientalis
ÖBS	Österreichische biblische Studien
OCA	Orientalia Christiana Analecta
OCP	*Orientalia Christiana Periodica*
OECT	Oxford Early Christian Texts
OTE	*Old Testament Essays*
OTL	Old Testament Library
OTS	Old Testament Studies/Oudtestamentische Studiën
PAAJR	*Proceedings of the American Academy of Jewish Research*
PG	Patrologia Graeca
PL	Patrologia Latina

PPS	Popular Patristic Series
ProEccl	*Pro Ecclesia*
PTR	*Princeton Theological Review*
PTS	Patristiche Texte und Studien
RSLR	Rivista di storia e letteratura religiosa
SBLDS	Society of Biblical Literature Dissertation Series
SC	Sources Chretienne
SCJ	*The Sixteenth Century Journal*
SECT	Sources of Early Christian Thought
SFC	Selections from the Fathers of the Church
SJOT	*Scottish Journal of Theology*
SNVAO	Skrifter utgitt av Det Norske Videnskaps-Akademi i Oslo
SST	Studies in Spirituality and Theology
ST	Studia Theologica
StBL	Studies in Biblical Literature
STNJT	*Studia Theologica: Nordic Journal of Theology*
STR	*Southeastern Theological Review*
STT	Studia Traditionis Theologiae
TB	*Tyndale Bulletin*
TGUOS	*Transactions of the Glasgow University Oriental Society*
TOTC	Tyndale Old Testament Commentaries
TWOT	Theological Wordbook of the Old Testament
VC	*Vigiliae Christianae*
VT	*Vetus Testamentum*
VTSup	Supplements of Vetus Testamentum
WBC	Word Biblical Commentary
WGRW	Writings of the Greco-Roman World
WSA	Works of Saint Augustine: A Translation for the 21st Century
WW	*Word & World*
YJS	Yale Judaica Series
ZAW	*Zeitschrift für die alttestamentliche Wissenschaft*
ZNW	*Zeitschrift fur die neutestamentliche Wissenschaft*

1
The Figure of David and a Canonical Approach to Psalms 3–14

To assert that the figure of David plays an important role in the book of Psalms may sound like common sense to some, but ridiculous to others. On the one hand, David is the subject of several psalms and is named in the superscription of nearly one-half of them. On the other hand, modern historical study of the Psalter has all but left David behind. Approaching the book using higher critical and both form criticism and cult-functional criticism, scholars have discounted the historical connection between the psalms and David, rendering the role of David in the superscriptions obsolete. The past thirty-five years, however, have seen the rise of a "canonical approach" that seeks to understand the purpose and meaning of a psalm within its context in the final form of the book. Here, the role or function of the figure of David again has become a significant subtopic within contemporary psalm studies.

In the struggle to understand the figure of David, scholars have shown an interest primarily in how David functions in the larger theological program of the book. According to one influential model, David functions differently depending on which sections are being read. In Books 1–3 (Pss 1–89), which are usually construed as historical commentary on the failure of the Davidic covenant, David functions as a historical and sapiential figure: his sufferings and deliverance are interpreted as an example of the faithfulness of YHWH for his promises to David, understood in terms of the monarchy in the pre-exilic period. With the failure of the Davidic monarchy at the end of Book 3 (Ps 89), in Books 4–5 (Pss 90–150) David changes roles, now understood as a bygone righteous figure, one worthy of imitation as Israel sings, reads, studies, and meditates on the Psalms. Here, David is no longer the "David of history," but a literary figure who exhorts Israel towards a faith in YHWH alone as king. Related to this latter role, the use of expanded biographical (or historical) superscriptions attached to thirteen psalms is taken as a hermeneutical clue to allow readers a better understanding of the inner mind of the David found in the books of Samuel. They create a complementary portrait of David, so that when read together with 1–2

1

Samuel, the reader better appreciates the spirituality and motives undergirding David's actions.

In this book, I am asking whether contemporary psalm scholarship has properly grasped how the figure of David is utilized within the book of Psalms. My argument will address several related concerns, including the question of "speaking voice" (or "literary persona") and canonical context. Through an analysis of literary voice in the history of interpretation, the introductory role of Pss 1–2, and the hermeneutical value of the superscriptions, I will use Pss 3–14 to trace the relationship between literary voice and the development of the figure of David in the Psalter. I will argue that the figure of David functions multivalently in Pss 3–14, suggesting that to pigeonhole the literary voice of David into only a "historical" or "sapiential" voice is to misunderstand his role in Pss 3–14 specifically, and Book 1 (Pss 3–41) more generally.

As my analysis will show, beginning even with Book 1, the Davidic figure should be understood as exploring the faith of Israel concerning the failure of the Davidic line of kings in Judah and an ongoing hope in Yhwh for the establishment of a just kingdom in the context of the Davidic promises. Book 1, then, is not an anthology meant to uphold and show Yhwh's *past* faithfulness to the Davidic promises and king, but was carefully-constructed to address and explore those concerns expressed in the theological heart of the book (Book 4, Pss 90–106), including Yhwh's faithfulness to his covenant promises, the ongoing role and function of the Davidic dynasty, and the relationship between the successes and failures of the Davidic line with the laments and praises of ancient Israel. Moreover, within the context of Pss 1–2, the figure of David developed in Pss 3–14 not only functions as a bygone righteous figure to be imitated by faithful readers, but also takes on additional figural roles directly related to these concerns. As such, I will show that one cannot properly interpret the larger theological program of the book without also understanding how the figure of David has been utilized in Pss 3–14. These psalms have been purposefully placed at the beginning of the Psalter to provide a kind of "pressure" on the reader, the Psalter's first exploration of the themes and concerns introduced in Pss 1–2.[1]

1.1. The Rise of the Canonical Approach

The study of the Psalms has changed dramatically over the course of the past two centuries.[2] Generally speaking, there have been three main periods, the first

---

[1] The term "pressure" is one used by C. Kavin Rowe and Christopher R. Seitz, linked with Brevard Childs's language of the "coercion" of the biblical text. See C. Kavin Rowe, "Biblical Pressure and Trinitarian Hermeneutics," *ProEccl* 11 (2002): 295–312; Christopher R. Seitz, *The Character of Christian Scripture: The Significance of a Two-Testament Bible* (Grand Rapids: Baker Academic, 2011), 67–69.

[2] Consistent use of terminology related to psalms is difficult to attain. I have made every attempt to render references to the entire book as either "book of Psalms," "Psalms," or "Psalter," and to "psalms" and "psalm" in lowercase when making generic

marked by higher or literary criticism (nineteenth- and early-twentieth centuries), the second marked by form criticism and cult-functional criticism (early to mid-twentieth century), and the third marked by a broadly-construed canonical and/or final-form approach (late-twentieth and early-twenty-first centuries). In the nineteenth century, one of the first waves of higher criticism reached the Psalter through the 1811 commentary of W. M. L. de Wette.[3] De Wette's work marked a tectonic shift in the study of the Psalms. While he was by no means the first to question traditional views, he was among the first to expressly use an array of historical tools to put forward a coherent, convincing argument away from the traditionalism which still marked his predecessors.

By the mid-to-late nineteenth century, most of the psalms had been relegated to the late postexilic period and the editorship of the Psalter was consigned to the Maccabean period. The psalm superscriptions, losing their historical worth, at best were valuable in showing the ways a psalm might have been used. They were viewed as created by the editors of the book and were not even attached to the "original" form of a psalm.[4] This did not mean that a focus on the historical situation was given up, simply that the superscriptions were not any help in getting there. Indeed, at this time a psalm was considered to be a literary work of art, with interpretive focus falling on the author's historical situation (i.e., the events and environment which the psalm itself references) and inner feelings (i.e., one's psychological and religious beliefs within a particular social setting).[5] While there continued to be some pushback in various corners, the higher-critical understanding of the Psalter gained sway throughout Europe, England, and the United States.[6]

By the end of the nineteenth century, convictions were changing, with a new "religio-historical school" (*religionsgeschichtliche Schule*) calling for the reevaluation of history, culture, and religion.[7] Within this milieu, a ground-

---

references. I will also be rendering the divine name with small capitalized letters, Yʜwʜ. When quoting other works, I have left their own use of these terms unedited.

[3] W. M. L. de Wette, *Commentar über die Psalmen* (Heidelberg: Mohr & Zimmer, 1811).

[4] C. A. Briggs and E. G. Briggs, *A Critical and Exegetical Commentary on the Book of Psalms*, ICC (Edinburgh: T&T Clark, 1906), 1:lvii, describes this process well. The commentary of Diodore expresses a similar view, so it is not entirely new to the modern age. See Diodore of Tarsus, *Commentary on Psalms 1–51*, trans. Robert C. Hill, WGRW 9 (Atlanta: SBL, 2005).

[5] Erhard S. Gerstenberger, "Psalms," in *Old Testament Form Criticism*, ed. John H. Hays (San Antonio, TX: Trinity University Press, 1974), 180.

[6] See the so-called "reactionary" commentators of this period, who continued in the spirit of traditional interpretation, such as: E. W. Hengstenberg, *Commentar über die Psalmen* (Berlin: Ludwig Oehmigke, 1849–52) [ET: *Commentary on the Psalms* (Edinburgh: T&T Clark, 1846–48)]; J. A. Alexander, *The Psalms* (Edinburgh: Andrew Elliot & James Thin, 1864); Albert Barnes, *Book of Psalms* (New York: Harper & Brothers, 1868); and C. H. Spurgeon, *The Treasury of David* (London: Marshall Brothers, 1870).

[7] Gerstenberger, "Psalms," 180–81.

breaking approach to the Psalms was formulated by the German scholar Hermann Gunkel.[8] For him, a psalm could only be rightly understood through the examination of its "genre" (*Gattung*), alongside a recognition of a psalm's "setting in life" (*Sitz im Leben*), the situations in which a psalm would have been used. In this regard, a psalm's genre was understood within a more general ancient Near Eastern study of the "history of types" (*Gattungsgeschichte*).

Gunkel argued that there were four major *Gattungen* corresponding to celebrations and events in life,[9] and although each *Gattung* had its origin in the cult, the vast majority of psalms in the Psalter, being individual songs, no longer belonged in that environment, but were more expressive of a personal and private piety than their original settings.[10] Through his influence, the classification of psalms into different genres has stood the test of time, even if some scholars have nuanced them a bit differently over the course of the past century.[11] There has, however, been considerable opposition to Gunkel's understanding of *Sitz im Leben*.

The first major argument against Gunkel came from Sigmund Mowinckel, whose approach faithfully relied on the foundational elements of Gunkel's form criticism, but went in significant new directions concerning their original setting.[12] Whereas Gunkel maintained that most psalms were composed by individuals no longer formally involved in the cult, Mowinckel argued that the psalms were cultic in both origin and intention, composed by members of the temple personnel.[13] In relocating them to the pre-exilic period, Mowinckel also proposed a new *Sitz im Leben* for many psalms: an annual autumn New Year festival.[14] Situating this festival within the early monarchy, he argued that it celebrated the enthronement of YHWH as the universal king, whereby YHWH made all things new, liturgically enacting both his triumph over primeval chaos

---

[8] Hermann Gunkel, *Die Religion in Geschichte und Gegenwart* (Tübingen: J. C. B. Mohr, 1930) [ET: *The Psalms: A Form-Critical Introduction*, trans. Thomas M. Horner (Philadelphia: Fortress, 1967)]; Hermann Gunkel and Joachim Bergich, *Einleitung in die Psalmen: die Gattungen der religiösen Lyrik Israels* (Göttingen: Vandenhoeck & Ruprecht, 1933) [ET: *An Introduction to the Psalms*, trans. James Nogalski (Macon, GA: Mercer University Press, 1998)].

[9] Gunkel, *Introduction to the Psalms*, 19.

[10] Ronald E. Clements, *One Hundred Years of Old Testament Interpretation* (Philadelphia: Westminster, 1976), 81.

[11] The most notable has been Claus Westermann, *Praise and Lament in the Psalms*, trans. Keith R. Crim and Richard N. Soulen (Atlanta: John Knox, 1981).

[12] Sigmund Mowinckel, *Psalmenstudien I–IV*, SNVAO (Kristiania: Jacob Dybwa, 1921–24) [ET: *Psalm Studies*, trans. Mark E. Biddle, 2 vols., SBLHBS 2–3 (Atlanta: SBL, 2014)]; Mowinckel, *Offersang og sangoffer* (Oslo: H. Aschehoug & Co., 1951) [ET: *The Psalms in Israel's Worship: Two Volumes in One*, trans. D. R. Ap-Thomas (Grand Rapids: Eerdmans, 2004)].

[13] A. R. Johnson, "The Psalms," in *The Old Testament and Modern Study: A Generation of Discovery and Research*, ed. H. H. Rowley (Oxford: Clarendon, 1951), 190, 205.

[14] Mowinckel, *Psalms in Israel's Worship*, 1:106–92.

and the work of creation.[15] In the ritual drama, YHWH is shown to reign over those kings and rulers allied with chaos, vindicating the faith of Israel by renewing his covenant with them and with the house of David. Given the scarcity of evidence for this festival within Scripture, much room was created in scholarship for developing Mowinckel's conclusions in several different directions.[16]

Surveying the literature which sprang up in the wake of Gunkel and Mowinckel, there is little doubt that great progress has been made in understanding the relationship between the forms of Israel's poetry and the cultic life of the pre-exilic community in which these songs and poems found their original setting. As Gerstenberger has observed, "All the evidence gathered until now... points to the fact that cultic performances of some kind have been background and fertile soil for most of the OT psalms."[17] One of the main characteristics of these approaches has been to read psalms independently of one another, with little to no attention given for the collection as a whole or its arrangement.[18] While Claus Westermann did some initial work in this area, the turn towards the canonical shaping of the book by its final editors is usually attributed to Brevard Childs.[19]

As Childs had noted, by the late 1960s the methods of form-criticism and cult-functional criticism had begun to produce diminishing returns.[20] Exegetical understanding of the text was resting on an increasingly fragile and hypothetical base, and he sought the secondary setting of the book of Psalms itself as more significant for exegesis. In his view, individual psalms had been loosed from their original cultic context and subsumed (or, subordinated) into a new "canonical" context with a new theological function for the future generations of worshiping Israelites. In this new setting, as part of a canon of sacred Scripture, psalms began to function normatively within the various parts of the early Jewish community.[21] Childs thought that one of the keys to

---

[15] Mowinckel, *Psalms in Israel's Worship*, 1:136–39.

[16] See Artur Weiser, *The Psalms: A Commentary*, OTL (Philadelphia: Westminster, 1962); H.-J. Kraus, *Die Königsherrschaft Gottes im Alten Testament*, BZHT 13 (Tübingen: J. C. B. Mohr, 1951). Perhaps the most developed view of the Autumn Festival is represented by the work of the so-called "Myth and Ritual School." See Johnson, "The Psalms"; John H. Eaton, *Kingship and the Psalms*, 2nd ed (Sheffield: JSOT Press, 1986); Steven J. L. Croft, *The Identity of the Individual in the Psalms*, JSOTSup 44 (Sheffield: Sheffield Academic, 1987).

[17] Gerstenberger, "Psalms," 197.

[18] Gordon Wenham, "Towards a Canonical Reading of the Psalms," in *Canon and Biblical Interpretation*, ed. Craig G. Bartholomew, et al. (Grand Rapids: Zondervan, 2006), 334.

[19] See Westermann, *Praise and Lament*; Brevard S. Childs, *Introduction to the Old Testament as Scripture* (Philadelphia: Fortress, 1979).

[20] See Brevard S. Childs, "Reflections on the Modern Study of the Psalms," in *Magnalia Dei, the Mighty Acts of God: Essays on the Bible and Archaeology in Memory of G. Ernest Wright*, ed. Frank Moore Cross, Werner E. Lemke, and Patrick D. Miller, Jr. (Garden City, NY: Doubleday, 1976), 378.

[21] Childs, "Modern Study," 382.

determining this function lay in how the editor(s) of the Psalter collected psalms and organized them into the final form of the book. This included both the shape of the book—its fivefold division, doxologies marking those divisions, the psalms which introduce and conclude the book, and the strategic placement of royal psalms—and the redactions made on individual psalms, resulting in an eschatological orientation given to psalms of mixed forms, corporate reference, and the addition of biographical titles to several Davidic psalms.

In observing these editorial markers, Childs concluded that the development of the Psalter was a long and complex process, one that was not simply the result of liturgical influence.[22] Beyond being a fresh articulation of praise to God through the medium of older forms, the traditional prayers of Israel now assumed a new role, and were made immediately accessible to every faithful generation of suffering and persecuted Israel, testifying to all the common troubles and joys of human life.[23] Without a need for cultic actualization psalms could be used in a variety of new situations without losing their meaning.[24] Most importantly, the Psalms no longer address God alone, but are the medium through which God speaks to his people.[25]

This new understanding of the purpose and function of psalms within the life of the people of God was quite a turn from previous scholarship. The first sign that the study of psalms had taken a new direction was the success of a monograph by Childs's student, Gerald H. Wilson.[26] Wilson touched on a number of concepts and themes which would themselves become foundational for contemporary studies of the Psalter. In the first part of his monograph, he argued that the book of Psalms was a purposefully organized collection, using a comparative study of the Psalter with other ancient song collections. In the second half, he sought to show what editorial purpose lay behind the Psalter in its final form, paying close attention to how royal and wisdom motifs were developed along the so-called "seams" of the book.

In his further work, Wilson countered Childs's claim that the Psalter was edited towards a more eschatological orientation. This was achieved, in part, by his understanding of the introduction to the book. For him, the Psalter can be divided into two interlocking frameworks: a royal frame (Pss 2–89) which has been enclosed by a sapiential frame (Pss 1, 90–150). There is a notable difference in orientation between these two frames, and thus, between Pss 1–2. Books 1–3 (Pss 2–89) are historical in nature, using royal psalms to affirm and uphold YHWH's commitment to the Davidic promises (Pss 2, 72, 89). The experience of the exile, however, raised important questions concerning the future of the

---

[22] Childs, *Old Testament as Scripture*, 512.

[23] Childs, *Old Testament as Scripture*, 521.

[24] Childs, "Modern Study," 584; Childs, *Old Testament as Scripture*, 515.

[25] Childs, *Old Testament as Scripture*, 513. He wrote: "The prayers of Israel directed to God have themselves become identified with God's word to his people."

[26] Gerald H. Wilson, *The Editing of the Hebrew Psalter*, SBLDS 76 (Chico, CA: Scholars, 1985).

Davidic dynasty, and the ancient Israelite community sought a more fundamental foothold for hope. The answers, argued Wilson, can be found in Books 4–5. Here, one finds a strong call to repentance and an exhortation towards faith in YHWH alone as the true king of Israel. Israel is urged back to its more fundamental and simple Mosaic faith, with the figure of David emerging in Book 5 as an exemplary (literary) figure of repentance and faith for the postexilic community. Hope for a future under a reigning Davidide fades into the background—and may even disappear altogether—while a call for repentance enters the foreground. With repentance, YHWH will bring Israel back from exile, restore their fortunes, and rebuild Zion (cf. Ps 102). Psalm 1, as introduction to the whole book, aligns well with the focus of Books 4–5, urging meditation on the Torah of Moses (1:2).

In the thirty years since his initial monograph, dozens of important contributions have been made within this new approach of "reading the Psalms as a book."[27] Perhaps a great indication of the value of the canonical approach to the study of the Psalter is the growing number of commentaries which take seriously a psalm's setting in the book as a clue to its meaning.[28]

---

[27] See J. Clinton McCann, Jr., ed., *The Shape and Shaping of the Psalter*, JSOTSup 159 (Sheffield: JSOT Press, 1993); Peter W. Flint and Patrick D. Miller, eds., *The Book of Psalms: Composition & Reception*, VTSup 99 (Leiden: Brill, 2005); David Firth and Philip S. Johnston, eds., *Interpreting the Psalms: Issues and Approaches* (Downers Grove: InterVarsity, 2005); Erich Zenger, ed., *The Composition of the Book of Psalms*, BETL 238 (Leuven: Peeters, 2010); William P. Brown, ed., *The Oxford Handbook of the Psalms* (Oxford: Oxford University Press, 2014); Nancy L. deClaissé-Walford, ed., *The Shape and Shaping of the Book of Psalms: The Current State of Scholarship*, AIL 20 (Atlanta: SBL, 2014). Beyond edited volumes, note the following summaries of recent research: David Howard, "Recent Trends in Psalms Study," in *The Face of Old Testament Studies: A Survey of Contemporary Approaches*, ed. David W. Baker and Bill T. Arnold (Grand Rapids: Baker, 1999), 329–68; Patrick D. Miller, "Current Issues in Psalms Studies," *WW* 5 (1985): 132–43; James Nogalski, "From Psalm to Psalms to Psalter," in *An Introduction to Wisdom Literature and the Psalms: Festschrift for Marvin E. Tate*, ed. Harold Wayne Ballard and W. Dennis Tucker (Macon, GA: Mercer University Press, 2000), 37–54.

[28] See especially Frank-Lothar Hossfeld and Erich Zenger, *Die Psalmen, Vol. 1: Psalmen 1–50*, NechtB (Würzburg: Echter Verlag, 1993); Hossfeld and Zenger, *Psalms 2: A Commentary on Psalms 51–100*, trans. Linda M. Maloney, Hermeneia (Minneapolis: Fortress, 2005); Hossfeld and Zenger, *Psalms 3: A Commentary on Psalms 101–150*, trans. Linda M. Maloney, Hermeneia (Minneapolis: Fortress, 2011); James L. Mays, *Psalms*, IBC (Louisville: Westminster John Knox, 1994); J. Clinton McCann, Jr., "The Book of Psalms: Introduction, Commentary, and Reflections," in *New Interpreter's Bible: A Commentary in Twelve Volumes*, vol. 4 (Nashville: Abingdon, 1996), 641–1280; Gerald H. Wilson, *Psalms: Volume 1*, NIVAC (Grand Rapids: Zondervan, 2002); Samuel Terrien, *The Psalms: Strophic Structure and Theological Commentary* (Grand Rapids: Eerdmans, 2003); Geoffrey Grogan, *Psalms*, Two Horizons (Grand Rapids: Eerdmans, 2008); Howard N. Wallace, *Psalms* (Sheffield: Sheffield Phoenix, 2009); and Walter Brueggemann and William H. Bellinger, Jr., *Psalms*, NCBC (New York: Cambridge University Press, 2014).

1.2. Psalms 3–14 and the Figure of David

Given the above description of the state of psalm scholarship, it may appear that Pss 3–14 are an odd place to begin one's investigation of the role of the figure of David within the Psalter. Considering psalm studies more generally, the leading reason for choosing to work with this group of psalms is its significant placement at the beginning of Book 1. Its positioning within the shape of the Psalter intensifies its hermeneutical significance and pressure on the reader. In psalm scholarship, it is well-acknowledged that Pss 1–2 are introductory, setting the agenda for the book and introducing the reader to its larger theological concerns. As will be discussed below, while scholars have had some difficulty dividing Book 1 into smaller groupings of psalms, there is a strong majority who consider Pss 15–24 as forming a distinct grouping of psalms. This, at the very least, sets Pss 3–14 off at the beginning of Book 1.

Given this position, one might have expected that research on Pss 3–14 (or some grouping of psalms that resembles it) had been undertaken to explore the development of the themes and topics within this context. It is surprising, then, that so few studies on these psalms have actually carried this hermeneutical insight through.[29] One peruses the available resources to find that, having dealt with Pss 1–3, an author will usually skip to Ps 41, perhaps touching on one or two additional psalms along the way; such studies speak in generalizations and are not much help in showing development from psalm to psalm, or even from one cluster of psalms to another.[30] This is not to say that the contributions have thus far been unhelpful—far from it. But one of the shortcomings has been that, in articulating a larger editorial purpose for the book of Psalms, they have

---

[29] Joseph P. Brennan, "Psalms 1–8: Hidden Harmonies," *BTB* 10 (1980): 25–29; Friedhelm Hartenstein, "'Schaffe Mir Recht, JHWH!' (Psalm 7, 9): Zum Theologischen und Anthropologischen Profil der Teilkomposition Psalm 3–14," in Zenger, *The Composition of the Book of Psalms*, ed. Erich Zenger, BETL 238 (Leuven: Peeters, 2010), 229–58; Patrick D. Miller, "The Beginning of the Psalter," in *The Shape and Shaping of the Psalter*, ed. J. Clinton McCann, JSOTSup 159 (Sheffield: JSOT Press, 1993), 83–92; Miller, "The Ruler in Zion and the Hope of the Poor: Psalms 9–10 in the Context of the Psalter," in *David and Zion: Biblical Studies in Honor of J. J. M. Roberts*, ed. Bernard F. Batto and Kathryn L. Roberts (Winona Lake: Eisenbrauns, 2004), 187–97; Rolf Rendtorff, "The Psalms of David: David in the Psalms," in *The Book of Psalms: Composition & Reception*, ed. Peter W. Flint and Patrick D. Miller, VTSup 99 (Leiden: Brill, 2005), 53–64; Howard N. Wallace, "King and Community: Joining with David in Prayer," in *Psalms and Prayers*, ed. Bob Becking and Eric Peels, OTS 55 (Leiden: Brill, 2007), 267–77.

[30] See W. Dennis Tucker, Jr., "Beyond Lament: Instruction and Theology in Book 1 of the Psalter," *Proceedings EGL & MWBS* 15 (1995): 121–32; J. Clinton McCann, Jr., "The Shape of Book I of the Psalter and the Shape of Human Happiness," in *The Book of Psalms* (ed. Flint and Miller), 340–48; William H. Bellinger, Jr., "Reading from the Beginning (again): The Shape of Book I of the Psalter," in *Diachronic and Synchronic: Reading the Psalms in Real Time*, ed. Joel S. Burnett, W. H. Bellinger, Jr., and W. Dennis Tucker, Jr., LHBOTS 488 (London: T&T Clark, 2007), 114–26.

largely ignored how the concerns of Pss 1–2 have been initially developed in Pss 3–14. It is time for Pss 3–14 to receive a proper treatment, one which may perhaps reorient (or at the very least *inform*) the discussion which has already taken place.

Another significant reason for choosing these psalms is the lack of consensus concerning the function or role the figure of David plays within the book of Psalms. Two views are influential, but no one has yet been able to show how they relate to one another, or even if they can be held together. The first view, following Gerald Wilson (cf. my brief review above), considers Books 1–2 as historically-oriented and concerned with promoting the faithfulness of Yнwн towards the reigning Davidic king and the Davidic promises. For him, Book 3 raises theological questions regarding Yнwн's commitment to David given the ultimate failure of the Davidic dynasty, with Books 4–5 exhorting Israel towards faith in Yнwн as the universal king. In this scheme, the figure of David is understood as an historical figure in Books 1–2, and becomes an exemplary (bygone) figure of repentance and faith in Book 5.[31] A second view, building off the work of Childs, constructs the figure of David not through the shaping of the book *per se*, but in how several Davidic psalms were given expanded biographical titles pointing to various episodes in his life as recounted in 1–2 Samuel (and perhaps Chronicles).[32] In these studies, the expanded titles help to unite the narratives of David with the Psalms, giving the reader a privileged glimpse into the mind of David.

While there is something to be said for both of these views, each needs to be reworked to provide a more lasting contribution to psalm studies. Wilson argued that the voice of David in Book 1 is a past voice, a voice that can only speak concerning the unique relationship David enjoyed with Yнwн. This is due to his understanding of the introductory psalms, since for him they set up the Davidic voice within a particular historical setting in relationship to the ascension of David and the time of the united monarchy. Thus, the voice of David

---

[31] Wilson, *Editing*, 220–28.

[32] A number of contributions can be noted here: Brevard S. Childs, "Psalm Titles and Midrashic Exegesis," *JSS* 16 (1971): 138–51; Elieser Slomovic, "Toward an Understanding of the Formation of Historical Titles in the Book of Psalms," *ZAW* 91 (1979): 350–80; Alan M. Cooper, "The Life and Times of King David according to the Book of Psalms," in *The Poet and the Historian: Essays in Literary and Historical Biblical Criticism*, ed. Richard Elliot Friedman, HSS 26 (Chico, CA: Scholars, 1983), 117–31; James L. Mays, "The David of the Psalms," *Int* 40 (1986): 143–55; Jean-Marie Auwers, "Le David des Psaumes et les Psaumes de David," in *Figures de David: À Travers la Bible*, ed. Louis Desrousseaux and Jacques Vermeylen (Paris: Cerf, 1999), 187–224; Susanne Gillmayr-Bucher, "The Psalm Headings: A Canonical Relecture of the Psalms," in *The Biblical Canons*, ed. Jean-Marie Auwers and H. J. de Jonge (Leuven: Leuven University Press, 2003), 247–54; Rendtorff, "The Psalms of David: David in the Psalms"; Vivian L. Johnson, *David in Distress: His Portrait through the Historical Psalms*, LHBOTS 505 (London: T&T Clark, 2009).

is unique and historical.[33] In this book, however, I will argue that the voice of David has not been relegated to the past, but, through the introductory setting (Pss 1–2) and the use of biographical headings, speaks with a present and future voice. That is, in Pss 3–14 we meet a "voice without end" who speaks to the present and future of God's people.[34]

Concerning Childs's view of David, it is significant that the expanded psalm titles are not believed to inform one's reading of the Psalms, but one's reading of "David" within a united, complementary portrait of the figure of David in 1–2 Samuel. In doing this, scholars have failed to appreciate how the intertextuality of the psalm titles hermeneutically shapes one's reading of psalms themselves in the context of the Psalter. In my view, the hermeneutical move must be flipped, with 1–2 Samuel being used to shape the Psalms via the superscriptions, and not *vice-versa*.[35] By turning the formula around, I will show that the figure of David in the book of Psalms is not appropriated to give us a glimpse into the mind of David but in order to set up the Psalter's own "David," which has a significant impact on the theological movement of the book.[36]

1.3. A Canonical Approach to Psalms 3–14

As I noted above, the canonical approach to the Psalms proposes that "the ordering and placement of the psalms is not entirely random, but that the Book of Psalms has been shaped by the work of editors in order to emphasize the importance of certain theological themes."[37] The implications of this shift for interpreting individual psalms are significant. As Wenham explained: "If the psalms have been arranged thematically, by title, and by keywords to form a

---

[33] In his commentary, Wilson never draws out these earlier observations and is satisfied with a more generic psalmic voice in his interpretation of Books 1–3. See Wilson, *Psalms*.

[34] See Brevard S. Childs, "Analysis of a Canonical Formula: 'It Shall be Recorded for a Future Generation,'" in *Die Hebräische Bible und ihre zweifache Nachgeschichte: Festschrift für Rolf Rendtorff zum 65. Geburtstag*, ed. E. Blum, C. Macholz, and E. W. Stegeman (Neukirchen-Vluyn: Neukirchener Verlag, 1990), 357–64.

[35] For the larger discussion, see Christopher R. Seitz, "Psalm 34: Redaction, Inner-biblical Exegesis and the Longer Psalm Superscriptions—'Mistake' Making and Theological Significance," in *The Bible as Christian Scripture: The Work of Brevard S. Childs*, ed. Christopher R. Seitz and Kent Harold Richards, BSNA 25 (Atlanta: SBL, 2013), 279–98.

[36] I was delighted to find the publication of Stefan M. Attard, *The Implications of Davidic Repentance: A Synchronic Analysis of Book 2 of the Psalter (Psalms 42–72)*, AnBib 212 (Rome: Gregorian & Biblical, 2016). In this work, Attard reads Book 2 in much the same way as I have advocated reading Pss 3–14 (pp. 25–28). He writes, "Our working hypothesis is that the resulting ambiguity suggests that these Davidic psalms are not merely meant to fill out lacunae in Samuel and Kings, but are rather meant to create a body of literature in its own right that possesses its own logic, namely the Book of Psalms" (27).

[37] Jamie A. Grant, *The King as Exemplar: The Function of Deuteronomy's Kingship Law in the Shaping of the Book of Psalms*, AcBib 17 (Atlanta: SBL, 2004), 13.

deliberate sequence, it is imperative to read one psalm in the context of the whole collection and in particular in relationship to its near neighbors."[38] As such, this new literary context has subordinated the original *Sitz im Leben* of the psalms in the cult under its canonical situation as part of Israel's scriptural traditions. Here,

> the net effect of the canonical reading of the Psalms is that each composition is now read within a literary context.... The Psalms are no longer to be read as the song book of Israel, they are instead to be read as a book like any other book of the Bible.... This means that each poem is influenced by the context within which it is found—either simply by its juxtaposition alongside a neighbouring psalm or neighbouring psalms, or by its inclusion in a collection such as the Song of Ascents, or by its placement and positioning within one of the five books of the Psalter.[39]

In a 1993 essay, Gerald Wilson articulated succinctly the four methodological components of a canonical approach to the book of Psalms.[40] For him, "Any progress in understanding the purposeful arrangement of the psalms in the Psalter must begin...with a detailed and careful analysis of the linguistic, literary and thematic linkages that can be discerned among the psalms." First, then, one must attempt "the recognition of clear indications of psalms groupings where discernible." Second, one must make a "detailed and systematic investigation of linguistic and thematic connections between psalms within these groupings and their subgroups." Third, and only after finishing the above steps, one can begin a "judicious speculation...regarding the purpose or effects of the arrangement of the whole Psalter." And fourth, with less certainty, one can "make suggestions as to the appropriate social/historical matrix that may illuminate the theological function and purpose revealed by the editorial arrangement." These methodological concerns will be utilized in my analysis of Pss 3–14.

1.3.1. *Psalms 3–14 as a Distinct Group*
Wilson's initial call is for the recognition of clear indications that Pss 3–14 are in fact a distinct group of psalms in the Psalter, with a subsequent investigation into the shaping of this group of psalms to discern any smaller sub-groupings or psalm clusters. Beginning at the macro-level, biblical commentators stretching back to antiquity have observed that the book of Psalms has been divided into

---

[38] Wenham, "Towards a Canonical Reading of the Psalms," 347. See Hossfeld and Zenger, *Psalms 51–100*, 7. They write, "Each psalm is a text in itself with an individual profile, and at the same time it is open to the context in which it stands within the book of Psalms, which gives it an additional dimension of meaning."

[39] Jamie A. Grant, "Determining the Indeterminate: Issues in Interpreting the Psalms," *Southeastern Theological Review* 1 (2010): 11–12.

[40] Gerald Wilson, "Understanding the Purposeful Arrangement of Psalms in the Psalter: Pitfalls and Promise," in McCann, *Shape and Shaping*, 50–51.

five separate sections, usually referred to as "books."[41] The marks of division occur in doxological formulae found at the end of four psalms: Pss 41:14; 72:18–19; 89:53; and 106:48. In virtually all modern introductions and commentaries, this fivefold shape of the book of Psalms is given account. Modern accounts usually consider Pss 1–2 and 146–150 as introduction and conclusion, respectively, dividing them off from Books 1 and 5.[42] Using this framework, a common way to divide the book of Psalms is as follows: Introduction (Pss 1–2), Book 1 (3–41), Book 2 (42–72), Book 3 (73–89), Book 4 (90–106), Book 5 (107–145), and Conclusion (146–150).

Within this fivefold shape smaller groupings of psalms can be observed, usually based on genre considerations and/or elements within the psalm headings. For instance, in Book 5 there are a several groupings of psalms based on associations with David (Pss 108–110; 138–145), ancient liturgical practices (113–118), and the Songs of the Ascents (120–134). Book 1, however, has been notoriously difficult to divide into smaller groups of psalms. This is largely because these principal factors of division offer meagre guidance. Nearly every psalm in Book 1 has been associated with David, leaving little to no room based on this criterion, and of the thirty-nine psalms in Book 1, twenty-three are typically classified as laments (Pss 3–7, 9/10, 12–14, 17, 22, 25–28, 31, 35, 36, 38–41), and do not seem to offer any satisfactory division into smaller groups. Without such guides, scholars have been forced to consider other clues concerning its shape.

As a starting point, many consider Pss 15–24 to be a grouping of psalms, based on their chiastic structure: 15 and 24 are paired up as psalms of a temple entrance liturgy, 16 and 23 as psalms of confidence (trust), 17 and 22 as psalms of lament, 18 and 20–21 as royal (kingship) psalms, and 19 receiving the focus of the chiasm as a hymn about the benefits of Torah.[43] In fact, Hossfeld and Zenger aver the chiastic pattern observed for Pss 15–24 provides a template for understanding the structure of Book 1 as a whole.[44] For them, Book 1 divides into

---

[41] See William G. Braude, *The Midrash on Psalms*, YJS 13 (New Haven: Yale University Press, 1959), 1.5 (on Ps 1:2); Eusebius of Caesarea, "Hypothesis on the Psalms" (PG 23.66); Gregory of Nyssa, *Treatise on the Inscriptions of the Psalms*, trans. Ronald E. Heine (Oxford: Clarendon Press, 1995).

[42] See Hossfeld and Zenger, *Psalms 101-150*, 1–7, 605–7; Brueggemann and Bellinger, *Psalms*, 2.

[43] Pierre Auffret, *La sagesse a bati sa maison: Etudes structures litteraires dans l'Ancien Testament et specialement dans les Psaumes*, OBO 49 (Gottingen: Vandenhoeck & Ruprecht, 1982), 407–38; Patrick D. Miller, "Kingship, Torah Obedience, and Prayer: The Theology of Psalms 15–24," in *Neue Wege der Psalmenforschung: Festschrift für W. Beyerlin zum 65. Geburtstag*, ed. K. Seybold and E. Zenger, HerdBS 1 (Freiburg: Herder, 1994), 127–42; Jamie Grant, *King as Exemplar*, 235–36; Matthias Millard, *Die Komposition des Psalters*, FAT 9 (Tübingen: Mohr, 1994), 24–25.

[44] Hossfeld and Zenger, *Die Psalmen 1-50*, 12–14. The same divisions are also used in Gianni Barbiero, *Das erste Psalmenbuch als Einheit: Eine synchrone Analyse von Psalm 1-41*, OBS 16 (Berlin: Peter Lang, 1999).

four sub-groupings: Pss 3–14; 15–24; 25–34; and 35–41. In each grouping, the "corner psalms" (*Eckpsalmen*) are correlated, with a third psalm marked out as the thematic center. These marked psalms in turn project the form and content of the psalms which surround them. For instance, Pss 3 and 14 are identified as *Eckpsalmen*, each asking Y_HWH for help and blessing for God's people Israel from the God of Zion.[45] Psalm 8, then, is marked out as the thematic center of the group, a hymn within a grouping of lament psalms.[46] Not all, however, are convinced by Hossfeld and Zenger's concept of *Eckpsalmen* and "center" psalms.

Jamie Grant, for example, has argued that in order for their divisions to hold any weight, they must be able to identify elements of disjuncture and conjuncture to show that one group of psalms can and should be distinguished from another group of psalms.[47] The concept of *Eckpsalmen* at best offers proof of disjunction, marking off the group from other groups. In order to give definitive proof of division, elements of conjunction within a group must also be observed. This, Grant argues, can *only* be detected within Pss 15–24.[48] From his analysis, a tentative structure within Book 1 would yield three sections, not four: Pss 3–14; 15–24; and 25–41.[49] These two theories on the structure of Book 1 illustrate both the complexity of the issue as well some of the major concerns regarding conjuncture and disjuncture.

Turning to Pss 3–14, the methodological need is to establish points of conjunctive editorial activity and elements of disjuncture which may indicate further sub-divisions into smaller psalm clusters. Scholars have currently only taken seriously two theories about the shape of Pss 3–14, those of Hossfeld/Zenger and Matthias Millard. After reviewing them, I will offer an alternative third theory, which will serve as the foundational building block of my later analysis.

1.3.1.1. Hossfeld and Zenger on the shape of Pss 3–14. According to Hossfeld and Zenger, Pss 3–14 is an independent grouping of psalms which has been marked out by two corner psalms (Pss 3 and 14) and a thematic center (Ps 8). For them, the entire unit has been thematically oriented towards the poor and the suffering of the righteous by "outside threats."[50] Nevertheless, hope remains, as seen in the closing prayers of Pss 3 and 14, which petition for Y_HWH's help and God's blessing upon his people (3:9; 14:7).[51] Similarly, in Ps 8, despite the threat of persecution, human "honor" is indestructible for it is a participation in divine honor, the mightiness of Y_HWH himself.[52]

---

[45] Hossfeld and Zenger, *Die Psalmen 1–50*, 56.
[46] Hossfeld and Zenger, *Die Psalmen 1–50*, 12.
[47] Grant, *King as Exemplar*, 234–40.
[48] Grant, *King as Exemplar*, 238.
[49] Grant, *King as Exemplar*, 239.
[50] Hossfeld and Zenger, *Die Psalmen 1–50*, 13–14.
[51] Hossfeld and Zenger, *Die Psalmen 1–50*, 14, 56.
[52] Hossfeld and Zenger, *Die Psalmen 1–50*, 12, 14.

For them, to truly understand the inner relationships between the psalms in the group one must also understand something about the diachronic processes which brought them together. They explain that Pss 3–14—as well as Book 1 as a whole—is the result of a four-stage "growth process" (*Wachstumsprozesses*) spanning the late pre-exilic to Hellenistic periods.[53] The first stage comes in the composition of independent prayers of request, lament, and thanksgiving, written within the late pre-exilic period. This would have included Pss 3, 4, 5, 6, 7, 11, 12, 13, and 14, and perhaps an early version of Ps 8. In the late exilic or early post-exilic period, a second stage consisted of the compilation of these psalms into small groups, incorporating with them additional late pre-exilic or exilic psalms, expansions within individual psalms, and psalms written by the redactors themselves.

The first small grouping of psalms, Pss 3–7, forms a series of laments of someone being pursued. As an outside bracket, Pss 3 and 7 provide a paradigm for the situation of distress (*Notsituationen*), with the petitioner praying as a (politically-)pursued worshipper using regal language. Inside this bracket, Ps 4 illustrates the invocation of a poor person, Ps 5 one who is in need of justice (*Rechtsnot*), and Ps 6 that of a sick person. These specific kinds of afflictions are meant to be paradigmatic for various aspects of a sorrowful or painful human existence. The second small grouping, Pss 11–14, has been brought together in order to focus on a "theology of the poor." As a group, these psalms are arranged as a process of prayer which one undertakes to practice "the certainty that YHWH is the patron-God [*Schutzgott*] of the poor."[54] Psalms 11 and 14 form a frame, using the image of YHWH as the king who brings justice amidst a chaotic world (11:7; 14:1–3; cf. 12:13). Within this frame, Ps 12 is a lament depicting the heavenly judge as a patron God of the poor, while Ps 13 is placed after Ps 12 in a purposeful response to its promises: that YHWH would "now arise" (12:6) is answered with a fourfold question of "how long?" In this literary position, it can be read as a lament of one who is poor and oppressed, who desires to be included amongst the poor named in Ps 12.

Within this same late exilic redaction, Ps 8 was included between these two groups of psalms as its center, spreading throughout the entire grouping a theology of human dignity. As part of the redaction process, verse three was added to better fit the psalm into its place, picking up on themes of YHWH as heavenly king found in both Pss 7 and 11. This edition of Pss 3–14* articulated an awareness of the poor and persecuted with an acute perception of their

---

[53] Hossfeld and Zenger, *Die Psalmen 1–50*, 14. The following discussion has relied principally on their introduction to the commentary (pp. 14–16), as well from comments in the preface to each psalm (pp. 56, 59, 64, 68, 72, 77, 82–83, 89, 93, 96, and 100). It should be noted that their treatment of the diachronic growth of Pss 3–14 is related on a larger scale to the growth of the entirety of Book 1. For our concerns, I have only summarized that material relevant to Pss 3–14.

[54] Hossfeld and Zenger, *Die Psalmen 1–50*, 100.

distresses, which have been named according to their causes (e.g., persecution, poverty, slander, false accusation, the brutality of the rich, etc.).

The third stage took place in the post-exilic period, likely in the fifth or fourth century BCE. The focus of this expansion is not Pss 3–14 but other groupings in Book 1, altering our understanding of Pss 3–14 by emphasizing the "piety of the poor" (*Armenfrömmigkeit*), who are no longer understood simply as a social entity, but now have their own religious category. By changing the perception of the "poor" in the Psalms, this edition of Book 1 attempts to use the poor as representative of the "true Israel." Just like the poor, Israel itself is treated with hostility, and by identifying with the poor is able to lay claim to YHWH's close relationship to the righteous ("the poor"), knowing that God's authority and rule will prevail.

A fourth (and final) stage of redaction occurs during the Hellenistic period, which again broadens the notion of the "poor" (and its synonyms) to include all Israel in its threats from within and without. It is at this time that Pss 9–10 (as a single psalm) are included within Pss 3–14, transforming the group into its present shape. Though Ps 9/10 had already been written prior to its inclusion, its editors had adapted the original "to a new historical situation and opens up the entire Davidic Psalter as prayers of the poor and of the poor people Israel."[55] In its final redaction, Book 1—including Pss 3–14—attempts to define the whole of Israel as the "poor," threatened from both internal and external enemies.

The most striking element of this proposal for understanding Pss 3–14 is its sheer comprehensiveness. Hossfeld and Zenger's attempt to understand the dynamics of how these texts function in view of their redactional growth is both laudable and exceptional. Even so, it is remarkable that they have not concluded their analysis with an attempt to describe the text synchronically as it now stands. Their comments, as such, are incomplete.[56] In my view, this is not due to their redactional model, but their understanding of the final form (or lack thereof). In their view, Ps 9/10 was added alongside the previous center of the group (Ps 8) and establishes lexical and thematic connections with psalms on

---

[55] Hossfeld and Zenger, *Die Psalmen 1–50*, 83.

[56] On this point, even though Hossfeld and Zenger identified themselves with an approach akin to that of Childs, they fail to do final form analysis of Pss 3–14. See Childs, "Analysis of a Canonical Formula," 363–64. The emphasis of a canonical approach is not simply to track with the developmental growth of a certain collection of texts, but also to see how this "reconstructed depth dimension" actualizes the tradition for its own ends. A canonical approach accounts for diachronic development, but only as this better helps to inform the text in its received shape. While Hossfeld and Zenger expertly trace the development of various themes throughout the different stages of the text—and even note how Pss 9/10 attempts to redefine the identification of the "poor" from previous stages of redaction—they fail to account for how all of these elements work together in the received text. To see how a synchronic reading might apply to the redactional-critical work of Hossfeld and Zenger for Pss 3–14, see Barbiero, *Das erste Psalmenbuch als Einheit*, and Hartenstein, "Zum Theologischen und Anthropologischen Profil."

both sides of its placement. But there is no discussion of how the inclusion of the psalm might have affected the overall balance of the grouping which, in my assessment, has been thrown off. While Pss 3–7 may have formed a sub-unit in its original grouping, the clear binding together of Pss 7–9 (cf. 7:18; 8:2, 10; 9:2–3) shows that Ps 7 has been reassigned a different role in the structure of the group. Instead of forming part of the frame surrounding Pss 4–6, it now functions as the beginning psalm in a new grouping of psalms (Pss 7–14). This new function is at least partially marked by the biographical elements in the superscriptions of Pss 3 and 7.

1.3.1.2. Matthias Millard on the shape of Pss 3–14.   A second important theory on the structure of Book 1 has been put forward by German scholar Matthias Millard.[57] In his view, the book of Psalms is made up of a series of "compositional arcs" (*Kompositionsbögen*). Against Hossfeld and Zenger, Millard argued that Book 1 is composed of three major *Kompositionsbögen* (Pss 1–10; 11–31; and 32–41), divided by psalms without superscriptions.[58] While he does not speak much about Pss 11–14 in his monograph, he devoted an entire section to Pss 1–10. For him, Pss 1–10 fit into the category of "post-cultic sapiential liturgy of thanksgiving" (*weisheitlichnachkultischen Dankliturgie*).[59] Like Hossfeld and Zenger, he argued that the first major sub-grouping of psalms in this section is the lament cluster of Pss 3–7. Before this group, Pss 1–2 form an introduction (*Einleitung/Anfang*) to the entire book (not just Pss 1–10), and have been given a sapiential shape (cf. 2:12). Following the group is a hymn (*Lob/Hymnus*, Ps 8), a song of thanksgiving (*Dank*, Ps 9), and a concluding lament (*Klageschluß*) which also evidences a sapiential setting (Ps 10).[60]

Unlike Hossfeld and Zenger, Millard took the biographical superscriptions seriously as clues to the interpretation of psalms, as a "midrash of the Davidic history."[61] In his view, the principal role of biographical titles in Pss 1–10 is to set up David as one who prays (*Beter*), introducing direct speech to God within the episode of Absalom's rebellion (2 Sam 15–18). Concerning structure, Millard argued that Pss 3–7 form a chiastic pattern: Pss 3 and 7 have Midrashic superscriptions, Pss 4 and 6 share the element בנגינות, with Ps 5 as the center point.[62] Supporting this structure, he noted that Pss 3–6 contain a morning/evening motif, which highlights the critical nature of David's extra night in the desert:

> The motif of laying himself down and getting up in Ps 3–6 is,
> therefore, a central component of the interpretation of the context

---

[57] Millard, *Die Kompositions des Psalters*. See also the helpful exchange between Millard, Rendtorff, and Hossfeld and Zenger in *BibInt* 4 (1996).

[58] Millard, *Die Kompositions des Psalters*, 127.

[59] Millard, *Die Kompositions des Psalters*, 127.

[60] Millard, *Die Kompositions des Psalters*, 127. See his charts on pp. 163 and 168.

[61] Millard, *Die Kompositions des Psalters*, 131.

[62] Millard, *Die Kompositions des Psalters*, 131.

of Ps 3ff. as midrash to the history of Absalom. Accordingly, this motif is lacking in Ps 7, where the victory of David is already referred to in the superscription. From this interpretation of Ps 3ff., David prays in this night, which is crucial for his victory.[63]

There is, then, a kind of story being told through the biographical superscriptions, working from David's flight in Ps 3 through the death of Absalom in Ps 7. In Millard's view, the "Midrashic" superscriptions bookend a *Kompositionsbögen* which opens up the Psalter with a particular textual context.

Perhaps indicative of the problems with his theory, however, Millard observed that Ps 8 is "unwieldy" (*sperriger*), since it is "a hymn of the individual and has relatively little connection with the context."[64] While it does share some thematic links with Pss 3-7 in terms of the enemy, its reflection is not on an adult son, but children. It does not, then, fit very well into Millard's thesis that Pss 1-10 are concerned primarily with the story of Absalom's rebellion. The story continues into Ps 9, which he interpreted as a thanksgiving that the psalmist's enemies have retreated and were killed (vv. 4, 7), with the superscription again offering a midrash of Absalom.[65] The compositional arc closes with Ps 10, which is read as separate from Ps 9. In it, Millard observed a sapiential bookend with Pss 1-2, and a close relationship to Ps 2 since both psalms lack a superscription and begin, as a rarity in the Psalter, with the interrogative (למה).

In assessing Millard's view, I find his connections between psalms insightful, especially his argument that the superscriptions of Pss 3 and 7 carry a weight that moves beyond the individual psalm, setting a context for the whole *Kompositionsbögen*. His theory suffers, however, in its attempt to overlay modern notions of genre on an ancient collection whose editors simply did not work with our categories. His overarching theory that Pss 3-9 correspond chronologically with the Absalom narrative (2 Sam 15-18) also leads him into trouble with Ps 8, which has difficulty fitting into his scheme. Moreover, he never addresses how Pss 11-14 fit into his chiastic understanding of Pss 11-31. In my view, he has neglected some important lexical and thematic links between Ps 10 and Pss 11-14, of which I will speak in a later chapter.[66]

---

[63] Millard, *Die Kompositions des Psalters*, 131-32.

[64] Millard, *Die Kompositions des Psalters*, 132.

[65] Millard, *Die Kompositions des Psalters*, 133. He reads the superscription, "*wegen des Sterbens, in Bezug auf den Sohn, ein Psalm Davids.*"

[66] I would offer a similar criticism of the redactional model in Kevin G. Smith and William R. Domeris, "The Arrangement of Psalm 3-8," *OTE* 23 (2010): 367-77. They argue that Pss 3 and 7 may have been juxtaposed at one time, after which Pss 4-6 were inserted, and Ps 8 even later as a conclusion. While I appreciate a number of points they make in the article, particularly concerning the verbal links between psalms, they fail to take into account verbal links which extend into Pss 11-14, while also admitting that Ps 7 is the "odd one out" (369) in their understanding of the superscriptions. Their justification of the placement of Ps 7 within Pss 3-10 (interrupting a sequence of מזמור psalms) and Pss

1.3.1.3. Two psalm clusters: Pss 3-6 and 7-14.   In view of the problematic areas in both previous accounts of the structure of Pss 3–14, I argue for an alternative theory which is built on the editorial value of the superscriptions. This theory is closely related to that of Hossfeld and Zenger but shifts the placement of Ps 7. Rather than closing an initial group as a "corner psalm" (Pss 3–7), I argue that it begins a second psalm cluster (Pss 7–14). This would create two psalm clusters within Pss 3–14, with no center psalm: Pss 3–6 and Pss 7–14. These two sub-groupings account for elements of continuity within a given set of psalms and discontinuity with previous and subsequent groups of psalms, following Grant's earlier criterion. As with other portions of the Psalter, the best place to look for shaping begins in the editorial superscriptions. Using the headings of Pss 1–17, we can make several observations about the shape of Pss 3–14 (cf. chart on next page).

In terms of discontinuity, our first observation is that Pss 1–2 have been set apart from Pss 3–14 by their lack of a superscription. Second, on the other side of the group, there are clear markers of disjuncture between Pss 3–14 and 15–17. Even though we continue to find a Davidic association in Pss 15–17 (לדוד), Ps 15 breaks patterns found in Pss 3–14. In Pss 3–14, every psalm besides 3 and 7 begins with למנצח, and only 7, 11, and 14 lack מזמור.[67] While Ps 15 is a מזמור לדוד, Pss 16 and 17 are designated מכתם לדוד and תפלה לדוד, respectively.   The introduction of these alternate types indicates some kind of break, which is further marked by the absence of למנצח in Pss 15–17.[68] On top of this, one must also note the widely-held chiastic structure which holds Pss 15–24 in a tight unity.[69]

In terms of continuity, we can first observe that nearly every psalm begins with למנצח. On its own, this might not appear to be significant,[70] but the only two places it is absent in Pss 3–14 are where we find biographical superscriptions related to the life of David.[71] Psalms 3 and 7, then, are marked within the larger

---

4–14 (interrupting a sequence of למנצח psalms) as due to redaction history is not suffi-cient (371–72).

[67] Several Hebrew manuscripts and the LXX include מזמור for Pss 11 and 14 (cf. BHS).

[68] See Gerald H. Wilson, "Evidence of Editorial Divisions in the Hebrew Psalter," *VT* 34 (1984): 337–52, esp. 340–44.

[69] See Philip Sumpter, "The Coherence of Psalms 15–24," *Bib* 94 (2013): 186–209; Sumpter, *The Substance of Psalm 24: An Attempt to Read Scripture after Brevard S. Childs*, LHBOTS 600 (London: Bloomsbury T&T Clark, 2015), 185–202; Carissa M. Quinn Richards, *The King and the Kingdom: The Message of Psalms 15–24* (PhD diss., Golden Gate Baptist Theological Seminary, 2015).

[70] Over half the psalms in Books 1–3 have למנצח in their superscriptions: Book 1 (Pss 4–6, 8, 9/10, 11–14, 18–22, 31, 36, 39–41), Book 2 (42/43, 44–47, 49, 51–62, 64–70), and Book 3 (75–77, 80–81, 84–85, 88). Only three psalms have it in Books 4–5 (109, 139, 140).

[71] When considered as a group, the presence of למנצח for the thirteen biographical superscriptions does not appear significant: five lack it (Pss 3, 7, 34, 63, 142), and eight

whole. According to both Hossfeld-Zenger and Millard, such marking indicates that they are *Eckpsalmen* framing Pss 4–6 as a unit. In both arguments, modern form-critical analysis is the primary factor of psalm grouping, complemented by the presence of biographical headings. This, however, is not the only option. One could also argue that Pss 3 and 7 begin their own psalm clusters. To support this alternative view, we must turn to the superscriptions themselves.

The Superscriptions of Pss 1–17			
Pss 1–2	(none)		
Psalm Cluster (3–6)		**Psalm Cluster (7–14)**	
Ps 3	A *mizmôr* of David, when he fled from before Absalom his son.	**Ps 7**	A *šiggayôn* of David, which he sang to Yʜwʜ on account of the words of Cush, a Benjamite.
Ps 4	*lamnaṣṣēaḥ, bingînôṯ.* A *mizmôr* of David.	**Ps 8**	*lamnaṣṣēaḥ, ʿal-haggittîṯ.* A *mizmôr* of David.
Ps 5	*lamnaṣṣēaḥ, ʾel-hannᵉḥîlôṯ.* A *mizmôr* of David.	**Ps 9/10**	*lamnaṣṣēaḥ, ʿalmûṯ labbēn.* A *mizmôr* of David.
Ps 6	*lamnaṣṣēaḥ, bingînôṯ, ʿal-haššᵉmînîṯ.* A *mizmôr* of David.	**Ps 11**	*lamnaṣṣēaḥ.* Of David.
		Ps 12	*lamnaṣṣēaḥ, ʿal-haššᵉmînîṯ.* A *mizmôr* of David.
		Ps 13	*lamnaṣṣēaḥ.* A *mizmôr* of David.
		Ps 14	*lamnaṣṣēaḥ.* Of David.
New Section (Pss 15ff.)			
Ps 15	A *mizmôr* of David.		
Ps 16	A *miktām* of David.		
Ps 17	A *tᵉpillâ* of David.		

In Pss 3–6, each psalm is titled with the elements "A psalm of David" (מזמור לדוד), with Pss 4–6 also including liturgical and musical elements. These performance elements always precede the ancient literary indication (מזמור) and association with a biblical figure (לדוד). Psalm 7, however, breaks this line of continuity. Not only is למנצח absent, but instead of מזמור, Ps 7 has been designated a שגיון, and includes a different biographical notice.

---

include it (18, 51, 52, 54, 56, 57, 59, 60). Ancient literary type does not appear to be significant either: four are מכתם (56, 57, 59, 60), three are מזמור (3, 51, 63), three are משכיל (52, 54, 142), one is שגיון (7), one is שיר (18), and one lacks a literary type (34).

After this break, we again find very strong continuity within Pss 8–14. Each includes למנצח and לדוד, and only Pss 11 and 14 are missing מזמור.[72] As with Pss 3–6, the ordering of elements within the superscriptions may also have value, as performance elements again precede the ancient genre designation and association with David.[73] Further marks of continuity will be noted in my later analysis between Pss 7–8–9 and Pss 8 and 14, which strengthen the bond in this grouping. Here, it should be noted that form-critical categories have been overshadowed by the editors of the Psalter. The hymnic bridge focusing on the name of Yhwh (Pss 7:18; 8:2, 10; 9:2–3) has neatly allowed Ps 8, as a psalm of praise, to fit seamlessly into a group of lament psalms (7–14). On top of this, further lexical and thematic continuity will be noted in both Pss 3–6 and 7–14.

In sum, Wilson's method for canonical analysis initially called for the recognition of clear markers that a group of psalms are distinct from previous and subsequent psalm groupings, followed by an investigation into the how this group of psalms has been shaped. I conclude that Pss 3–14 stand apart from Pss 1–2 and Pss 15–17 through elements of disjuncture, but also show elements of conjuncture within the group. I have also argued that the biographical elements of Pss 3 and 7 mark out these psalms as beginning two different psalm clusters within Pss 3–14: Pss 3–6 and 7–14.

1.3.2. *Psalms 3–14 and Canonical Analysis*

Wilson's second methodological concern is for an investigation of linguistic and thematic connections between psalms. While I have already noted some of these connections in the previous section, my own analysis will be found below in chapters four and five. Since Pss 3–14 are the first exploration within the Psalter of the themes and textual world presented in Pss 1–2, establishing their relationship to these psalms is also a pressing concern. The study of such links between psalms (*concatenatio*) is an established practice in the analysis of juxtaposed psalms, especially when the links contain noteworthy "catchwords" (*Stichwort*). But the significance of lexical parallels (*Wortverbindungen*) and thematic parallels (*Motivverbindungen*) beyond immediate juxtaposition is much doubted in current research. This is not a new concern but had already been raised by Gunkel in his introduction: "The danger of arbitrariness is suggested by the exposition of a thoughtful relationship as when seeking the alleged connecting catchwords.... Connections by catchwords and similarities can therefore perhaps be recognized in individual cases, but the principle fails in relation to the whole psalter."[74] Likewise, Norman Whybray expressed his own concerns for the contemporary canonical approach:

---

[72] As noted before, while מזמור lacks in the MT in Pss 11 and 14, LXX includes ψαλμὸς. The LXX, then, further tightens the continuity in this group of psalms.

[73] Incidentally, this might be an indication that Millard's interpretation of Ps 9's superscription, while ingenious, is not correct. It is not another biographical reference, but an indication of an ancient melody.

[74] Gunkel, *Introduction*, 334–35.

Such attempts to force psalms into a pattern of meaning that does not exist in the text illustrate the great danger of subjectivity in psalm interpretation and also show how a psalm that contains mixed, not to say contradictory, statements can be interpreted quite differently depending on the stress that is placed on particular verses. The impression is given that with a sufficient amount of ingenuity it would be possible to find links between almost any pair or group of psalms selected at random.[75]

These criticisms are constructive and need careful consideration.[76] It is clear that a methodology which works with the idea of sequence must have some safeguards in place.

On the one hand, historical-critical scholarship has proven the value of understanding a psalm on its own terms, with its own genre, intentions, concerns, and *Sitz im Leben*. On the other hand, it is equally clear that the editor(s) of the Psalter saw reason to group (or leave grouped) particular psalms in the final form of the book. Each psalm, then, has a place within its literary context. The sense of this literary whole takes on a cumulative weight, with recurring vocabulary, phrases, motifs, and themes, all contributing to the meaning and trajectory of the larger picture. There is justification, then, for thinking that once we have established these more general connections, we may move into a closer analysis of how particular elements build off one another and create new meaning through their juxtaposition. I adopt the hypothesis that *concatenatio* could very well be at work beyond immediately neighboring psalms, but is limited to psalms only within the same sub-grouping or cluster. Rather

---

[75] Norman Whybray, *Reading the Psalms as a Book*, JSOTSup 222 (Sheffield: Sheffield Academic, 1996), 82. He did not dismiss the idea that the book of Psalms is an editorial collection, but that current methods try to do too much and ultimately fail. His own suggestion was as follows: "There is, however, another method by which the Psalter may be shown to have a kind of literary unity. This does not require a minute examination of each psalm and its relationship with its neighbors, but is concerned with a much broader treatment of the material. It is well known that one effective way of reinterpreting collections of heterogeneous literary material used by ancient Near Eastern and Old Testament scribal editors was to enclose such material within an introduction and a conclusion to the whole work" (84). Thus, Whybray appears to value a broader understanding of editorial purpose which does not extend normatively to the relationship between each psalm in the final form of the book. In my own approach, I see the psalm cluster as the main object of interpretation, with each psalm in the cluster performing its own role. In Pss 3–6, I argue that this happens in a parallelistic fashion, while in Pss 7–14 there appears to be more of a trajectory to the cluster, with some psalms appearing to respond directly to others (e.g., Ps 9/10, or Ps 13 to Ps 12).

[76] Harry Nasuti has been quite helpful in this regard. See Harry P. Nasuti, *Defining the Sacred Songs: Genre, Tradition, and the Post-Critical Interpretation of the Psalms*, JSOTSup 218 (Sheffield: Sheffield Academic, 1999), 128–62; Nasuti, "The Interpretive Significance of Sequence and Selection in the Book of Psalms," in Flint and Miller, *Book of Psalms*, 311–39.

than focusing exclusively on the individual psalm, one can look to psalm clusters as meaningful units for interpretation.[77]

The final two steps advocated by Wilson create a concern for a judicious discernment of the relationship between Pss 3–14 and the book of Psalms as a whole, as well as the social matrix which may be responsible for the final form of the book. While the latter will always be a product of speculation, and is not my focus, I will make a number of suggestions in later chapters on ways in which Pss 3–14 inform a reading of the book as a whole.

1.4. The Concept of Literary Persona

A second major methodological concern is the identification of the speaker in a psalm, or literary persona. In addressing this concern, I will spend the second chapter reviewing representative interpreters in the history of interpretation, and will make an argument in the third chapter that the book of Psalms itself is an important component in identifying the speaker in a given psalm. To make this argument, I will be drawing upon a theory of literary persona used by Nathan Maxwell in his recent doctoral dissertation at Baylor University.[78] This concept has a rich and diverse history in the literary tradition, and proves helpful when applied to the book of Psalms. At the core of literary persona theory is a distinction between the historical author of a text and the literary voice of that text.[79] Their relationship is complex, and Maxwell's lengthy treatment of its history can hardly be summarized here.[80] His conclusions, though, form part of the basis of my own method.

He argues that two constants are critical for a responsible theory of literary persona. First, a literary persona "is always derivative and can never be wholly separate from the poet"; and second, it is "always a voice created for the world of the poem and can never be fully equated with the poet."[81] Given these constants, Maxwell develops a fourfold definition of literary persona:

- A literary persona is the creation of the poet. It is a "formalized representation of the poet's cognition and result of the poet's aesthetic design that functions to govern, regulate, and manipulate the imagery, affective qualities, and language that constitute the 'subject' or material of the poem." Here, the poet uses a literary voice to achieve a desired effect.

---

[77] See Attard, *Implications of Davidic Repentance*, 27–28. See also above comments.

[78] Nathan Dean Maxwell, "The Psalmist in the Psalm: A Persona-Critical Reading of Book IV of the Psalter" (PhD diss., Baylor University, 2007). Within biblical studies, Maxwell noted two works which have also employed the concept of literary persona: Michael V. Fox, *The Song of Songs and the Ancient Egyptian Love Songs* (Madison: University of Wisconsin Press, 1985); Fox, *Ecclesiastes* (Philadelphia: JPS, 2004).

[79] Maxwell, "The Psalmist in the Psalm," 14.

[80] Maxwell, "The Psalmist in the Psalm," 8–95.

[81] Maxwell, "The Psalmist in the Psalm," 88, 89.

- A literary persona lives and survives within the text, such that, long after the historical author passes away or is even forgotten, the literary persona can be realized in the experience of the reader.
- Even though a literary persona derives from an historical author, it is yet autonomous from the author. This is a product of the creative process in which the author used the literary persona to achieve a rhetorical or aesthetic end. Through the persona the author produces something derivative of one's self, but also other than one's self.
- A literary persona is hermeneutically bound to the text, relying on the world of the text rather than the reader's knowledge of or access to the world of the historical author.[82]

When applied to the book of Psalms, one first must acknowledge that the voice of the speaker in a psalm is, though derived from the historical author, distinct from him. Interestingly, this idea was a key component of Mowinckel's cult-functional criticism, where the "I" of the psalm is not the composer himself, but the person for whose use he has written the psalm.[83] For cult-functional criticism, social context played a key role in identifying the speaker as an official in the temple. In my appropriation of literary persona theory, however, this context is different.

As discussed above, in the canonical Psalter the original cultic prayers "are changed into liturgical pieces of scriptural meditation and devotion."[84] In this new setting, its collectors and editors have given the literary persona of a psalm a new contextual setting, one distinct from the historical author of the psalm. Thus, the question about the identity of the speaker, even though it may be informed by historical-critical approaches of the last few centuries, is ultimately one which rests on the context given to the psalm in the final form of the text. Practically, this means that a psalm does not have to be written by David in order for the psalm to use the voice of the Davidic figure in its canonical context. It also shows us that the pursuit of the "historical" voice of a psalm in its original *Sitz im Leben* is not the only avenue available to give voice to a psalm.[85] The value

---

[82] These four points are my own summaries. See Maxwell, "The Psalmist in the Psalm," 92–93.

[83] Mowinckel, *Psalms in Israel's Worship*, 2:133. He wrote, "The psalm has been composed and put into the mouth of the one who has to use it." And later in the same work, "Even if it was the task of the psalm composer to enter into the situation for which the psalm was composed, in such a way that he could give expression to that which the ill-fated king then felt and ought to feel and say, still the poet was in fact a part of it" (2:134).

[84] Erhard S. Gerstenberger, *Psalms: Part 1 with an Introduction to Cultic Poetry*, FOTL 14 (Grand Rapids: Eerdmans, 1988), 52.

[85] The history of interpretation in both Jewish and Christian traditions amply shows that commentators were willing to hear, and advocated hearing, different literary personae in their understanding of the Psalms. Modern approaches are but one avenue on which psalm interpretation has traveled over the past 2,500 years, and its conclusions are not definitive.

of Maxwell's method is that it steps back from the simple identification of author with voice, and allows one to consider just what voice is being used in a psalm.

Literary persona theory allows one to open the door to hearing Pss 3–14 within the literary context of the book of Psalms. At the same time, it raises questions about how to identify its literary setting: what is the textual world of the book of Psalms? How is this textual world similar to or different than other books in the Old Testament? Does each psalm work within its own textual world, or is there one overarching textual world for the book within which each psalm plays a role? What are the indicators in the book about how psalms relate to one another, if any? These and other questions play an important part in our identification of the literary persona(e) in Pss 3–14.

1.5. Psalm Titles and Inner-Biblical Interpretation

In an earlier section, I briefly discussed modern developments in how to approach the psalm headings (superscriptions). Generally speaking, modern scholarship has understood the superscriptions in two different ways. The earlier tendency was to reject them as late additions to the book, concluding that they had little to no use for understanding the original setting of a psalm. More recent scholars, however, have understood them not in terms of their historical value, but in terms of their exegetical or hermeneutical value, in how they set up a psalm for interpretation.[86] Following Childs, the biographical superscriptions connect the "David" of the psalm titles to the "David" we find in narratives of the Old Testament. The goal is not to understand the "David" of the psalm titles *per se*, but to obtain a clearer picture of the mind of "David" within the historical narratives. Having gained this understanding, the reader can better identify with him in his suffering and persecution, and in imitation of him is better enabled to respond with faithful trust in Yhwh regardless of her situation. In the fifty years since Childs's article, however, the function of a "title" in literature has been much discussed by literary scholars. Their conclusions have yet to be included in Psalms research, but there is much to gain by incorporating them into how we understand the hermeneutical value of psalm superscriptions.

Gérard Gennette has noted that at the very least a title in a work of literature is composed of three different elements: the title itself (the "message"), a sender (its author), and an intended recipient.[87] The sender does not necessarily need to be the producer of the work, as an editor could give a title to a previously untitled work; but regardless of authorship, the sender of the title (the "intitulator") adopts the title. The intended recipient of the title is

---

[86] See Childs, "Psalm Titles and Midrashic Exegesis."

[87] Gérard Gennette, "Structure and Functions of the Title in Literature," *Critical Inquiry* 14 (1988): 705–6.

generally some notion of the public, and could potentially be greater than the sum of its readers, including those who contribute to the diffusion and reception of a work without ever reading it.[88] Considering the canonical Psalter, one could conclude that the intended recipient includes the entirety of God's people, and more broadly, any who are willing to sit under the authority of sacred Scripture.

Genette also details three main functions for titles, some of which are mandatory and others optional.[89] The first is designation or identification. This sets the work apart from other similar works, and can take many forms (e.g., a serial number, or a multi-line description of a treatise). In the Psalter, the title of the work is given in order to allow one to reference the work in an efficient way. As Stephen Kellman points out, numbers can be efficient ways of identifying a work, and perhaps the various enumerations of psalms throughout reception history are an example of this kind of titling.[90]

A second main function of titles is description. Genette notes that this function is optional but is often inescapable in practice. The descriptive function identifies how the title of a work can provide rhematic (generic) and thematic descriptions of the piece of literature. For instance, in the title, *A Treatise on Human Understanding*, the rhematic element indicates that the work is a "treatise." For psalms, ancient type distinctions (e.g., משכיל, מכתם, סיר, מזמור, תפלה) are perhaps examples of rhematic description. Thematic description is more complex but is used to designate the central theme or subject of the work through literal, symbolic, or ironic descriptions. Using the above example, *On Human Understanding* is a literal thematic description which identifies the central subject matter of the treatise. With sacred texts (such as the Psalms), opening and closing formulae function as "an intertextual framework that allows people to identify the kind of textual situation they are about to enter."[91]

The third main function of a title is its connotative function. Here, the title reminds the reader about other works, whether to recall other authors, other periods of writing, or other works of a specific genre. This information is always attached to the title of a work, willingly or not. It also seems to have the most direct impact on the study of psalm superscriptions since the connotative function is hermeneutical in its orientation.[92] As Jerrold Levinson has argued, one of the main hermeneutical roles of titles is how they "focus" a work: "What a focusing title does is select from among the main elements of core content one theme to stand as the leading one of the work.... [suggesting] which of the

---

[88] Gennette, "Title in Literature," 706–7.

[89] Gennette, "Title in Literature," 712–19.

[90] Steven G. Kellman, "Dropping Names: The Poetics of Titling," *Criticism* 17 (1975): 156–57.

[91] Wolfgang Karrer, "Titles and Mottoes as Intertextual Devices," in *Intertextuality*, ed. Heinrich F. Plett (Berlin: de Gruyter, 1991), 128.

[92] John Fisher, "Entitling," *Critical Inquiry* 11 (1984): 288.

contending themes should be given center place in interpreting the work and organizing one's appreciation of it."[93]

Technically, the superscriptions or headings are not "titles" in the modern sense, at least in how we think about literary works. They are not identifications (e.g., the numerical numbers given in MT and LXX), nor are they the focusing titles given to various psalms as, for example, in many English translations.[94] Rather, their associative value focuses the psalms by connecting them to the cultic life of Israel through musical and ancient genre indication and their association with leading figures in the establishing of the cult during the reign of David (e.g., David, Asaph, the sons of Korah). Moreover, the biographical headings given to Davidic psalms "pressure" interpretation in certain directions. Such headings are "allusive" and are "dependent on our collective memory, our sense of tradition"; and as far as we can identify them, "activate potential references."[95] Kellman explains several literary titles which are illustrative: "Stoppard's *Rosencrantz and Guildenstern Are Dead* insists that we recall our experience of *Hamlet* before encountering this new work. Huxley's title *Brave New World* obliquely signals Miranda's innocence in *The Tempest*, but it in any case points both outward and inward."[96] In my view, this well illustrates what is happening with the biographical elements associated with David. Indeed, Kellman describes perfectly the effect of the inclusion of the Psalter within Israel's scriptural traditions: "A large class of books achieves this effect by plucking bits of earlier works out of their familiar surroundings and pressing them into service on a new title page."[97] The effect is that the present text utilizes the earlier text to create something new.

This means that biographical superscriptions do not actualize the stories of David in order to fill in the blanks about David's inner thoughts; rather, their primary purpose is to "press" the narratives "into the service" of a new literary work, the book of Psalms. This point will be expanded later, but, for now, my argument is that this "pressing into service" is the development of the Psalter's own figure of David. The "David" described in the narratives of Samuel certainly informs that figure, but the figure of David in the Psalms is the "David of the Psalms," not the "David" of Samuel or Chronicles or Kings or the New Testament (or some combination thereof). They supply an initial context in which the figure of David can be heard and developed.

In Pss 3–14, the initial psalms in each psalm cluster are critically important as they both contain biographical elements in their superscriptions, calling into service different episodes in the life of David from 1–2 Samuel. In Ps 3, the

---

[93] Jerrold Levinson, "Titles," *Journal of Aesthetics and Art Criticism* 44 (1985): 35.

[94] For example, the English Standard Version entitles Ps 3, "Save Me, O My God," and Ps 4, "Answer Me When I Call." One is reminded of the Syriac tradition of psalm headings, which are also thematically titled.

[95] Kellman, "Dropping Names," 163.

[96] Kellman, "Dropping Names," 163.

[97] Kellman, "Dropping Names," 163.

episode is the rebellion of Absalom, found in 2 Sam 15–18. The goal is not to identify the exact moment David composed or sang this psalm, but how the Absalom narrative sets up a literary context within which to hear the literary persona of Ps 3, which is literarily bound *not* by the Deuteronomistic History, but by Pss 1–2. Similarly, while Ps 7's title has been notoriously difficult to understand, I will argue that it could fit several different episodes in the story of David associated with the cursing words of the Benjaminites, and each could provide a context in which to hear the psalm.

For both Pss 3 and 7, one must bear in mind the "allusive" narrative text, reading it alongside and in comparison with the psalm, to see which elements are fitting and which are incongruous. That a psalm does not fit perfectly in the context of the life of David is not an indication that the biographical titles are shortsighted or historically useless, but that their main purpose is not to help us understand the episodes of David in Samuel or the historical David.[98] The work of Wolfgang Müller has been particularly helpful in thinking through this process, which he calls "interfigurality."[99] He has argued that when an author utilizes "a figure from a work by another author into his own work, he absorbs it into the formal and ideological structure of his own product, putting it to his own uses, which may range from parody and satire to a fundamental revaluation or re-exploration of the figure concerned."[100] He emphasized the necessity of recognizing that "such figures are more than mere duplicates and that they are marked by a characteristic tension between similarity and dissimilarity with their models from the pre-texts."[101] Though they may bear the same names, "it would be wrong to take for granted an identity of the figures from the pre-text with the corresponding figures in the subsequent text."[102] For the book of Psalms, then, points of incongruity are extremely valuable. They show us that the Psalter is developing its *own* portrayal of David, and as readers, we are to attempt to understand this new literary persona within the context of the Psalter itself.

In this endeavor, recalling the summary of Matthias Millard earlier, we must ask whether the biographical titles are meant to provide a literary context only for the psalm to which they are ascribed, or could they rather stand behind an entire sub-group or cluster of psalms? Should we understand, for example, Pss

---

[98] As will be discussed in subsequent chapters, an untidy fit between the psalm and the narrative may also indicate that the psalm has been given a secondary setting which could be different than its original purpose within a cultic and/or social context in ancient Israel. The final form of the text provides a new frame of reference for the psalm, adding diachronic depth, showcasing its new function using the persona of the figure of David.

[99] Wolfgang G. Müller, "Interfigurality: A Study on the Interdependence of Literary Figures," in *Intertextuality*, ed. Heinrich F. Plett (Berlin: de Gruyter, 1991), 101–21.

[100] Müller, "Interfigurality," 107.

[101] Müller, "Interfigurality," 109.

[102] Müller, "Interfigurality," 110.

4–6 to have the same setting in Absalom's rebellion as Ps 3? When I began my research, I had assumed that the title of a psalm governs *only that psalm*; that is, the title for Ps 3 is the title for Ps 3, not Ps 4. After completing my analyses, however, I have become convinced that one can propose the same kind of setting for subsequent psalms in the same psalm cluster.[103] In fact, for Pss 3–14, the overwhelming number of linguistic and thematic connections between psalms justifies a reading of Pss 4–6 within the same biographical context as Ps 3, and Pss 8–14 as Ps 7.

---

[103] See Gary A. Anderson, "King David and the Psalms of Imprecation," *ProEccl* 15 (2006): 267–80. He applies a similar theory of the superscriptions in his account of the imprecatory psalms.

2

The Speaking Persona(e)
in the History of Interpretation

In the previous chapter I appealed to the literary concept of "persona" as a fruitful avenue of research into understanding the figure of David in the Psalms. This method opens the door for analysis by understanding the voice of the psalmist as derivative of the author—and thus, not wholly separable from him—but also as autonomous from the author—and thus, not equated with him. As such, we are able to distinguish between the attributed author of a psalm and the voice we hear when we read, listen to, chant, or pray a psalm.

In this chapter we will investigate how the history of interpretation has described the speaking persona. Chronologically, it has been organized with a basic distinction between premodern and modern (historical-critical) exegesis, identifying the major turning point with the publication of de Wette's commentary at the beginning of the nineteenth century.[1] While several premodern and early modern interpreters share some of his historical-critical sensibilities (in nascent and perhaps superficial form), he was one of the first to describe in detail what we can recognize as a fully-fledged "historical" approach to the Psalms. Conceptually, I have also divided premodern interpreters along the lines of two different interpretive methods: prosopological exegesis and typological exegesis. Using these as lenses, I will show how interpreters have understood the speaking persona(e) in a psalm.

Given the nearly inexhaustible catalog of premodern interpretation of the Psalms, I have limited my discussion to five representative interpreters. These

---

[1] I recognize that not all "modern" exegesis is of the historical-critical variety. Using the categories of premodern and modern, however, avoids the language of "pre-critical," which could be taken as pejorative. In practice, "modern" is virtually synonymous with historical-critical methods, with "early modern" used to denote the time between the Protestant Reformation and the nineteenth century. I am including Calvin with premodern interpreters, though he is technically in the *early* early modern period.

are figures who cannot be overlooked, whose accomplishments as exegetes are innovative, and from whom generations of interpreters are derivative. For prosopological exegesis, the two interpreters which offer the greatest breadth and influence are Origen and Augustine. Each has a very different approach to the Psalms but fit under the same basic methodological umbrella. For typological exegesis, I will be surveying both Thomas Aquinas and John Calvin. Each understand David as a type, but construct David's relationship to Christ and to the church along different figural lines. I will also survey the work of Athanasius, whose unique approach utilizes elements of both prosopological and typological exegesis. I hope to show that, far from being monolithic, the premodern period was filled with interpreters who understood the speaking persona(e) of the Psalms to be determined by a number of different variables.[2]

2.1. Prosopological Exegesis in the Premodern Period

In perhaps the earliest complete treatment we have on any psalm, Justin Martyr argued that in Ps 22, David spoke of the passion and cross of Christ ἐν παραβολῇ μυστηριώδει, "in a mysterious parable."[3] His extended verse-by-verse discussion of this psalm in *Dialogue with Trypho* 97–106 and *First Apology* 35 offers us one of the first reflections on how to negotiate between the author of a psalm and its speaking persona. He begins his discussion by noting that one's identification of the speaking persona must take place through a correspondence between the content of the psalm and history:

> You are indeed blind when you deny that the above-quoted psalm was spoken of Christ, for you fail to see that no one among your people who was ever called *king* ever had his hands and feet pierced

---

[2] I will not be surveying the work of the Antiochenes (Diodore, Theodore, Chrysostom, and Theodoret) or the Cappadocians (Basil, Gregory of Nyssa) in the patristic period, nor major figures in the Medieval and Reformation periods, such as Cassiodorus, Erasmus, Luther, Bellarmine, or de Ligouri. To do so would have been a book all by itself (a book that should be written!). This does not mean such interpreters are unimportant, or that they did not make any original contributions. Rather, in my opinion, their methods are sufficiently illustrated or can be found within the breadth of interpretative room created by the chosen representative figures. For instance, Hilary of Poitiers, Eusebius of Caesarea, and Jerome are all reliant on Origen for their basic approach, as are Cassiodorus and a number of Medieval commentators on Augustine. Again, the chosen interpreters are representative of the breadth of Christian interpretation, and by no means exhaust it. Some reference will be made to the work of Diodore and Theodore in later discussion.

[3] Justin Martyr, *Dialogue avec Tryphon: Édition critique, traduction, commentaire*, ed. Philippe Bobichon, Paradosis 47/1 (Fribourg, Switzerland: Academic Press Fribourg, 2003), 455 [§97.3]. The French translation reads, "en une mystérieuse parabole." Cf. Justin Martyr, *Dialogue with Trypho*, trans. Thomas B. Falls, rev. Thomas P. Halton, SFC 3 (Washington, DC: Catholic University of America Press, 2003), 148. He translates the phrase, "in mystical parable."

while alive, and died by this mystery (that is, of the crucifixion), except this Jesus alone.[4]

In other words, since we no-where read about any king in Israel's history
undergoing the kind of suffering spoken of in the psalm, David must be speaking
prophetically of the crucifixion of Jesus Christ. The same principal is at work in
First Apology 35 (after quoting Ps 22:16 and 18):

> And David, the king and prophet who said this, suffered none of these
> things, but Jesus Christ had his hands stretched out when he was
> crucified by the Jews gainsaying him and asserting that he was not
> the Christ.[5]

The key in both quotations is historical correspondence: we find no
correspondence between the psalm and David (or any other king) in the Old
Testament narratives, but accordance with the Gospel's witness to Jesus Christ.
With this in place, Justin walks Trypho through the entire psalm, attempting to
prove how "the whole psalm referred to Christ."[6]

He begins his exposition on Ps 22:1 by observing:

> The opening words of the psalm, *O God, my God, look upon me, why have
> you forsaken me*, foretold of old what would be said by Christ. For,
> while hanging on the cross, he exclaimed, *My God, my God, why have
> you forsaken me?*[7]

This brief summary of the prophetic act is perhaps the simplest summary of
prosopological exegesis that I have found. As we will see below in the
explanation of Matthew Bates, Justin's understanding of David's prophetic act
involves three different horizons or settings: (1) the prophetic setting, "foretold
of old"; (2) the theodramatic setting, "what would be said by Christ"; and (3) the
actualized setting, "while hanging on the cross, he exclaimed." This "staging"
of the prophetic dialogue, if you will, is a second key in prosopological exegesis.

A third key involves divine inspiration, and in particular, the Spirit speaking
prophetically through a human agent in the voice of another person. This, too,
we find in Justin, as he notes how God teaches us through the prophets: "The
prophetic Spirit (τὸ προφητικὸν πνεῦμα) speaks from the character of Christ
(ἀπὸ προσώπου τοῦ Χριστοῦ)."[8] Prosopological exegesis, then, involves three

---

[4] Justin Martyr, *Dialogue with Trypho*, 149 [§97.4].

[5] Justin Martyr, "Justin's Apology on Behalf of Christians," in *Justin, Philosopher and
Martyr: Apologies*, ed. Denis Minns and Paul Parvis, OECT (Oxford: Oxford University Press,
2009), 176–77 [§35.6].

[6] Justin Martyr, *Dialogue with Trypho*, 150 [§99.1].

[7] Justin Martyr, *Dialogue with Trypho*, 150 [§99.1]. The French reads, "Son début... an-
nonçait anciennement ce qui devait être dit au temps du Christ. Car, sur la Croix, il
s'écria," or "Its beginning...formerly announced what was to be said in the time of Christ.
For, on the Cross, he cried out" (*my own translation*). See *Dialogue avec Tryphon*, 452–53.

[8] Justin Martyr, "Justin's Apology on Behalf of Christians," 180–81 [§38.1].

keys: non-correspondence between the prophet and his own history, theodramatic staging, and divine inspiration.

For most of the modern period this aspect of psalm exegesis has been ignored, but it has been receiving more attention in recent scholarship.[9] Prosopological exegesis has its roots in the Greek concept of prosopopoeia, which in literary theory refers to "the speech of an imaginary person."[10] Built from the Greek words *prosopon* ("face, person") and *poiein* ("to make")—hence, "character-making"—the concept is closely connected to the idea of a "persona," which we explored in the previous chapter.[11] In Greek education, exercises called *prosopopoeiae* called for a writer to take on "the persona of a famous historical or mythological figure in a composition with the end of exhibiting his character."[12] In the Christian exegetical tradition, the key terms— used by Justin above—are ἀπὸ/ἐκ προσώπου (Greek) and *ex persona* (Latin), translated "in/from the person/character of."

Even though its roots were found in prosopopoeia, prosopological exegesis had a slightly different application than its pagan counterpart. As noted above, in Greek tradition prosopopoeia is properly speaking a rhetorical device, a literary fiction. But in Christian tradition, because of divine inspiration, prophets did not take on fictionalized personae. Note the description of prophecy from Irenaeus on Ps 2:

> Since David says, "the Lord says to me," it is necessary to affirm that it is not David nor any other one of the prophets, who speaks from himself—for it is not man who utters prophecies—but [that] the Spirit of God, conforming Himself to the person concerned, spoke in the prophets, producing words sometimes from Christ and at other

---

[9] See Marie-Josèphe Rondeau, *Les Commentaires Patristique du Psautier (IIIe-Ve siècles): Vol. II—Exegèse Prosopologique et Théologie*, OCA 220 (Rome: Pontifical Institutum Studioroum Orientalium, 1985); Matthew Bates, *The Hermeneutics of the Apostolic Proclamation: The Center of Paul's Method of Scriptural Interpretation* (Waco: Baylor University Press, 2012); Bates, *The Birth of the Trinity: Jesus, God, and Spirit in New Testament and Early Christian Interpretations of the Old Testament* (Oxford: Oxford University Press, 2015); Craig A. Carter, *Interpreting Scripture with the Great Tradition: Recovering the Genius of Premodern Exegesis* (Grand Rapids: Baker Academic, 2018), 191–201.

[10] T. V. F. Brogan, A. W. Halsall, and J. S. Sychterz, "Prosopopoeia," in *The Princeton Encyclopedia of Poetry and Poetics*, ed. Stephen Cushman, Clare Cavanagh, and Paul Rouzer, 4th ed (Princeton: Princeton University Press, 2012), 1120. See also Gavin Alexander, "Prosopopoeia: the Speaking Figure," in *Renaissance Figures of Speech*, ed. Sylvia Adamson, Gavin Alexander, and Katrin Ettenhuber (Cambridge: Cambridge University Press, 2007), 97–115; Hannibal Hamlin, "My Tongue Shall Speak: The Voices of the Psalms," *Renaissance Studies* 29 (2015), 509–30.

[11] See William F. Lanahan, "The Speaking Voice in the Book of Lamentations," *JBL* 93 (1974), 41. He wrote that a "persona" is a "mask or characterization assumed by the poet as the medium through which he perceives and gives expression to his world."

[12] Brogan, Halsall, and Sychterz, "Prosopopoeia," 1121.

times from the Father. So, in a very fitting manner Christ says, by David, that the Father Himself speaks with Him.[13]

According to Irenaeus, the Spirit speaks realities *via* the prophets, producing words which the Spirit has conformed "to the person concerned." As such, it is not David "who speaks from himself," but by the Spirit. The basic process of prosopological exegesis, then, is described well by Hubertus Drobner:

> David does not speak the Psalms in a concrete historical situation but, because of the divine inspiration, does so from a different πρόσωπον; hence his words are to be referred to the person so speaking and are to be understood as from that person (God, Christ, the person, the church, etc.).[14]

But how does prosopological exegesis conceptually work? As illustrated with Justin Martyr, Bates explained that this takes place on three textual horizons or settings. Picking up from Justin Martyr above, we will use Ps 22 as a way to illustrate the method.

The first horizon is the "prophetic setting." This is the time of the ancient prophets themselves, within the circumstances of ancient Israel. In this setting, the prophet could speak with a different voice (*prosopon*), participating in a speech or dialogue that preceded him, is contemporaneous to him, or has yet to occur. As inspired, the prophet's speech can be envisioned as a kind of script authored by the Holy Spirit, and these scripts "[have] been, are, or will become a reality when performed."[15] For Ps 22, we would identify the "prophetic setting" as David's own historical context when he composed the psalm.

The second horizon is the "theodramatic setting" or "theodrama." This is the time in which the speech is delivered from within the narrative world, the time of the *prosopon.* Conceptually, this is most difficult part of prosopological exegesis to envision. As Bates explained, a theodrama is "the visionary scene ancient interpreters felt that a prophet could really inhabit."[16] We should not think of it as if a window in reality were opened and the prophet was seeing *the* future scene in its fullness. Rather, the prophet has been given an "oracular experience" or "visionary-level of reality" which will share correspondence to future lived-out reality. It is within this experience that the prophet "enters into a character-role and is speaking or being addressed as that person."[17] Again, this goes beyond pagan prosopopoeia. The prophet is more than a playwright composing a Spirit-script and envisioning what it *might* look like for characters in

---

[13] Irenaeus of Lyons, *On the Apostolic Preaching*, trans. John Behr, PPS 17 (Crestwood, NY: St. Vladimir's Seminary Press, 1997), 73 [§49–50].

[14] Hubertus R. Drobner, *The Fathers of the Church: A Comprehensive Introduction*, trans. Siegfried S. Schatzmann (Peabody, MA: Hendrickson, 2007), 321.

[15] Bates, *Birth of the Trinity*, 34. I rely primarily on his presentation of this material over the next few paragraphs.

[16] Bates, *Birth of the Trinity*, 34n61.

[17] Bates, *Birth of the Trinity*, 35.

the story to perform it at a future time. Rather, the prophet David feels "inspired by God to step into the role of the future Messiah, and is given words, but... David himself would not have securely understood the whole scene or the full referential significance."[18] For Ps 22, if David is speaking in the person of Christ during his passion, then the theodrama is his oracular experience of the crucifixion scene.

The third horizon is the "actualized setting," when the theodrama is performed, not by the prophet, but by the person the prophet was truly voicing in the theodrama. Using Ps 22, we would identify Jesus's utterance of "my God, my God," from the cross in first century CE, as bringing to pass what the prophet David anticipated in his performance of the theodrama of Ps 22.

Taking the earlier quotation from Justin, we can highlight these three horizons or settings as follows:

Prophetic Setting	The opening words of the psalm, *O God, my God, look upon me, why have you forsaken me*, foretold of old
Theodramatic Setting	what would be said by Christ.
Actualized Setting	For, while hanging on the cross, he exclaimed, *My God, my God, why have you forsaken me?*

The prosopological method of exegesis was quite common throughout the premodern period, but given the theological and historical differences between ancient and modern hermeneutics, it is not surprising that modern methodologies lack the assumptions necessary to interpret the text using this approach.[19] Even so, prosopopoeia continues to have an important function within psalm studies, especially those who concentrate on the cultic origin of the psalms. For instance, Sigmund Mowinckel understands the psalm authors to have written them with the intention of being spoken by other people:

> If... the psalms have in the main originated among the temple singers and are intended for use by a king, a national leader or a private person, who in connexion with public worship should present a psalm of

---

[18] This way of explaining the prophetic setting is quoted from personal email correspondence with Bates (24 May 2019). Perhaps an analogy might be how a storyboard is used by film directors to sequence and visualize a script before it is performed for filming. For example, I am reminded of how Peter Jackson purposefully framed scenes in his adaptation of *The Lord of the Rings* to bring to life sketches by illustrator Alan Lee. The principle difference is that prosopological staging is a storyboard for non-fictional actualization.

[19] In particular, premodern interpreters understood prophecy as an author writing God's revelation about the past, present, and future under the inspiration of the Holy Spirit. Modern interpreters understand prophecy more in terms of social discourse; any "future" predictions are written *ex post facto*.

prayer or praise, it is also evident that we have to distinguish between the poet and the "I" who prays in the psalm.[20]

For Mowinckel, the basic principle of "speaking in the character of another" is present, but this is simply a rhetorical fiction which may or may not be acted out in the worship of Yʜᴡʜ at some point in Israel's history. Prosopological exegesis, on the other hand, is built on the understanding that the Spirit of God has spoken through a prophet in the *actual voice* of another person, such that the inscribed dialogue is a reality.

To illustrate further how the prosopological method was utilized by premodern interpreters to describe the speaking persona in the Psalms, we will now survey two of the most important interpreters in the history of Christian interpretation: Origen and Augustine.

2.1.1. Origen: The "Journey of the Soul"

The importance of Origen for psalm exegesis is hard to overstate. According to one patristic scholar, his work "conditioned decisively all subsequent patristic exegesis."[21] Even though much is known about Origen's voluminous output on the Psalms, relatively little has survived.[22] A modern reevaluation of Origen began in the late nineteenth century, and a number of valuable contributions have been made to better make sense of his exegetical techniques and aims.[23] The

---

[20] Sigmund Mowinckel, *The Psalms in Israel's Worship: Two Volumes in One*, trans. D. R. Ap-Thomas (Grand Rapids: Eerdmans, 2004), 2:133.

[21] Manlio Simonetti, *Biblical Interpretation in the Early Church: An Historical Introduction to Patristic Exegesis*, trans. John A. Hughes (Edinburgh: T&T Clark, 1994), 39.

[22] See Ronald E. Heine, "Restringing Origen's Broken Harp: Some Suggestions Concerning the Prologue of the Caesarean Commentary on the Psalms," in *The Harp of Prophecy: Early Christian Interpretation of the Psalms*, ed. Brian E. Daley and Paul R. Kolbet (Notre Dame: University of Notre Dame Press, 2015), 47–74. Origen's writings on the Psalms include two commentaries, a number of homilies, and *scholia* prepared near the end of his life. Scholarly literature is still debating how to organize all the fragments which remain. If we follow Heine's chronology (above), Origen composed a commentary on Pss 1–25 while still living in Alexandria (see *First Principles* 2.4.4; Jerome, *Letter 33*; Eusebius, *Church History* 6.24). Then, shortly after moving to Caesarea, he preached a number of homilies on the Psalms, also writing a second, more extensive commentary and later *scholia*. Heine, following others, suggests that the Palestinian *catenae* preserves fragments of the Caesarean commentary, while the *scholia* are preserved in manuscript Vindobonensis 8. For an alternative view, see John A. McGuckin, "Origen's Use of the Psalms in the Treatise *On First Principles*," in *Meditations of the Heart: The Psalms in Early Christian Thought and Practice; Essays in Honour of Andrew Louth*, ed. Andreas Andreopoulos, Augustine Casiday, and Carol Harrison, STT 8 (Turnhout: Brepols, 2011), 97–98.

[23] See Jean Daniélou, *Origen*, trans. Walter Mitchell (London: Sheed & Ward, 1955); Henri de Lubac, *History and Spirit: The Understanding of Scripture according to Origen*, trans. Anne Englund Nash (San Francisco: Ignatius, 2007); and the anthology by Hans Urs von Balthasar, *Origen, Spirit and Fire: A Thematic Anthology of His Writings*, trans. Robert J. Daly (Washington, DC: The Catholic University of America Press, 1984).

success of his approach to the Psalms in both the Christian East and West is directly related to its exegetical end, the reader's own lifelong "journey of the soul."[24] As such, to gain a better understanding of his treatment on the Psalms I will first summarize what this "journey" meant for Origen's exegesis.

The soul's journey begins in its creation, called "divination," in which the human being was made in complete likeness to God. Throughout one's life, progress is made towards the goal of the journey: the restoration of this created divine likeness, the (re)union of the soul with God.[25] The journey itself consists of three principal stages, or kinds of knowledge.[26] As Karen Jo Torjesen summarized, the first stage is called "purification," consisting of the knowledge of humanity in which "the soul struggles against sin and overcomes it, resisting and renouncing the world."[27] A second stage consists of a growing knowledge of divinity, in which one advances in "knowledge of the mysteries, knowledge of the Logos, of the intelligible and eternal."[28] And finally, a third stage consists of a "face-to-face" knowledge of God, a state of perfection as the soul returns to its original form of existence, "to participation in God as the goal of its journey."[29]

Using these stages, Torjesen has argued cogently that Origen's tripartite exegetical rhetoric of "body," "soul," and "spirit," does not refer to three senses in the text (the literal, moral, and mystical senses), but to three levels of meaning in relation to each reader's journey.[30] It is in this context that one can properly account for Origen's own introduction to his hermeneutic in *On First Principles* 4.2.4. Using Prov 22:20–21—"You are to register them thrice in counsel and knowledge, to answer words of truth to those who challenge you"—he explained:

> It is, therefore, necessary to register in one's soul the senses of the sacred writings thrice: so that the simple may be edified from the flesh, as it were, of Scripture, for so we designate the obvious interpretation; while one who has ascended a certain measure may be edified from the soul, as it were; and the person who is perfect... [may be edified] from the *spiritual law, having a shadow of the good things to come.* Just as the human being consists of body and soul and spirit, in the same way so also does Scripture, arranged by God to be given for the salvation of human beings.[31]

---

[24] See Karen Jo Torjesen, *Hermeneutical Procedure and Theological Method in Origen's Exegesis*, Patristiche Texte und Studien 28 (Berlin: de Gruyter, 1986). I will make much use of her work in what follows.

[25] Torjesen, *Origen's Exegesis*, 71–72.

[26] Torjesen, *Origen's Exegesis*, 84.

[27] Torjesen, *Origen's Exegesis*, 76.

[28] Torjesen, *Origen's Exegesis*, 76.

[29] Torjesen, *Origen's Exegesis*, 76.

[30] Torjesen, *Origen's Exegesis*, 40–41.

[31] Origen, *On First Principles*, trans. John Behr, OECT (Oxford: Oxford University Press, 2017), 2:497–98 [§4.2.4 Gk]. Proverbs 22 quotation also from this translation.

To be sure, as Morwenna Ludlow pointed out, Origen did not argue that the text itself depicts the threefold journey of the soul; rather, "the idea of that progress serves as his interpretative framework for connecting the seemingly diverse and discrete elements of scripture."[32] In practice, when Origen came to a text, he first explained its grammatical sense, where he focused on its literal and historical reality as well as identifying places where the text is unclear or "impossible."[33] To resolve these difficulties, he typically made reference to other relevant biblical passages, followed by an appeal to the journey of the soul to bring meaning to the text, examining the text's fuller spiritual meaning and application to the present hearer.[34]

Origen's approach to the Psalms and to the speaking persona in a psalm can be illustrated well by his nine homilies on Pss 37–39 [36–38 LXX].[35] His first homily on Ps 37 opens by reminding his listeners that each passage can speak in different ways:

> Sometimes He teaches us ineffable mysteries through the things which he speaks, and yet at other times it is about the Savior and His coming that He instructs us, but from time to time He corrects and reforms our behavior. For this reason, we will attempt to point out differences of this kind in each passage of divine Scripture and to distinguish when there are prophecies and it speaks of things to come, or when some mystical realities are being announced, or when the passage is moral.[36]

For Ps 37, Origen argued that "the entire psalm is moral and that it has been given as a kind of cure and medicine for the human soul, since it rebukes our

---

[32] Morwenna Ludlow, "Theology and Allegory: Origen and Gregory of Nyssa on the Unity and Diversity of Scripture," *International Journal of Systematic Theology* 4 (2002): 52.

[33] Brevard Childs, *The Struggle to Understand Isaiah as Christian Scripture* (Grand Rapids: Eerdmans, 2004), 69. See also Origen, *The Philocalia of Origen: A Compilation of Selected Passages from Origen's Works made by St. Gregory of Nazianzus and St. Basil of Caesarea*, trans. George Lewis (Edinburgh: T&T Clark, 1911), 1. In Gregory and Basil's diagram of Origen's threefold approach, they divide the "Literal (Body)" sense into "Actual History" and "Fictitious History," qualifying the latter: "Invented by the Holy Spirit to convey moral and mystical truths which earthly things could not sufficiently typify. In the law some things were literally to be observed; others were in the letter impossible or absurd, but were intended to convey moral and mystical teaching" (1).

[34] See Ludlow, "Theology and Allegory," 52; Childs, *Struggle*, 69; Origen, *Philocalia* 1. In the latter, the "Mystical (Spirit)" sense is divided into "Allegory," which prefigures "the history of Christ and His Church," and "Anagoge," which typifies "the things of a higher world in which everything of this earth has its anti-type."

[35] I am working from the versions which were preserved in the Latin translations of Rufinus. See *Origène: Homelies sur les Psaumes 36 à 38*, ed. E. Prinzivalli, SC 411 (Paris: Cerf, 1995). English translation is taken from Michael Heintz, "The Pedagogy of the Soul: Origen's Homilies on the Psalms" (Phd diss., Notre Dame, 2008).

[36] Heintz, *Pedagogy of the Soul*, 90.

sins and instructs us how to live according to the Law."[37] Its meaning, then, would fit well within the "purification" stage of the soul's journey. The same conclusion is also offered for Pss 38–39, as each has been given "as a kind of cure and medicine for the human soul." Concerning the speaker, Origen used prosopological reasoning to argue that David is speaking in the voice of another. In Ps 38:6, for example, he argued that the prophet David speaks as a "repentant sinner,"[38] and that "we, although we hear these things, still stink of the sins and vices concerning which the penitent speaks through the prophet."[39] In the same psalm, at verse eighteen, he further commented, "This, too, is the voice of the sinner—a good one, the best kind, so to speak—who has indeed sinned, but who awaits scourging for his failures, by which he wishes to be reformed here and now, so that in the future he might not be punished and perish."[40]

By speaking in the person of a repentant sinner, Origen understood David as giving us a remedy, a way in which the Christian can see his or her own self in the wording of the psalm and move forward in progression towards perfection. As he wrote in his introduction to Ps 39:

> But now let us see what the voice of the just one [David] has brought forth. As if gazing at ourselves in a mirror, let us look to see if we are capable of being like this, or whether much is lacking in us, or if we are already quite close, although we have not fully attained [our goal].[41]

More than this, however, not only does David pray as a repentant sinner, but the penitent in the church can speak through the prophet to God. Using Ps 38:6 as his foundation, Origen wrote programmatically about prosopological reading in his commentary on the book of Romans:

> That it is customary in the Holy Scriptures for saints to take on the *personae* of sinners and for teachers to take upon themselves the weaknesses of disciples, we are indeed taught in greatest detail in the book of Psalms when it says, *There is no peace in my bones before my sins, for my iniquities have gone over my head; they have weighed down on me like a burden. My wounds have grown foul and have festered before my foolishness. I am afflicted with wretchedness and utterly bowed down,* etc. Almost the entire Psalm is written in this way…. It is fitting for us, when we read the things said by the saints, when we see something like this said by them, to interpret and understand that in themselves they are describing our passions and our sins; and the reason they weep is in order that we might be invited to shed tears by their weeping. For

---

[37] Heintz, *Pedagogy of the Soul*, 90.

[38] Origen, *Homilies on Genesis and Exodus*, trans. Ronald E. Heine, FOC 71 (Washington, DC: The Catholic University of America Press, 1982), 170.

[39] Origen, *The Song of Songs Commentary and Homilies*, trans. R. P. Lawson, ACW 26 (Westminster, MD: Newman, 1957), 269.

[40] Heintz, *Pedagogy of the Soul*, 256.

[41] Heintz, *Pedagogy of the Soul*, 266–67.

they were considering that no one could possibly be found who is so hardened and ungrateful, who, when he sees his own wounds being lamented by others, should fail to receive a sense of grief from his own wounds.[42]

Within the Psalms, Origen's prosopological reading is not limited to the persona of a sinner but can take on several other personae,[43] such as the Father,[44] Christ,[45] or the church.[46] Interestingly enough, the majority of references to a speaking persona are to the prophet David himself, but here it is difficult to determine whether Origen is identifying David as the speaking persona or using David as a way of quoting from or alluding to a psalm.[47]

---

[42] Origen, *Commentary on the Epistle to the Romans, Books 6–10*, trans. Thomas P. Scheck, FOC 104 (Washington, DC: The Catholic University of America Press, 2002), 42–43 [§6.9.12]. For a similar discussion, see Origen, *Commentary on the Epistle to the Romans, Books 1–5*, trans. Thomas P. Scheck, FOC 103 (Washington, DC: The Catholic University of America Press, 2001), 343–44 [§5.5.6].

[43] Key explanations of literary persona and prosopological exegesis can be found in the following: Origen, *Commentary on the Epistle to the Romans, Books 1–5*, 135–36 (§2.11.2, 3), where he discusses how to do dialogical analysis; Origen, *Philocalia*, 44–45 [§7.2], from his fourth homily on Acts, on how personification is "devised" by the Spirit; and Origen, *Commentary on the Gospel According to John: Books 1–10*, trans. Ronald E. Heine, FOC 80 (Washington, DC: The Catholic University of America Press, 1989), 91–93 (§1.280–88), where he discusses the speaker in Ps 45 [44 LXX].

[44] In almost every instance, the Father speaks to the Son in Ps 2 (see *Against Celsus* 3.8; 5.32; *Homilies on Genesis* 9.3; *Homilies on Numbers* 17.5.1; *Homilies on Joshua* 11.3), but there are other examples, such as in Ps 40 (*Treatise on the Passover* 47) and Ps 82 (*Commentary on Romans* 9.1.15).

[45] For example: *Against Celsus* 2.6.2 (Ps 16:9–10); *On Prayer* 6.5 (Ps 109); 15.4 (Ps 22:23); *Treatise on the Passover* 41 (Ps 22:23); 48 (Ps 24:7–10); *Philocalia* 1.5 (Ps 45:1); 23.12 (Ps 109); *De Principiis* 2.8.1 (Ps 22:19–20); *Commentary on Romans* 5.10.10 (Ps 16:9–10).

[46] See *Homilies on Genesis* 2.4 (Ps 139:17).

[47] See *Against Celsus* 1.56 (Ps 45:2–7); 4.37 (Ps 119:73); 6.13 (Ps 49:9–10, "...to quote from the words of David what he says regarding the man who is wise"); 6.19 (Ps 148:4, "for David long ago brought to view the profundity and multitude of the thoughts concerning God entertained by those who have ascended above visible things, when he said in the book of Psalms"); *On Prayer* 9.2 (Ps 123:1; 25:1; 4:7; 25:1); 24.4 (Ps 34:4); 27.12 (Ps 74:13–14); 29.3 (Ps 34:20); 12.2 (several quotes of David speaking in prayer); *Dialogue with Heraclides* 17–18 (Ps 58:3–5; 38:5); *On First Principles* 1.3.2 (Ps 51:11); 1.6.1 (Ps 72:1); 1.6.4 (Ps 102:26); 2.6.7 (Ps 89:50–51); 3.2.4 (Ps 76:10; 84:5); 3.4.1 (Ps 102:26–27); *Homilies on Exodus* 3.2 and 4.5 (Ps 81:11, "But God also says through David"); *Homilies on Exodus* 4.8 (Ps 25:7, "But another prophet, speaking about himself"); *Homilies on Leviticus* 3.4, 7; 4.5; 5.2, 4, 9, 12; 7.6; 8.3; 9.9; 12.3; *Homilies on Numbers* 1.1.4; 5.3.3–4 (Ps 91); 6.3.6 (Ps 51); *Homilies on Joshua* 8.7 (Ps 101:8, "Some such thing seems to me to be designated also by the holy prophet in the Psalms, where he says of himself"); *Homily 5 on 1 Samuel* 5.9 (Ps 51:11, "This is what David feared when, after his sin"); *Homilies on Jeremiah* 8.2 (Ps 51, "So David, in the psalm of the confession concerning these spirits, asks the Father, when he says"); *Commentary on Romans* 4.1.19 (Ps 51, "But if instead the Apostle should be understood as having called our

In summary, we have observed that Origen's concern to identify a speaking voice in the Psalms is part of his larger hermeneutic related to the journey of the soul towards perfection. Using prosopological exegesis, we might spell out his model as follows: the prophet David, through divine design, speaks in the person of a repentant sinner, in order that later Christian readers will actualize the psalm in their own lives as a kind of medicine for the soul, rebuking sins and instructing one in how to live. As Origen wrote:

> And therefore, if you receive the word of God which is preached in the Church with complete faith and devotion, that word will become whatever you desire. For instance, if you are afflicted, it consoles you saying, "God does not despise a contrite and humble heart." [Ps 51:19] If you rejoice in your future hope, it heaps up joys for you saying, "Rejoice in the Lord and exult, O righteous." [Ps 32:11] If you are angry, it calms you saying, "Cease from wrath and leave indignation behind." [Ps 37:8] If you are in pain, it heals you saying, "The Lord heals all your weaknesses." [Ps 103:8] If you are consumed by poverty, it consoles you saying, "The Lord lifts up from the earth the helpless and snatches the poor from the dung." [Ps 113:7] So, therefore, the manna of the word of God imparts into your mouth whatever taste you wish.[48]

The interpretive methods employed by Origen heavily influenced many Psalm commentators in his wake. Of special importance is Gregory of Nyssa, whose programmatic treatise on the superscriptions is fascinating insofar as it represents one of the only examples in the history of interpretation which attempts to treat the book of Psalms as a canonical whole.[49] Using the fivefold shape of the book and the superscriptions as hermeneutical clues, Gregory applied Origen's approach of the journey of the soul to the entire Psalter, showing how it is clued into this movement of the soul towards virtue.[50]

---

body the body of sin, it will assuredly be taken in agreement with the understanding which David speaks of in reference to himself").

[48] Origen, *Homilies on Genesis and Exodus*, trans. Ronald E. Heine, FOC 71 (Washington, DC: The Catholic University of America Press, 1982), 313–14.

[49] Gregory of Nyssa, *Treatise on the Inscriptions of the Psalms*, trans. Ronald E. Heine (Oxford: Clarendon, 1995); see also Casimir McCambley, "On the Sixth Psalm, Concerning the Octave by Saint Gregory of Nyssa," *Greek Orthodox Theological Review* 32 (1987): 39–50. Aquinas would later undertake an alternative scheme, but unfortunately died before being able to comment on the entire Psalter.

[50] See Patrick D. Miller, "Gregory of Nyssa: The Superscriptions of the Psalms," in *Genesis, Isaiah, and Psalms*, ed. Katharine J. Dell, et al., SVT 135 (Leiden: Brill, 2010), 215–30.

2.1.2. *Augustine: The* Totus Christus

Like Origen, Augustine represents one of the most important voices in the history of interpretation of the Psalms.[51] While Origen was geographically and spiritually contextualized within Eastern, Greek-speaking communities of the early church (and later, through translation in Western, Latin-speaking churches), Augustine was thoroughly part of Western, Latin church, where his approach to the Psalms dominated Christian interpretation for the next millennium.[52] That the two held differing views on the Psalter is no secret, a point made by Jerome in a somewhat tense epistolary exchange with Augustine:

> I am not saying this because I now think there is anything to object to in your works, for I have not applied myself to reading them; I have no copies of them, except the books of your Soliloquies and some short commentaries on the Psalms. If I wished to discuss these I would not say that they differ from my views—since I am nothing—but I would show that they are at variance with the interpretations of the ancient Greeks.[53]

While the reference to "ancient Greeks" is vague, Jerome likely has in mind Origen and those who followed in his footsteps, and on this score he thought Augustine was venturing into new interpretive territory. While his observation should be read with a grain of salt, it is clear when comparing Origen and Augustine that Augustine's approach is the far more Christological. Indeed, the chief mark of his entire interpretive program is bound up in what he called the "total" or "complete" Christ (*totus Christus*).[54]

Augustine's life was quite literally bookended by his study of the Psalter.[55] His *Confessions* demonstrates a theological outlook and spiritual vocabulary thoroughly engrained in the language of the Psalms, evidences not only of his daily practice of psalmic prayer but a lifetime of preaching and teaching the

---

[51] See Jason Byassee, *Praise Seeking Understanding: Reading the Psalms with Augustine* (Grand Rapids: Eerdmans, 2007).

[52] See Frederick Van Fleteren, "Principles of Augustine's Hermeneutic: An Overview," in *Augustine: Biblical Exegete*, ed. Frederick Van Fleteren and Joseph C. Schnaubelt (New York: Peter Lang, 2004), 1–32.

[53] Augustine, *Letters, Volume I (1-82)*, trans. Sr. Wilfrid Parsons, FOC 12 (Washington, DC: The Catholic University of America Press, 1951), 332.

[54] See Michael Cameron, "The Emergence of *Totus Christus* as Hermeneutical Center in Augustine's *Enarrationes in Psalmos*," in *The Harp of Prophecy* (ed. Daley and Kolbet), 222n13. He noted Augustine's reliance on Tyconius in this regard; see Tyconius, *The Book of Rules of Tyconius*, 1.19–2.1.

[55] See Michael Cameron, *Christ Meets Me Everywhere: Augustine's Early Figurative Exegesis* (Oxford: Oxford University Press, 2012), 165.

Psalms.[56] As with Origen, Augustine did not regard the Psalms simply as devotional reading, but as affecting healing in his soul.[57] In the words of Rowan Williams, the psalmist's voice "unseals deep places, emotions otherwise buried, and it provides an analogy for the unity or intelligibility of a human life lived in faith."[58] Augustine expressed this in several places using the analogy of a "mirror" or "remedy" of the soul. For example, in Ps 124 [Lat. 123] he commented:

> In the psalm we hear the voices of jubilant singers; it is the exulting members of Christ who are changing. But who exults in this world except people whose joy springs from hope...? Let this hope be unhesitating in us, and let us sing for joy. It is not as though these singers were strangers to us or as though our own voice were missing from this psalm. Listen to it as though your were hearing yourselves. Listen as though you were looking at your own reflection in the mirror of the scriptures. When you gaze into the scriptural mirror your own cheerful face looks back at you. When in your exultant hope you observe the likeness between yourself and other members of Christ, the members who first sang these verses, you will be certain that you are among his members, and you too will sing them.[59]

The Psalms, then, were a deeply personal text through which Augustine was able to express his most inward thoughts, while also encountering a vision of his true self.

The *Expositions of the Psalms* (*Enarrationes in Psalmos*) are Augustine's longest work, compiled from homilies and writings he composed throughout his life. These began ca. 391–95 CE, during his initial years in the priesthood, when he undertook to explain the meaning of Pss 1–33.[60] After becoming bishop, he continued to preach and teach on the Psalms, occasionally treating them in numerical order (Pss 111–118, 120–134), but most often non-sequentially. After nearly three decades his final exposition was completed on Ps 119 in 421/22 CE, at

---

[56] Augustine undertook the compilation of these and published them under the title *Enarrationes in Psalmos*. Critical editions can be found in CCSL 38–40, ed. by E. Dekkers and J. Fraipont (Turnhout: Brepols, 1956), formerly in *PL* 36–37. English translations include *Expositions on the Psalms*, 6 vols (Oxford: John Henry Parker, 1847–57); *St. Augustine on the Psalms*, trans. Felicitas Corrigan, ACW 29–30 (Westminster, MD: Newman, 1960–61); and *Expositions of the Psalms*, ed. John E. Rotelle, trans. Maria Boulding, WSA 3/15–20 (Hyde Park, NY: New City Press, 2000–4).

[57] See Michael Fiedrowicz, "General Introduction," in Augustine, *Expositions of the Psalms*, 15:37–38.

[58] Rowan Williams, "Augustine and the Psalms," *Interpretation* 58 (2004): 18. See also *Confessions* 9.4.7–12, where Augustine goes into great length on how Ps 4 helped to uncover and express his soul.

[59] Augustine, *Expositions on the Psalms: 121–150*, trans. Maria Boulding, WSA 3/20 (Hyde Park, NY: New City Press, 2004), 45 [§123.3].

[60] I will be using the modern MT enumeration, though Augustine used the traditional Latin divisions.

which time the *Enarrationes* were compiled as a unified work. As one might suspect, his theological and hermeneutical principles developed during these decades, and recent scholarship has attempted to trace them out.[61] According to Michael Cameron, Augustine's earliest work on the Psalter (Pss 1–33) was more of an "exegetical workshop" than a clear demonstration of his later hermeneutical principle.[62] One can find in these treatments an Augustine who is still getting a feel for the Psalter and how it might be an avenue of grace for his parishioners. Yet, even at this early stage, he employs a thoroughgoing prosopological exegesis, one which will be developed into the characteristic concept of his approach, the *totus Christus*.

The fundamental assumption underlying the *totus Christus* is that the Psalms are a prophecy of Christ.[63] Augustine believed David composed the entire Psalter under the inspiration of the Holy Spirit,[64] and thus he was able "to choose words in such a way that they would be fully capable of expressing the mystery of Christ."[65] The characteristic which set Augustine apart from previous interpreters, however, was his close affiliation between Christ and his church, the Head and the Body, together the "whole Christ." For him, the speaking voice of the Psalms is a conjoining of multiple voices within the same *prosopon*; "Christ" does not simply refer to the Son of God, but the intimate relationship between Christ as Head of the church, and the church itself, which is his Body.[66]

In several homilies Augustine explicitly wrote how this principle of interpretation works, grounding them in Scripture. One of the more complete explanations is found in his second exposition of Ps 30, where he noted the complexity of the speaking voice when the Head and Body are so closely united:

> He who deigned to assume the form of a slave, and within that form to clothe us with himself, he who did not disdain to take us up into himself, did not disdain either to transfigure us into himself, and to speak in our words, so that we in our turn might speak in his... When he said that his soul was sorrowful to the point of death, we all unquestionably said it with him. Without him, we are nothing, but in him we too are Christ. Why? Because the whole Christ consists of the Head and Body. The Head is he who is the savior of his Body, he who has already ascended into heaven; but the Body is the Church, toiling on earth.[67]

He goes on to explain a few paragraphs later, using several biblical texts:

---

[61] See Cameron, *Christ Meets Me Everywhere*; Cameron, "The Emergence of *Totus Christus.*"

[62] Cameron, *Christ Meets Me Everywhere*, 166–67.

[63] Fiedrowicz, "Introduction," 44.

[64] See *City of God* 17.14.

[65] Fiedrowicz, "Introduction," 44.

[66] Fiedrowicz, "Introduction," 51.

[67] Augustine, *Expositions on the Psalms: 1–32*, trans. Maria Boulding, WSA 3/15 (Hyde Park, NY: New City Press, 2000), 322–23 [§30.3].

> Some of the things said here may not even seem suitable for him in the form of a servant, that form which he took from the Virgin; and yet it is Christ who is speaking, because in the members of Christ there is Christ. I want you to understand that Head and body together are called one Christ. To make this quite clear he says, when speaking of marriage, *They will be two in one flesh; so they are two no longer, but one flesh* (Mt 19:5). But perhaps it might be thought that he only means this to apply to any ordinary marriage? No, because listen to what Paul tells us: *They will be two in one flesh,* he says. *This is a great mystery, but I am referring it to Christ and the Church* (Eph 5:31–32). So out of two people one single person comes to be, the single person that is Head and body, Bridegroom and bride.... And if two in one flesh, why not two in one voice? Let Christ speak, then, because in Christ the Church speaks, and in the Church Christ speaks, and the body speaks in the Head and the Head in the body. Listen again to the apostle as he expresses this even more plainly: *As the body is a unit and has many members, and yet all the members of the body, many though they be, are one body, so too is Christ* (1 Cor 12:12).... A body is one single unit, with many members, but all the members of the body, numerous as they are, constitute one body; and it is the same with Christ. Many members, one body: Christ.[68]

Using prosopological exegesis, this framework for the *totus Christus* allowed him to dig deeply into the heart of what was for him a Christological and ecclesiological text.

Augustine's prosopological model is brilliantly constructed. Within the *prosopon* of the *totus Christus* there is a duality: the Head (Jesus) and the Body (the church, both collectively and individually). Cameron explained this as something like "a second voice speaking *within* the first voice," such that "Christ and church are thus a single entity whom Augustine hears talking in the psalm's speaking *ego*."[69] On this score, Augustine "makes Christ's duality-in-unity a mode of scripture interpretation."[70] This is true to an extent, but I would push Cameron a bit further to draw out the model even more.[71] Employing Bates's distinction between various horizons, Augustine's *totus Christus* can be mapped out as

---

[68] Augustine, *Psalms 1–32*, 324 [§30.4].

[69] Cameron, *Christ Meets Me Everywhere*, 210, 213.

[70] Cameron, *Christ Meets Me Everywhere*, 213.

[71] See Cameron, "The Emergence of *Totus Christus*," 208–14; Cameron, *Christ Meets Me Everywhere*, 171–73, 179–85. While his discussion is enlightening, it does not clearly distinguish between prosopopoeia and prosopological exegesis in a way which I think is accurate. For him—if I'm reading correctly—prosopopoeia is the rhetorical device of impersonation employed by an author, while prosopological exegesis is the analysis one does to recognize the different voices in the text. I'm not quite sure this is the correct categorization (i.e., device vs. method). Rather, the difference lies more in prosopopoeia referring to *fictions personarum* ("imagined persons"), while prosopological exegesis is not *impersonation*, but "personation," if you will, the author speaking in the actual voice of another.

follows. On the "prophet" horizon, David speaks in the person of Christ (he is not *impersonating* Christ, but *personating* him); but when this is actualized, the figure of Christ speaks in a kind of dual actualization: the Son of God (the Head) speaks as the church (the Body), "in our words," while the Body "in our turn might speak" as the Head. There is a kind of back and forth, or, as Cameron put it, an "interactive or transpositive dynamic...in which the head and body exchange voices or dialogue together."[72]

We need to remember, however, that Augustine does not apply the "whole Christ" *completely* in each psalm; it does not serve as an interpretive grid that he programmatically lays over the Psalter. Rather, "in practice the various perspectives intermingle, so that often one and the same psalm speaks to God, speaks about God, and represents God himself as speaking."[73] Augustine intimates this himself in his exposition on Ps 37. While he argued that in Ps 37 the whole Christ is speaking, he also noted that

> when Christ speaks, he sometimes does so in the person of the Head alone, the Savior who was born of the virgin Mary; but at other times he speaks in the person of his body, holy Church diffused throughout the world.... We are within his body, we are members of it, and we find ourselves speaking those words.[74]

Indeed, Fiedrowicz has been able to systematize Augustine's interpretive voicing patterns into five options: psalms as a word to Christ (*vox ad Christum*), as a word about Christ (*vox de Christo*), as a word spoken by Christ himself (*vox Christi*), as a word about the church (*vox de ecclesia*), or as a word spoken by the church (*vox ecclesiae*).[75] Moreover, he further delineated the *vox Christi* into several schemata: Christ speaking in his own name (*ex persona sua*), or Christ speaking in our name (*ex persona nostra*) or "in the name of the body" (*ex persona corporis*) or "in the name of his members (*ex membris*).[76] Such flexibility in the voice of David allows Augustine to be a careful reader, and keeps him away from the trap of hermeneutical grids.

In practice the hermeneutic of the *totus Christus* is perfectly illustrated using Ps 3. For Augustine, "this psalm should be understood as spoken in the person of Christ."[77] He then takes the reader through the entire psalm, showing how it relates to Jesus's death and resurrection. The biographical link to the rebellion of Absalom in the psalm heading gives him an opportunity to speak initially of Judas' betrayal of Jesus, allegorically using the Passion of Christ as the narrative

---

[72] Cameron, "The Emergence of *Totus Christus*," 223n26.

[73] Fiedrowicz, "Introduction," 45.

[74] Augustine, *Expositions of the Psalms: 33-50*, trans. Maria Boulding, WSA 3/16 (Hyde Park, NY: New City Press, 2000), 150 [§37.6].

[75] See Fiedrowicz, "Introduction," 44-45.

[76] See Fiedrowicz, "Introduction," 52-55.

[77] Augustine, *Psalms 1-32*, 76 [§3.1].

background of the psalm.[78] At the end, however, he adds, "This psalm can also be understood with reference to the person of Christ in another way, namely, that the whole Christ is speaking: Christ in his totality, I say, in concert with his body of which he is the Head."[79] Here he envisions the church as a collective whole, noting how the psalm helps "the Church beset by the storms of persecution throughout the whole earth."[80] Additionally, he concludes by showing how the individual Christian prays the psalm: "Each one of us can also say, when a whole host of vices and desires leads the struggling mind under the law of sin."[81]

One of the more interesting aspects of Cameron's study of Augustine is that he argued for a shift in Augustine's application of the *totus Christus* comparing his treatment of Pss 1–15 to Pss 16–33. For him, this shift occurred because Augustine "was not yet playing with a full Christological deck; that is, he had not yet sorted out all the dynamics necessary for constructing a coherent understanding of how Christ's humanity conjoined his divinity."[82] According to him, the aim of Augustine's treatment of Pss 1–15 was "to map the road of spiritual ascent for advanced readers."[83] In contrast, Pss 16–33 shift our focus away from spiritual ascent and more towards "the looking glass of Christ's death." He wrote: "Augustine's emphasis on moral purification in the first block of Psalms expositions contrasts the second block's stronger theological analysis of salvation accomplished by Christ."[84]

The impetus for this change of focus is that Augustine learned how to apply the "co-crucifixion" principle of Rom 6:6 ("we were crucified with him"), which theologically emphasized the mystical union between Christ and the church.[85] Cameron is correct to say that Augustine interprets the words of Pss 16–18, 22, 28, and 30–31 in terms of Christ's paschal suffering, such that in them we hear Christ speaking as the Head from the cross.[86] Nevertheless, eight other psalms in this section do not fit so nicely into Cameron's theory: in Pss 23–26 and 29 we hear an acclamation of Christ; the voice of a new convert in the church is heard in Ps 27; the voice of a repentant sinner speaks in Ps 32; and in Ps 33 David speaks an exhortation to praise *in his own voice*. While Cameron has certainly noticed a

---

[78] Augustine, *Psalms 1-32*, 76–77 [§3.1]. For him, there is no sense of an underlying typological connection between the story of David in 1–2 Samuel and the story of Jesus in the Gospels. The superscription allows Augustine to apply his allegorical reading of Ps 3 more fully, but not typologically; the story of David means nothing on its own terms. For him, David is only the prophet who speaks in the person of Christ.

[79] Augustine, *Psalms 1-32*, 81 [§3.9].

[80] Augustine, *Psalms 1-32*, 81 [§3.9].

[81] Augustine, *Psalms 1-32*, 83 [§3.10].

[82] Cameron, *Christ Meets Me Everywhere*, 187.

[83] Cameron, *Christ Meets Me Everywhere*, 167.

[84] Cameron, *Christ Meets Me Everywhere*, 190.

[85] Cameron, *Christ Meets Me Everywhere*, 190, 195.

[86] Cameron, *Christ Meets Me Everywhere*, 196. Likewise, Pss 20–21 speak about Christ's death, but from the third person.

change in Augustine's interpretation, in my opinion this change is not necessarily due to an "ah-ha" moment from time spent in the Pauline epistles. Rather, perhaps it was due to Augustine sitting under the content of the Psalms in the school of David. It is striking that, even in the New Testament use of the Psalms, there are virtually no quotations Pss 3–14 as applied to Christ, whereas Pss 16–24 are a repository for understanding Christ and his Passion. Moreover, when Pss 3–14 are quoted in the New Testament, it is principally for their moral exhortations. This matches Augustine's own focus, as we hear the words of the church, with no mention of the Head, in Pss 5–6, and the "perfected soul" in Ps 7. In other words, Augustine might not have changed his whole interpretive program between these two blocks of psalms, but was capturing the sense of the texts themselves, especially as they were read and applied in the wider canon.

In summary, Augustine made his mark on psalm interpretation by putting forward a robust example of prosopological exegesis. Within the figure of Christ, one could hear a duality of voices: Christ himself (Head), the church (Body), the individual (member of the Body), or all simultaneously (*totus Christus*). By giving room for distinctive voices within one collective persona, Augustine achieved one of the most unique yet influential readings of the Psalter in history. Moreover, he does not seem to have applied the *totus Christus* statically, as a grid placed over the text, but was a careful reader who could hear nuanced Christocentric persona speaking through the prophet David.

2.2. Typological Exegesis in the Premodern Period

A distinct, but equally important approach to the Psalms within the history of interpretation has been called "typological exegesis." Its foundational tenet is that the figure of David is understood as a type of the future Messiah, identified by Christian tradition as Jesus Christ. At the same time, as Matthew Bates noted, proponents of this approach also extend the Davidic type corporately: "[Because] the king embodied Israel's national sorrows and hopes he was also a type in the sense of a corporate symbol, allowing early Christians to see an imitative correspondence between David, Israel, and the future Christ."[87] As such, the words of the Psalms were indeed spoken by David *and were appropriately expressions of David*; yet, through the providence of God and the inspiration of the Holy

---

[87] Bates, *Birth of the Trinity*, 9. See also Christopher R. Seitz, "Psalm 2 in the Entry Hall of the Psalter: Extended Sense in the History of Interpretation," in *Church, Society, and the Christian Common Good: Essays in Conversation with Philip Turner*, ed. Ephraim Radner (Eugene: Cascade, 2017), 96. He notes here the importance of this corporate figure: "An ethics that would lose the corporate life of Israel as a figure for the corporate life of the church would seriously impoverish us, and would make the Old Testament a book that exists only *en route* to a second installment and not a direct word to the church from out of the bosom of the cherished people of God."

Spirit, the truest and most ultimate speaker of David's words is found in his anti-type, Jesus Christ.[88]

For example, in a discussion on the vision of the Messiah in Ps 18, James Mays wrote: "Deliverance from all enemies is an eschatological hope of the people of God. This was hope realized one day in David's career as a proleptic manifestation of what God intends to accomplish through David's seed for the servants of the Lord."[89] In other words, what happens in the deliverance of David is messianic in the sense that it anticipates "that which in fact is still only a future possibility"[90]: the deliverance of Jesus Christ. Christopher Seitz articulated well how a careful typological-figural reading of the text holds in tension a past referentiality connected to David and an extended sense connected to Christ, both of which are already at work in the Psalter itself: "The reader of the Psalms will see that a specific concern will be the particularity of David and Israel in the realistic portrayal of the Psalter, which gives rise to extended sense-making but in so doing never loses its own specific concrete reality for Jewish-Christian reception."[91]

In the contemporary discussion, New Testament scholar Richard Hays is a well-known proponent of the typological model.[92] He approached the topic of typological exegesis in the Psalms through a discussion of Paul's use of the Psalms in Rom 15:3–7. For him, the key to Paul's argument is that Christ is understood as "the true and ultimate speaker of Israel's laments and praises."[93] On one level, the New Testament Christian community believed that "Jesus, in his death, enacts the destiny of the Righteous Sufferer whose voice is heard at prayer in the Psalms."[94] There is a direct correspondence between the voice of David in the Psalms—a righteous sufferer—and the voice of Christ as he most fully expresses the Psalms as *the* Righteous Sufferer. In this respect, the Psalms can be understood as the Messiah's prayer book.[95] On a second level, he also noted a separate correspondence between David and Christ found in their corporate personalities, as noted above: "[David] becomes a symbol for the whole

---

[88] See Childs, *Struggle to Understand Isaiah*, 144–46. In discussing the use of the typological sense by Theodoret, he described it as follows: "The method is one that tries to guard the theological significance of the events of the Old Testament while allowing these events to be seen as prefigurations of later ones. The Old Testament events in the life of Israel, constituted as prophetic, offer a type that recurs as an antitype within a prophecy-fulfillment pattern" (144).

[89] James L. Mays, *The Lord Reigns: A Theological Handbook to the Psalms* (Louisville: Westminster John Knox, 1994), 103.

[90] Richard N. Soulen and R. Kendall Soulen, *Handbook of Biblical Criticism*, 3rd ed (Louisville: Westminster John Knox, 2001), 142.

[91] Seitz, "Psalm 2 in the Entry Hall of the Psalter," 96.

[92] Richard Hays, *The Conversion of the Imagination: Paul as Interpreter of Israel's Scripture* (Grand Rapids: Eerdmans, 2005), 101–18.

[93] Hays, *Conversion of the Imagination*, 109.

[94] Hays, *Conversion of the Imagination*, 106.

[95] Hays, *Conversion of the Imagination*, 110, 117.

people and—at the same time—a prefiguration of the future Anointed who will be the heir of the promises and the restorer of the throne."[96] Indeed, the whole endeavor of hearing the Psalms as the prayers of Christ hangs on whether, in the Psalter itself, the Messiah representatively embodies "the fate of the whole people Israel."[97]

For Hays, the royal psalms paradigmatically account for Israel's corporate suffering, and their "triumphant conclusions" point to God's "eschatological restoration of Israel."[98] He described the narrative as follows:

> Israel's historical experience had falsified a purely immanent literal reading of the texts; the line of David had in fact lost the throne, and Israel's enemies had in fact seized power. Thus, the promise that God would raise up David's seed and establish his kingdom forever... *had* to be read as having reference to an eschatological future.... The distinctive hermeneutical move of early Christianity was to see the sufferings of Israel in these psalms (or, to say the same thing differently, the sufferings of the king who represents Israel) as having been accomplished in an eschatologically definitive way by Jesus on the cross, *and* to see the vindication of Israel accomplished proleptically in his resurrection.[99]

In this way, the past King David has been fused with the future Messiah, identified by the early church as Jesus of Nazareth. By doing so, "David's songs can be read retrospectively as a prefiguration of the Messiah's sufferings and glorifications."[100] For Hays, this is not an example of Christian re-appropriation of the Old Testament. The interpretation of Jesus's death and resurrection in the New Testament grows "organically out of the matrix of the psalms of the Righteous Sufferer."[101] The corporate understanding of the royal and lament psalms, then, must be a component of the editorial purpose of the Psalter.

He further extended his typological understanding of psalms by including the individual believer. In his reading of Rom 15, the goal of Paul's use of the Psalms was to hold up the death of Christ as a paradigm for Christian obedience.[102] A typological model for the Psalms, then, proposes a close connection between the voice of Christ, the church, and the individual believer. While this bears great resemblance to the prosopological model described earlier, the vital difference between the two models lies in how one construes the original utterance of the psalm and its later use. In prosopological exegesis, the prophet David speaks in the voice of another, with no need for correspondence between the

---

[96] Hays, *Conversion of the Imagination*, 111.
[97] Hays, *Conversion of the Imagination*, 118.
[98] Hays, *Conversion of the Imagination*, 110–11.
[99] Hays, *Conversion of the Imagination*, 110, 111.
[100] Hays, *Conversion of the Imagination*, 115.
[101] Hays, *Conversion of the Imagination*, 117–18.
[102] Hays, *Conversion of the Imagination*, 113.

experience of David and the one who actualizes his words; in typological exegesis, however, the correspondence between David and Christ is of utmost importance, as the speech of the anti-type brings the type's words to their fullest
and truest expression.

To demonstrate the practical interpretive difference between the two models we can compare the treatment of Ps 22 by Justin Martyr (discussed above)
and by John Calvin. For Justin, David spoke in the person of Christ, not having
experienced any of the trials related in the psalm. Calvin, on the other hand,
allows for a figure of Christ to be portrayed in David's person:

> David complains in this psalm, that he is reduced to such circum-
> stances of distress that he is like a man in despair. But after having
> recounted the calamities with which he was so severely afflicted, he
> emerges from the abyss of temptations, and gathering courage, com-
> forts himself with the assurance of deliverance. At the same time, he
> sets before us, in his own person [*en sa personne*], a type of Christ [*la
> figure de Christ*], who he knew by the Spirit of prophecy behooved to
> be abased in marvelous and unusual ways previous to his exaltation
> by the Father.[103]

I have provided Calvin's original French to better capture the conceptual differences between him and Justin: for Justin, the prophet David speaks "from the
prosopon of Christ" (ἀπὸ προσώπου τοῦ Χριστοῦ); for Calvin, David speaks "in his
own person, a type of Christ" (*en sa personne, la figure de Christ*). In the prosopological model, through the voice of David one *hears* the person of Christ; in the
typological model, the person of David *represents* the person of Christ.[104] With
prosopological exegesis David's own life events carry no bearing in the significance of a psalm, but with typological exegesis there is a correspondence, an "at
the same time" parallel between David and the Messiah.

To illustrate the application of a typological model within the history of interpretation I have chosen to look at two representative interpreters: Thomas
Aquinas and John Calvin. Both, while making their own specific contributions,
articulate a view of the Psalter which allows for "a fusion of referents" in such a
way that, as Seitz described, "the particularity of each is not lost, but through
extended sense-making is capable of greater integration and theological
achievement."[105]

---

[103] John Calvin, *Commentary on the Book of Psalms*, trans. J. Anderson, 5 vols. (Edinburgh: Calvin Translation Society, 1845), 1:356.

[104] See Wulfert de Greef, "Calvin as Commentator on the Psalms," trans. Raymond A.
Blacketer, in *Calvin and the Bible*, ed. Donald K. McKim (Cambridge: Cambridge University
Press, 2006), 103.

[105] Seitz, "Psalm 2 in the Entry Hall of the Psalter," 95.

2.2.1. Thomas Aquinas: Literal David and Mystical Christ

We begin with Thomas Aquinas, whose contribution on the Psalms in the history of interpretation is more modest than both Origen and Augustine, yet represents a robust typological model which came into play centuries before Calvin.[106] As Ryan noted, Thomas is both "traditional and innovative," but "to be sure, he is not *sui generis*."[107] Relying conceptually on predecessors such as Peter Lombard and Hugh of St. Cher,[108] he developed a threefold programmatic scheme for the entire Psalter, all the while advocating a typological-figural approach.

Thomas explained his hermeneutical aims and the general characteristics of the Psalms within the Prologue to his commentary, which uses a typical fourfold Aristotelean division.[109] In the opening sections he highlights the universal nature of the Psalms as well as their reparative value, which he ties to the incarnation of Christ: "Everything which pertains to faith in the incarnation is clearly treated in this work that it almost seems to be a gospel, rather than prophecy."[110] Concerning its mode, he also distinguished the Psalms from other books of the Bible by its use of "praise and prayer" (*laudis et orationis*). Prayer—the "end or purpose" of the Psalter—is critical as it is through prayer that we find "the lifting up of the mind to God" (*elevatio mentis in Deum*).[111] Ryan summarized adeptly the ways in which prayer represents an ascent for Thomas: "It involves wonder at God's greatness, which is the elevation of faith; a tendency towards beatitude, which is the elevation of hope; adherence to divine goodness and sanctity, the

---

[106] Critical editions of Aquinas's *Postilla Super Psalmos* include *Opera Omnia*, ed. Vernon J. Bourke (New York: Musurgia, 1948–50), and *Opera Omnia, Vol. 5: Commentaria in Scripturas*, ed. Roberto Busa (Stuttgart-Bad Cannstatt: Frommann-Holzboog, 1980). There is no published translation of Aquinas's entire commentary in English, but an unofficial effort is being made by several translators with the Aquinas Translation Project at DeSales University (http://hosted.desales.edu/w4/philtheo/loughlin/ATP/). An English translation in progress by Sr. Albert Marie Surmanksi, O.P., from the Latin-English *Opera Omnia* in the Aquinas Institute. A critical French edition is available: Thomas D'Aquin, *Commentaire sur les Psaumes*, ed. Jean-Eric Stroobant: Paris: Cerf, 1996). For translations of his Prologue and Ps 45 in English, see Thomas Aquinas, *The Gifts of the Spirit: Selected Spiritual Writings (Chiefly from his Biblical Commentaries)*, ed. Benedict M. Ashley, trans. Matthew Rzeczkowski (Hyde Park, NY: New City Press, 1995), 95–133.

[107] Thomas F. Ryan, *Thomas Aquinas as a Reader of the Psalms*, SST 6 (Notre Dame: University of Notre Dame Press, 2000), 8.

[108] See Ryan, *Aquinas as Reader*, 5–7. A translation of Lombard's preface to his commentary can be found in A. J. Minnis and A. B. Scott, eds., *Medieval Literary Theory and Criticism c. 1100-1375: The Commentary Tradition* (Oxford: Clarendon, 1988), 105–12. Several parts of this preface, including the basic threefold schema, are reproduced almost verbatim in Aquinas's prologue.

[109] For an in-depth explanation of what follows, see Ryan, *Aquinas as Reader*, 13–17.

[110] Thomas, "Prologue," in Aquinas, *Gifts of the Spirit*, 96.

[111] Thomas, "Prologue," 97.

elevation of charity; and finally imitation of divine justice in work... the elevation of justice."[112] Thomas concludes this opening section by summarizing the "four causes" of the Psalter:

> Its matter concerns all the works of God; its genre is deprecatory or laudatory; its purpose is to join those who have been exalted to union with the Most High and Holy One; the author is the Holy Spirit himself revealing all these things.[113]

In this way, the Psalms provide a means by which the one who reads them ascends to the mind of God, which in turn influences how one lives a life in imitation of God.

Having described the general characteristics of the Psalms, Thomas then turned to his basic hermeneutical principles, referencing the so-called "Rule of Jerome" in contrast to the exegetical tendencies of Theodore of Mopsuestia. As Daniel Flores noted, this section in the Prologue represents his "most sophisticated analysis of textual significations."[114] We will do well, then, to dwell on it to understand the subtleties of his figural reading. He begins by relating his understanding of Theodore's error:

> We need above all to avoid one error which was condemned by the Fifth Ecumenical Council.... Theodore of Mopsuestia said that in sacred scripture and the prophets nothing is said explicitly about Christ [*expresse dicitur de Christo*]; rather, these books really speak of certain other matters, which statements have only been accommodated to refer to Christ [*sed adaptaverunt Christo*], for example, Ps 22:19, *They divided my garments among them,* {is said not about Christ, but literally said about David} [*sed ad litteram dicitur de David*].[115]

Whether or not Theodore actually made the errors attributed to him at the Second Council of Constantinople (553 CE)—and, the legitimacy of his resulting posthumous condemnation—have been a matter of contemporary debate within the larger conversation on so-called Alexandrian and Antiochene exegesis.[116] Regardless, the kind of reading Thomas wants us to avoid is crucial to his

---

[112] Ryan, *Aquinas as Reader*, 15.

[113] Thomas, "Prologue," 99.

[114] Daniel E. Flores, "Thomas on the Literalness of Christ and the Interpretation of Scripture," *St. Thomas Day Lecture*, 29 Jan 2019, http://thomasaquinas.edu/print/18579.

[115] Thomas, "Prologue," 99–100. Translation in braces { } is from Flores.

[116] Thomas is comfortable repeating the Council *anathema*, as are some contemporary scholars. See John J. O'Keefe, "'A Letter That Killeth': Toward a Reassessment of Antiochene Exegesis, or Diodore, Theodore, and Theodoret on the Psalms," *JECS* 8 (2000): 83–103. At the same time, others have attempted to better appreciate Antiochene *theoria* as a legitimate hermeneutical aim. See Bradley Nassif, "'Scriptural Exegesis' in the School of Antioch," in *New Perspectives on Historical Theology: Essays in Memory of John Meyendorff*, ed. Bradley Nassif (Grand Rapids: Eerdmans, 1996), 342–77.

own hermeneutic. The error hinges on what he means by the "adaptation" or "accommodation" of a prophetic text concerning Christ.

Generally speaking, adaptation suggests that "the Old Testament authors did not intend to refer to New Testament things, rather, New Testament authors appropriated the words at will: they made them fit."[117] In his commentary on Matthew, Thomas also mentioned Theodore's error, there comparing it to how some had "adapted" Virgil so that one of his texts (*Aeneid* 2.650) can be read concerning Christ. Such a move disregards the intention of the author, showing a "radical manipulation of words based upon verbal ambiguities and the equivocal use of language."[118] In the case of Ps 22, this meant that while the text could literally only speak of David, it was available for later "adaptation" concerning Christ. The problem for Thomas is that this would implicate the apostles and evangelists "in a falsification of textual integrity," and would run against Jesus's own words concerning the Psalms (cf. Luke 24:44); namely, that they are "about me."

In contrast to this hermeneutic, Thomas suggests we follow the "Rule of Jerome," which states that "the things related are to be interpreted as prefiguring [*figurantibus*] something about Christ or the Church."[119] He further explained:

> As 1 Cor 10:11 says, *These things happened {to them in a figure} [Omnia in figura contingebant illis]*. Prophecies, were, of course, sometimes pronounced about things of that time, but they were not said principally about them, except insofar as they were a prefigurement of future things [*figura sunt futurorum*]. The Holy Spirit ordained that when such things were spoken of, certain things were included that {exceeded} the condition of the event [*excedunt conditionem illius rei gestae*]; that way the soul would be lifted up to what was being prefigured [*ad figuratum*].[120]

The approach advocated by Thomas differs from Theodore principally in his understanding of the relationship between the present historical reality (of the prophet) and the future historical reality (pertaining to Christ). Whereas Theodore connected them together through "adaptation," Thomas connects them by recognizing how the former events were a "prefigurement of future things." Thus, the words of David have both a historical referent to his own life and a literal sense that extends to Christ. The *Rule* from which Thomas based this hermeneutic comes from Jerome's commentary on Hosea, at Hos 1:3:

> The prophets promised about the coming of Christ after many centuries and the calling of the gentiles in this way, in order that they might not overlook the present time, lest they seem not to teach the convoked assembly [of their time] about the things that occur

---

[117] Flores, "Thomas on the Literalness of Christ."
[118] Flores, "Thomas on the Literalness of Christ."
[119] Thomas, "Prologue," 100.
[120] Thomas, "Prologue," 100. Translation in braces { } is from Flores.

through their fault, on account of the other [future realities], but instead seem to [neglect the present] and rejoice about obscure and future things.[121]

In this passage, Jerome argued that the prophet intended "to signify both the
present historical reality (*res*) and the future historical reality (*res*) with the
same words."[122] The concept which binds these two realities together is *extension*
or *completion*. For Thomas, Ps 72 perfectly illustrates this principle:

> We can read certain things about the reign of David and Solomon
> which were not to be fulfilled in the reigns of such kings but were to
> be fulfilled in the reign of Christ. These things were said as a figure of
> Christ [*in cujus figura dicta sunt*]...since the Holy Spirit also puts in that
> psalm certain things which exceed {its capacity} [*et aliquid ponit in eo
> quod excedit facultatem ipsius*].... Thus, Psalm 72 is to be interpreted as
> being about the reign of Solomon insofar as it is a figure [*figura*] of
> the reign of Christ; in that reign all the things the psalm says will be
> {completed} [*complebuntur*]."[123]

According to Thomas, the "exceeding" language of the psalm points to a literal
extension or bridge between David and Christ. The result is that we are able to
find literal references to Christ in the prophets, yet at the same time not pre-
cluding a genuine Old Testament historical reality. That is, David or Solomon do
not cease to be historical because they figure something else which will bring
the text to completion.

We see the same kind of typological move in Thomas's treatment of Ps 2.
For him, the "psalm is David's, because it was composed by him, and it treats of
his kingdom in the figure of the kingdom of Christ. For by David, Christ is suita-
bly signified."[124] At verse seven, he noted: "*The Lord said to me*, which is not always
fulfilled concerning David [*completur de David*]; and thus it is understood concerning Christ [*ideo intelligitur de Christo*] to whom belong dominion over the
Gentiles by right."[125] Through this extension both David and Christ continue to
have relevance for the reader.

In Ps 22—where Thomas criticizes Theodore—we have a special version of
his typological extension. He begins his comments on this psalm as follows:

> As was said above, as in the other prophets, also this one treats of
> certain things then present inasmuch as they were figures of Christ
> [*figura Christi*], and which pertained to the prophecy itself. And thus,
> sometimes some things are put forth [in the text] which pertain to

---

[121] Translation from Flores, "Thomas on the Literalness of Christ."
[122] Flores, "Thomas on the Literalness of Christ."
[123] Thomas, "Prologue," 100. Translation in braces {} is from Flores.
[124] Thomas, "Psalm 2 and commentary," trans. Stephen Loughlin, Aquinas Translation Project, http://hosted.desales.edu/w4/philtheo/loughlin/ATP/.
[125] Thomas, "Psalm 2 and commentary."

Christ, which exceed [*excedunt*], so to speak, the condition of the histories [*virtutem historiarum*]. And among others, this very psalm treats about the Passion of Christ in a spiritual manner [*spiritualiter*]. And thus, this is its literal sense [*sensus literalis*]. Hence, specifically He spoke this Psalm in the passion when He cried out *Heli, Heli, Lammasabactani*: which is the same as *God, my God, etc.*, as this psalm begins. And thus, granted this Psalm is said figuratively about David [*et ideo licet figuraliter hic Psalmus dicatur de David*], nevertheless specifically it refers to Christ in a literal sense [*ad litteram*]."[126]

Perhaps because of the importance of Ps 22 in its witness to Christ, Thomas departs from his typical use of *historiae* in reference to David's historical reality and *mystice* in reference to Christ's future reality. Instead, he equates the "spiritual" with the "literal," so that, unlike what he does elsewhere (cf. below), the narrative of Christ in the Gospels supplies the primary context within which he interprets the psalm. He will also take great advantage of Augustine's *totus Christus* to allow for a duality of voices within the person of Christ: the Head and the Body. Nevertheless, unlike Augustine, Thomas will continue to refer to David's context, albeit figuratively. For instance, in explaining the title to Ps 22, he wrote:

The title here refers to the time when David was a fugitive, and was hiding in desert places like a stag. Thus, he previously said, *And he set my feet as of a stag.* Therefore, this psalm itself is entitled for the very tribulation which symbolized the passion of Christ [*figurabat passionem Christi*]. Nevertheless, this mode is referred better to Christ, so that by the stag is understood human nature in Christ, because the stag crosses a thicket of thorns without injury to its foot, just as Christ crossed through this present life without defilement.

We can see, then, that Thomas is able to employ a rich variety of typological relationships between David and Christ. In most cases the literal sense is identified as David's own history, but, as in the case of Ps 22, the literal sense is not David's but Christ's. For Thomas, the problem with Theodore is that his interpretive principles only allow for a single literal referent: either David or Christ. In the case of Ps 22, since the literal referent was David, Theodore's hermeneutic only allowed for Christ to speak through an adaptation of the words.[127]

---

[126] Translation from Flores, "Thomas on the Literalness of Christ."

[127] See Seitz, "Psalm 2 in the Entry Hall of the Psalter," 98–99. He noted that the Antiochenes are willing—as seen in the case of Ps 2—to read David as a prophet speaking about future events, even the time of Christ, but only in terms of "single sense making: David always sees one thing intelligibly and prophetically" (98). He goes on to suggest that even in the case of Ps 22, for Theodore the issue is not one of adaptation, but utilization: "The utilization by Christ of Psalm 22 is just that: a utilization, appropriate for him, and also appropriate for us in the church in a situation of kindred affliction being borne 'in Christ'" (99). For Seitz, Theodore is allowing the figure of David to function in a typical rather than a typological fashion. Speaking in the context of his own experiences

The final component of Thomas's Prologue sets out his programmatic threefold scheme for the entire Psalter. He divided it into three sets of fifty psalms which correspond to three different stages in one's progress from penitence to praise: Psalms 1–51 [Lat. 1–50] correspond to the state of penitence; Pss 52–101 [51–100] to the judgment of God; and Pss 102–150 [101–150] to the praise of God's eternal glory. Resembling the earlier approach of Gregory of Nyssa, Thomas's model "conceives of the Psalms as a sort of map that charts out the human journey to salvation that begins with penance, continues with progress, and concludes with praise."[128]

Within these three sections, Thomas also noted that the historical titles do not occur in chronological order, and must "signify something other than history alone." This builds off his previous comments, highlighting again that while the literal sense of the text is important, one still needs to attend to a secondary, mystical sense. As an example, in the first set of fifty he argued that all of David's sufferings and subsequent liberations are to be understood figuratively, according to how they signify Christ and the church. In particular, he named the persecutions of Absalom and Saul as signifying "the persecution which the saints suffer either from those of their own household or from outsiders: so Christ suffered from Judas, and from the Jews." He broke this down by looking at the literal sense of the text: Psalms 1–11 [Lat. 1–10] concern the persecutions of Absalom—note that both Pss 3 and 7 are connected to Absalom's rebellion—while Pss 12–21 [11–20] concern the persecutions of Saul (cf. Ps 18). The biographical superscriptions, then, direct Thomas in his understanding of the literal sense not simply on the superscripted psalms, but on entire sections in which they are

---

of suffering at the hands of Absalom, which was the consequence of his previous sins in the matter of Uriah and Bathsheba, David's prayer provides all "pious people" with words "to recite when they suffer something of this kind." See Theodore of Mopsuestia, *Commentary on Psalms 1-81*, trans. Robert C. Hill, WGRW 5 (Atlanta: SBL, 2006), 243.

Nevertheless, it is important for us to acknowledge that Theodore has moved beyond his teacher Diodore in this regard. See Diodore of Tarsus, *Commentary on Psalms 1-51*, trans. Robert C. Hill, WGRW 9 (Atlanta: SBL, 2005), 69–74. While Diodore too argued that Ps 22 was not applicable to Christ because of its mentioning of the speaker's sins and their subsequent punishment, and thus should be read as from the viewpoint of David, he continues to allow for Christological "resemblances" at certain points: "Now, this was fulfilled more properly in the case of the Lord to the extent of lots being cast to divide his very clothes. But it is not in opposition to the psalm's theme: it is possible, as I said, for the resemblance to emerge in greater detail in that case and for it to happen here in actual fact. Hence the sequel applies more properly to David" (72, on verses 18–19). These extensional resemblances—the barest form of figural reading—are not found in Theodore. For Thomas, the issue does not seem to be Theodore's utilization of the psalm by Christ and the church *per se*, but the denial of an extension of the literal sense. As we will see below, in his own commentary he will often appeal to a moral sense, but it is one found as an extension of the literal sense rather than as part of later typical utilization.

[128] Ryan, *Aquinas as Reader*, 21.

found. This literal sense sets up his figural reading, which informed his own understanding of the speaking personae. I will illustrate these by attending to his comments on Pss 3–6.

Thomas approached Ps 3 in view of its biographical superscription about the rebellion of Absalom. He noted that Ps 2 speaks about the effort of David's adversaries, while Ps 3 is presented as a prayer imploring God for help against their efforts. The psalm, then, can be explained with three different senses: as based in history (*historae*), as giving an allegorical sense (*sensum allegoricum*), and as giving a tropological or moral sense (*moralem*). Following the comments in his preface, Aquinas located the historical sense in the title of the psalm, such that the psalm is about David and Absalom. At the same time, however, "this persecution prefigures the persecution that Christ suffered from his son Judas."[129] Furthermore, this can be extended to also include the tribulations the church faces according to a moral sense: "In the moral sense, it is the tribulations that the man suffers from temporal or spiritual enemies. And this is why this psalm expresses the sentiments of the man who implores."[130] Concerning the speaking persona, this means that at the historical level we are to hear the voice of David praying to God about the rebellion of his son Absalom, while at the same time we are to also hear the voice of Jesus Christ (Head) praying concerning the treachery of Judas and the church (Body) praying against its temporal and spiritual enemies. While retaining the Augustinian understand of the *totus Christus* (as he does in Ps 22), there is a noted contrast to the prosopological reading of Augustine discussed earlier. For Thomas, since the *totus Christus* is a typological extension of the literal sense, both David and Jesus retain their voices in the praying of the psalm. Here, in contrast to Ps 22, Aquinas explains the psalm wholly from the viewpoint of David, whereas in Ps 22 he explains it from the viewpoint of Christ.

Turning to Ps 4, which lacks the biographical heading, Thomas again initially argued for a literal Davidic reading: "In the previous psalm David implored God's help with his prayer; understanding that he has been heard, he now urges others to trust in God. This psalm expresses the sentiment of the man who, having experienced divine mercy, his benefits and his justice, exhorts others not to despair."[131] He explained the different elements of the psalm title in both their literal (*litteralis*) and mystical (*mystice*) senses, noting that "unto the end" should be understood as ultimately pointing to Christ: "If we consider the phrase in the figurative sense, we can understand that we were singing to celebrate the completion of some work or for some business, just as this psalm was composed upon the completion of the liberation of David who was persecuted by Absalom, in other words, his victory."[132] In the commentary itself, Thomas never speaks of

---

[129] Thomas, *Commentaire sur les Psaumes*, 55.

[130] Thomas, *Commentaire sur les Psaumes*, 56.

[131] Thomas, *Commentaire sur les Psaumes*, 60.

[132] Thomas, *Commentaire sur les Psaumes*, 61. See the Latin, as the French translation appears to have skipped a phrase due to haplography.

the mystical sense explicitly, perhaps relying on the reader to make the connection. Again, we here note that the mystical voice of the Body (the church) is an extension of the literal voice of David.

A similar approach was taken for Ps 5. Thomas summarized the psalm by noting how the psalmist previously prayed against those pursuing him (Ps 4), and here "prays against those who spread deceit, so as not to be deceived."[133] He again explained the title ("Unto the end. For her that obtains the inheritance") in terms of its literal figure (*figura*) and mystical sense (*mysterium*), as referring to the Jewish people inheriting the promises through David and Christians through Christ, respectively. As with the previous psalm, Thomas only commented on the literal sense: David had returned from his victory over Absalom, having lost his inheritance, and is now recovering it.

And finally, in Ps 6 David prays to be restored from a failure on his part, through which we can see "the feelings of the man who, chastised for his sins and delivered into the hands of his enemies, obtained his liberation after performing a penance."[134] For the title, he interpreted "the octave" to refer historically to David's composition of the psalm for the Feast of Tabernacles, on which it was sung during an octave of days (eight days). As a celebration of harvest, the Feast mystically indicates the resurrection of Christ and the gathering of all humankind from the four winds in their own resurrection. Still, Thomas spent no time developing the mystical interpretation in his comments. Rather, he was content to explain the nature of prayer using David, within his own literal context, as an exemplar.

Within Pss 3–6, Thomas consistently envisioned at least a twofold meaning of each psalm within his introductory comments. The first related in a literal sense (*historiae/ad litteram*) to David within his own history, and the second in a mystical sense (*mystice/mysterium*) to Christ as both Head and Body (*totus Christus*). In this, he envisioned speaking personae which are related to each of these senses: the voice of David (literal) and the voice of Christ/church (mystical). Beyond the superscription, we see Thomas taking different avenues for commentary. In Pss 4–6 he remained solely within the literal sense, perhaps anticipating the reader to make the extension themselves. In Ps 3, and at other times (e.g., Pss 9/10 and 11 [Lat. 9–10]), he expresses his full hermeneutic, explicitly moving back and forth between the literal and mystical senses, even going so far as to unite these senses within the literal in the case of Ps 22.

In sum, Thomas thought that Christians could look to either David or Christ to achieve union with God, which was the chief aim of reading the Psalter. The theme of penitence is important here, as a concentration solely on the voice of Christ would render the penitential voice of the psalms speechless.[135] The typological link between David and Christ draws together their mutual sufferings

---

[133] Thomas, *Commentaire sur les Psaumes*, 68.

[134] Thomas, *Commentaire sur les Psaumes*, 79.

[135] This is a different conclusion than Ryan, *Aquinas as a Reader*, 107–44. He contended that Thomas's approach to the Psalter not only holds Christ in a central position, but that

and deliverance at the hands of their sons (Absalom/Judas), the nations (Saul/Pilate), and the general population. In this, both David and Christ are exemplars as Christian readers contemplate the work of God in order to achieve union with God, progressing from penitence to praise.

2.2.2. John Calvin: David in the Shadow of Christ

Our second typological interpreter is Reformation theologian and exegete John Calvin. His work on the Psalms comes primarily in his lengthy commentary on the book, written throughout the 1550s.[136] He also oversaw the formation of the Geneva Psalter (begun in 1537, and only finished in 1562), helped revise Olivetan's translation of the Psalms into French, and preached regularly from the Psalter between 1546 and 1554. The Psalms, then, were a consistent part of Calvin's thought for a lengthy portion of his life. I briefly introduced Calvin's typological model earlier, but to understand his distinctive approach we need to situate him within the context of the Reformation, when traditional approaches to Scripture (i.e., the *Quadriga*) were being supplanted for a more robust understanding of the literal sense.[137]

For Calvin, the problem with traditional approaches to Scripture did not lie with a spiritual understanding of the text *per se*, but with a neglect of the historical situation of the authors of Scripture. As one scholar explained:

> In Calvin's perspective, the way that these exegetes filled the Psalms with Christological content did violence to their historical context, and thus nullified what the psalmists experienced in their relationship to God. To fail to take God's dealings with Israel seriously, Calvin warns, is to do an injustice not only to Israel, but much more so to God himself.[138]

Calvin's greater regard for the historical sense of the text is not the result of an historical consciousness or of history *as history*—he is not a modern exegete—but came from his "desire to do complete justice to the total biblical message which is cast in historical form."[139] Replacing the *Quadriga*, Calvin preferred what

---

Christ and *not David* is put forward as the one the Christian should imitate in prayer. In a telling section, "Christ as Example in *Super Psalmos*" (112–22), Ryan consistently showed that David, and not Christ, is most often used as the *exemplum*. Still, Ryan is correct that Thomas explicitly links together David and Christ to show how Christ provides believers an example of suffering. See Michael Cameron's review in *JR* 83 (2003): 138–39.

[136] The first edition of the commentary was published in Latin in 1557 (*In librum Psalmorum commentarius*), followed by two French editions: *Le Livre des Psaumes exposé par Jehan Calvin* (1558) and *Commentaires sur le livre des Psaumes* (1561).

[137] See David C. Steinmetz, "John Calvin as an Interpreter of the Bible," in *Calvin and the Bible*, ed. Donald K. McKim (Cambridge: Cambridge University Press, 2006), 284–85.

[138] Wulfert de Greef, "Calvin as Commentator," trans. Raymond A. Blacketer, in *Calvin and the Bible*, ed. Donald K. McKim (Cambridge: Cambridge University Press, 2006), 89.

[139] S. H. Russell, "Calvin and the Messianic Interpretation of the Psalms," *SJT* 21 (1968): 38.

he called a "plain" or "natural" sense of the biblical text. In our vernacular, one might say that he interpreted the Psalms for their "grammatical" and "historical" meanings, if by this one means that he gave serious attention to the words on the page and the location of a psalm within the psalmist's scriptural setting.[140] His plain sense, however, was not woodenly literal. As Steinmetz has noted: "By modern standards, Calvin adhered to what can only be regarded as a generous reading of the 'plain sense' of the text."[141]

In the preface to Calvin's commentary, he stated that his chief purpose in the work was the edification of the church. He also noted that this edification primarily takes place through his (and his readers') imitation of David.[142] In his approach to the book of Psalms, Calvin first speaks of their spiritual benefit. In an oft-quoted passage he wrote:

> I have been accustomed to call this book, I think not inappropriately, "An Anatomy of all parts of the soul"; for there is not an emotion of which any one can be conscious that is not here represented as in a mirror. Or rather, the Holy Spirit has here drawn to the life all the griefs, sorrows, fears, doubts, hopes, cares, perplexities, in short, all the distracting emotions with which the minds of men are wont to be agitated.[143]

The Psalms as "an anatomy of all parts of the soul" is the hallmark of Calvin's approach. In some respects, it is reminiscent of the approach of Athanasius (cf. below), but for Calvin the relationship between the reader and the speaking voice is construed differently. In Athanasius's model, the reader puts the words of the speaker on her own lips, making the words her own, while Calvin thought that readers were listening in on how the psalmists spoke to God, and, as they did, "laying open all their inmost thoughts and affections," the words draw in the reader to their own examination. The result is that the reader's own infirmities and vices are laid bare, urging them to seek God in faith:[144]

> Genuine and earnest prayer proceeds first from a sense of our need, and next, from faith in the promises of God. It is by perusing these inspired compositions, that men will be most effectually awakened to a sense of their maladies, and, at the same time, instructed in seeking remedies for their cure. In a word, whatever may serve to encourage us when we are about to pray to God, is taught us in this book.[145]

---

[140] de Greef, "Calvin as Commentator," 92.

[141] Steinmetz, "Calvin as an Interpreter," 285.

[142] G. Sujin Pak, *The Judaizing Calvin: Sixteenth-Century Debates over the Messianic Psalms* (Oxford: Oxford University Press, 2010), 78.

[143] John Calvin, *Commentary on the Book of Psalms*, trans. J. Anderson, 5 vols. (Edinburgh: Calvin Translation Society, 1845), 1:xxxvi-xxxvii.

[144] Calvin, *Commentary on the Book of Psalms*, 1:xxxvii.

[145] Calvin, *Commentary on the Book of Psalms*, 1:xxxvii.

One can hear echoes of all our previous commentators in this language that de-scribes the Psalms as providing "remedies" to human maladies.

Unlike other interpreters, Calvin argued that the principal means by which to find our cure was through the person of David and all his experiences. Truly, David is worthy of imitation, providing us a model for a faithful life:

> For although I follow David at a great distance, and come far short of equaling him; or rather, although in aspiring slowly and with great difficulty to attain to the many virtues in which he excelled, I still feel myself tarnished with the contrary vices; yet if I have any things in common with him, I have no hesitation in comparing myself with him... [It has] been of very great advantage to me to behold in him as in a mirror... so that I know the more assuredly, that whatever that most illustrious king and prophet suffered, was exhibited to me by God as an example for imitation.[146]

Calvin followed this passage with a rather lengthy recounting of his own life, and finished by noting how David's footsteps had shown him a way of life and provided him much consolation. The commentary functions, then, as a kind of exercise that allows his readers to catch a glimpse of David's "internal affec-tions," that they too might be edified by his words as in a mirror.[147]

As such, David is something like a type or figure, "not in the sense of being an empty figure of things to come, but as an example of beliefs and teachings that remain the same under the new covenant."[148] As Pitkin observed: "David is like a mirror in which believers can contemplate all that should lead them to pray well and to praise God when he has heard them."[149] Throughout his com-mentary Calvin will use plural first-person pronouns—"we" and "us"—showing both his and David's solidarity with the church: "David has furnished an exam-ple to others, that they should freely and without fear approach God."[150] But this is not the only way Calvin approached the book of Psalms.

Combined with this "David as exemplar" approach, Calvin also developed David as a figure, or type, of Christ. This is almost entirely isolated to the royal psalms (or those psalms interpreted in the New Testament as prophesying Christ), but the popularity of this reading strategy has led some scholars to go so far as to say that his main hermeneutical principle is that "David and his king-dom are shadows and types of the kingdom of Christ."[151] In truth, his typological

---

[146] Calvin, *Commentary on the Book of Psalms*, 1:xl.

[147] Calvin, *Commentary on the Book of Psalms*, 1:xliv.

[148] Barbara Pitkin, "Imitation of David: David as a Paradigm for Faith in Calvin's Exe-gesis of the Psalms," *SCJ* 24 (1993): 848.

[149] Pitkin, "Imitation of David," 847.

[150] Calvin, *Commentary on the Book of Psalms*, 1:560 [on Ps 34:5]. See also Pitkin, "Imita-tion of David," which provides a wealth of examples of how David acts as a mirror for Calvin and for all believers.

[151] See Russell, "Messianic Interpretation," 38–39. He argued that the "master key" is "the solidarity of Christ and His members before and after the incarnation" (42).

reading of the royal psalms is only an extension of his goal of lifting up David as an exemplar for the church. In this respect, as we saw above, Thomas is perhaps the more consistently typological than Calvin. The clearest place to begin is with Calvin's treatment of Ps 2.

For Calvin, Ps 2 is about David and his kingdom, but also moves beyond David's kingdom since it was "typical and contains a prophecy concerning the future kingdom of Christ."[152] He explained the typological connection between David to Christ as follows:

> That David prophesied concerning Christ, is clearly manifest from this, that he knew his own kingdom to be merely a shadow. And in order to learn to apply to Christ whatever David, in times past, sang concerning himself, we must hold this principle, which we meet everywhere in all the prophets, that he, with his posterity, was made king, not so much for his own sake as to be a type of the Redeemer.... As David's temporal kingdom was a kind of earnest to God's ancient people of the eternal kingdom, which at length was truly established in the person of Christ, those things which David declares concerning himself are not violently, or even allegorically, applied to Christ, but were truly predicted concerning him.[153]

From this passage, we can see that there are a few principles which lie beneath his typological model. First, David was not a prophet who wrote unknowingly about the future, but "knew his own kingdom to be a shadow." As such, since the typological connection was intended by David, what David predicted concerning Christ is not "violently" or even "allegorically" applied to Christ, but was "truly predicted concerning him." Indeed, David was made king "not so much for his own sake as to be a type of the Redeemer." In this way, the temporal kingdom of David was *for David* a kind of pledge. For both Thomas and Calvin, then, David's intent for the text rescues it from violently being applied to Christ. Both contexts are part of a robust spiritual-literal sense. As Russell noted: "The Davidic kingdom indeed must not be thought of as a mere representation of that of Christ.... [Because] it was a pledge of Christ's coming...the substance of His kingdom must in some way be regarded as present."[154] We have, then, a paralleling between the kingdom of David and the kingdom of Christ, such that "those things which David testified concerning his own kingdom are properly applicable to Christ."[155] As Seitz observed: "David spoke of something God would intend to refer to something else as well, but which has meaning in his own frame of reference all the same."[156] For Thomas, this is called the "Rule of Jerome."

---

[152] Calvin, *Commentary on the Book of Psalms*, 1:9.

[153] Calvin, *Commentary on the Book of Psalms*, 1:11.

[154] Russell, "Messianic Interpretation," 42.

[155] Calvin, *Commentary on the Book of Psalms*, 1:11–12.

[156] Seitz, "Psalm 2 in the Entry Hall of the Psalter," 102. He continues: "[The] literal sense exists within its covenantal context in Israel, but which has a further extensional capacity that is built into its original gifting to David" (102).

Second, Calvin also demonstrated that he was careful in listening to whom might be speaking. In verse three, for example, he wrote, "This is a prosopopoeia, in which the prophet introduces his enemies as speaking; and he employs this figure the better to express their ungodly and traitorous design."[157] Calvin, then, joins many others in reception history by hearing different voices in this psalm. Such a reading, in fact, leads to another typological connection between David and Christ. In verse seven, "David... assumes the office of preacher in order to publish the decree of God; or at least protests that he did not come to the throne without a sure and clear proof of his calling." And yet, this protest "was more truly fulfilled in Christ, and doubtless, David, under the influence of the spirit of prophecy, had a special reference to him." In other words, "Christ proved himself to have been endued with lawful power from God, not only by his miracles, but by the preaching of the gospel."[158] This leads to a third principle in which Calvin connects David to Christ; namely, that when hyperbolic language cannot be understood fully in a historical sense (i.e., applied to David), it must have a deeper meaning that is only fulfilled in Christ.[159] Again, this highlights the conceptual similarities between Calvin and Thomas.

Calvin followed the above three principles when he commented on the messianic psalms (e.g., 16, 22, 41, 72, 109, and 110). Outside of these psalms, however, he was committed to explaining a psalm principally within the context of David's life, applied to the lives of Christians as they reflect on the whole doctrine of God in Scripture. The distinctive mark of Calvin's interpretation of the Psalms, then, lies in his insistence on hearing a Davidic voice within its Old Testament situation. When David speaks in the Psalms, Calvin expects us to hear this with reference to David and his kingdom. On occasion, when there is justification, he will also allow a broader typological connection between David and his kingdom with Christ and his kingdom.[160]

This is a noteworthy turn away from the approaches used by our first three interpreters. As Pitkin observed, perhaps the lack of a need for a comprehensive Christological approach to the Psalms arose from Calvin's "unwillingness to risk making a sharp distinction between the faith of David in his historical situation and that of sixteenth-century Christians in theirs."[161] In maintaining this figural link between David and later faithful readers, he is able to console and strengthen his own parishioners, who, like him, had experienced similar troubles and struggles. In reading the Psalms, we are to imitate David, but a David who also lived, like us, in the shadow of Christ.

---

[157] Calvin, *Commentary on the Book of Psalms*, 1:13. Note the language. Calvin is employing prosopopoeia, not prosopological exegesis.

[158] Calvin, *Commentary on the Book of Psalms*, 1:16.

[159] See de Greef, "Calvin as Commentator," 99; Russell, "Messianic Interpretation," 39.

[160] See Pitkin, "Imitation of David," 858–59.

[161] Pitkin, "Imitation of David, 862.

2.3. Eclectic Approaches in the Premodern Period

In my above review of the prosopological and typological models of premodern interpretation, one might get the impression that an interpreter must be committed wholesale to either model. In practice, however, interpreters are generally flexible, allowing their methods to bend when appropriate. Augustine, for example, did not find a rigid *totus Christus* in every psalm; and Calvin, whose *modus operandi* was a typical-typological model, applied a thoroughgoing prosopological reading to Ps 109. Indeed, it should be stressed that within the history of interpretation these two models were never understood as mutually exclusive. My later analyses of Pss 3–6 and 7–14, in fact, will show that each subgrouping of psalms employs a different figural relationship between David, his promised heir, and the reader, which involves multiple models. As a case in point, before we move on to the modern period, I want to highlight one final premodern interpreter who uniquely interprets the Psalms with an approach that is at the same time prosopological and typological.

2.3.1. Athanasius: The Psalms as a "Mirror to the Soul"
Athanasius is perhaps most famous for his treatise *On the Incarnation* or his biography *The Life of Antony*.[162] Equally important, however, is his treatment of the Psalms in *The Letter to Marcellinus*, which prefaces the Psalter in *Codex Alexandrinus* alongside Eusebius of Caesarea's introductory notes.[163] Even though Athanasius is situated in the East, his reading of the Psalms is different from what we find in Origen. In the following overview, I will be paying attention to this *Letter*, but also to other passages in his wider theological and epistolary works which bear witness to his approach to the Psalms.[164]

---

[162] Athanasius, *On the Incarnation*, PPS (Crestwood, NY: St. Vladimir's Seminary Press, 1996); Athanasius, *The Life of Antony and the Letter to Marcellinus*, trans. Robert C. Gregg, CWS (New York: Paulist Press, 1980).

[163] The *Letter to Marcellinus* (PG 27:12–45) is almost universally acknowledged as authentic to Athanasius but has yet to receive a modern critical edition (PG 27 remains the only edition). English translations include: *The Life of Antony and Letter to Marcellinus* (Gregg translation, cf. above); "On the Interpretation of the Psalms," in *Early Christian Spirituality*, trans. Pamela Bright, Sources of Early Christian Thought (Philadelphia: Fortress, 1986), 56–77; and "Appendix: The Letter of St. Athanasius to Marcellinus on the Interpretation of the Psalms," in *On the Incarnation*, trans. 'a religious of CSMV' (Crestwood, NY: St. Vladimir's Seminary Press, 1982). In citations of the *Letter* below, I will always use the Gregg translation.

[164] While the *Letter* is authentic to Athanasius, most of the other psalm material contained in PG 27 has been deemed spurious. Rondeau assigned a substantial portion of *Expositio in Psalmos* (PG 27:60–545) to Evagrius of Pontus, while *De titulis Psalmorum* (PG 27:591–1343) has been attributed to Hesychius of Jerusalem (whose longer and shorter commentaries are found in PG 93). See Marie-Josephe Rondeau, "Le commentaire sur les Psaumes d'Evagre le Pontique," *Orientalia Christiana Periodica* 26 (1960): 307–48; Gilles

A significant component of Athanasius's approach to the book of Psalms is his biography, which is full of trials, tribulations, exiles, and conflict. Around the age of twenty-five he was ordained as a deacon, and became the attendant to Alexander, the bishop of Alexandria. He accompanied Alexander as an advisor to the council of Nicaea in 325 CE (aged thirty), and only three years later succeeded Alexander as bishop. During the tumultuous political and ecclesiastical situation in the decades following Nicaea, Athanasius would be exiled on five separate occasions over a thirty-year period. These provided him the chance to reflect on similar experiences by a number of biblical figures. For our purposes, his acknowledged affinity with David and the other psalmists lies at the forefront. For instance, we read in *Festal Letter* 3.5:

> Let us, being followers of such men, pass no season without thanksgiving, but especially now, when the time is one of tribulation, which the heretics excite against us, will we praise the Lord, uttering the words of the saints: "All these things have come upon us, yet have we not forgotten Thee" [Ps 44:17]. For as the Jews at that time, although suffering an assault from the tabernacles of the Edomites, and oppressed by the enemies of Jerusalem, did not give themselves up, but all the more sang praises to God; so we, my beloved brethren, though hindered from speaking the word of the Lord, will the more proclaim it, and being afflicted, we will sing Psalms, in that we are accounted worthy to be despised, and to labour anxiously for the truth. Yea, moreover, being grievously vexed, we will give thanks.[165]

In these and similar instances, Athanasius looked to the singing of the Psalms as an example of how to respond to tribulation. In the *Letter to Marcellinus*, these experiences have given him the ability to know which psalms are most appropriate for one's inner dispositions and external circumstances. Indeed, "there is

---

Dorival, "Athanase ou Pseudo-Athanase," *RSLR* 16 (1980): 80–89; and G. C. Stead, "St. Athanasius on the Psalms," *VC* 39 (1985): 65–78. Moreover, the remaining sections of PG 27:60–545 not ascribed to Evagrius have likewise been reassigned to "Pseudo-Athanasius," who apparently wrote after Athanasius but relied on a number of his contemporaries. To add to the "attribution confusion," a critical edition and English translation of two Syriac versions of the *Expositio in Psalmos* has been published, but its editor and translator noted its untidy relationship to the Greek original. See *Athanasiana Syriaca IV: Expositio in Psalmos*, ed. and trans. R. W. Thomson, CSCO 386–387 (Louvain: Secrétariat du Corpus, 1977). According to Thomson, the "longer" version (B.M. Add. 14568; ca. 597 CE)—while missing many folios and thus fragmented—is very similar but not identical to the composite Greek of PG 27:60–545, containing "material not found in the published Greek." The "shorter" abridgement of this commentary is complete (B.M. Add. 12168; ca. 700s), and while it frequently corresponds to the wording of the longer Syriac version, it also contains material not found in it. No one to my knowledge has sought to explain the relationship between the Syriac versions and the composite texts in PG 27, and what bearing such a comparison would have to the reassignment of the material to Evagrius and Hesychius.

[165] Athanasius, "Festal Letter III," in *NPNF* 2.14.

not a single experience of life and death without an appropriate psalm as a response to it."[166]

A second component of Athanasius's biography came earlier in his life, when he spent time with the Egyptian desert monk Antony. He played an important role for Athanasius because his meditative discipline centered on daily recitation and reflection of the Psalter.[167] Given the ascetic life practiced by the Egyptian monks, one of the distinctive elements of their interpretation of the Psalms was their "incarnational" model for exegesis. Instead of engaging in sophisticated and technical interpretive methodology, they "sought a way to let the words of the Psalms, the Words of salvation, incarnate their bodies and souls through the repetitive reading of the Psalms."[168] As we will see below, this influenced Athanasius's interpretive model and significantly shaped his instruction on the Psalms. Athanasius's construction of the relationship between the soul of the reader and its true Image, the Incarnate Christ, highlights the Psalter's profound accessibility for the Christian life.[169]

As its title indicates, the *Letter to Marcellinus* was composed for a certain man named Marcellinus. Scholars have been unable to identify him, but from the letter itself we know that he was training in a monastic order and had recently fallen ill.[170] Athanasius discovered that Marcellinus had a great fondness for the Psalms, but was having difficulty comprehending their meaning.[171] Sharing that fondness, he wrote to him in an attempt to aid him in this endeavor. As such, the *Letter* represents "the earliest extant handbook for gaining spiritually by personal, devotional meditation on, as distinct from congregational singing of, the Psalms."[172]

The uniqueness in Athanasius's approach is in how he distinguished between two kinds of psalms: those which speak directly concerning Jesus Christ as prophecy, and those the reader is meant to take upon their own lips as their own words.[173] In the former category, Athanasius will often use prosopological

---

[166] Charles Kannengiesser, *Handbook of Patristic Exegesis: The Bible in Ancient Christianity* (Leiden: Brill, 2004), 2:709–10.

[167] See Hikaru Tanaka, "Athanasius as Interpreter of the Psalms: His *Letter to Marcellinus*," *ProEccl* 21 (2012): 422–23.

[168] Tanaka, "Athanasius as Interpreter of the Psalms," 423.

[169] See Kannengiesser, *Handbook*, 2:709.

[170] See Paul R. Kolbet, "Athanasius, the Psalms, and the Reformation of the Self," *HTR* 99 (2005): 85–86.

[171] See Robert C. Gregg, "Introduction," in Athanasius, *The Life of Antony and the Letter to Marcellinus*, trans. Robert C. Gregg, CWS (New York: Paulist Press, 1980), 12. He noted that Marcellinus's main concern was how the Psalms related to the Christian life.

[172] William A. Clebsch, "Preface," in Athanasius, *The Life of Antony and the Letter to Marcellinus*, trans. Robert C. Gregg, CWS (New York: Paulist Press, 1980), xiii.

[173] Athanasius, *Letter to Marcellinus*, 110, 123 [§11, §27]. In §5–8, he identified the following psalms as prophetic in some capacity: 2, 9, 22, 24, 45, 47, 50, 69, 72, 82, 87, 88, 107, 110, 118, and 138.

exegesis to hear Christ speaking without recourse to David own's life.[174] In these psalms, he clearly has larger theological points to make, and is using the Psalter for these dogmatic purposes. In the latter category, however, he introduced a unique approach to the Psalms, perhaps his greatest contribution to the history of psalm interpretation, by combining together typological and prosopological methods.

For Athanasius, the Psalter is similar to other books in Scripture, narrating historical events (§3–4) and containing prophecies about the Savior (§5–8), and yet is unique, having a "certain grace of its own, and a distinctive exactitude of expression."[175] He began by speaking of how it both identifies and regulates the emotions of the soul:

> [The book of Psalms] possesses... this marvel of its own—namely, that it contains even the emotions of each soul, and it has the changes and rectifications of these delineated and regulated in itself. Therefore anyone who wishes boundlessly to receive and understand from it, so as to mold himself, it is written there. In the Book of Psalms, the one who hears comprehends and is taught in it the emotions of the soul, and, consequently, on the basis of that which affects him and by which he is constrained, he also is enabled by this book to possess the image deriving from the words.[176]

In this critical paragraph, Athanasius first noted how the Psalms not only "possess" the emotions of each soul but have the unique ability to rectify and regulate the soul of the reader. In the process of reading, singing, and meditating on the Psalms, the reader is affected and constrained, herself now possessing "the image deriving from the words." Athanasius described this mutuality of possession in a later paragraph:

> And it seems to me that these words become like a mirror to the person singing them, so that he might perceive himself and the emotions of his soul, and thus affected, he might recite them. For in fact he who hears the one reading receives the song that is recited as being about him, and either, when he is convicted by his conscience, being pierced, he will repent, or hearing of the hope that resides in God, and of the succor available to believers—how this kind of grace exists for him—he exults and begins to give thanks to God.[177]

There is, then, a certain mutuality of possession: the Psalms *possessing* the emotions of the soul, and then the reader *possessing* the Image found within the

---

[174] Corresponding with his wider works, Athanasius often uses many of these same above psalms to describe the work and person of the Son. See *On the Incarnation* 25; 35; *Against the Arians* 1.12, 40, 41, 46, 49; 2.4, 13, 14, 57, 66; 3.57; 4.24, 26; *On the Councils of Ariminum and Seleucia* 27; and *Festal Letters* 6.8.

[175] Athanasius, *Letter to Marcellinus*, 107 (§10).

[176] Athanasius, *Letter to Marcellinus*, 108 (§10).

[177] Athanasius, *Letter to Marcellinus*, 111 (§12).

Psalms through disciplined and attentive meditation. As such, the contents of the Psalms are peculiarly tailored to the one who prays them, accepting them and reciting them "not as if another were speaking" but as if she were speaking about herself:

> After the prophecies about the Savior and the nations, he who recites the Psalms is uttering the rest as his own words, and each sings them as if they were written concerning him, and he accepts them and recites them not as if another were speaking, nor as if speaking about someone else. But he handles them as if he is speaking about himself.[178]

By making the words our own, we partake of the "image" we find therein, which then comes to life as we recite them.

As Paul Kolbet argued, one needs to be aware of the Nicene Christology which undergirds and shapes this element of Athanasius's teaching in this section.[179] Indeed, it is easy to miss in his tightly woven presentation that this Image (the "Mirror") is inextricably bound to the incarnation of Christ.

> The same grace is from the Savior, for when he became man for us he offered his own body in dying for our sake, in order that he might set all free from death. And desiring to show us his own heavenly and well-pleasing life, he provided its type in himself... It was indeed for this reason that he made this resound in the Psalms before his sojourn in our midst, so that just as he provided the model of the earthly and heavenly man in his own person, so also from the Psalms he who wants to do so can learn the emotions and dispositions of the soul, finding in them also the therapy and correction suited for each emotion.[180]

In this paragraph, Athanasius set out the innerworkings of the typological connection between the soul of the reader and the image of Christ, whose type can be found resounding throughout the Psalms. This is not a minor point: Athanasius's entire endeavor hangs on this typology. As Khaled Anatolios explained:

> [The] Psalms provide a "mirror" or "image" wherein the soul can recognize a perfected image of itself, [and] the same is true of the act whereby the Word became flesh and "typified in himself" human virtue. Henceforth, humanity can find "in itself"—that is, in the model of its own humanity in Christ—the perfect image of virtue.[181]

---

[178] Athanasius, *Letter to Marcellinus*, 110 (§11).
[179] See Kolbet, "Reformation of the Self," 90–93.
[180] Athanasius, *Letter to Marcellinus*, 111–12 (§13).
[181] Khaled Anatolios, *Athanasius: The Coherence of His Thought* (London: Routledge 1998), 201–2.

Through disciplined, daily vocalization of the Psalter, the reader not only comes to know what to do, but has the means by which to do it.[182] His discussion here is quite extraordinary: the Son of God takes on flesh by living out the image of the Psalter in his own person. If someone wants to learn how to live as Christ does, in his image, then one needs to spend time in the Psalms, "finding in them the therapy and correction suited for each emotion."

In the second half of the *Letter*, Athanasius illustrated how this approach worked by showing the usefulness of each psalm within whatever situation the reader may find herself (§15–26), as well as how the singing of the Psalms brings the soul into concord with its created intention (§27–31). In these sections, David is utilized as an exemplar (Pss 7, 51, 53, 55, 144, 145), and a number of psalms are understood as having strong support for those who suffer persecution (Pss 3, 17, 24, 26, 30, 39, 53, 55, 56, 58, 61, 76, 84, and 125).[183]

So how does Athanasius's model conceptually hold together, as it involves David as author, the "mirrored image" (i.e., Christ), and the reader? The first move, as we saw with both Origen and Augustine, is that the psalmist speaks using a different persona. Though Athanasius did not use the typical prosopological language in the *Letter*, we have already seen that the reader is meant to recognize a certain "image" when reading the Psalms, connected, presumably, to the voice we hear:

> [The] one who hears comprehends and is taught in it the emotions of the soul, and, consequently, on the basis of that which affects him and by which he is constrained, he also is enabled by this book to possess *the image deriving from the words.*

> And it seems to me that these words become like a mirror to the person singing them, so that he might perceive himself and the emotions of his soul.[184]

Thus, David can be understood as writing in the person of the Image. This image, as we have seen, is not David playing the part of a typical sinner (*a la* Origen), nor his life seen as a parallel with Christ's life (*a la* Aquinas or Calvin), but as an instance of the Son of God's eternal existence revealing itself before his taking on human flesh. The incarnate Son is the perfected Image of the self, and so is the proper speaker of the Psalms, the one who *actualizes* the theodrama of the "mirror" in his own person during his "sojourn in our midst."

At this point, Augustine's *totus Christus* and Athanasius's *mirror* are close conceptually, though Athanasius is working from a different foundational concern than Augustine. For Augustine, David speaks in the person of Christ, where

---

[182] Athanasius, *Letter to Marcellinus*, 108 (§10). He wrote: "Therefore, through hearing, it teaches not only not to disregard passion, but also how one must heal passion through speaking and acting." See also Kolbet, "Reformation of the Self," 94.

[183] See David M. Gwynn, *Athanasius of Alexandria: Bishop, Theologian, Ascetic, Father*, Christian Theology in Context (Oxford: Oxford University Press, 2012), 151.

[184] Athanasius, *Letter to Marcellinus*, 108 (§10), 111 (§12).

we find the dual voice of Christ the Head and Christ the Body (the church). For Athanasius, however, the *function* of the Psalms is foremost: they are properly meant to heal the passions. In order to do that, they use the Image of the Son of God to speak a mirrored image of the perfected soul. So, the move from "Christ as Speaker" to "Church as Speaker" is conceptualized differently in Athanasius. For Augustine it involved what Cameron referred to as a "transpositive dynamic," where Head speaks in the voice of the Body; for Athanasius, the next move is typological:

> And desiring to show us his own heavenly and well-pleasing life, he provided its type in himself... A more perfect instruction in virtue one could not find than that which the Lord typified in himself.... Just as he provided the model of the earthly and heavenly man in his own person, so also from the Psalms he who wants to do so can learn the emotions and dispositions of the souls, finding in them also the therapy and correction suited for each emotion.[185]

For Athanasius, the incarnation of the Word provides the most perfect instruction in virtue, and in this way the life of Christ is the model human being. But since Christ speaks the Psalms in his own person, we have unique access to this Image in our own praying of the Psalms, which too contain this perfected Image of the human soul. There is, then, a typological connection between the *mirrored Image* and the person praying the Psalms, so that we are able to put these words directly on our own lips without first navigating through other persona. Whereas the Head and the Body come together in the person of Christ for Augustine, in Athanasius, while the reader does speak the Image's words, she does so *via* the correspondence between Christ's image and her own. In this way, the Psalms are able to both confront the reader with the perfected image of the soul, but also bring healing to the soul in their daily recitation as they begin to inhabit the one praying.

Bringing these discussions together, we have seen that Athanasius approaches the Psalms in a very personal manner. Concerning the speaking persona, in most cases he would identify the speaking voice as our own. He does not advocate such a voicing based on principles akin to modern reader-response models, but on a typological relationship between the reader's soul and the incarnation of the Word, in whose voice the prophet David speaks. To recite the psalms as a "mirror" to the soul is to speak them in one's own relationship to the Word, whose image is reflected before us, both revealing and healing our deformities in a journey towards the equanimity of the soul.[186] At the same time, Athanasius will often interpret psalms as direct prophecy of Jesus Christ. In these cases, he consistently applies a prosopological reading of the Psalms in

---

[185] Athanasius, *Letter to Marcellinus*, 112 (§13).
[186] Athanasius, *Letter to Marcellinus*, 124 (§28).

which we hear the voices of each divine person.[187] These readings most often occur in theological treatises, and are limited to the royal psalms and/or those already associated prophetically with Christ in earlier Christian tradition.

2.3.2. Summary of the Premodern Period

My survey has walked through the history of premodern interpretation by describing five different representative figures of Christian interpretation: Origen and Augustine represent prosopological approaches to the Psalms; Aquinas and Calvin represent typological models; and Athanasius represents a more eclectic approach, beginning with a prosopological model but introducing a complex typology. With each interpreter I have attempted not only to illustrate how they envisioned the speaking persona in their interpretations, but also give some context as to why they might have done so. We have seen that while each was concerned with the spiritual progress of the reader, one's relationship to David and/or Christ was constructed differently depending on how an interpreter utilized a prosopological or typological model.

At the same time, they each share some distinctive marks of premodern interpretation that will be contrasted in our next section. First, each interpreter demonstrated a strong view about the prophetic voice of the Psalms, connected to divine inspiration. Second, to a varying degree, each assumed that the psalm titles, especially the biographical ones, related to the content and meaning of a psalm. This is most apparent in Augustine and Aquinas, who described even the musical elements of the titles as imparting a Christological meaning. Calvin, on the other hand, principally relied on the Davidic titles to justify seeking a context in the life of David. Third, each interpreter developed his own spiritual reading of the text which helped to bring the words of the Psalms into the life of its readers. For Origen, this principally related to a tropological reading of the text; in Athanasius we see an immediate connection to the Incarnate Word in the words of the Psalms, as in a "mirror." As we will see, these concerns shaped our premodern interpreters' view of the speaking voice in the Psalms, including certain directions which will be forfeited by modern scholarship.

2.4. The Speaking Voice in the Modern Period

In this final section of the chapter, I will now summarize engagements with the literary voice in the Psalms during the modern period. As noted in the first chapter, psalm scholarship took a major turn during the nineteenth century. Whereas earlier views on the speaker relied on the superscriptions—confining

---

[187] Though not always stated, David is often also included in the reference as the person through which each *persona* speaks. For instance: Ps 2 (*Against the Arians* 2.23; *Nicene Definition* 13; *Festal Letters* 11.5; 10.5); Ps 8 (*Against the Arians* 2.52); Ps 16 (*Against the Arians* 1.61); Psalm 41 (*Festal Letters* 3.4); Ps 45 (*Against the Arians* 3.59; 3.67; *Nicene Definition* 21); and Ps 110 (*Nicene Definition* 13). Outside of these psalms normally understood in a prophetic manner, we also have Ps 30 (*Festal Letters* 6.4).

interpretation either to incidents in the life of David, when David was considered the author and speaking persona of a psalm, or to analogous incidents in the life of Jesus Christ, when Davidic authorship was prophetic and the words belonged to the Messiah—in the nineteenth century, scholars began to look beyond these narratives to other episodes within ancient Israelite and Second Temple Jewish history.[188] Denying the historical veracity and genuineness of the superscriptions, scholars interpreted psalms as having been written at later periods. Early on this included late pre-exilic contexts, but by the end of the nineteenth century scholars had gradually extended historical contexts to include the exilic and post-exilic periods, until most were dated into the Maccabean period. Giving up a Davidic context for the psalms, scholars also left behind a Davidic speaking persona, as this had been envisioned earlier. As representative of the initial modern turn, I will be giving special attention to W. M. L. de Wette, followed in quick succession with a variety of subsequent views in the late nineteenth and early twentieth centuries.

2.4.1. W. M. L. de Wette: Davidic Doubts and Speaker Ambiguity
I begin my survey with W. M. L. de Wette. As mentioned above, de Wette was a figurehead for the higher criticism which followed in his wake, illustrated well in the introduction to his 1811 Psalms commentary.[189] He opened by repeating an oft mentioned aspect of the Psalter throughout the history of interpretation:

> Among all the books to the Bible, there is, perhaps, no one so rich in [a religious aspect] as the Psalter. Others, as the Pentateuch, or the Prophets, may furnish the religious inquirer with more materials relating to the positive views of religion, symbolic forms, etc. but the Psalter is the great fountain and source of *religious experience*, and on this account, worthy of very special attention in all inquiries into the history of religion.[190]

The difference between de Wette and his more traditional predecessors was that *religious experience* was no longer worthy in and of itself, as it once had been; its value, rather, was only in how it may factor into the history of religion. So, while de Wette could quote Luther at length on this point, he also felt the need to add: "But even in a doctrinal point of view also, the Psalter is of great importance,

---

[188] As also noted in the first chapter, there were exceptions to this rule in the premodern period, evidenced in the work of interpreters such as Diodore of Tarsus and Theodore of Mopsuestia. They were quite willing to suggest periods much later than David as the contexts for interpretation; but even for these interpreters this meant that David was simply speaking as a prophet about later times.

[189] The first edition was prepared in 1811. References to his commentary are to the fifth edition: W. M. L. de Wette, *Commentar über die Psalmen*, ed. Gustav Baur, 5th ed (Heidelberg: J. C. B. Mohr, 1856). Quotations from the introduction come from an 1833 English translation: "Introduction to the Psalms," trans. J. Torrey, *The Biblical Repository* 3/11 (1833): 445–518.

[190] De Wette, "Introduction," 449. Emphasis his.

although modern historical interpretation has pronounced to be inadmissible, as it is obliged to do, many doctrinal allusions, especially to the Messiah."[191] With this final hammer strike the premodern and early modern eras were left behind: the Psalter no longer gives us insights into doctrinal issues, but should only mined for its contributions to history.[192]

In his treatment of the origin and cultivation of poetry, we find similar points of departure from earlier perspectives. De Wette began by entertaining what views one might hold, provided one follows the titles of the Psalms and the common opinion concerning them.[193] He found the psalm titles suspicious, in that they do not ascribe any psalms to authors belonging to any period after Solomon. For him, the psalm-like poetry one finds by Hezekiah and within Habakkuk clearly evinces that psalm composition continued into later periods.[194] For these and a variety of other reasons he concluded that many psalms must be assigned to the times of the captivity and beyond.[195] Unsurprisingly, given his initial conclusions de Wette was quite pessimistic about the superscriptions, which he thought were making historical claims. Since the majority ascribed authorship to David, "some gross mistakes were committed by the authors of these titles, from which in other respects they cannot be pronounced wholly free."[196] Many of his contemporaries, in fact, had already unconditionally rejected the headings, whether in whole or in part.[197] De Wette did not go that far, but certainly doubted their genuineness.[198] Indeed, since several titles prove incorrect, a dark shadow has been cast, exposing "all to the suspicion of being spurious."[199]

After casting all these doubts, in the final section of his introduction de Wette discussed the basic procedures of "historical" interpretation. He expressed its goal as an endeavor "by the aid of history [*Geschichte*] to refer the Psalms to the situation [*die Situation*] of the author, by which they were occasioned, and in which they were composed, and to make this the ground of their

---

[191] De Wette, "Introduction," 450.

[192] See Michael Goulder, *The Prayers of David (Psalms 51–72): Studies in the Psalter, II*, JSOTSup 102 (Sheffield: JSOT, 1990), 13. He noted that while others before de Wette argued that not all psalms could go back to David on historical grounds, he was the first to include the entire Davidic tradition even where there were none of the same historical problems. The transition between the premodern and modern eras is complex. See Hans W. Frei, *The Eclipse of Biblical Narrative: A Study in Eighteenth and Nineteenth Century Hermeneutics* (New Haven: Yale University Press, 1974).

[193] De Wette, "Introduction," 450–56.

[194] De Wette, "Introduction," 455.

[195] De Wette, "Introduction," 456.

[196] De Wette, "Introduction," 458.

[197] De Wette, "Introduction," 467.

[198] De Wette, "Introduction," 467–69.

[199] De Wette, "Introduction," 469.

exposition."[200] Without such knowledge, it is impossible to comprehend what the "soul of the poet" is attempting to communicate:

> It is impossible that *any* feeling or emotion should be rightly and fully comprehended, without some knowledge of the individual who expresses it, in his distinct personality, and in his relation to the objects which have occasioned it; it is only by such a knowledge one is placed in a situation to sympathize in the emotion expressed, and to enter fully into the soul of the poet.[201]

Having expressed these grounds for interpretation, he speaks of a twofold procedure. First, one must provide a characteristic sketch of the subject-matter of the psalm by identifying what constitutes its peculiarity of the feelings and perspective. And second, one must determine whether any allusion to external relations, objects, and/or occasions, whether personal or national, can be found, and then compare these to the account of the author and subject intimated in the superscriptions. When the two agree, one can adhere to the superscription and fill up the "deficiencies" from other probable facts of history; when they disagree, however, "we abandon the attempt at a definite historical interpretation, and content ourselves with general references."[202] To make such an attempt would only serve to "obscure the sense and prevent the enjoyment of these poems; for there are many subjects which may be understood with greater advantage in a broad and general view, than they can be when considered in a more definite but false point of light."[203]

To illustrate this method, he described the process for a typical Davidic psalm, a process which he followed throughout his commentary:

> We first endeavor to ascertain what were the dangers, sufferings, persecutions, in a word, what was the situation of the poet; we next compare this with the history and relations of David; if they do not correspond we abandon the reference to David as improbable, but make no further attempt to verify the personal and historical allusions, except in a general way, and as a matter of conjecture pointing out the various probabilities.[204]

This proved true for most of the Davidic psalms, including those with biographical superscriptions.

De Wette's treatment of Ps 3 illustrates his interpretive profile well. As a first step, he analyzed the superscription, which relates to the events of Absalom's rebellion in 2 Sam 15–18.[205] Finding no hint of this episode within the contents of the psalm, he then focused on the military dangers which seem to

---

[200] De Wette, "Introduction," 514.
[201] De Wette, "Introduction," 514–15.
[202] De Wette, "Introduction," 515.
[203] De Wette, "Introduction," 515–16.
[204] De Wette, "Introduction," 516.
[205] De Wette, *Die Psalmen*, 18.

threaten the one praying. Looking at the wider Davidic narratives in Samuel he continued to find problems connecting psalms to history, concluding that the poet should be identified generally as an Israelite king in the face of hostile enemy armies. From here, he also suggested that the psalm finds a private connection to any suffering saint whose fate was devoured by those who surrounded him. Even without a Davidic identification, then, de Wette could argue for a royal interpretation which provided him access to the spiritual mindset of the psalmist. In the end, however, the speaking persona can be understood as an "Everyman," someone who is difficult to place historically but has appeal for readers in any age.

2.4.2. Modern Interpreters in the Wake of de Wette

Those interpreters who continued in the wake of de Wette repeated many of his same doubts about the traditional understanding of the Psalms. Nevertheless, as we progress through the nineteenth century, we find that scholars increasingly were less willing to maintain the ambiguity he proposed. This is especially true when we consider how scholars attempted to understand the relationship between the voice of the individual and a communal voice.

In 1888, Rudolf Smend published a lengthy article arguing that the "I" of the Psalms should not be understood as an individual, but as a personification of the community.[206] This view transforms the individual psalms into community psalms, allowing each instance of distress or oppression to take on national proportions; conflicts are no longer personal in nature, but are public and international in scale. In his 1892 article, Alfred Rahlfs agreed in measure, but instead of seeing the enemies of the allegorical "I" as national enemies, he proposed something more internal to Israel itself: the "I" personifies loyal, downtrodden Jews who were caught up in some form of class warfare.[207]

The first major study to refute these positions was undertaken in 1912 by Emil Balla, who argued that the real individuality of the psalmist must be upheld.[208] Hermann Gunkel followed suit, arguing that when an "I" is speaking it refers to an individual, but when a "we" speaks, there is a corporate voice; in psalms where the psalmist alternates between "I" and "we," it often means that the individual speaker is praying on behalf of the whole congregation.[209] Thus, in many of the psalms we encounter the individual laments of a psalmist who was writing out of a situation of distress.

Sigmund Mowinckel took a somewhat moderating position. While he initially followed Gunkel's view of the speaking persona, through the influence of

---

[206] Rudolf Smend, "Über das Ich der Psalmen," *ZAW* 8 (1888): 48–147. See also Justus Olshausen, *Die Psalmen* (Leipzig: Hirzel, 1853).

[207] Alfred Rahlfs, *'Ani und 'Anaw in den Psalmen* (Göttingen: Dieterichsche Verlagsbuchhandlung, 1892).

[208] Emil Balla, *Das Ich der Psalmen*, FRLANT 16 (Göttingen: Vandenhoedt & Ruprecht, 1912).

[209] Gunkel, *Introduction*, 122–23.

Birkeland he changed his position.[210] The problem was that Gunkel's mechanical distinction between the "I" and "we" did not take into account that, in reality, there were many individual laments in which the "I" is not just an "Everyman," but the king. This new dynamic changed the situation, since a king would pray with the needs, duties, and privileges of his office. Moreover, combined with the ancient Israelite notion of "corporate personality," the king stood before God, speaking *as* the entire congregation.[211] Embodying the congregation in himself, the king is a representative personality, weakening the distinction between public (congregational) and private (individual) psalms.[212] The continued focus on the king or cult leader as the representative was most fully incorporated into the approach of the Myth and Ritual school.[213]

Fully enthralled with form-critical and cult-functional criticism over the next several decades, scholars' views of the speaking persona in the psalms changed very little.[214] New views would only come with the introduction of the canonical approach by Childs and a renewed interest in early Jewish exegesis (especially inner-biblical interpretation). For them, the expanded historical psalm titles associated with David and linked to various episodes recounted in Samuel and Chronicles help to connect the psalm and the story. David, then, was reintroduced into psalm scholarship, but not in the same way as in premodern interpretation, nor as in the Myth and Ritual school. Now, readers are given a privileged glimpse into his mind, with David becoming exemplary, typical figure.

Christological interpretation is still possible within a typical approach, illustrated masterfully by James Mays's commentary on Ps 22.[215] Yet, without premodern theological commitments, it is unclear whether David is considered a prophet, nor if it matters one way or the other; what matters is that the voice is exemplary and can be accessed by any reader, including Jesus.[216] Nevertheless,

---

[210] Harris Birkeland, *Ānî und ānāw in den Psalmen* (Oslo: J. Dybwad, 1933).

[211] Mowinckel, *Psalms in Israel's Worship*, 1:46. While the translation has "on behalf of," this is not exactly what he is communicating. The representative speaks *as* the congregation; in the one representative figure we have the voice of the leader *and* the congregation. There is perhaps, then, an intriguing parallel here between Mowinckel's view of the cultic speaker and Augustine's *totus Christus*.

[212] Mowinckel, *Psalms in Israel's Worship*, 2:18.

[213] See A. R. Johnson, "Book of Psalms," in *The Old Testament and Modern Study: A Generation of Discovery and Research*, ed. H. H. Rowley (Oxford: Clarendon, 1951), 162–209; Ivan Engnell, "Book of Psalms," in *A Rigid Scrutiny: Critical Essays on the Old Testament by Ivan Engnell*, ed. John T. Willis (Nashville: Vanderbilt University Press, 1969), 68–122; Steven J. L. Croft, *The Identity of the Individual in the Psalms*, JSOTSup 44 (Sheffield: JSOT, 1987).

[214] This is due, in part, to the methods themselves, which work best with a more generic understanding of the speaking persona. Having identified a *Sitz im Leben* for a psalm's type, any speaker found in that situation could speak the psalm themselves.

[215] James Mays, *Psalms*, Int (Louisville: Westminster John Knox, 1994), 105–15.

[216] See Ellen T. Charry, *Psalms 1–50: Sighs and Songs of Israel* (Grand Rapids: Brazos, 2015), 108–15. She is clear that the psalm "is not a prediction of the events in the first

commentaries rarely, if ever, carry through on these observations (even with psalms containing biographical superscriptions), contented with a generic, typical voice. In some ways, then, the modern period has come full circle. Contemporary commentaries show a lack of confidence in asserting an original setting for a psalm, whether in a reconstructed cult or in the scriptural narrative, and continue to refuse a hermeneutical role for David. In such an environment, interpreters are left with little to work with besides de Wette's "Everyman," unless the reader supplies her own context in which to hear the psalm.

2.4.3. Summary of the Modern Period

Reviewing the history of interpretation in the modern period helps us see more clearly that the primary issue for the speaking persona remains fixed on how interpreters understand a psalm's context. In the eighteenth and nineteenth centuries, the Psalms began to be read within a wider secular account of the history of the ancient Near East. No longer satisfied with the context of a psalm within the canonical history (e.g., 1–2 Samuel with David), modern scholarship began to interpret the Psalms within a new notion of "historical context."[217] Having rejected the psalm titles as not having any value, they removed the book's own affiliation with David. As a result, new avenues for understanding the speaker emerged within the development of Israel's religion.[218] The speaker was the *historical* speaker, the one who spoke as these psalms were used in their *Sitz im Leben*—whether this was construed as an individual or collective voice, within the cult or without. When confidence waned for supplying such a context, interpreters have returned to a more typical, generic speaking persona.

2.5. Conclusion

In this chapter I have attempted to show the great variety of speaking personae in the Psalms from the history of interpretation. It has become clear that one's interpretive context has enormous implications for how one understands the speaker within a psalm. In premodern interpretation, this context presumed a number of theological commitments, such as prophetic speech, the hermeneutical value of psalm titles, and a basic rule of faith that Jesus of Nazareth is identified as the heir of Davidic promise. With modern interpreters these commitments have not only been displaced, but replaced with an attempt to understand the speaker within a history of Israel as part of a developing religious tradition in the context of the ancient Near East.

Christian century," but "authenticates the theological continuity of the latter events not only with scripture but also with the sensibility of the community shaped by many experiences of deliverance, the example in Ps. 22 being but one of them" (114).

[217] See Frei, *The Eclipse of Biblical Narrative*.

[218] See Clements, *One Hundred Years*, 76.

What we have seen is that premodern interpreters worked along two key methodologies: prosopological exegesis and typological exegesis. These two approaches were not mutually exclusive, but provided interpreters an environment in which the Psalms could be prophecy related to Christ and accessible to Christians in their own spiritual life. For Augustine this access was provided through his prosopological *totus Christus* model, while for Calvin and Athanasius it was through a typical-typological relationship to the speaker. In the modern period, historical interpretation of the Psalms has resulted in a speaker who at best has a typical voice, but in many cases is a historical voice not meant to be imitated by the reader.

Regardless of the correctness and legitimacy of these views, it is important to acknowledge how interpretive context is often the determining factor when hearing a psalm. In the next chapter our main question is not what people have done with the speaking persona in the Psalms, but what the book itself is doing. That is, in what ways has the literary context of the final form of the text been set up in order to shape our understanding of the speaking persona in a psalm?

3

The Shaping of the Figure of David in the Psalms

My aim in this chapter is to pose a canonical question: does the book of Psalms itself provide a literary context that shapes our understanding of the speaking persona in a given psalm? In order to answer this question, we need to recognize the changing function of a psalm within the context of ancient Israel. That is, once a psalm was removed from the context of the cult and placed within sacred Scripture, how does the pressure exerted by the canon affect not only one's understanding of, for instance, the eschatological and messianic concerns of the royal psalms, but also how one listens to the Psalms themselves?[1] Even though the Psalms continued to be used in the cultic life of both early Judaism and Christianity, the canonical question recognizes a shift in perception about them. They are not simply an anthology of traditional prayers one might lift to God, but now stand as an authoritative word *from* God to the individual and the community.

I will be focusing my attention on two key areas scholarship has identified as significant for understanding the editorial purpose of the book: its dual introduction (Pss 1–2) and the superscriptions. In both areas, my aim is to uncover what hermeneutical signals these texts cast over the Psalter, especially in terms of the speaking persona. For instance, Ps 1 is spoken by a didactic voice which introduces to us a number of characters and themes which will appear in throughout the book, such as the righteous, the wicked, the "Blessed Man," and the Two Ways and their respective ends. Psalm 2, on the other hand, places these characters within the context of ancient Israel, and specifically within YHWH's appointment of the Davidic king as his co-regent at Zion. On the world stage, the righteous and the wicked take on further attributes, associated with those who trust in YHWH and the rebelling nations against YHWH, respectively. At work in

---

[1] See Gerald Sheppard, *The Future of the Bible: Beyond Liberalism and Literalism* (Toronto: United Church, 1990), 49–94.

the introduction is an integration of the "Blessed Man" of Ps 1 and the anointed king ("Son") of Ps 2, resulting in a Davidic figure who can speak as both the historical David and, through extension, his promised heir. This aligns closely with the typological models introduced in the second chapter. Moreover, in these opening psalms we also have the inner-workings of an identification model which unites the king with the community of the righteous: he is blessed in his delight in the *torah* of Yʜᴡʜ, and they share in his blessings as they follow in his footsteps. As part of their stage-setting function, the opening psalms put forward these characters as part of the literary context of the entire Psalter. Whether David speaks or not, his own life and experiences have been figurally extended to the life and experiences of his heir; what happens to David will parallel what happens to his promised heir.

I will also argue that the superscriptions continue to have an ongoing function in the final form of the book, both in helping associate psalms with certain biblical figures—in Pss 3–14 this figure is David—and in overlaying psalms with certain thematic and spiritual concerns connected to ancient literary categories and musical direction. Most important for Pss 3–14, however, are the biographical elements in Pss 3 and 7, which are part of an editorial shaping process which included exegetical activity with other parts of Scripture. As noted in the first chapter, many take these as clues to read the psalm in connection with the alluded episodes in David's life in 1–2 Samuel. While I am sympathetic to the idea that these inner-biblical links help to create a Davidic portrait in which the psalm complements the narrative, I am more convinced this intertextual reading needs to be inverted. Here, the Davidic narratives further configure the Davidic profile being developed by the Psalter. As Pss 3 and 7 are part of the first implementation of the characters introduced by Pss 1–2, their configuration of the Davidic profile is critical to our understanding of the speaking persona in the Psalter.

3.1. Psalms 1–2 and the Speaking Persona

In the contemporary discussion, a near consensus of scholars has argued that Pss 1–2 have been set apart as an introduction to the book of Psalms. Though each is to be read individually,[2] there is much to commend their integration, such as their lack of superscriptions and the bracketing presence of אשרי in Ps 1:1 and Ps 2:12.[3] Beyond this, there are a number of shared lexical terms which have interpretive value.[4] Such correspondence, especially at the beginning of

---

[2] See John T. Willis, "Psalm 1—An Entity," *ZAW* 9 (1979): 382–401.

[3] In Book One (Pss 1–41), only Pss 1, 2, 10, and 33 are without title. Of these, Pss 10 and 33 are often read as a single psalm with their forerunners: Ps 9/10, 32/33. Regardless, Pss 1–2 are set apart from Pss 3–9 as "orphan" psalms. See Gerald Wilson, *The Editing of the Hebrew Psalter*, SBLDS 76 (Chico, CA: Scholars, 1985), 173–81; Patrick D. Miller, *Interpreting the Psalms* (Philadelphia: Fortress, 1986), 87.

[4] Primarily ישב (1:1; 2:4), הגה (1:2; 2:1), נתן (1:3; 2:8), דרך (1:6; 2:12), and אבד (1:6; 2:12).

the book, is a strong indication that they were meant to be read together, not as a single psalm but as an integrated introduction. Like an entryway, it is through them that readers enter the rest of the book, and, as such, we can speak of them as something like a guide or as stage-setting.[5] Though some have recently pushed back against hearing Pss 1–2 in this way,[6] Nahum Sarna encapsulated well the modest claims I wish to advocate here: "The selection [of Ps 1 to head the Book of Psalms] must communicate an intention to make a statement, to inculcate at the outset certain fundamental ideas, and to promote some essential teachings."[7] Or, as Artur Weiser wrote:

> The first psalm, standing at the entrance to the Psalter as a signpost, gives clear guidance regarding the way in which [God-fearing people] shall conduct their lives. Presumably the compiler of the Psalter deliberately assigned first place to this psalm in order to call the reader to obedience to God's will and to trust in his providential rule.... The psalm endeavors to guide, educate and press for a decision.[8]

While in my opinion both Pss 1–2 function in this capacity, these authors helpfully point out how Ps 1 acts as a "signpost," articulating both important conceptual categories and the kind of person the reader ought to be. Its function, then, is like a map and compass, laying out the way in which the reader should go and the consequences of going off course.[9] Similarly, Eugene Peterson explained their function as something like "pre-prayer":

> Psalms 1 and 2 pave the way. They get us ready to pray. The Psalms are an edited book. All these prayers were collected and arranged at one point in Israel's history, and then Psalms 1 and 2 set as an entrance to them, pillars flanking the way into prayer. We are not unceremoniously dumped into the world of prayer, we are courteously led across an ample

---

[5] See James L. Mays, *The Lord Reigns* (Louisville: Westminster John Knox, 1994), 108–16, 119–27; Robert Cole, "An Integrated Reading of Psalms 1 and 2," *JSOT* 98 (2002): 75–88; Grant, *King as Exemplar*, 41–70.

[6] See Michael Lefebvre, "'On His Law He Meditates': What is Psalm 1 Introducing?" *JSOT* 40 (2016): 439–50; David Willgren, "Why Psalms 1–2 Are Not to Be Considered a Preface to the 'Book' of Psalms," *ZAW* 130 (2018): 384–97. Willgren is against the idea altogether, while Lefebvre avers against viewing Ps 1 as a hermeneutical lens, shaping how we read the Psalter as a whole. Both articles argue that Ps 1:2 is not self-referential, and as such, preclude Ps 1 from acting as a preface for the book. Such a conclusion is unduly restrictive. The broader understanding developed here is more productive.

[7] Nahum M. Sarna, *Songs of the Heart: An Introduction to the Book of Psalms* (New York: Schocken, 1993), 27.

[8] Artur Weiser, *The Psalms: A Commentary*, trans. Herbert Hartwell, OTL (Philadelphia: Westminster, 1962), 102.

[9] See Hans-Joachim Kraus, *Psalms 1–59: A Commentary*, trans. Hilton C. Oswald (Minneapolis: Augsburg, 1988), 122. He wrote: "That person is pronounced happy who, in his reading and reflection about the Psalms, lets himself be guided by the message that shows the path."

porch, a way that provides space and means by which we are adjusted to
the realities of prayer.[10]

In my discussion of these psalms below, my goal is to show how each has its own
particular contribution to make to the introduction, guiding and preparing the
reader not only in her expectations of theme and content, but also in her understanding of the speaking persona(e) which she will encounter throughout.

3.1.1. *Psalm 1 and the Speaking Personae*

Psalm 1 has been classified as "some sort of didactic poem... composed for edu-
cational purposes by wise men."[11] Its message is structured around a contrast
between two different ways of life: the "way of the righteous" (1:6) and the "way
of the wicked" (1:1, 6).[12] The psalm opens with a reflection on the happiness or
blessedness of a particular "man" (vv. 1–2) and his destiny (v. 3), and closes by
contrasting the ends of the Two Ways (vv. 4–6):

> [1] Blessed is the man
>> who does not walk in the counsel of the wicked,
>> nor stands in the way of sinners,
>> nor sits in the seat of scoffers.
>
> [2] But rather, in the *torah* of Y<small>HWH</small> is his delight,
>> and in his *torah* he ruminates day and night.
>
> [3] Thus, he will be like a tree transplanted upon streams of water,
>> which yields its fruit in its season,
>> and its leaves do not whither;
>> and everything he does will prosper.
>
> [4] Not so the wicked:
>> Rather, (they are) as chaff, which is blown away by the wind.
>
> [5] Therefore, the wicked will not rise in the judgement,
>> nor sinners in the congregation of the righteous.

---

[10] Eugene H. Peterson, *Answering God: The Psalms as Tools for Prayer* (New York: Harper-
Collins, 1989), 23–24.

[11] Erhard S. Gerstenberger, *Psalms: Part 1, with an Introduction to Cultic Poetry*, FOTL 14
(Grand Rapids: Eerdmans, 1988), 42. He goes on to note that those allowing for cultic us-
age call it a "didactic song," or, connecting with royal use, a "coronation liturgy." Others,
more concerned with the private sphere, simply use "wisdom psalm."

[12] These "Two Ways" are an important part of the wisdom tradition in Israel and can
go by different names. For instance, the "way of the righteous" (Ps 1:6; Prov 8:20) can also
be called "the way of his saints" (Prov 2:8), "the way of the good" (Prov 2:20), "the way of
wisdom" (Prov 4:11; 9:6), "the way of life" (Prov 6:23), or "the way of YHWH" (Prov 10:29).
The "way of sinners/the wicked" (Ps 1:1, 6; Prov 4:19; 12:26) can be called "the way of
evil" (Prov 2:12; 4:14; 8:13), "the way to Sheol" (Prov 7:27), "the way of a fool" (Prov 12:15),
and "the way of the treacherous" (Prov 13:15).

⁶ For YHWH knows the way of the righteous,
  but the way of the wicked will perish.

Throughout the psalm the speaker uses third-person pronouns, and there is no indication that more than one voice is speaking, or to whom the psalm is addressed. It lacks any sense of prayer, rendering it unlikely to be addressed to God. In fact, Ps 1 is heard much like one would hear Ps 14:1–6 or Ps 15, as instruction.[13] As such, I understand there to be a wide audience for the psalm, encompassing both the blessings promised to the righteous and the warnings given to the wicked.[14]

In terms of voicing, the speaker waxes authoritatively regarding the distinction between the Two Ways and their respective ends. Within the context of the Old Testament, the speaker is best understood as either the divine voice itself (YHWH), a prophetic voice speaking on behalf of YHWH, or, given the psalm's close affiliation with wisdom motifs, a sapiential instructor. In the premodern period, interpreters settled almost universally on the voice of the psalmist himself, most often identified as the prophet David. For example, Hilary of Poitiers wrote that "we are to recognize the person of the Prophet by whose lips the Holy Spirit speaks," whose purpose is to extol "the happiness of that man whose will is in the Law of the Lord."[15] Given the instructive nature of the psalm and its firm convictions on the destiny of the righteous and wicked, I am inclined to identify the voice of Ps 1 as an ambiguous prophetic-sapiential (didactic) figure, who, for the lack of a better term, we can generically call the "psalmist."[16] His main roles are to introduce the theological and thematic context of the book, as well as give its readers a sense of who they might encounter as they enter into prayer. Our ability to observe how different "characters" or "participants" are introduced in Ps 1 helps us in identifying further speaking personae. We will keep this in mind as we walk through the psalm.

3.1.1.1. Psalm 1:1–2. Psalm 1 begins with a three-verse reflection on the figure of "the man" (הָאִישׁ). While some translations provide a plural reading of these

---

[13] See Gerstenberger, *Psalms: Part 1*, 40. He categorizes it as a "liturgical admonition."

[14] But also see Charry, *Psalms 1–50*, 1–4. She argued that the audience is principally the people of Israel as a whole, the wicked being understood as "faithless" Israelites, while the righteous are "faithful" Israelites.

[15] Hilary of Poitiers, *Homilies on the Psalms* 1.1 (NPNF² 9:236).

[16] See Beat Weber, "'Herr, wie viele sind geworden meine Bedränger...' (Ps 3,2a): Psalm 1–3 als Ouvertüre des Psalters unter besonderer Berücksichtigung von Psalm 3 und seinem Präskript," in *Der Bibelkanon in der Bibelauslegung: Methodenreflexionen und Beispielexegesen*, ed. Egbert Ballhorn and Georg Steins (Stuttgart: Kohlhammer, 2007), 232–34. He prefers to speak of a Moses-like figure as the speaker of Ps 1, with the "man" of Ps 1:1 as the addressee of the psalm, whom he identified as a Davidic king. Interestingly, while noting David as a possible addressee, he emphasized Solomon as better suited, especially given the Solomonic addressee in Pss 70–72. My further analysis below will also argue for identifying this "man" as a Davidic king.

verses ("blessed are those..."), the underlying Hebrew and all ancient versions consistently use third-person masculine singular pronouns to refer to him. In combination with the definite article, there is a strong argument that הַאִישׁ refers to a specific male person.[17] Important clues to his identity are given in the opening verses of the psalm. The first comes in the first clause, "Blessed/Happy [אַשְׁרֵי] is the Man" (1:1).[18] As the psalm unfolds, it describes the character traits of the one considered blessed/happy (1:1–2) as well as the kind of future expected for such a person (1:3). As part of the staging for the Psalter as a whole, the description of the "man" in these verses will model the "way of the righteous" referenced in the second half of the psalm (vv. 4–6).

After the initial note of blessing, the final three clauses in verse one and the whole of the second verse explain why this man has been described as blessed. Verse one does so negatively, listing three activities the man refuses to participate in: walking in the counsel of the wicked, standing in the way of sinners, and sitting in the seat of scoffers. The second verse does so positively, naming the man's delight in the *torah* of YHWH and his meditations over it throughout the days of his life.[19] Without yet naming them, the psalmist has already begun painting two contrary ways of living: one based on human counsel (1:1), and the other on divine counsel, the *torah* of YHWH (1:2). The use of different terminology to describe this negative path, both in terms of personal description—"wicked" (רְשָׁעִים), "sinners" (חַטָּאִים), and "scoffers" (לֵצִים)—and action—"walk" (הָלַךְ), "stand" (עָמַד), and "sit" (יָשַׁב)—denote something of the progress and positioning of the ungodly in contrast to the stability of divine *torah*. This is reinforced by the use of the strong adversative particle at the beginning of verse two, "but rather" (כִּי אִם).[20]

We find an interesting parallel to this opening verse in Prov 1:8–19. The father begins his instruction to his son, highlighting the speech of "sinners" (הַטָּאִים; 1:10–15), their movement ("their feet run to evil, and they hurry to shed blood"; 1:16), and the end of their way (1:17–19). The subsequent call of Lady Wisdom (1:20–33) includes scoffing and delighting, "How long will scoffers

---

[17] To be sure, "the man" 1:1 takes on a certain representative character given his connection with "the righteous" of 1:5–6, but this is *interpretation*, not translation. There is a marked difference between "Blessed is *a* man" and "Blessed is *the* man." By incorporating interpretation into the text, translators have not allowed English readers to reflect on the relationship between this specific "man" and the later groups of the wicked and the righteous. See also Patrick D. Miller, *Interpreting the Psalms* (Philadelphia: Fortress, 1986), 84.

[18] Alternatively, this first clause could be a construct noun phrase: "O the blessings/happiness of the man!" See Gerstenberger, *Psalms: Part 1*, 40–41, for a summary of the history of this congratulation/beatitude formula.

[19] The verb הגה is normally translated as "meditate," but the root imagery is that of chewing or savoring the flavor of something. When applied to *torah*, the idea is that one is mulling things over or even muttering them to oneself.

[20] See McCann, "Psalms," 684.

[לצים] delight [חמד] in their scoffing [לצון]?" (1:22). This helps us to get a sense of how the terminology in Ps 1:1 has broader use within texts sharing wisdom motifs.[21] The psalm is not talking about innocuous influence or being a little rough around the edges; the psalmist is describing nefarious activities designed to injure. As the father notes: "Such are the ways [ארחות] of all who make their cut [בצע] unjustly [בצע]" (1:19). Within the Psalter, Ps 10 further elaborates the kinds of activities which characterize the ungodly: they "chase down those who suffer" (10:2); "they brag about the things they want; they bless the greedy but hate YHWH" (10:3); "their mouths are full of curses, lies, and threats; they use their tongues for sin and evil; they hide near the villages; they look for innocent people to kill; they watch in secret for the helpless" (10:7–8); and, "the poor are thrown down and crushed; they are defeated because the others are stronger" (10:10).

Contrasting this imagery, the life which is considered "blessed" has a two-fold positive characterization in Ps 1:2: delight [הפץ] in the *torah* of YHWH, and daily "rumination" [הגה] in it. Contemporary discussion of Ps 1 has been keenly interested in identifying the reference to *torah*, as its identification has had a large impact on understanding the influence of Ps 1 over the entire book. A number of options are open to the interpreter: (1) teaching or instruction which has its source in YHWH; (2) a specific text—oral or written—which bears the authority of YHWH, with several sub-options: the deuteronomic code, Deuteronomy as a whole, the *Torah* of Moses, the Pentateuch, the Law and Prophets, or sacred Scripture more generally; (3) to the book of Psalms itself, as a new kind of Davidic *torah*; or (4) some combination of these options. A few factors from Ps 1 can help to navigate our choices. First, verse two does not refer to the *torah* of YHWH as a "book" or "scroll," nor does this occur anywhere else in the Psalter. This could suggest that at most the psalmist is referring to oral *torah* which has come from YHWH. Yet, second, the latter half of the verse assumes that one is able to memorize the *torah* of YHWH and ruminate [הגה] on what it is teaching. As many have pointed out, this verb does not refer to silent, mindful meditation, but is a physical act in which one murmurs (cf. Ps 63:7; 90:9; 143:5), speaks aloud (cf. 2:1; 37:30; 38:13; 71:24; 77:13), or even sings (cf. Ps 35:28). Thus, the *torah* of YHWH "must define a recognizable, established, and crystallized text that can be committed to memory and recited."[22] Even still, there has been much room for interpretation, as can be seen from the flurry of new essays on the topic.[23]

---

[21] For a recent re-assessment of wisdom literature, see Will Kynes, *An Obituary for "Wisdom Literature": The Birth, Death, and Intertextual Reintegration of a Biblical Corpus* (Oxford: Oxford University Press, 2019). My observation is only to draw attention to similar conceptions of the wicked at both the beginning of the Psalms and Proverbs.

[22] Sarna, *Songs of the Heart*, 38.

[23] See Phil J. Botha, "Intertextuality and the Interpretation of Psalm 1," *OTE* 18 (2005): 503–20; Beat Weber, "Psalm 1 and Its Function as a Directive into the Psalter and Towards a Biblical Theology," *OTE* 19 (2006): 237–60; Lee Roy Martin, "Delighting in the Torah: The Affective Dimension of Psalm 1," *OTE* 23 (2010): 708–27; Beat Weber, "Die Buchouvertüre

While I am inclined to take the reference to the Mosaic *Torah* (as we will shortly discuss with verse three), I am at the same time convinced that the referent is not limited to it, but by synecdoche is broadened to the entirety of Scripture, including the Psalms. As Calvin explained:

> When David here speaks of *the law*, it ought not to be understood as if the other parts of Scripture should be excluded, but rather since the whole of Scripture is nothing else than an exposition of the law, under it as the head is comprehended the whole body. The prophet, therefore, in commending the law, includes all the rest of the inspired writings. He must, therefore, be understood as meaning to exhort the faithful to the reading of the Psalm also.[24]

Brevard Childs would extend Calvin's argument in light of his canonical approach. In his view, the primary reference of *torah* must be "the commandments of Moses," but because Ps 1 has been placed as an introduction to the book, there is a fascinating interplay between Ps 1:2 and the prayers of Psalter: the prayers are seen *as* the "ruminations" of Ps 1:2. He wrote: "Israel's prayers are not simply spontaneous musings or uncontrolled aspirations, but rather an answer to God's word which continues to address Israel in his Torah."[25] They are, in a sense, expositional prayers.

The subsuming of the Psalter within the *torah* of Y{\sc hwh} allowed Childs to argue that the blessing pronounced on the godly man (1:1) now extends over those who read the Psalms. Benjamin Sommer neatly summarized this effect:

> Psalm 1 attempts to convert the book of Psalms into another form of Torah. It suggests that one ought to learn this text, just as one learns the Pentateuch. By intimating that one can receive teaching from the Psalter,

---

Psalm 1–3 und ihre Bedeutung für das Verständnis des Psalters," *OTE* 23 (2010): 834–45; Benjamin D. Sommer, "Psalm 1 and the Canonical Shaping of Jewish Scripture," in *Jewish Bible Theology: Perspectives and Case Studies*, ed. Isaac Kalimi (Winona Lake: Eisenbrauns, 2012), 199–222; Phil J. Botha, "Interpreting 'Torah' in Psalm 1 in the Light of Psalm 119," *HTS* 68 (2012): 1–7, doi:10.4102/hts.v68i1.1274; Lefebvre, "On His Law He Meditates"; Robert L. Cole, *Psalms 1–2: Gateway to the Psalter*, HBM 37 (Sheffield: Sheffield Phoenix, 2013); Susan Gillingham, *A Journey of Two Psalms: The Reception of Psalms 1 and 2 in Jewish and Christian Tradition* (Oxford: Oxford University Press, 2013); Scott Jones, "Psalm 1 and the Hermeneutics of Torah," *Bib* 97 (2016): 537–51; Adam D. Hensely, *Covenant Relationships and the Editing of the Hebrew Psalter*, LHBOTS 666 (London: T&T Clark, 2018), 135–36; Willgren, "Why Psalms 1–2 Are Not to Be Considered a Preface"; Daniel R. Driver, "On Difficulty and Psalm 2," in *The Identity of Israel's God: Theology, Reality, and the Scope of the Christian Bible*, ed. Donald Collett, *et. al.* (Atlanta, GA: SBL, fc).

[24] John Calvin, *Commentary on the Book of Psalms*, trans. J. Anderson, 5 vols (Edinburgh: Calvin Translation Society, 1845), 1:4. See Kraus, *Psalms 1–59*, 116.

[25] Brevard S. Childs, *Introduction to the Old Testament as Scripture* (Philadelphia: Fortress, 1979), 513.

Psalm 1 also makes the somewhat surprising move of transforming prayers into instruction. What one might have regarded as a human's words to the deity become a form of divine revelation to humanity.[26]

We begin to see, then, how Ps 1 plays a critical role in mapping out the whole book. Lefebvre and others, who either limit the use of *torah* to only one referent or refuse the literary device of synecdoche, fail to appreciate the sense in which these songs and prayers really have become *more* than an anthology of ancient cultic poetry.[27] As Childs argued, "The prayers of Israel directed to God have themselves become identified with God's word to his people."[28]

Regardless of one's view on this, the immediate purpose of verse two is to highlight a very different approach to life for the "Blessed Man" in contrast to the ungodly of verse one. The centerpiece of this contrast rests on the *torah* of YHWH. Instead of heeding the call and counsel of the ungodly, the "Blessed Man" has set his mind and body to the rumination of God's words with "diligent, gratifying application" (חפץ).[29]

3.1.1.2. Inner-biblical interpretation of Ps 1:3. Following the description of these two contrary ways of life, the third verse speaks of the future of the "Blessed Man" using figurative language: "Thus, he will be like a tree [כעץ] transplanted [שתל] upon streams of water [על־פלגי מים], which yields [נתן] its fruit [פרי] in its season, and its leaves [עלה] do not whither [נבל]; and everything he does [עשׂה] will prosper [צלה]." The language draws upon standard imagery in the ancient Near East,[30] and yet, through inner-biblical allusions and quotation, speaks beyond that language to bring in additional dimensions to our "Blessed Man."

First, we begin with Jer 17:7–8, which shares not only certain phrasing, but a parallel stretching back into verses one and two. It reads:

> [7] Blessed is the man [ברוך הגבר] who trusts [בטח] in YHWH,
>> and YHWH is his trust.
>
> [8] He shall be like a tree [כעץ] transplanted [שתול] along water [על־מים],
>> and along a stream [על־יובל] he sends out [שלח] his roots;
>> and he does not fear when the heat comes,

---

[26] Sommer, "Psalm 1 and the Canonical Shaping of Jewish Scripture," 207–8.

[27] See Lefebvre, "On His Law He Meditates," 443–44. One's understanding of this referent, then, seems to rest on how one understands the nature of the Psalms as Scripture. For Lefebrve, they are not God's words at all, but "a compilation of songs to sustain *torah*-faithfulness according to the function of psalmody appointed in Deut 31–32, and the Law of Moses is the *torah* on which these songs meditate" (444). On the other hand, as I am arguing, while they do certainly sustain *torah*-faithfulness, providing examples of ruminations on the Law of Moses—though they do much more than that, cf. Ps 106—we need to recognize that they are authoritative in this regard, as Scripture. And, what is Scripture if not the *torah* of YHWH?

[28] Childs, *Introduction to the Old Testament as Scripture*, 513.

[29] Sarna, *Songs of the Heart*, 36.

[30] See Sarna, *Songs of the Heart*, 40–41.

for his leaves [עָלֵהוּ] remain green [רַעֲנָן];
and in a year of drought he is not anxious,
and he does not cease [מוּשׁ] from the bearing [עֲשׂוֹת] of fruit [פֶּרִי]."

In the surrounding context, Jeremiah is condemning the sins of Judah, explaining how their idolatry is going to be punished by YHWH. After threatening them with exile (17:1–4), he recounts a description of those who trust in human beings (17:5–6) in contrast with those who trust in YHWH (17:7–8). The contrast shows that those who turn away from YHWH will fail in their strength, while those who trust in YHWH will be sustained in the midst of trouble.[31] This accords well with the meaning of Ps 1:1–2, especially in its wisdom parallels. Dependence on and delight in the *torah* of YHWH both has set the "Blessed Man" apart from his ungodly peers and provided him with continual sustenance in the presence of YHWH. As he becomes more like those whom the ungodly intend to injure, his rootedness "along the water" becomes all the more substantial. The well of his strength does not depend on his outward circumstances but is based on his trust in YHWH.

One aspect of this imagery which is not as explicit in Ps 1 relates to the presence of YHWH. In Jer 17, the threat of exile was not simply a loss of one's livelihood, land, and community, but also the presence of YHWH in their midst at the temple. Using the imagery of the tree, a few parallels in the Psalter show that the language of Ps 1:3 does indeed symbolize God's presence there. For instance, in Ps 52:10, the image of a tree is used to describe the flourishing of the psalmist in the temple: "But I am like a green olive tree in the house of God [בְּבֵית אֱלֹהִים]." Closer still to Ps 1:3, in Ps 92:13–15 the tree simile has been democratized to describe the entire community of the righteous flourishing in the temple of YHWH:

> [13] The righteous [צַדִּיק] flourish [פרח] like the palm tree [כַּתָּמָר],
> and grow [שׂגה] like a cedar in Lebanon;
>
> [14] they have been planted [שׁתל] in the house of YHWH [בְּבֵית יהוה],
> they will flourish [פרח] in the courts of our God [בְּחַצְרוֹת אֱלֹהֵינוּ].
>
> [15] They still bear fruit [נוב] in old age;
> they are ever juicy [דָּשֵׁן] and fresh [רַעֲנָן].

Beyond the plural subject, when compared to Ps 1:3 we see a substitution of the phrase "the house of YHWH" for "streams of water" (92:14).

This understanding of "streams of water" as temple is further substantiated by its use within a second prophetic text, Ezek 47. This chapter offers strong parallels to Ps 1:3, using tree imagery within its grand vision of a future temple-city-garden, where the people of God find their home:

---

[31] See William L. Holladay, "Indications of Jeremiah's Psalter," *JBL* 121 (2002): 245–61; Creach, "Like a Tree," disagreed with Holladay's construction in his *Hermeneia* commentary, but the cited article by Holladay offers a much stronger argument in favor of Jeremiah's use of Ps 1 and not *vice-versa*.

On the banks, on both sides of the river [נהל], there will grow all kinds of trees for food. Their leaves [עלה] will not wither [נבל], nor their fruit [פרי] fail, but they will bear fresh fruit every month because for them the water [מים] flows from the sanctuary [מקדש]. Their fruit [פרי] will be for food [מאכל], and their leaves [עלה] for healing [תרופה]." (Ezek 47:12)

In his eschatological vision, Ezekiel sees fruit trees planted alongside a river which flows out of a new temple complex. While temporally located in the future, the imagery stresses the special providence of God to nourish, sustain, and even heal. In Ps 1, the "Blessed Man" will be *like* these eschatological trees, planted along Edenic rivers flowing from the temple mount, in a city named "Yhwh is there" (Ezek 48:35). He, too, will nourish and bring healing. While it may also suggest that the "Blessed Man" is promised a place in this eschatological future, the imagery is more about Yhwh enabling him to bring that future into the present. In short, because of his trust in Yhwh rather than human beings, Yhwh has blessed him, that he will be firmly rooted in the presence of Yhwh, bearing the beneficent fruit of that presence in ministries of flourishing and healing.[32]

3.1.1.3. Inner-biblical interpretation and kingship in Ps 1:2-3. Though we have done quite a bit of inner-biblical reading to help understand the full complexity of imagery in Ps 1:3, we have one more phrase to discuss: "and everything he does [עשה] will prosper [צלה]." This phrase is one of the most important for helping us identify the figure of the "Blessed Man." The connection with other texts is linked also to the mention of *torah* and its rumination "day and night," from verse two.

The first inner-biblical link comes from Deut 17:18–20, within the laws given to the future kings of Israel (the so-called "kingship law"):

And it will be, when he will sit on the throne of his kingdom, he shall have a copy of this *torah* written for him upon a scroll in the presence of the Levitical priests. And it shall be with him and he shall read [קרא] in it all the days of his life [כל־ימי חייו], so that he may learn to fear Yhwh his

---

[32] According to some scholars, the "streams of water" in Ps 1:3 symbolize not the temple but the *torah* of YHWH. For them, the imagery is that "our individual is resilient, stable, and steadfast because he is deeply rooted in the spiritual and ethical soil of the Torah" (Sarna, *Songs of the Heart*, 42). See also Jerome F. D. Creach, "Like a Tree Planted by the Temple Stream: The Portrait of the Righteous in Psalm 1:3," *CBQ* 61 (1999): 34–46. Elsewhere in the Psalter *torah* does have this sustaining and reviving capacity (cf. Pss 19; 119), so perhaps we have *torah* and not the presence of YHWH as the meaning of the image. In my opinion, the decisive factor comes in recognizing the different functions of *torah* and temple in Ps 1. In 1:2, the *torah* of YHWH is used not as a substitute for the temple in 1:3, but to contrast the ungodly of verse one with the delight and ruminations of the "Blessed Man." Once this contrast is made, a new subject is in view, with a different future time frame: "thus, he will be" (והיה; 1:3). In 1:3, then, the imagery points to a future for the "Blessed Man" within the presence of YHWH in the temple.

God, observing all the words of this *torah* and these statutes, to do them,
that his heart be not lifted up above his brothers, and that he not turn
aside from the commandment, either to the right or to the left, so that
he may prolong the days over his kingdom, he and his sons, in the midst
of Israel.

Paralleling Ps 1, these verses tell us that kings must pay heed to *torah*, reading it
daily and for the rest of their lives. In doing so, they will learn to observe (שמר)
and do (עשה) its commandments, resulting in humility before their people and
establishing a strong dynasty. As Patrick Miller pointed out, this passage sets up
the king as a leader of God's people, that he might "exemplify and demonstrate
true obedience to the Lord for the sake of the well-being of both the dynasty and
the kingdom. King and subject share a common goal: to learn to fear the Lord."[33]
The figure of the king was meant to take on a typical role for the people of Israel.
Jamie Grant explained:

> The kingship law indicates that, above all else, the king is meant to be the
> paradigmatic Israelite believer. How does he become such? By internal-
> izing Yahweh's *torah* and allowing it to influence every aspect of his life
> and rule. This is what all kings in Israel were meant to be like—archetypal
> believers, examples for all other Israelites to follow.[34]

The development of this kingship law in Josh 1:6–8 and 1 Kgs 2:2–4 suggests that
the same is expected of the Blessed Man in Ps 1.

In Josh 1:6–8, YHWH speaks to Joshua as he is about to lead Israel into the
Promised Land:

> Be strong [חזק] and courageous [אמץ], for you shall cause this people to
> inherit the land that I swore to their fathers to give to them. Only be
> strong [חזק] and very courageous [אמץ מאד], being careful to observe
> [לשמר לעשות] in accordance with all the *torah* that my servant Moses
> commanded you: do not turn from it to the right hand or to the left, so
> that you may be successful [שכל] wherever you go. The scroll of this *torah*
> shall not depart from your mouth; but you shall ruminate [הגה] on it day
> and night [יומם ולילה], so that you may be careful to act [תשמר לעשות] in
> accordance with all that is written in it. For then you shall make your way
> [דרך] prosperous [צלח], and then you shall be successful [שכל].

Both Josh 1 and Ps 1 are concerned with the prosperity of its referent (צלח),
which results from his daily meditation on *torah*. There is also a strong lexical
correspondence between Josh 1 and Deut 17:18–20. YHWH admonishes Joshua to
observe (שמר) and do (עשה) the *Torah of Moses*, turning not to the right or left
(ימין ושמאול), ruminating/speaking it (הגה/קרא) daily (יומם ולילה/כל-ימי חייו).
While Joshua is not Israel's king, he is its spiritual leader and general, and thus,
would be expected to exemplify the kingship code's concern that the people of

---

[33] Patrick Miller, *Deuteronomy*, IBC (Louisville: Westminster John Knox, 1990), 149.

[34] Jamie A. Grant, "The Psalms and the King," in *Interpreting the Psalms: Issues and Approaches*, ed. David Firth and Philip S. Johnston (Downers Grove: InterVarsity, 2005), 115.

God follow in the footsteps of their leaders in their obedience of *torah*.[35] Joshua 1 also emphasizes something that Deut 17 leaves unmentioned: the rewards of obedience. If Joshua does as Yʜᴡʜ requests, then his way (דרך) will be prosperous (צלח) and he will have success (שכל). The links between Ps 1 and Josh 1 may be a deliberate attempt to tie the Psalms to the deuteronomic emphasis on the *torah* and its rewards.

Building on this motif, 1 Kgs 2:2–4 brings the kingship code within the context of the Davidic dynasty. Here, David is passing the torch of kingship to Solomon, giving him final words of advice:

> I am going in the way of all the earth, but you will be strong [חזק] and become a man [והיית לאיש], and you will keep [שמר] the charge of Yʜᴡʜ your God, to walk [הלך] in his ways [דרך], to keep [שמר] his statutes, his commandments and his ordinances, and his testimonies, as it is written in the *torah* of Moses, so that you may prosper [שכל] in all that you do [עשה] and wherever you turn; in this way, Yʜᴡʜ will establish his word which he spoke concerning me, saying, "If your sons keep watch [שמר] of their way [דרך], to walk before me in faithfulness with all their heart and with all their soul, then there will not fail you a man from upon the throne of Israel."

In this passage, we are met again with similar phrases and terminology found in Deut 17, Josh 1, and Ps 1. David's advice sticks closely to the kingship code in Deut 17, especially its emphasis on obedience to the *torah* of Moses. It also recalls Yʜᴡʜ's speech to Joshua, repeating the same command for Solomon to be strong, with the same promises of success. On top of this is also added the summary of the Davidic promises from 2 Sam 7. For the author of Kings, this means that the Davidic dynasty is not only fulfilling the kingship code, with its promise of a long line of kings, but also that Joshua's promised "success" should be further qualified as the outworking of God's promises to the line of David.

After David, no other king in the history of Israel and Judah would ever repeat this advice (or anything like it). This suggests that there is a special connection between the figures of David and Solomon and the kind of king envisioned in Deut 17. Though far from perfect, they capture important elements of ideal kingship. Indeed, throughout the book of Kings David has been set up as the standard by which all subsequent kings are compared. For example, in 1 Kgs 9:4–5 we read the following summary about Solomon's reign: "And as for you, if you will walk before me, *as David your father walked*, with integrity of heart and uprightness, doing according to all that I have commanded you, and keeping my statutes and my rules, then I will establish your royal throne over Israel forever, as I promised David your father." Even though Solomon would ultimately fail to walk before God, David remained the benchmark for judgment over the kings of

---

[35] See Grant, *King as Exemplar*, 47n15.

Judah (cf. 1 Kgs 11:4–6; 15:1–5, 9–11; 2 Kgs 14:1–3; 16:2; 18:1–3; 22:1–2). This portrays David as *the* exemplary king envisioned in the kingship law of Deut 17: the exemplary king for the exemplars, the ideal king, the ideal Israelite.[36]

This has a profound effect on the way we read Ps 1. By recalling these texts in its description of the "Blessed Man," he emerges as an exemplary figure, one who takes upon himself the mantle of Deut 17, patterned after the leadership role of Joshua, and following in the footsteps of Israel's most idealized royal figure, David. There are, however, notable differences. As Robert Cole argued, whereas the earlier speeches given to Joshua (and Solomon) are given as commands and enjoined with conditional promises of success, their description in Ps 1 portrays them as facts (note the perfect verbs in 1:1), whose successes are described as both "absolute and unqualified." The "Blessed Man" is "portrayed as an ideal royal figure greater than Joshua in his unswerving devotion to Yahweh's Torah and enjoying consequent success."[37]

Pulling these observations together, the "Blessed Man" in Ps 1 should not be understood as an "Everyman" or even a generic exemplar, but as having a pedigree as a royal figure from the line of David.

3.1.1.4. Psalm 1:4–6. In the closing verses of the psalm (vv. 4–6), the psalmist takes up the figure of the "Blessed Man" and uses it to further contrast two different ways of life. The focus, however, lies not on individuals, but on two groups of people: the wicked (רשעים, vv. 4–5a, 6b) and the righteous (צדקים, vv. 5b, 6a).

Verse four begins by contrasting the destiny of the "Blessed Man" with the judgment given to the wicked: "Not so [לא־כן] the wicked." Whereas the "Blessed Man" is described using imagery which emphasizes his strength, durability, and vigor, the imagery used for the wicked suggests their fragility and instability: "They are like chaff which the wind drives away." This simile is consistently used throughout the Old Testament to characterize the judgment given to enemies who appear to be immovable (cf. Ps 35:5; 83:13–15; Job 21:18; Isa 17:13; Jer 13:24); before YHWH their strength and power are reduced to dust and chaff, easily driven away by the wind.

Verse five builds on this contrast of images (1:3–4) by drawing conclusions about the destiny of the wicked. While the "Blessed Man" will be firmly planted within the presence of YHWH in the renewed temple, the wicked will not "rise up" [קום] in YHWH's judgment, finding no place in the congregation of the righteous (1:5). The psalm concludes by introducing a final contrast between the two different ways of life taken by the righteous (v. 6a) and the wicked (v. 6b). These Two Ways are an important clue to understanding the entire Psalter, and Book

---

[36] See Grant, *King as Exemplar*, 46. He noted that the above texts were given to the leaders of God's people, and as such, they were meant to be "exemplars of devotion to YHWH."

[37] Cole, "Integrated Reading," 79.

1 in particular.[38] In 1:5b, the psalmist had already introduced us to the righteous congregation, and in 1:6a he tells us that Yʜᴡʜ keeps providential watch over their "way" (דרך). The way of the wicked, however, will end in destruction (אבד).

Given the earlier reference to Ps 92:13–15, there is an implicit connection between the kind of life described of the "Blessed Man" and "the way of the righteous" (1:5–6). Looking at the wider context of Ps 92, we note that the military success of the king over his enemies (vv. 10–11), as part of Yʜᴡʜ's pattern of deliverance (vv. 1–9), allows for the flourishing of the righteous (vv. 12–15).[39] Psalm 92, then, provides a strong link between the prosperity of the king, the destructive ends of the wicked, and the flourishing of the righteous. In short, the blessings of the king have become the blessings enjoyed by the righteous. In Ps 1, the same pattern is found. In verses five and six, the righteous are portrayed as following along the path of life laid out by the "Blessed Man," avoiding the disastrous influence of the wicked (1:1) and trusting in Yʜᴡʜ for support (1:2). The "Blessed Man" is their exemplar; they follow in his ways and share in his destiny.

3.1.1.5. Psalm 1 and the speaking persona(e). In closing my discussion on Ps 1, I want to consider how it contributes to our understanding of the speaking personae in the Psalms. First, we have the principal speaker, the sapiential-prophetic (didactic) voice who describes the figure of the "Blessed Man," the characteristics of the righteous and the wicked, and their respective ends. Even though no explicit clues are given this identity, the introductory nature of Ps 1 and the focus on the *torah* of Yʜᴡʜ as part of the way of the righteous allows the speaker to help shape our understanding of the Psalter as a whole. Second, the characterization of important figures in Ps 1 greatly shapes how we hear the psalms which follow. We start with the "Blessed Man," an ideal royal figure associated with the Davidic dynasty, whose pattern of life is exemplary to the righteous, and whose beneficent ministry and destiny will be shared by the righteous. Next, we are introduced to the wicked, whose counsel and way of life are at odds with what has been revealed in the *torah* of Yʜᴡʜ (1:1–2), and whose destiny is contrasted with that of the "Blessed Man" (1:3–4) and righteous (1:5–6). And last, we have the righteous, who are only briefly described. Their way of life is patterned after the "Blessed Man," which is guarded by the providential care of Yʜᴡʜ (1:6). It is important to distinguish them from the "Blessed Man," following the pronouns used in the psalm, and to note their contrast with the wicked found in verses five and six. In Ps 1, then, we have been given important

---

[38] See Jerome Creach, *Yahweh as Refuge and the Editing of the Hebrew Psalter*, JSOTSup 217 (Sheffield: Sheffield Academic, 1996), 79–80.

[39] See Walter Brueggemann and William H. Bellinger, Jr., *Psalms*, NCBC (New York: Cambridge University Press, 2014), 398–401. Their comments cogently describe the main issues and interpretive possibilities of the psalm.

indications on who might be speaking in the Psalter: a divine perspective mediated through the sapiential-prophetic voice of the psalmist, the "Blessed Man," the wicked, and the congregation of the righteous.

3.1.2. Psalm 2 and the Speaking Personae

As I have argued above, Ps 2 should be considered a discrete psalm, independent from Ps 1. Even so, their juxtaposition, lack of superscriptions, and binding elements show that the two psalms have now been integrated in some way as a dual entryway into the Psalter. My reflections here will not tease out all the implications of this setting but will be focused on how it has developed the concept of speaking persona(e) in the Psalms.

The psalm begins by referencing nations and peoples in rebellion against YHWH and his anointed king, vainly plotting to be free from their sovereign rule (2:1–3). YHWH reacts with mocking derision, establishing his king on Mount Zion despite their plans (2:4–6). A decree is recounted between the king and YHWH, closely associated with the Davidic covenant (cf. 2 Sam 7), granting worldwide sovereignty to bring rebel nations into subjection (2:7–9). It concludes with a change in tone. Several imperatives are given to defiant kings, admonishing them to act with wisdom and submit willingly to the rule of YHWH, lest the Son (the anointed ruler) unleash his fury in establishing his kingdom (2:10–12a). Those who take refuge in him, however, are considered blessed (2:12b).

In my discussion of Ps 1, the concept of kingship was not absent but was only accounted for through inner-biblical reading. In Ps 2, kingship sits on the surface, with a focus both on the sovereign rule of YHWH and the role of the king as YHWH's co-regent. Throughout the psalm, the precedence of YHWH and the derivative nature of the king is felt on every level.[40] As such, even the statement of blessing in 2:12b is strongly connected to this theme of dependence: as the king relies on YHWH, so do those who take refuge in him.

In terms of the speaking persona, it is helpful to compare Ps 1 with Ps 2. Psalm 1 is spoken by a sapiential-prophetic voice to a general audience composed of both the righteous and the wicked. There are no indications of a change of voice or audience. Psalm 2 is much different, presenting us with several changes in speaking voice and addressee. Surprisingly, in a book known for containing the prayers of God's people, we have yet to see prayer's presence.[41]

3.1.2.1. A dialogical analysis of Ps 2.

In the first section of the psalm (vv. 1–3), we hear a voice who reports the rebellion of the nations against YHWH and his anointed. As of yet, we are given no indications on the identity of this speaker, so for the time being I will simply refer to him as the "psalmist." Unlike Ps 1, a clue for the audience is given in these opening verses, as they report the rebellion in the form of a question. Erhard Gerstenberger has argued that this reflects

---

[40] See Grant, *King as Exemplar*, 59.
[41] Weber, "Psalm 1–3 als Ouvertüre des Psalters," 235.

a forensic speech form in which the psalmist brings his complaint before the divine Judge, with the aim of persuading Yʜᴡʜ to assist him in his suffering. In this case, we should identify the principal audience as Yʜᴡʜ, with the psalm taking the form of a complaint.[42] John Goldingay, however, has pointed out that the question is more rhetorical in force, expressing a statement of conviction; as such it is likely addressed to the whole people Israel.[43] Further, the report of Yʜᴡʜ's response in verses four and five would be difficult to assess if the speaker is addressing them to Yʜᴡʜ. It seems best, then, to identify the addressee in these verses as the people of Israel. Following this report, in verse three there is an unmarked change of persona (prosopopoeia) as the psalmist quotes the speech of those who are in rebellion. They speak using plural volitional verb forms, announcing their plans to any willing to care about their cause.

In the second section (vv. 4–6) we find a similar patterning of voices.[44] In verses four and five we have an unmarked return to the psalmist reporting the response of Yʜᴡʜ to those in rebellion, presumably with the same audience as in verses one and two. We have another unmarked change in persona in verse six, as the psalmist reports the speech of Yʜᴡʜ in the first person. This speech is directly addressed to those in rebellion, and indirectly to all who can hear Yʜᴡʜ speak.

The speaking persona changes considerably in the next section (vv. 7–9). At the beginning of verse seven we hear the voice of the king, who was announced in verse six as installed on Zion and referred to in verse three as one of the objects of rebellion. He proclaims a decree that Yʜᴡʜ had given him concerning his coronation and the authority this rule gives him in relation to the kings and rulers of the earth (vv. 7b–9). The audience of the decree is unclear, though its all-encompassing character would have not only affected neighboring kings but all peoples within and without Israel. Within this section, while the king's voice is heard in verse 7a, the voice of Yʜᴡʜ comes to the fore in verses 7b–9, marked and reported by the king. An important question we will need to consider is whether verses seven through nine as a whole are considered reported speech, in which case the psalmist would be doing the reporting (so Craigie), or whether this is a complete shift to the persona of the king.[45] If the latter is true, then it is likely that the voice of the psalmist and the voice of the king are one and the same; we should identify the king speaking in 2:1–2, 4–5, and reporting speech in 2:3, 6.

The final section of the psalm (vv. 10–12) offers us a clue that favors the view that the entire psalm is spoken in the voice of the anointed king. The speaker addresses both the rebelling rulers, commanding fealty to Yʜᴡʜ (vv. 10–12a), as

---

[42] Gerstenberger, *Psalms: Part 1*, 45.

[43] Goldingay, *Psalms 1–41*, 96, 98. See also Charry, *Psalms 1–50*, 5–9. She argued that the psalm is also addressed to the people of Israel, but for different reasons.

[44] See Gerstenberger, *Psalms: Part 1*, 45–46; Goldingay, *Psalms 1–41*, 99.

[45] See Craigie, *Psalms 1–50*, 65. For the latter view, see Goldingay, *Psalms 1–41*, 96, and Mays, *Psalms*, 44.

well as those who seek refuge, that they should take joy in his presence (v. 12b). While it is certainly possible that the voice we hear belongs to the psalmist, now addressing those he referenced at the beginning (vv. 1–3), it is more fitting that it would be the king addressing those over whom Yнwн has given him authority. Before "breaking them with a rod of iron" or "dashing them in pieces like a potter's vessel," the nations and rulers are given the opportunity to return to Yнwн. In my opinion, then, throughout Ps 2 we should identify the voice of the king with the voice of the psalmist.

In sum, the psalm represents a model case of prosopopoeia. An author speaks in the person of the anointed king, who also reports the speech of other characters: the voice of the king (vv. 1–2, 4–5, 7a, and 10–12), the voice of the rebellious kings and rulers (reported in v. 3), and the voice of Yнwн (reported in vv. 6 and 7b–9).[46] This presents us with an important development from Ps 1, where we only heard the voice of the psalmist. Moreover, the psalm presents an imperative challenge to those in rebellion and a note of encouragement to those in refuge, that they would both place themselves under the authority of the Anointed, trusting in the reign of Yнwн. In Ps 1, we only received a descriptive account of the "Blessed Man," the Two Ways, and their end.

3.1.2.2. Semantic transformation and the king in Ps 2.   Identifying a royal figure as the speaker helps us understand the dialogical relationships in the psalm, but we are also concerned with identifying who this king might be. To do so, we will need to carefully distinguish between the earlier use of the psalm within the cultic life of ancient Israel and the psalm's function in the final form of the book. Gerald Sheppard framed the question as follows: "Why and how did the oldest prayers which once belonged to a hymn book of the first temple become part of a Jewish scripture? What alterations in the meaning or transformation in the semantic import of such pre-biblical traditions took place when they came to be read as part of a larger scripture?"[47] The key to identifying the kingly speaker in Ps 2 lies in our distinction between the pre-scriptural use of the psalm and its enduring function as sacred Scripture.

A reconstruction of the pre-scriptural use of Ps 2 has been well-documented throughout the twentieth century.[48] As part of the formal grouping of royal psalms, its main subject was the reigning king of Judah. While the purpose of each of the royal psalms should be considered on a case-by-case basis, they each "speak of the place the office of the king had in the faith of Israel" and "witness

---

[46] See Kraus, *Psalms 1–59*, 125. Augustine, commenting on this psalm, limits the voice to Jesus Christ, and therefore, understands the psalm with a more thoroughgoing prosopological model; David is a prophet speaking in the voice of Christ. Calvin, on the other hand, as we saw earlier, sees a closer connection between the person of David and Christ, using a typological model.

[47] Sheppard, *The Future of the Bible*, 54.

[48] For a fuller summary, see Sam Janse, *"You Are My Son": The Reception History of Psalm 2 in Early Judaism and the Early Church*, CBET 51 (Leuven: Peeters, 2009), 10–13.

that the king had a focal role in Israel's status, welfare, and destiny under God."[49] Concerning the specific purpose of Ps 2, scholars have argued that it would have been sung at the enthronement of the king (cf. 2 Kgs 11:12–14), or perhaps even at an annual royal festival.[50] The accession of a king in the ancient Near East consisted first of his crowning, at which time he was given a divine decree containing his commission to rule, and second, of his ritual accession to the throne where the beginning of his reign was proclaimed.[51] In this context, 2:7–9 stand out. As Craigie noted, these verses "may well be the words which were formally declared by the new king after his anointing and installation, during the course of the coronation."[52] Here, the language of "anointed" and "son" were understood as titles given to the king, referring to the surrogacy of the king in his leadership of the people.[53] In this account, 2:1–6 reflect the divine response to vassals who may see a change in leadership as an opportunity for rebellion. It was a decisive moment:

> When the psalm was recited by a Davidide in Jerusalem, it was a proclamation that the Lord had chosen to provide life through the office which the Davidide was installed. The inauguration of his reign created the opportunity for blessing or perishing, depending on the response to the announcement of kingship.[54]

Each time a new Davidic king was installed on Zion, a psalm, perhaps even an earlier form of Ps 2, would have been read as part of his ritual coronation.

According to Sheppard, while this reconstruction of the cultic use of the text may be accurate, it speaks nothing of the present form of Ps 2 and its function as part of an authoritative book of Psalms. He wrote:

> In this treatment, the psalm itself does not belong to scripture. It undoubtedly carries some authority... but it belongs to the material of an ancient liturgy and not to a body of writings on par with the Torah of Moses. Though God is quoted within the psalm and these authoritative words form part of a larger argument within it, the literary context is not yet that of scripture.... When traditions that were originally pre-scriptural become part of scripture they change their context and their semantic import.[55]

---

[49] Mays, *The Lord Reigns*, 110.

[50] For the former view, see Hermann Gunkel, *The Psalms: A Form-Critical Introduction*, trans. Thomas M. Horner (Philadelphia: Fortress, 1967), 24; Hermann Gunkel and Joachim Begrich, *Introduction to the Psalms: The Genres of the Religious Lyric of Israel*, trans. James D. Nogalski (Macon, GA: Mercer University Press, 1998), 99–120. For the latter view, see Kraus, *Psalms 1–59*, 126–35.

[51] Mays, *The Lord Reigns*, 111.

[52] Craigie, *Psalms 1–50*, 67.

[53] See Gerstenberger, *Psalms: Part 1*, 46–47.

[54] Mays, *The Lord Reigns*, 112–13.

[55] Sheppard, *The Future of the Bible*, 61–62.

Crucially, we need to ask what "semantic transformations" might take place when a psalm which was originally part of a traditional cultic situation was taken up into the Psalter as Scripture. For my purposes, how does this affect the way we understand the king who speaks in Ps 2?

To begin, the editing of the Psalms into its final form only took place within the postexilic period, when the Davidic dynasty had collapsed and the cultic use of Ps 2, as reconstructed, would have altogether disappeared. Thus, the psalm's "exceeding" language, to borrow from Aquinas, would have "now seemed to be an impossible dream."[56] Moreover, the very office of kingship would have been questioned. As Mays noted, "There was an unbearable contradiction between the royal office borne by David's successors and the way they used its authority and privilege. They were both bearers and betrayers of the calling to make it possible for their subjects to live in the reign of God."[57] It is curious, then, that Ps 2 took such a prominent place at the beginning of the book.[58] As McCann explained, the loss of the Davidic monarchy was "an ongoing theological crisis that made it necessary for the people of God to come to a new understanding of God and of their existence under God."[59] For him, "The shape of the Psalter indicates that its editors intended the psalms to participate in the theological dialogue that resulted in new perspectives on both divine and human sovereignty and suffering."[60]

In contemporary scholarship, these "new perspectives" have been understood in two ways. The first argues that the role of kingship had been reassessed during the exilic and postexilic periods. The prophetic outlook which emerged spoke of a new covenant, with expectations of a new "David" given the eternal nature of YHWH's promises. This change in conception of kingship resulted in a change in the understanding of the "anointed" of YHWH, which took on messianic and eschatological overtones.[61] As Fabry and Scholtissek explained:

> The royal psalms... originate from an interest group that propagated an expectation of a restorative dynastic king. The psalms originally had the king in mind who was currently reigning and were made to refer to the coming ruler of the eschaton in the post-exilic era.[62]

Similarly, Gerstenberger asked:

---

[56] Craigie, *Psalms 1–50*, 68.

[57] Mays, *The Lord Reigns*, 114.

[58] As noted by Childs, *Introduction to the Old Testament as Scripture*, 516.

[59] McCann, "Psalms," 661.

[60] McCann, "Psalms," 662.

[61] Craigie, *Psalms 1–50*, 68.

[62] Heinz-Josef Fabry and Klaus Scholtissek, *Der Messias*, NEBT 5 (Würzburg: Echter-Verlag, 2002), 27. Cited in Hossfeld and Zenger, "Considerations on the 'Davidization' of the Psalter," in *The Shape of the Writings*, ed. Julius Steinberg and Timothy J. Stone, Siphrut 16 (Winona Lake: Eisenbrauns, 2015), 119.

How could the defeated people be restored if not by a Davidic savior? And what other chance could there be to be liberated than by overthrowing the world powers that held Israel captive? To oppose all the kings of the world, as visualized in Psalm 2, makes sense only in a political situation of universal dependency.[63]

The salvation of Yʜwʜ would now only be realized when a Davidic heir would once again take the throne at Zion as the universal king. The royal psalms, while activating "old monarchical traditions of the divine election of David," were not able to be explained "by the aspirations of Israel's historical monarchies"; rather, Ps 2 corresponds to a postexilic theological universalism in which Yʜwʜ would one day be revealed as the real master of all the world.[64] For Gerstenberger, this is why Ps 2 should be categorized as a "messianic hymn" instead of its usual designation as a royal or kingship psalm.[65] In this context, the decree of Yʜwʜ in Ps 2:7 is still connected to the Davidic promises in 2 Sam 7:12–16, but is now heard as promises made *to* David about his descendant(s), and not about David himself.[66]

Alternatively, a second view has been formulated which reassesses kingship in the postexilic period as it now relates not to the Davidic dynasty but to the universal reign of Yʜwʜ. It admits that these kinds of messianic concerns were indeed expressed within the late prophetic layers of the Old Testament and within early Judaism, yet the focus in Ps 2 is not on the installment of the messianic king *per se*, but on the kingship of Yʜwʜ. Childs wrote:

> The weight of the psalm falls on God's claim of the whole earth as his possession, and the warning of his coming wrath against the presumption of earthly rulers. In other words, the psalm has been given an eschatological ring, both by its position in the Psalter and by the attachment of new meaning to the older vocabulary through the influence of the prophetic message.[67]

In this new context, Ps 2 would have helped to provide an identity and stabilized the lives of the people of God by urging them to rely on the rule of Yʜwʜ (2:11–12) and obey his *torah* (1:2).[68] The result of this ideological change is that the referent for the anointed king in Ps 2 could no longer be a reigning Davidide, but a future Davidic heir. The royal speaker of Ps 2 is not the historical David nor any of the kings who reigned after him, but the prophetic "David," the heir who would actualize the promises of 2 Sam 7.

---

[63] Gerstenberger, *Psalms: Part 1*, 48.

[64] Gerstenberger, *Psalms: Part 1*, 49.

[65] Gerstenberger, *Psalms: Part 1*, 48.

[66] See Childs, *Introduction to the Old Testament as Scripture*, 517.

[67] Childs, *Introduction to the Old Testament as Scripture*, 516.

[68] Nancy deClaissé-Walford, *Reading from the Beginning: The Shaping of the Hebrew Psalter* (Macon, GA: Mercer University Press, 1997), 44–48.

In both above cases one could make an argument for a messianic royal voice as the speaker of Ps 2. A third option, however, observes that when we consider the language of Ps 2 compared to other royal psalms in the Psalter, the speaking voice is not the future Davidic heir, but David himself. In Ps 89, for instance, the first half of the psalm holds together the praise of YHWH (89:2–3, 6–19) and the election of David (89:4–5, 20–38). Within the retelling of God's choice of David (vv. 20–29), we find clear conceptual parallels with Ps 2: David is the "chosen" (בחור, v. 20) and "anointed" (משׁח) servant of YHWH (v. 21); YHWH will protect him and break his enemies (vv. 22–24); and will exalt his office (v. 25), making him the "firstborn" (בכור), the highest of all kings (v. 28), with an enduring kingdom (v. 29). That David himself is in view, and not one of his descendants is clear from verse thirty, "I will establish forever his seed, his throne as the days of the heavens." Verses 31–38 follow by recalling the promises of 2 Sam 7:12–16, focusing on the faithfulness of YHWH in upholding his promises concerning the everlasting nature of David's throne. Furthermore, in a reversal of the language of the promise from 2 Sam 7:14—"I will be to him a father, and he shall be to me a son" (cf. Ps 2:7)—the psalmist envisions David pledging to YHWH, "You are my father, my God, and the rock of my salvation" (Ps 89:27). Clearly, then, even though in Ps 2 we have a recollection of the promises made to David concerning his royal line, so that it would be appropriate to hear the voice of one of his heirs reading the decree (2:7–9), in the memory of Ps 89 David himself was the first to utter such words.

Similarly, although Ps 72 is superscripted with the heading "Of Solomon" (לשׁלמה), the postscript refers explicitly to the "prayers of David, son of Jesse" (v. 20). This colophon suggests that we are hearing David praying the psalm over his son Solomon, that the promises YHWH has made with him would be actualized within Solomon's reign. As with Ps 89, we find several conceptual parallels with Ps 2: the just rule of the king (vv. 1–4, 12–14), his everlasting reign (vv. 5–7), his worldwide dominion (vv. 8–11), prosperity and bounty (vv. 15–17), and the precedence of YHWH's works above the rule of the king (vv. 18–19). Just as with Ps 89, the thematic similarities between Ps 2 and Ps 72 help to make the case that the voice of the king in Ps 2 could be the same voice in Ps 72, the voice of David himself.[69]

The semantic transformation of Ps 2 in the book of Psalms, then, allows for two options in identifying the royal speaking voice of Ps 2: either David himself or the messianic heir of promise. Throughout history, interpreters have most often chosen *between* these two voices, but perhaps the Psalter is leaving the option open. As Christopher Seitz has observed, Ps 2 could be holding in its right hand a historical voice—David within his own covenantal context—and in its left an "extended" voice—the Davidic heir, who speaks in a "capacity that is built

---

[69] Likewise, Ps 18:51 identifies David as the one praying in Ps 18 (cf. 18:1), while also referring to him with the titles "anointed one" and "king." This, too, could suggest a Davidic voice for Ps 2. See Hossfeld and Zenger, "Davidization," 121.

into its original gifting to David."[70] When we consider Pss 1–2 together as an integrated introduction, there is a certain fittingness of this twofold Davidic persona, the "figure of David." The "Blessed Man," referred to in Ps 1, is now given a voice in Ps 2. We discover that the voice is figural, allowing both David and his expected heir to speak simultaneously.

3.1.3. Final Reflections on the Speaking Personae from Pss 1–2

To conclude my reflections on Pss 1–2, I want to further draw out some of the implications of their juxtaposition due to shared lexical terms and characterization. For Sheppard, the clearest signs of editorial purpose in the Psalter are found in texts identified as later redactions, especially those which show either lexical or thematic linking with juxtaposed psalms.[71] For Ps 2, he primarily located this in 2:12b, "Blessed [אשרי] are those who take refuge in him," which creates an *inclusio* with Ps 1:1, "Blessed [אשרי] is the man." Sharing the term אשרי ("blessed/happy"), these verses apply it first to the "man" in Ps 1:1–3, while in 2:12 it is used for those identified as taking refuge in Yʜᴡʜ. This reinforces my earlier observation that there is a distinct, yet close relationship between the "Blessed Man" and the righteous, the "Blessed Congregation." Once we recognize this bracket of blessing, there is an implicit invitation to seek out further correspondences and contrasts between Pss 1–2.[72]

One of most stark contrasts we find in these psalms is between the "Blessed Man" (1:1–3) and those who plot against Yʜᴡʜ and his anointed (2:1–3). In 1:2 and 2:1, the verb הגה is used first to describe the "Blessed Man's" ruminations (הגה) on the *torah* of Yʜᴡʜ, and second with the nations and people ruminating (הגה) vanity. This contrast is further heightened by the use of the terms דרך ("way") and אבד ("perish") in 1:6 and 2:12. In the former, we are told that Yʜᴡʜ watches over the "way" of the righteous, but that the "way" of the wicked will "perish"; in the latter, the reference is made concerning the end of those who refuse to serve Yʜᴡʜ and give fealty to his Son, who will "perish" in their "way." Through these lexical correspondences the more generic statements in Ps 1 are developed and given more explicit specification in Ps 2.[73] For instance, the wicked of Ps 1 can be identified with the nations, people, kings, and rulers of Ps 2:1–3. Similarly, the righteous of Ps 1 can be identified with "those who take refuge" in 2:12. The imperatives given to the rulers and judges in 2:10–12 also imply that there is a certain fluidity between these two groups of people; the wicked

---

[70] Seitz, "Psalm 2 in the Entry Hall of the Psalter," 102.

[71] Sheppard, *Future of the Bible*, 63.

[72] For the history of the study of concatenation, see David C. Mitchell, *The Message of the Psalter: An Eschatological Programme in the Book of Psalms*, JSOTSup 252 (Sheffield: Sheffield Academic, 1997), 45–57. For an explanation of the method, see David M. Howard, Jr., *The Structure of Psalms 93–100*, BJS 5 (Winona Lake: Eisenbrauns, 1997), 99–100; Grant, *King as Exemplar*, 14–19.

[73] Gerald Sheppard, *Wisdom as a Hermeneutical Construct: A Study of the Sapitentializing of the Old Testament*, BZAW 151 (Berlin: de Gruyter, 1980), 140.

are given opportunities to change their course, giving up vain rumination and submitting to the reign of Yhwh. These identifications also help us understand the two different ways of life. From Ps 1, the example of the Blessed Man (1:1–3) is used to provide a glimpse into what it means to take refuge in Yhwh, to walk the path over which Yhwh watches. From Ps 2, likewise, the example of the nations and peoples conspiring and plotting against the rule of Yhwh (2:1–3) is used to give us a glimpse of what it means to walk in the way of the wicked (1:1, 6). The two psalms mutually benefit one another.

A final specifying relationship between Pss 1–2 allows the reader to link together the "Blessed Man" (1:1–3), whose royal characteristics are implicitly suggested through inner-biblical references, and the figure of David, who speaks in Ps 2. What is often missed in their connection, however, is that both figures are placed upon Mount Zion by Yhwh.[74] In Ps 1, this occurs as the psalmist describes the "Blessed Man" as being "transplanted" (שתל) into the presence of Yhwh at the (eschatological) temple complex (1:3); in Ps 2, it reads more literally, "I have installed (נסך) my king upon Zion, my holy mountain" (2:6). Further, the deep-rooted and beneficent life of the "Blessed Man" is described in terms of his success (1:3), which, as we saw, is used in Josh 1 to describe the success of his military campaign in the conquest of the land. In Ps 2, these inner-biblical suggestions become explicit in the divine decree recounted by the king, pertaining to a worldwide sovereignty (2:7–9).[75]

The correspondence between these two personae strengthens our understanding of the "Blessed Man": identified with the figure of David of Ps 2, he is not just any ideal king of Israel, but is intimately connected to David and to David's promised messianic heir. With David, the "Blessed Man" becomes an exemplar of exemplars for the people of Israel; through the character of the "Blessed Man," the figure David becomes a cipher representing the people of Israel, an exemplar of both penitence and piety. Moreover, connected to the Davidic heir, the figure of David takes on a further nuance. As Grant observed, the editors of the Psalter "direct the reader's attention to a future king who goes beyond even the best examples of kingship found in Israel's history—the future king will be the one who actually fulfills the ideal of kingship, Deuteronomy's kingship law."[76] Here, the Davidic figure has been extended from the historical reality of David's life to plot out the eventual life of his heir.

To summarize, we have seen that the figure of David has a critical role to play as a speaking persona in the Psalms. He speaks in Ps 2, and his exemplary role is laid out for the reader in Ps 1. At the same time, Pss 1–2 together introduce us to several other personae who will loom large in what is to come: (1) the righteous (or, "Blessed Congregation"), who bear affiliation with those who trust in Yhwh, give fealty to his anointed king, and receive similar blessings to their exemplar, the "Blessed Man" and anointed king; (2) the wicked, whose way

---

[74] See Gillingham, *Journey of Two Psalms*, 7–9, 15–17; Cole, "Integrated Reading."
[75] See Cole, "Integrated Reading," 75; Gillingham, *Journey of Two Psalms*, 8.
[76] Grant, "The Psalms and the King," 114.

is opposed to the way of the righteous, and who act in open rebellion against YHWH and his king; and (3) YHWH himself, to whom both prayer and praise will be offered, and who will continue to speak to his people through prophetic speech. In answer to our opening question, Pss 1–2 have much to say regarding the voice of the psalmist. Given our review of the history of interpretation in the previous chapter, it is remarkable how interpreters followed the current of this pressure in their conceptual models of the speaking persona, even if they could not quite articulate it as such.

3.2. The Superscriptions and the Speaking Personae

Alongside the introductory role of Pss 1–2, the psalm headings provide herme-neutical clues to the speaking personae. All but the most conservative interpret-ers argue that they are not original to the text of their respective psalms, but are additions made by later editors or scribes.[77] In this respect, they represent traditions in the life of ancient Israel, and are most likely connected to the Le-vites.[78] The difficulty one encounters with the psalm headings is that the mean-ing of technical terms are largely indeterminable, and even simpler elements such as the preposition ל ("of") are far from clear.[79] Even so, beginning with the earliest extant interpreters of the psalm titles the vast majority of the history of interpretation consistently understood them as indicative of a psalm's con-tent.[80] It is only within modern scholarship that the situation has changed. As noted previously, in the nineteenth century, there was a paradigm shift which

---

[77] See the discussion in Allen P. Ross, *A Commentary on the Psalms: Volume 1 (1–41)* (Grand Rapids: Kregel, 2011), 42–47.

[78] See Susan E. Gillingham, "The Levites and the Editorial Composition of the Psalms," in *The Oxford Handbook of the Psalms*, ed. William Brown (Oxford: Oxford Univer-sity Press, 2014), 201–13; Gary N. Knoppers, "Hierodules, Priests or Janitors? The Levites in Chronicles and the History of the Israelite Priesthood," *JBL* 118 (1999): 49–72.

[79] See C. Hassell Bullock, *Encountering the Book of Psalms: A Literary and Theological In-troduction*, 2nd ed (Grand Rapids: Baker Academic, 2018), 7–8. The preposition changes meaning depending on its context, such as: "to/for" (dedicating a psalm to an individual), "by" (indicating authorship), "for" (indicating the performer of the psalm in a cultic set-ting), "of" (an indication of quality), "belonging to" (indicating the collection to which a psalm belongs), etc.

[80] For instance, see Hippolytus, "Homily on the Psalms," in *On the Apostolic Tradition*, trans. Alistair Stewart-Sykes, PPS (Crestwood, NY: St. Vladimir's Seminary Press, 2001), 175–82. This is one of the earliest recorded comments on a superscription. See also 4QpPs^a (4Q171), dated ca. 20–70 CE, a *pesher* on Ps 45. Beginning in 1–10 IV 23, it cites the super-scription in full, and though little remains of its interpretation, we do have the following: "[The interpretation of it: th]ey are the seven divisions of the returnees of Is[rael, who...]" (1–10 IV 23–24). This is very likely a reference to the Korahites. Though we have no idea what is said about them, it at least shows early interpreters using the headings to aid in interpreting the psalm.

discounted the importance of the superscriptions, having deemed them unhistorical. Some scholars have written them off, then, as one of the latest layers of redaction, either vestiges of ancient liturgical practice (e.g., musical elements)[81] or, at best, one of the earliest examples of ancient Israelite interpretation (e.g., the biographical titles).[82] In their opinion, the psalm titles are not to be trusted in any kind of "historical" sense and should not be consulted as part of proper psalm interpretation.[83] Others, however, following the lead of Childs, find hermeneutical value in at least those titles containing allusions to episodes in the life of David.[84]

In this section, I will discuss the significance of the psalm titles for understanding Pss 3–14. There are ten different elements in them, which can be divided into five categories:[85] (1) an association with a biblical figure (לדוד, "of David");[86] (2) two biographical descriptions which refer to episodes within David's life;[87] (3) a reference to the leader of the performance of the psalm (למנצח);[88] (4) musical directions;[89] and (5) two different designations of either a style of music or category of song (שגיון; מזמור).[90] In my discussion of these elements, my main concern is to trace what hermeneutical value they may have retained or even gained in the final form of the text. The basic principle I am working from was well-stated by Childs:

---

[81] See Sigmund Mowinckel, *Psalm Studies*, trans. Mark E. Biddle, SBLHBS 3 (Atlanta: SBL, 2014), 2:599–650; Mowinckel, *The Psalms in Israel's Worship*, trans. D. R. Ap-Thomas (Grand Rapids: Eerdmans, 2004), 2: 79–103, 207–17.

[82] See F. F. Bruce, "The Earliest Old Testament Interpretation," in *The Witness of Tradition: Papers Read at the Joint British-Dutch Old Testament Conference held at Wouschoten, 1970*, ed. A. S. Van Der Woude, OTS 17 (Leiden: Brill, 1972), 52; Tremper Longman, III, *How to Read the Psalms* (Downers Grove: IVP Academic, 1988), 41.

[83] See the discussion of Kraus, *Psalms 1–59*, 31–33, 65–68.

[84] Brevard S. Childs, "Psalm Titles and Midrashic Exegesis," *JSS* 16 (1971): 138–51. See also James L. Mays, "The David of the Psalms," *Int* 40 (1986): 143–55; Gerald T. Sheppard, "Theology and the Book of Psalms," *Int* 46 (1992): 143–55; Rolf Rendtorff, "Psalms of David, David in the Psalms," in *The Book of Psalms: Composition and Reception*, ed. Peter W. Flint and Patrick D. Miller, SVT 99 (Leiden: Brill, 2005), 53–64; Brian T. German, "Contexts for Hearing: Reevaluating the Superscription of Psalm 127," *JSOT* 37 (2012): 185–99.

[85] In the larger book, there is a sixth category: those elements indicating a cultic occasion or the purpose of use (cf. Pss 30, 38, 60, 70, 92, 100, 102, 120–134).

[86] In total, David will be associated with seventy-three psalms in the superscriptions. There are six other associations besides David: Asaph (twelve: Pss 50, 73–83), the Sons of Korah (eleven: Pss 42, 44–49, 84, 85, 87, 88), Jeduthun (Pss 39, 62, 77), Solomon (Pss 72, 127), Heman the Ezrahite (Ps 88), Ethan the Ezrahite (Ps 89), and Moses (Ps 90).

[87] There are thirteen psalms in the MT Psalter which include this biographical element: Pss 3, 7, 18, 34, 51, 52, 54, 56, 57, 59, 60, 63, and 142. All of them are also preceded by an association with David (לדוד).

[88] In the larger book, למנצח is found at the beginning of fifty-five psalms.

[89] There are fifteen (perhaps sixteen) of these instructions in the book.

[90] There are six other designations often considered literary types: שיר, משכיל, מכתם, תהלה, תפלה.

I would argue that the need of taking seriously the canonical form of the Psalter would greatly aid in making use of the psalms in the life of the Christian Church. Such a move would not disregard the historical dimensions of the Psalter, but would attempt to profit from the shaping which the final redactors gave the older material in order to transform traditional poetry into Sacred Scripture for the later generations of the faithful.[91]

The goal is not for a purely synchronic reading of the Psalter, but in tracing out how various elements present in the pre-scriptural use of the psalms were transformed or recast in its function as scripture for future generations. For instance, given my discussion of the figure of David in Pss 1–2, does the association with David (לדוד) in Pss 3–14 have any effect on their interpretation? Similarly, what role does "for the leader" (למנצח) or any of the so-called musical terms play, or one of the ancient type descriptions (e.g., מזמור or שגיון)?

3.2.1. Biblical Associations and Biographical Headings

The first element of the superscriptions that I will discuss is the association with a biblical figure, "of David" (לדוד). This is the only element found in every psalm, supposing Pss 9–10 hold together (cf. LXX). Scholars have debated at great length the meaning of the preposition *lamed* (ל), as well as the referent "David" (דוד). Throughout the premodern period, the association with David within the book of Psalms was understood on two levels. First, as designating the author of a psalm: as a prophet of Yhwh, David composed psalms under the inspiration of the Holy Spirit. His words are authoritative, and the Psalms could be used as foundation stones for expressions of spiritual devotion and liturgical practice.[92] Second, David was thought to have composed those psalms either with another speaker in mind (prosopopoeia), or, by writing about himself and his own experiences, creating a correspondence between himself and future persons (typology). As we saw in the previous chapter, the identification of "David" in this second level could be conceptualized in several different ways. This all changed in the modern period. Once scholars had discounted the psalm superscriptions' association with David, all ties with David were broken. Nevertheless, similar patterns of finding an "historical context" for a psalm continued. Now, however, instead of finding a context within the life of David as recounted in Samuel or the life of Christ in the Gospels, interpreters began to look for other biblical and

---

[91] Brevard S. Childs, "Reflections on the Modern Study of the Psalms," in *Magnalia Dei: The Mighty Acts of God: Essays on the Bible and Archaeology in Memory of G. Ernest Wright*, ed. Frank Moore Cross, Werner E. Lemke, and Patrick D. Miller, Jr. (Garden City, NY: Doubleday, 1976), 385.

[92] See Georg P. Braulik, "Psalter and Messiah: Towards a Christological Understanding of the Psalms in the Old Testament and the Church Fathers," in *Psalms and Liturgy*, ed. Dirk J. Human and Cas J. A. Vos (London: T&T Clark, 2004), 15–40.

early Jewish figures who would better fit the historical reconstruction.[93] Without superscriptions, debate surrounding the speaker in a psalm focused on whether to understand the speaking personae as an "I" or a "we," or some combination thereof.

3.2.1.1. The meaning of "David" in לדוד.   In the modern period, one of the first scholars to make a lasting contribution to our understanding of this superscription element was Sigmund Mowinckel, who sought to find meaning in its connection to the cultic life of ancient Israel. For him, the Davidic association was inextricably tied to how we conceptualize the connection between the individual ("I") and the community ("we").[94] The basic reality for an Israelite was that a person was not simply an individual within a larger community ("Israel"), but that one's existence was bound up as part of the larger group. In other words, the entity "Israel" was not understood as "a sum of individuals who had joined together, or who enjoyed an existence of their own apart from the whole to which they belonged; it was the real entity which manifested itself in each separate member."[95] Connected to this idea, he argued that certain individuals could represent the whole when they spoke:

> The priest or the king contains the whole and all its members when he appears as the leader of the cult. He really represents—in the old meaning of the word—the whole people. When he says 'I' it is the whole Israel, who speaks through him and who appears in his person 'in the presence of Yahweh.'[96]

The great moment when these personalities came together was in the annual enthronement festival, where the prayers of the cultic leader—the king—were intimately connected to the prayers of the people. The king becomes a kind of "corporate personality," with the whole cultic community together understood as a "great ego."[97]

In terms of the Davidic association, Mowinckel's major contribution came in identifying the Davidic king as this representative personality within the Jerusalem temple cult.[98] He wrote: "The psalms were composed for the use of, and were in due time used by 'David'—that is to say, in most cases, by a king of the house of David."[99] The Davidic element in a psalm heading was not originally meant to ascribe authorship of a psalm to David, but referred to the cultic use

---

[93] See Mowinckel, *Psalms in Israel's Worship*, 1:12.

[94] Mowinckel, *Psalms in Israel's Worship*, 1:42–80.

[95] Mowinckel, *Psalms in Israel's Worship*, 1:42. That is, "the whole is a greater 'I'" (43).

[96] Mowinckel, *Psalms in Israel's Worship*, 1:44, 61.

[97] Mowinckel, *Psalms in Israel's Worship*, 1:44; see also Mowinckel, *Psalmenstudien*, 1:164–65. He admitted his reliance on Robinson for the use of this term. See H. Wheeler Robinson, *Corporate Personality in Ancient Israel*, rev. ed. (Philadelphia: Fortress, 1980).

[98] Mowinckel, *Psalms in Israel's Worship*, 1:46–50.

[99] Mowinckel, *Psalms in Israel's Worship*, 1:77; see also *Psalm Studies*, 2:848–50.

of the psalm within the temple.[100] Once the connection was made with the traditional founder of the cult, the existence of לדוד on a psalm recommended its ongoing use and guaranteed its suitability.[101]

As Marko Marttila noted in his recent study of collective reinterpretation in the Psalter, Mowinckel's concepts of "corporate personality" and the "great ego" in ancient Israel have since been challenged on anthropological grounds.[102] Even so, his criticisms lie not in the concept of a corporate identity, but in earlier distinctions between "primitive" and "developed" practices and thinking, and in an overly ambitious reconstruction of the cult.[103] Moreover, he did not think that Mowinckel's insights were wrongheaded, but that they address issues concerned with the pre-scriptural use of the Psalms and not with the book in its canonical form (cf. earlier discussion of Sheppard). A more solid foundation for the "collective emphases" in the Psalms can be traced to the work of the redactors, whose operating principle was to adapt a collective idea which may have originally functioned as Mowinckel hypothesized.[104]

Within the redaction of the Psalter, he argued that van Oorschot's model of "role poetry" (*Rollendichtung*) was particularly helpful in establishing collective identities.[105] *Rollendichtung* claims that "a single person—for instance in his prayers—in fact represented the whole community."[106] Here, the post-exilic context of the redaction of the Psalter is significant, as the prayers and psalms which can be dated to this period show that the Second Temple community placed a strong significance on exemplary figures with whom they could identify and imitate (e.g., Ezra 9:6–15; Dan 9:4–19; Neh 9:6–37; Judith 9:2–14).[107] For the Psalter, the Davidic superscriptions enable David to become this kind of ideal, exemplary figure.[108] Marttila took these observations as indicative of collective reinterpretation of the Psalms *in opposition to a messianic reading*, such that David is a historical and sapiential collective figure.[109] This need not be the case. The pros-

[100] Mowinckel, *Psalms in Israel's Worship*, 2:98–101.

[101] See Jean-Marie Auwers, "Le David des psaumes et les psaumes de David," in *Figures of David: A Travers la Bible*, ed. Louis Desrousseaux and Jacques Vermeylen (Paris: Cerf, 1999), 187. He wrote, "As soon as the Davidic intitulation was interpreted as an attribution of psalms to the king-musician, David emerges as the presumed author of the collection: from that moment, the psalms were intended to be given the voice of David, possibly even speaking for his own person [*pour parler de sa proper personne*]" (translation my own).

[102] See Marko Marttila, *Collective Reinterpretation in the Psalms: A Study of the Redaction History of the Psalter*, FAT 2/13 (Tübingen: Mohr Siebeck, 2006), 10–25.

[103] Marttila, *Collective Reinterpretation in the Psalms*, 17.

[104] Marttila, *Collective Reinterpretation in the Psalms*, 21–22.

[105] Jürgen van Oorschot, "Nachkultische Psalmen und spätbiblische Rollendichtung," *ZAW* 106 (1994), 69–86 [esp. 84–86].

[106] Marttila, *Collective Reinterpretation in the Psalms*, 18.

[107] Marttila, *Collective Reinterpretation in the Psalms*, 19, 23.

[108] Oorschot, "Rollendichtung," 84–85.

[109] Marttila, *Collective Reinterpretation in the Psalms*, 78–81.

opological model of Augustine, for example, is a messianic, collective understanding of the speaking persona, in which Christ and the church are inextricably bound together as Head and Body.[110]

The instincts of these interpretive models, in my opinion, stem from the
shape of the Psalter itself. In my above treatment of Pss 1–2, I noted that the
persona of the idealistic "Blessed Man" from Ps 1 has been intimately connected
to the persona of the "figure of David" from Ps 2. At the same time, the way of
life and destiny of the "Blessed Man" (1:1–3) have been united to the way and
destiny of the righteous (1:5–6), "those who trust in him" (2:12b). The Psalter
itself provides the reader with the inner workings of an identification model
that intertwines the person of the king and the community of Israel. Moreover,
this is not limited to the historical figure of David; in an extended sense, we find
in the figure of David a type for his promised messianic heir and for the community which would take refuge in him. In the history of interpretation, both Aquinas and Calvin picked up on this model, in which David and the righteous are
bound figurally to the Messiah and his body, the church. My argument is that,
as part of the entryway into the Psalter, the ground-workings of this figural interpretive model in Pss 1–2 impart a transformative semantic force onto the association with David in the superscriptions of Pss 3–14. I will begin by considering this force on the biographical superscriptions—all of which are associated
with David—followed by a brief discussion of when the Davidic association
stands on its own.

3.2.1.2. David and the biographical superscriptions. The inclusion of the biographical elements within the editorial structure of the Psalter brings an added dimension to the portrait of the Davidic figure by drawing from biblical narratives
connected to the life of David from 1–2 Samuel. As I noted in the first chapter,
recent literary research of titles and intertextuality forces us to (re)consider
what significance the biographical links have for understanding a psalm. This is
especially important as these links are part of an editorial shaping process
which included exegetical activity with other parts of Scripture. Against typical
modern sensibilities, then, I argue that their value is not principally historical,
but hermeneutical. Within contemporary psalm research, scholars have attempted to trace out the implications of a hermeneutical understanding of the
biographical superscriptions.[111]

---

[110] In early Judaism, the principle of the Rabbis also envisions such a link; see *Midrash
Tehillim* on Ps 18; *Pesaḥim* 117a. See also James L. Mays, "A Question of Identity: The Threefold Hermeneutic of Psalmody," *AsTJ* 46 (1991): 87–94.

[111] See Childs, "Psalm Titles," 143–44; Rendtorff, "The Psalms of David," 54–55. For an
approach close to my own, see Stefan M. Attard, *The Implications of Davidic Repentance: A
Synchronic Analysis of Book 2 of the Psalter (Psalms 42–72)*, AB 212 (Rome: Gregorian & Biblical,
2016).

Vivian Johnson, for instance, argued the biographical headings give further explanation or clarification into what is happening in the narratives of 1–2 Samuel. She concluded her discussion of Ps 3 by saying: "A close reading of the narrative with Ps 3 brings out a heightened sense of danger for David at the time of Absalom's rebellion and suggests that he escapes his predicament with divine succor."[112] In this approach, the biographical title fills a *lacuna* of history; its hermeneutical value lies in bringing a fuller picture to the Davidic narratives. Alternatively, others have argued that the biographical titles help to give the reader a privileged glimpse into the mind of David. Childs was one of the first to hold this view in the modern period. He wrote: "By placing a psalm within the setting of a particular historical incident in the life of David, the reader suddenly was given access to previously unknown information. David's inner life was now unlocked to the reader, who was allowed to hear his intimate thoughts and reflections."[113] There is a certain benefit to such readings of the titles, as it helps the reader spiritually connect to the person of David either illustratively or, more substantially, as an exemplary figure worthy of imitation.[114]

Even though the two above approaches understand the purpose of the biographical referent differently, they both share a methodological approach which, given the narrative referent in the heading, uproots the psalm from its context within the book of Psalms to better serve the reader transplanted within the narrative context of 1–2 Samuel. A more consistent methodological application of intertextuality would reverse this process. Instead of placing a psalm in a different literary context, the biographical links recall the narratives of Samuel so that they give shape to the developing use of the figure of David within the book of Psalms. In other words, the psalm is not used to help give depth to the portrait of David within a narrative, but the narrative's portrait of David is used as relief to better project the persona of the figure of David within the larger concerns of the canonical book of Psalms.[115]

The inversion of the intertextuality of the biographical superscriptions is an important distinction I want to emphasize between my own approach and that represented by Childs and others. I will use James Nogalski as an interlocutor to help elucidate these differences.[116] In his analysis of the biographical superscriptions, he observed (much like Childs had earlier) that they were not composed at the same time as the psalms, but were attached to existing psalms

---

[112] Vivian L. Johnson, *David in Distress: His Portrait in the Historical Psalms*, LHBOTS 505 (London: T&T Clark, 2009), 16.

[113] Childs, "Psalm Titles," 150. Similarly, Mays, "The David of the Psalms," 152.

[114] For example, see Tremper Longman III, *Psalms*, TOTC (Downers Grove: InterVarsity, 2014), 65; Brueggemann and Bellinger, *Psalms*, 38.

[115] I am drawing on the taxonomy of engraving for this description. In relief carving, figures are carved in a panel of wood, adding a depth dimension based on how far they project from the background.

[116] James D. Nogalski, "Reading David in the Psalter: A Study in Liturgical Hermeneutics," *HBT* 23 (2001): 168–91.

so that they might be applied to the narratives of David.[117] The goal of these additions was not to develop the image of David across the Psalter, but to "connect specific narrative episodes with particular psalms."[118] In his view, given the seemingly random scattering of the biographical notices, as well as their lack of chronology, they appear to have been added "for a purpose other than the literary shaping of the Psalter."[119] The combination of the psalm with the story allows the psalm to shape the reader's perception of David, as if the David of the Psalms is the same persona as David of the narrative. This happens in two ways. First, Nogalski observed that the portrait of David in a psalm will often accentuate David's piety in ways that the reader is expected to emulate, clarifying the ambiguity of David in the narrative. Second, he noted that through the Psalms' influence, "Yʜᴡʜ takes on a more active role as protector, confidant, and avenger than the picture of Yʜᴡʜ that unfolds in the narrative alone."[120] The Psalms, then, complement the portraits of David and Yʜᴡʜ found within the biblical narratives, and more than the narratives alone, "highlight the need for utter dependence of Yʜᴡʜ in times of distress."[121] He continued, "They highlight the need for humility before God. They confidently affirm God's presence in times of persecution and trial."[122]

This analysis of the biographical superscriptions fits well within the trajectory laid out by Childs, and adds more force to his proposal. Yet, Nogalski's observations are more potent when we reverse the direction of intertextual references; that is, when the portrait of David within the Samuel narratives helps to complement the reader's perception of David within the context of the Psalter. For example, the first biographical superscription comes in the first psalm outside of the introduction, Ps 3. This superscription refers to the rebellion of Absalom in 2 Sam 15–18. Independent from its literary setting, the combination of the superscription and the psalm suggests that we hear the psalm as having some connection with the narrative, perhaps even in the way suggested by Nogalski. Yet, Ps 3 does not exist independently, nor is its literary context the book of Samuel; rather, it stands as the third psalm, the first outside of the integrated introduction. So while the Davidic reference in the superscription is in fact recalling the portrait of David from 2 Sam 15–18, that "David" is being mapped onto the already developing portrait of the figure of David in Pss 1–2. That is, by the time we arrive at the superscription of Ps 3, we already have certain expectations of the Davidic persona, expectations that do not suddenly disappear with a biographical superscription. The convergence of these two portraits is crucial to the development of the figure of David in the Psalms.

---

[117] Nogalski, "Reading David in the Psalter," 189.
[118] Nogalski, "Reading David in the Psalter," 190.
[119] Nogalski, "Reading David in the Psalter," 190.
[120] Nogalski, "Reading David in the Psalter," 190.
[121] Nogalski, "Reading David in the Psalter," 191.
[122] Nogalski, "Reading David in the Psalter," 191.

In the independent context of Ps 3, the combination of biographical super-scription and psalm allows us to hear the Davidic voice as he was fleeing from Absalom. But when set in juxtaposition with Pss 1–2, the characters of David and Absalom, as well as those who surround them, are recast so that they speak be-yond 2 Sam 15–18. Absalom is re-configured as a type for those nations and peo-ple who rebel against Yʜwʜ and his anointed (Ps 2:1–3). Likewise, the biograph-ical voice of David takes on additional typical and typological extensions in re-lationship to Pss 1–2. Nogalski's observations about the piety of David and the more active role of Yʜwʜ continue to have force, but instead of the Psalms giving these emphases to the Davidic narratives, in my approach the narratives provide relief within which the psalmic figure of David is projected. For Ps 3, one of the functions of the superscription is to recast the rebellion of Absalom as a figural lens through which to hear the dynamics between Pss 1, 2, and 3. When Ps 3 is uprooted from this context, the typological dimension is obscured (or even obliterated), rendering its transplanted use in 2 Sam 15–18 something quite dif-ferent.

3.2.1.3. "David" without biography. Moving beyond the thirteen biographical su-perscriptions, another sixty psalms include an association with David (לדוד). In the premodern period, this heading was understood as an authorial ascription, a view still held by many today (even if deemed historically inaccurate). Beyond Mowinckel's cultic representational view, modern interpreters have typically argued that this bare heading may have been added to psalms which were part of a previous, smaller Davidic Psalter, and thus, are an ancient rubric identifying the psalm as part of a collection. When these collections were combined, the titles remained as artefacts.[123]

In my view, the function of לדוד is defined by its first occurrence in the Psal-ter, as part of the biographical heading of Ps 3. Namely (and, admittedly, some-what vaguely), that a psalm entitled with לדוד associates it hermeneutically with the figure of David.[124] With the biographical superscription, לדוד more naturally indicates the psalm is spoken in the voice of the figure of David, but without the biographical notices we need to be more flexible. This is due, in part, to the am-biguity of the preposition ל. In some cases, it indicates that the voice of the fig-ure of David speaks ("by David"), while in others, for instance, that a psalm is

---

[123] See Brueggemann and Bellinger, *Psalms*, 2–3.

[124] While not settling the debate, the wider canon of Scripture corroborates an asso-ciation of David with music (1 Sam 16:18–23; 19:9; 1 Chr 23:5; 2 Chr 7:6; 29:26–27; Amos 6:5), psalmody (2 Sam 1:17–27; 3:33–34; 22:1–51; 23:1–7; 1 Chr 16:7–36; 2 Chr 29:30), and the establishment of the temple cult service (1 Chr 15:16–24; 16:4–7, 31–42; 25:1–5; Ezra 3:10–11; Neh 12:24, 46). One could also appeal to other early witnesses to this view of David (e.g., Sirach 47:8–10; 11Q5). See also the brief discussion of David Willgren, *The For-mation of the 'Book' of Psalms: Reconsidering the Transmission and Canonization of Psalmody in Light of Material Culture and the Poetics of Anthologies*, FAT 2/88 (Tübingen: Mohr Siebeck), 177.

"for David," in the sense of being offered up on behalf of the king (e.g., Ps 20). What is crucial is the hermeneutical association David; flexibility is important as it leaves room for discerning the proper voicing of a psalm within a set of choices provided by the Psalter itself. In the following chapters, I will argue that within Pss 3–14 the biographical superscriptions (Pss 3, 7) orient the reader towards a construction of the Davidic figure that will continue in subsequent לדוד psalms (Pss 4–6, 8–14, respectively).

3.2.2. *Cultic Terms and Musical Directions*

Alongside an association with a biblical figure, there are different cultic elements and musical directions given within the psalm headings. The most common of these is the rubric לַמְנַצֵּחַ, which has been pointed as a ל preposition, a definite article, prefixed to a *piel* participle of the root נצח. Modern interpreters have reached a strong consensus that it refers to a leader within the cult, and typically translate the phrase, "for the leader/precentor/chief musician." Additional rubrics often accompany it and are usually understood as musical directions. Notably, there is not a single occasion in the Psalms when musical direction is given without a preceding למנצח, which suggests that the two elements are closely related.[125] Within Pss 3–14, למנצח is found in Pss 4–6 and Pss 8–14, and is often followed by musical direction, such as: בנגינות, "upon stringed instruments" (Pss 4, 6); אל־הנחילות, "for the flutes" (Ps 5); על־השמינית, "upon the *Sheminith*" (Pss 6, 12); על־הגתית, "upon the *Gittith*" (Ps 8); עלמות לבן, "according to 'Death of the Son'" (Ps 9/10).[126]

In a canonical approach, these rubrics have often been left out of the discussion as they prove to be difficult: what ongoing function do they have? Willgren has recently argued that given the distribution of these terms in Books 1–3 (Pss 3–89), and their virtual absence in Books 4–5 (Pss 90–150), the pattern reflects "some change in how these psalms were perceived and used, rather than being the result of mere chance."[127] While he concluded that the present function of the musical directions is to "provide a general notion of antiquity and status," the vast majority of the history of interpretation viewed them as assisting in the interpretation of a given psalm. Ancient versions often provide alternative translations than today's consensus, which in turn directed interpreters to very different conclusions about their present function within the text. In what follows, I will briefly present some of the difficulties with the term למנצח and undertake my own hypothesizing about its ongoing function within the final form of the text.

---

[125] See John F. A. Sawyer, "An Analysis of the Context and Meaning of the Psalm-Headings," *TGUOS* 22 (1970): 36.

[126] Within the psalms proper we also find two rubrics that are also commonly understood as giving musical direction: סלה (Pss 3:3, 5, 9; 4:3, 5; 7:6; 9:17, 21) and הגיון (Ps 9:17).

[127] Willgren, *Formation*, 183.

The root נצח has a wide range of meaning and uses in the Old Testament. Older lexicons noted that the concepts of "brilliance" and "endurance" comprise the root meaning, and can yield a variety of verbal and nominal nuances, such as: preeminence, surpassing, glory, victory, leadership, perpetuity, forever, etc.[128] All lexicons agree that primary evidence for the meaning of למנצח in the psalm titles comes from 1–2 Chronicles and Ezra, where the root נצח is used in connection with supervising or overseeing work in the house of YHWH (1 Chr 23:4; 2 Chr 2:1, 17; Ezra 3:8, 9), as well as the Levites who were put in charge over musical performance in the tabernacle/temple (1 Chr 15:21; 2 Chr 34:12–13). In each of these cases, the *piel* stem is used with the meaning, "to lead, preside, oversee, superintend."[129] As a participle, the term would refer to the agent of the verbal action, "one who oversees, superintendents, directs, leads." With this background, the rubric found in the psalm titles would refer to the person who supervised or oversaw the performance of the psalm within the cult of ancient Israel, "for the leader" or "for the director of music."[130] The consensus of psalm scholarship since the beginning of the modern period has followed this interpretation of the rubric, but this was not always the case. In fact, none of the ancient versions of the psalm's titles, nor their Jewish and Christian interpreters, mention this interpretation.[131] They are often roughly criticized for this, but it must be remembered that they worked with an unvocalized text. Their translations are not unrelated to the root meaning and, in many cases, we find textual warrant for the interpretive paths they take.[132]

For instance, the Aramaic Targum consistently translated the term as referring to the praise or glorification of YHWH, לשבחא ("to/for praise, celebration" or "in glorification").[133] The Old Greek (LXX) consistently translated the

---

[128] *TWOT*, s.v. "נָצַח"; *BDB* s.v. "נָצַח".

[129] *TWOT*, s.v. "נָצַח".

[130] See *HALOT*, s.vv. "נצח I," "נצח II," "נֶצַח I," "נֶצַח II"; *DCH* 5, s.vv. "נצח I," "נצח II," "נצח III," "נצח IV," "נֶצַח I," "נֶצַח II," "נֶצַח III," "נֶצַח IV". See also T. K. Cheyne, *The Book of Psalms: Translated from a revised text with Notes and Introduction* (New York: Thomas Whittaker, 1904), xxxviii; J. J. Glueck, "Some Remarks on the Introductory Notes of the Psalms," in *Studies on the Psalms: Papers Read at the 6th Meeting Held at the Potchefstroom University for C.H.E., 29–31 January 1963* (Potchefstroom: Pro Rege, 1963), 31–32; W. O. E. Oesterley, *The Psalms* (London: SPCK, 1962), 10–11; Longman, *Psalms*, 30.

[131] See W. O. E. Oesterley, *A Fresh Approach to the Psalms* (London: Ivor Nicholson & Watson, 1937), 76; Cheyne, *Book of Psalms*, xxxix. As the translations of the relevant passages in Chronicles and Ezra show, the LXX and Targum translators were well-aware of the meaning "to oversee, superintend, to be a taskmaster," which makes their translations of the psalm titles (and Hab 3:19) even more intriguing. See the LXX for 1 Chr 23:4; 2 Chr 2:2, 18; 34:12–13; and Ezra 3:8–9.

[132] We would do well to learn a lesson in historical humility. See Sawyer, "Analysis of the Context and Meaning of the Psalm Headings," 26, 37.

[133] The same translation is given for Hab 3:19. Conceptually, it could be related to the root meaning, "brilliance." As such, it would be connected to מזמור, which is consistently translated with the same Aramaic root for praise, תושבחתא, "praise."

term εἰς τὸ τέλος, "unto the end" or "forever." This tradition is followed by the Old Latin/Roman text and Jerome's Gallican Psalter, which reads *in finem* ("towards an end"). As Kirkpatrick noted, both renderings understand למנצח not as a *piel* participle (per the MT, לַמְנַצֵּחַ) but as a substantive (לְמִנְצָּח), with the sense it gives the term throughout the Psalter (לָנֶצַח, "forever").[134] Supporting this reading, Cheyne argued that the word לנצח in 1 Chr 15:21 should not be pointed as a *piel* infinitive construct (per the MT, לְנַצֵּחַ), but adverbially as לָנֶצַח, "forever." For him, the parallel text in 1 Chr 16:6, which uses תמיד, suggests a meaning related to the underlying sense of "endurance."[135] A third alternative is offered by each of the three major recensions of the LXX, as well as Jerome's Hebrew translation. They translated the phrase with the root meaning of "victory" (cf. Hab 3:19): Aquila reads τῷ νικοποιῷ ("for the victor"); Symmachus, ἐπινίκοις ("a song of victory"); Theodotion, εἰς τὸ νῖκος ("for the victory"); and Jerome, *victori* ("to the victor" or "towards victory"). The root נצח is not used with this meaning elsewhere in the Old Testament, but is at Qumran (cf. 1QM 4.13; 12.5; 4QHod^a 7.1.14; 11QT 58.11; 4QBark^c 1.1.1). It also carries this meaning in Late Hebrew, Aramaic, Jewish Aramaic, Christian Palestinian Aramaic, Samarian, and Syriac.[136]

Given these alternative translations, early interpreters had a much different understanding of their function at the head of a psalm. Christian interpreters, working with the sense of "end" and/or "victory," often interpreted a psalm as a prophecy which pertained to the end, foretelling "events [that] will take place a long time afterwards."[137] This could apply both to Christ, the "glorious perfection of all good things," or even the church, "among whom the end of the world is come."[138] It was also understood morally as pointing to the end or goal of the Christian life, construed as the perfection of the soul or the blessed or virtuous end of human life.[139] Jewish interpreters worked on similar grounds,

---

[134] A. F. Kirkpatrick, *The Book of Psalms* (Cambridge: Cambridge University Press, 1906), xxi.

[135] Cheyne, *Book of Psalms*, xxxix. Unfortunately, the LXX does not translate 1 Chr 15:21 this way, but with ἐν κινύραις αμασενιθ τοῦ ἐνισχῦσαι, "to support them with *cinyras amasenith*." Note that they transliterate the musical directions in this verse. This could indicate that they were ignorant of their meaning. See also Otto Eissfeldt, *The Old Testament: An Introduction*, trans. Peter R. Ackroyd (New York: Harper & Row, 1965), 453.

[136] See David J. A. Clines, ed., *Dictionary of Classical Hebrew*, 8 vols (Sheffield: Sheffield Phoenix, 1993–2016), 5:738–40.

[137] Theodoret of Cyrus, *Commentary on the Psalms: Psalms 1-72*, trans. Robert C. Hill, FOC 101 (Washington, DC: The Catholic University of America Press, 2000), 62. See also Basil the Great, *Exegetic Homilies*, trans. Sr. Agnes Clare Way, FOC 46 (Washington, DC: Catholic University of America Press, 1963), 297.

[138] Cassiodorus, *Explanation of the Psalms*, trans. by P. G. Walsh, ACW 51 (New York: Paulist, 1990), 73. See also Martin Luther, *Complete Commentary on the First Twenty-Two Psalms*, trans. Henry Cole (London: Simplin & Marshall, 1826), 1:129–31.

[139] See Basil, *Exegetic Homilies*, 297; Gregory of Nyssa, *Treatise on the Inscriptions of the Psalms*, trans. Ronald E. Heine (Oxford: Clarendon, 2001).

most often indicating a meaning tied to the concept of "glory" or "victory." In the Midrash, for instance, we find two explanations for the term.[140] First, it could refer "to him most capable of glorifying Him whose glory endures for ever and ever." Second, the text is repointed as a *pual* participle (לִמְנֻצָּח) and refers "to Him who lets Himself be won over by His creatures." This second interpretation is followed by *Pesaḥim* 119a: "Rav Kahana said, citing Rabbi Yishmael, son of Rabbi Yosei: What is the meaning of that which is written: '*Lamenatzeaḥ* a psalm of David' (e.g., Psalms 13:1)? It means: Sing to the One who rejoices when conquered [*shenotzḥin oto*]."[141]

Saadiah Gaon, writing in the tenth century, is the first commentator (that I could find) who suggested that למנצח referred to those "who spurred on the work" at the temple (cf. 1 Chr 23:4; Ezr 3:8).[142] In his opinion the book of Psalms functioned as "one of the means by which the Temple was erected, for the Levites used it to spur on the building until its completion." In other words, the title "for the leader" refers the book of Psalms to the overseers who would address the workers with it. Rashi, writing at the end of the eleventh century, follows suit, but simplified it towards what would become the modern consensus: "David composed this psalm so that the Levites who lead the instrumental music for the song upon the stage would recite it."[143]

In summarizing these various positions, one can sense a marked difference in how the present function of the title was construed based on how the phrase למנצח was translated. Earlier interpreters, who vocalized the text differently than the MT, often interpreted the phrase as having a hermeneutical function for the psalm on which it was placed. Beginning with medieval Jewish interpreters, *now working with a vocalized MT*, the tide had shifted towards a meaning associated with the leaders of the cult in Chronicles and Ezra. From here, into the modern period, such an association has lost the hermeneutical force which was heard in Saadiah Gaon. The history of interpretation is important, then, as it urges us to consider more than how a prepositional phrase was translated. The premodern witness to alternative vocalizations of למנצח and their intuition to hear the superscriptions hermeneutically opens up the psalm titles for fruitful investigation.

Indeed, while I am convinced by the modern consensus around the MT vocalization, its connection to the Levitical overseers in 1–2 Chronicles and Ezra,

---

[140] William G. Braude, *The Midrash on Psalms* (New Haven: Yale University Press, 1959), 1:70, 2:411.

[141] "Pesachim 119a," Sefaria, https://www.sefaria.org/Pesachim.119a.

[142] Moshe Sokolow, "Saadiah Gaon's Prolegomenon to Psalms," *PAAJR* 51 (1984), 152–53.

[143] Mayer I. Gruber, *Rashi's Commentary on Psalms* (Leiden: Brill, 2004), 185. See also Abraham Ibn Ezra, *Commentary on the First Book of Psalms: Chapters 1–41*, trans. H. Norman Strickman (Boston: Academic Studies, 2009), 40; David Kimhi, *The Longer Commentary of R. David Kimhi on the First Book of Psalms (I–X, XV–XVII, XIX, XXII, XXIV)*, trans. R. G. Finch (London: SPCK, 1919), 26.

and a translation such as "for the one who leads (in music)," we are still left to contemplate the question: does this element, and the musical notations which follow it, have any present function in the text other than recommending a psalm's antiquity or association with the cult? The modern consensus would likely answer negatively, but early Jewish and Christian interpreters did not associate the titles in any respect with the cultic life of ancient Israel. This is very perplexing. As is seen in the prefaces of many early commentators, they were not ignorant of ancient Israel's cultic life, often ascribing Davidic authorship in connection with it. Rather than taking the headings in that direction, however, they sought hermeneutical value in them connected to etymology. Working from this general hermeneutical hypothesis, I want to promote two options for reading the rubric "for the one who leads" (למנצח) as having an ongoing, present function in the meaning of the Psalms. Each of these views agrees with the modern consensus in associating the title with those who oversaw work at the temple, but also moves beyond the idea that they are artefacts of ancient cultic practice.

The first option builds off the initial suggestions made by Saadiah Gaon, which paved the way for the modern consensus. As noted above, he argued that למנצח referred to the leaders of the people, who would have used the singing of psalms to encourage and "spur on the work" at the temple (cf. 1 Chr 23:4; Ezra 3:8–9). Given this background, later interpreters usually understood the psalm heading to refer to the one who oversaw music in the temple more generally. More narrowly, Johannes Reuchlin argued that למנצח should be understood as an "invitation" (*invitatorium*), "that is, for inviting, encouraging, urging concerning work" (*id est ad invitandu, hortandu, urgendu super opere*).[144] His principal justification is from Ezra 3:8, in which the Levites spurred on or encouraged the workers in their work, "They appointed the Levites... לְנַצֵּחַ the work of the house of YHWH." The participle refers to "the metrical voice [*proceleusmaticus*] of those encouraging and rousing the people to perform certain exercises, which causes one to do work and perform a pre-arranged duty." In his example from Ps 6, the phrase למנצח would be an invitation to "swift penitence," that readers might be roused from sleep and come quickly to their senses again. The general meaning ("invitation") is thus qualified by the psalm which it introduces.

Building on Reuchlin, but also incorporating earlier views, Martin Luther argued that psalms preceded by the title למנצח are analogous to the heroic songs and triumphal hymns of the Greeks (ἐπινίκιον; cf. 1 Chr 15:21).[145] He wrote: "For in all these the listless mind is sharpened and kindled, so that it may be alert and vigorous as it proceeds to the task." Hence, a psalm headed by למנצח would "awaken and encourage the spirit of man" in exhortation "to the work of the

---

[144] Johannes Reuchlin, *In septem psalmos poenitentiales hebraicos interpretation* (Tübingen: Thomas Anshelm, 1512) [no pagination]. A special thank you to Anthony Fredette for help in the translation of this difficult text.

[145] Martin Luther, *First Lectures on the Psalms I: Psalms 1–75*, trans. Herbert J. A. Bouman, LW 10 (Saint Louis: Concordia, 1974), 42–44.

Lord."[146] In this vein, David wrote the psalm "as something inciting, stirring, and inflaming, so that he might have something to arouse him to stir up the devotion and inclination of his heart, and in order that this might be done more sharply, he did so with musical instruments."[147] In my opinion, such an interpretation fits well into the concept of semantic transformation advocated above within the context of the book. Whereas the phrase "for the leader" would have at one time recommended the psalm for the use of the leader to spur on the people of God, in the final form it would suggest that readers themselves seek to be encouraged or spurred on by the psalm. Reuchlin's summative translation, "for invitation," while not semantically related to נצח, might indeed capture the function of the title as it now stands in the text.

An alternative, second view of the ongoing function of למנצח is founded on insights offered by Hans-Joachim Kraus.[148] Like his modern predecessors, he explained the title in light of the priests and Levites being the purveyors of Israel's cultic traditions (1 Chr 15:21). Instead of seeking an explanation of למנצח in Chronicles or Ezra, he argued that Deut 31:19–21 is helpful in envisioning what role these leaders played in the use of cultic music in ancient Israel. We read in 31:19, "Now therefore write this song [כתב את־השירה] and teach it [למד] to the people of Israel. Put it in their mouths [שים בפי] in order that this song might be for me as a witness [לעד] against the Israelites." When the events described in the song would come to pass (31:20–21a)—signaling its prophetic capacity—it would serve its purpose by testifying against the Israelites (31:21b). For Moses, this is all made possible because the song would not "be forgotten [שכח] from the mouths of their descendants [מפי זרעו]" (31:21c), and because YHWH is able to anticipate the inclinations of his people (31:21d).

As Kraus noted, four different activities stand out in this passage: (1) the Levites compose the song and (2) teach it to the people, so that the people would both (3) sing it as their own and (4) teach it to their children. The role of the Levites, then, was not limited to the *performance* of a psalm in the temple cult, but included a didactic purpose which allowed the people of Israel to sing these songs for themselves and make them part of their tradition.[149] Further examples within the Old Testament help to illustrate the ways in which this might be true for other songs in Israel, including the book of Psalms. For instance, we have the psalm-like prayer spoken by Hannah in 1 Sam 2:1–10.[150]

---

[146] Martin Luther, *Complete Commentary on the First Twenty-Two Psalms*, 1:130.

[147] Luther, *First Lectures on the Psalms I*, 43.

[148] Kraus, *Psalms 1–59*, 67.

[149] See Gerstenberger, *Psalms: Part 1*, 27–28. He argued that Levites had an important postexilic role in administering worship services throughout the Diaspora (cf. Ezra 8:15–20).

[150] Her prayer is but one of many examples of psalms being inserted into narrative contexts in the Old Testament. For a comprehensive treatment of these with relevant bibliography, see James W. Watts, *Psalm and Story: Inset Hymns in Hebrew Narrative*, JSOTSup 139 (Sheffield: Sheffield Academic, 1992).

At the outset, it is quite an odd psalm for her to pray: "A psalm which is primarily concerned with the position of the king in power and victory, acknowledging the supremacy of God and reflecting on the way in which the fortunes of men are at his disposal, has been used to provide a suitable prayer for a woman giving thanks for the gift of a son."[151] But even more odd, she prays the psalm not during the dedication of Samuel (1 Sam 1:26–28), but in a more private moment of prayer.[152] This is not unique to Hannah's psalm. Other psalms inserted into narratives almost always occur in non-cultic contexts, even though we can be relatively sure that the psalms themselves originated in the cult.[153] For Watts, this meant that those who inserted psalms into narratives believed "psalms could and should be used as reflections of personal, as well as collective, piety." Hannah's prayer shows that "private appropriation of liturgical psalmody was not only taking place, but [was] even being advocated."[154] In the wording of Deut 31, the psalm has been "put in her mouth." Moreover, the song has been reassessed and given a canonical function that no longer bears an exact resemblance to its pre-scriptural use.[155] Like Hannah's example, perhaps למנצח indicates that readers would put the psalm into their mouths, memorizing it, and making its words their own. Just as the Levites would teach a psalm to be used by an individual or group, למנצח now functions to democratizes the psalm for the benefit of the reader.[156]

In terms of Pss 1–2, this view would also connect the reader closely to how the righteous are to imitate the "Blessed Man" and his way. It invites the reader to join with "those who take refuge in him" (Ps 2:12). When used in conjunction with לדוד, not only are the prayers of the righteous taken up into the figure of David, but now his prayers are to be spoken by the readers themselves. More speculatively, further performative notes might also suggest that this occurs no longer in terms of the actual musical performance of the song, but in the reader's own actualizing of the psalm in personal situations. Erasmus offered the following reflection on the title of Ps 4, capturing this sense well:

---

[151] Peter R. Ackroyd, *Doors of Perception: A Guide to Reading the Psalms* (Leighton Buzzard, England: Faith, 1978), 29–30.

[152] Watts, *Psalm and Story*, 12.

[153] See the prayers of Moses and Miriam (Exod 15), Deborah (Judg 5), Jonah (Jonah 2), and David (2 Sam 22–23). Solomon's prayer at the dedication of the temple in 1 Kgs 8, after making petition to YHWH, includes seven different examples of times when Israel (and even foreigners) could gather together as a community or individually to make confession, petition, and praise to YHWH, either at the temple in Jerusalem or in the Diaspora (8:31–51). This gives us insight into ancient prayer practices, in which not only were the prayers of the king important (8:27–29), but also the prayers of the people (8:30).

[154] Watts, *Psalm and Story*, 39, 40. See also Ackroyd, *Doors of Perception*, 30. He wrote, "[What] belongs to the king and to his exalted position under God, can be true also of the ordinary worshiper."

[155] See Ackroyd, *Doors of Perception*, 32.

[156] See Norman Gottwald, *The Tribes of Yahweh* (Maryknoll, NY: Orbis, 1979), 119.

The Hebrews associated music with religion and used it in their ceremonies; it was clearly a particular interest of King David, who not only appointed musicians to make music for the Lord on their different instruments, but also did not consider it beneath his own dignity as a king to dance and sing before the Ark of the Lord. But all that they did was mere symbolism; we must strive to make that special kind of music which delights the ears of God... We should realize that our music is sweetest to God when every part of our lives is in harmony with his commandments, when our words are in tune with our lives, when the mellifluous chorus of brotherly concord is not marred by the discords of conflict and disagreement, when a plangent lyre bewails our misdeeds, when we give thanks with a clash of cymbals, and the trumpet boldly sounds the gospel message. [157]

Erasmus's tropological reading of the musical directions complements either of the above interpretations of למנצח and suggests a reading that urges readers towards doing the work of God in harmony with the way of the righteous.[158]

3.2.3. Ancient Literary Designations

The final category to consider is ancient literary designation, which in Pss 3–14 include מזמור and שגיון. Like the musical instructions, the literary designations are generally difficult to translate, as in the case of שגיון. This term appears only in the titles for Ps 7 and Hab 3:1 (plural). The LXX renders both occurrences as if the Hebrew word was מזמור, but modern scholars have made a more concerted effort to better explain שגיון etymologically. The most common understanding is that it derives from the root שגה, "to go astray, err, wander," from which it signals either a variety of emotions or feeling (in the praying of the psalm) or that the psalm itself has been written with an irregular meter. Other renderings are based on Assyrian and Akkadian roots, which designate the psalm as a lament, perhaps even an agitated lament. Given the tentative nature of the definition of שגיון, it is very difficult to offer anything of substance for its ongoing use. It is noteworthy, however, that it has been paired with a biographical notice in Ps 7. Perhaps this indicates something related to the context in respect to David's demeanor (cf. later discussion in chapter five), or even the reversal of expected blessings for the righteous.

---

[157] Erasmus, "A Sermon on the Fourth Psalm / *In psalmum quartum concio*," trans. Michael J. Heath, in *Expositions of the Psalms*, ed. Dominic Baker-Smith, CWE 63 (Toronto: University of Toronto Press, 1997), 175–76.

[158] In making this argument I have tried to find a way to retain the premodern practice of reading the psalm headings hermeneutically while escaping the Christological overreach often found in early Christian interpretation of the superscriptions. There is a certain level of speculation, admittedly, but one way to achieve this is by grounding the ongoing function of the superscriptions in their pre-scriptural use, especially if this explained in Old Testament narrative texts, and recognizing the semantic transformation of its elements within the final form of the Psalms.

The term מזמור is easier to understand. It is most often defined as indicating that the psalm was to be performed with instrumental accompaniment. This is derived from the basic meaning of its verbal root זמר, "to sing, play, praise," and by its consistent use outside the psalm titles in the context of musical instrumentation (cf. Pss 33:2; 71:22; 98:5; 144:9; 147:7; 149:3). But, as is sometimes pointed out, it appears to have become a technical term in the psalm headings, and may be understood as a special designation to denote cultic music.[159] Indeed, when used with the preposition ל it always refers to YHWH, to whom the מזמור is addressed.[160] In this way, then, the designation מזמור most likely indicates that a musical piece was meant to be performed for YHWH (as a cultic song) with the accompaniment of music. In terms of its ongoing function, the term would help to reinforce the idea that a psalm was ultimately meant for the worship of YHWH, no matter which form-critical category has been assigned to it.[161] If Pss 1–2 shape our understanding of מזמור, they would likely add that one addresses YHWH from a posture of fearful service and trembling joy (2:11), such that even lament is grounded in a place of refuge (2:12).

3.2.4. A Tentative Experiment with Psalm Headings in Pss 3–14

Thus far I have attempted to show that the psalm superscriptions may also have an ongoing function within the final form of the text. I have argued that the associations with David (לדוד and biographical notices) ask the reader to consider these psalms as associated with the figure of David, who emerges out of Pss 1–2 with both typical and typological characteristics. Likewise, the cultic elements in the psalm titles, related to direction and musical instruction, can be understood as an invitation for the reader to complete the work of God, bringing their lives in harmony with God's work in the world. And finally, the literary designations give further thematic context in which to hear the psalm voiced by both the figure of David and the reader.

To demonstrate how this might work, I propose these tentative and experimental explanations of the hermeneutical value of the superscriptions, which will be noted again in my later analysis:

> *Psalm 3*: A song of worship offered to YHWH ("A psalm"), spoken by the figure of David ("of David"), within the context of Absalom's rebellion in 2 Sam 15–18 ("when he fled from before Absalom his son").

> *Psalm 7*: An expression of the chaotic reversal of expected blessings (a *shiggaion*), spoken by the figure of David ("of David"), of his trust in YHWH despite lifelong verbal accusations and attacks from the Benjaminites ("which he sang to YHWH concerning the words of Cush, a Benjaminite").

---

[159] Mowinckel, *Psalm Studies*, 2:603–4. He also noted that שיר is used more broadly for both sacred and profane songs, and refers principally to the vocalization of a song, not its instrumentation.

[160] Kraus, *Psalms 1–59*, 22. This could provide a meaningful re-assessment of lament.

[161] See Sawyer, "An Analysis of the Context and Meaning of the Psalm-Headings," 32.

Psalms 4, 5, 6, 8, 9/10, 12: Recommended for encouragement and support ("for the leader"), that one's life might be aligned with God's work in the world (musical rubrics); a song of worship offered to YHWH ("A psalm"), related to the figure of David ("of David").

Psalms 11 and 14: Recommended for encouragement and support ("for the leader"), related to the figure of David ("of David").

Psalm 13: Recommended for encouragement and support ("for the leader"), a song of worship offered to YHWH ("A psalm"), related to the figure of David ("of David").

3.3. Conclusion

I began this chapter by asking a question: does the book of Psalms provide a literary context that shapes our understanding of the speaking persona in a given psalm? The answer, in short, is yes. The introductory psalms (Pss 1–2) and editorial superscriptions have been put in place as signposts, guiding the reader in certain hermeneutical directions. Psalms 1–2, for instance, bring to the forefront an important speaking persona that I have called "the figure of David." Psalm 1 lays out his exemplary role for the righteous (the "Blessed Man"), while in Ps 2 he is the speaking persona. In fact, Ps 2 constructs its Davidic figure allowing for polyphonic typology; both king David and his promised heir are heard speaking at the same time. Psalms 1–2 also introduce us to several other characters who will either be quoted or referred to in the psalms to come: YHWH, the righteous (the "Blessed Congregation"), and the wicked. The psalm headings further guide readers by recalling this Davidic persona (לדוד), sometimes within a specific biographical episode from 1–2 Samuel. I have argued that this intertextual link does not primarily help us to bring correspondence between the narrative and the psalm, but to identify the function of the Davidic voice within a certain cluster of psalms. My next two chapters will attempt to trace out how David speaks "without end" in Pss 3–6 and 7–14.

4

The Figure of David in Psalms 3–6

In this chapter and the next I will be discussing the figure of David in Pss 3–14. In each chapter I will first engage with Pss 3 and 7 independently, and then, in a more thorough manner, discuss a whole range of issues which help to uncover why the opening psalm in each sub-grouping plays an important orienting function for understanding the role of the Davidic figure in the remaining psalms in each psalm cluster. I will argue that the role or function of David in these two psalm clusters is closely connected to the Davidic figure which emerges out of Pss 1–2. In their own ways, Pss 3 and 7 further configure David through the introduction of biographical superscriptions connected to David's life in 1–2 Samuel.

In this chapter I will argue that, for Pss 3–6, this results in a Davidic figure who is shaped by Pss 1–2 and the Davidic profile of 2 Sam 15–18. Hermeneutically, the figure of David can be heard in three different ways. First, the "Biographical David" speaks as we read the psalm within the narrative context of 2 Sam 15–18. As explained in the previous chapter, the goal is not to fit the psalm into the larger literary structure of 1–2 Samuel, but to overlay the psalm with the specific narrative concerns of Absalom's rebellion. An important clue that this latter approach is correct is the untidy fit between the psalm and its ascribed story. The "Biographical David" is then filtered through the profile of the figure of David in Pss 1–2, which brings figural extension into two additional speaking voices. Second, we have the "Typical David," who speaks as the "Blessed Man" from Ps 1. This Davidic persona speaks as the ideal king whose way of life and delight in the *torah* of YHWH are meant to be emulated by the "Blessed Congregation." Alongside the "Typical David" we have a third voice, the "Typological David," aligned with Ps 2. With this voice we hear a figural extension which draws together the person of David with his promised heir.

An important component of my interpretation of these psalms and their role within Pss 3–14 is dialogical analysis. Several scholars over the past few decades have called attention to the social aspect of psalms, and in particular lament psalms.[1] The benefit of dialogical analysis is that it forces us to consider all aspects of the speaking voice, including addressee, audience, and motivation. These help us trace out the rhetorical effect of the use of pronouns and descriptions of various characters in the psalm, whether that be the psalmist himself, his opponents, his friends, other onlookers, or YHWH. My interest in dialogical analysis stems from the representative nature of the lament psalms in connection with the figure of David. The more we understand who is addressed and described in these psalms, the better we will understand their function within the book of Psalms (which has redressed the original pre-scriptural social drama under the figure of David).[2]

4.1. Hearing Psalm 3 Within the Context of the Psalter

4.1.1. The Superscription of Ps 3
Psalm 3 begins with one of the thirteen biographical titles referencing episodes within the life of David.[3] Such superscriptions have been understood in a variety of ways throughout the history of interpretation. In the modern discussion, most share Kraus's opinion that they are a "late editorial intrusion," and as such should not be appropriated to assert anything about the historical setting of the

---

[1] See Walter Brueggemann, *The Message of the Psalms: A Theological Commentary* (Minneapolis: Augsburg, 1984); Gerald T. Sheppard, "'Enemies' and the Politics of Prayer," in *The Bible and the Politics of Exegesis: Essay in Honor of Norman K. Gottwald on His Sixty-fifth Birthday*, ed. David Jobling, Peggy L. Day, and Gerald T. Sheppard (Cleveland: Pilgrim, 1991), 61–82; W. Derek Suderman, "The Cost of Losing Lament for the Community of Faith: On Brueggemann, Ecclesiology, and the Social Audience of Prayer," *JTI* 6 (2012): 201–18.

[2] This is something that has gone unrecognized in the contemporary discussion of dialogical analysis. For example, in Derek Suderman's insightful "The Cost of Losing Lament for the Community of Faith," his discussion addressing the "contemporary scriptural function" of laments extends over several pages (210–16) discussing Ps 55, but neglects the Davidic voice. To quote: "One could say that, whatever its historical provenance, the contemporary *Sitz im Leben* of the Bible as Scripture lies within believing communities that value and treat it as such. Recognizing the nature and extent of social address within lament psalms further underscores the significance of such a move and reveals yet another cost of losing lament. Lament psalms not only give voice to the voiceless; they also provide a scriptural means through which the broader community can empathetically hear and discern the cries of others" (211). The point he makes is an important one, but by failing to recognize the Davidic voice in these psalms of lament— a Davidic voice encoded into the very fabric of the "Bible as Scripture"—he fails to unite the contemporary social actualization of the lament with the scriptural figure through which that lament should be heard.

[3] That is, Pss 3, 7, 18, 34, 51, 52, 54, 56, 57, 59, 60, 63, and 142.

psalm.[4] Moreover, the superscription is "proved erroneous by the psalm itself and does not help to elucidate the text."[5] For interpretation, then, Kraus thought it should be ignored. Gerstenberger agreed that a biographical title is an addendum to an earlier heading, but he was willing to see it as "interpretive," referring to Ps 3's title as a "scholarly extension alluding to 2 Samuel 15:14."[6] In this way, the biographical title does not make *historical* claims about the psalm, but can be understood as its "earliest attested interpretation."[7] As such, Gerstenberger claimed that the original cultic prayer had been "changed into a liturgical piece of Scripture meditation and devotion."[8]

This way of understanding the biographical superscriptions as *informative* in nature moves in the direction that I endorsed earlier, namely, that the superscriptions have interpretive value as hermeneutical clues to the meaning of the psalm. The biographical information is meant to point us to the various episodes in David's life recounted in Samuel, adding a "depth of characterization" by means of an intentional inner-biblical exegesis.[9] Yet in recent commentators there are still subtle differences in how each would articulate the hermeneutical value of the biographical titles. A few of these were surveyed in the previous chapter: the title as a means to fill the *lacunae* of biblical narrative (Johnson), or more commonly, the title as a way to give the reader a privileged glimpse into the mind of David (Childs).

To help reiterate the distinctive claim I am making, the above approaches view the psalm headings as taking us out of the textual world of the Psalter and into the wider narrative world of 1–2 Samuel, aiding readers in the recognition of a kind of "complementary" David, a David whose external actions are given in the narrative and internal thoughts in the Psalms.[10] This Davidic figure is then

---

[4] Hans-Joachim Kraus, *Psalms 1–59*, trans. Hilton C. Oswald (Minneapolis: Fortress, 1988), 138.

[5] Kraus, *Psalms 1–59*, 139.

[6] Erhard S. Gerstenberger, *Psalms: Part 1 with an Introduction to Cultic Poetry*, FOTL 14 (Grand Rapids: Eerdmans, 1988), 50.

[7] Gerstenberger, *Psalms: Part 1*, 51.

[8] Gerstenberger, *Psalms: Part 1*, 52.

[9] See James W. Watts, *Psalm and Story: Inset Hymns in Hebrew Narrative*, JSOTSup 139 (Sheffield: Sheffield Academic, 1992), 183; Rolf Rendtorff, "The Psalms of David: David in the Psalms," in *The Book of Psalms: Composition and Reception*, ed. Peter W. Flint and Patrick D. Miller, VTSup 99 (Leiden: Brill 2005), 54–55.

[10] See Jean-Marie Auwers, "Les Voies de L'Exégèse Canonique du Psautier," in *The Biblical Canons*, ed. Jean-Marie Auwers and Henk Jan de Jonge, BETL 143 (Leiden: Leiden University Press, 2003), 22. Following Childs he wrote (my own translation): "One of the effects of the Davidic intitulation of the Psalter is to compensate for the silences of the *geste davidique* on the inner life of the son of Jesse. In other words, where the books of Samuel put us in the presence of a ringleader, the Psalter recalls that David was a man of prayer."

presented before the reader as worthy of imitation.[11] In my view, rather than using the titles as ways back into the narrative, a more consistent intertextual and interfigural move would be to treat them as something like narrative fishing hooks, cast from the Psalter into 1–2 Samuel, and reeling the narrative texts into the Psalter as constructive contextual background. Instead of the Psalter being used to help paint a complementary portrait of David, the "David of Samuel" is called upon to help serve the developing portrait of the figure of David in the Psalter. Though it may be an obvious point, Pss 1–2 are not equivalent to the Deuteronomistic history. Psalm scholarship, however, has not utilized this distinction in its understanding of the biographical superscriptions. For Ps 3 we need to recognize that Pss 1–2, in combination with the Absalom narrative (2 Sam 15–18), configure the profile of David in a different way than the narratives of 1–2 Samuel set up the Absalom episode.

Outside of this theoretical discussion, we must also discuss the content of the superscription itself. Syntactically, it includes "a psalm of David" (מזמור לדוד) followed by an infinitive clause, which is normally used in biblical Hebrew to express contemporaneity with whatever time frame is indicated by the rest of the clause. In this case, preceded by a nominal phrase, the infinitive clause places this psalm on David's lips during his flight from Absalom, inviting the psalm to be read in an inner-biblical relationship with that episode in David's life. It is helpful, then, to compare the details of the psalm to the story of Absalom's rebellion, as summarized below:[12]

The Details	Ps 3	2 Samuel
The fleeing of David	3:1	15:14 (cf. 19:10)
The increase of David's enemies	3:2, 7	15:12–17; 17:11; 18:31–32
Growing animosity and castigation against David	3:3	16:5–14 (esp. 7–8)
David's covered/raised head and trust in God	3:4–5	15:25–32
David's weary night at the river Jordan	3:6	16:14; 17:1, 16, 22
David's concern for the welfare of the people	3:9	15:14
David's eventual victory	3:9	19:1–2

---

[11] See James L. Mays, *Psalms*, IBC (Louisville: Westminster John Knox, 1994), 54; John Goldingay, *Psalms, Volume 1: Psalms 1–41*, BCOT (Grand Rapids: Baker Academic, 2006), 109.

[12] Among others, see Brevard S. Childs, "Psalm Titles and Midrashic Exegesis," *JSS* 16 (1971): 144–45; Peter C. Craigie *Psalms 1–50*, 2nd ed., WBC 19 (Dallas: Thomas Nelson, 2004), 72; Mays, *Psalms*, 53–54; Phil J. Botha and Beat Weber, "'Killing Them Softly with this Song…': The Literary Structure of Psalm 3 and Its Psalmic and Davidic Contexts; Part II: A Contextual and Intertextual Interpretation of Psalm 3," *OTE* 21 (2008): 285–87.

Such a strong correspondence between the psalm and the story indicates an inner-biblical connection between these texts. At the same time, Kraus was correct in saying that these correspondences should not mask the differences, which are numerous.

First, in Ps 3:3–6 David expresses a confidence in Yʜᴡʜ that simply is not found in the narrative; instead of having a raised head (3:4), the narrative expressly tells us of David's lowered head (2 Sam 15:25–32). Second, the psalm does not convey any sense of David's flight when considered on its own. This notion is introduced only by the superscription.[13] Third, the narrative explains that David escaped from Absalom's forces precisely because he did not sleep during the night he left Jerusalem (2 Sam 17:16), which seems to counter the sleep experienced by the psalmist in Ps 3:6.[14] Fourth, one could also appeal to the prayer for blessing in the final verse, which would correspond much better with a national crisis, and not a civil war.[15] Fifth, scholars have also objected to David's tenor in this psalm as compared to the narrative: how can we square his prayer for the smashing of his enemies' teeth (3:8) with his own efforts to save Absalom's life (2 Sam 18:5)?[16] And finally, historically speaking, scholars have noted that Jerusalem was not known as the "holy mountain" in David's time, before the temple.[17]

In view of such incongruences, one could take the advice of Childs, Mays, and others, to see the link to David as a kind of illustration only. Yet the impulse of premodern interpreters was different. They too acknowledged historical differences between the psalm and the story, but instead of appealing to David as illustration or exemplar, they took the differences as an invitation to reflect further on speaking persona in the psalm. For them, there was something *more* going on with the Davidic voice. The deviations between psalm and story were not meant to discount the intertextual connection established in the superscription, but to prod the reader into deeper theological reflection. As Seitz had observed with Ps 34:

---

[13] See Botha and Weber, "Killing them Softly," 286. They note that even though the flight is not recognizable in Ps 3 on its own, the "circumstances of having to cope with enemies that far outnumber the suppliant are definitely there." More, they suggest that elements of the night scene are present in verse six when compared to 2 Sam 17:1, 16.

[14] Botha and Weber, "Killing them Softly," 287. At best, one could understand the link to be that Yʜᴡʜ's response to David (Ps 3:5) enables "him the privilege of other nights of peaceful sleep."

[15] Goldingay, *Psalms 1–41*, 110. See also Howard Wallace, *Psalms* (Sheffield: Sheffield Phoenix, 2009), 21. He pointed out that the threat is different in the narrative, where David's enemies threaten the rule of David over Israel—a physical and political threat—while the psalm conveys a personal threat which is more theological in nature. He further wrote, "In the psalm, Yahweh is called to act for David, but in 2 Samuel 18 David himself, having set up spies and informants, eventually overcomes Absalom" (24).

[16] Robert L. Cole, *Psalms 1–2: Gateway to the Psalter*, HBM 37 (Sheffield: Sheffield Phoenix, 2013), 145; Wallace, *Psalms*, 24.

[17] Mays, *Psalms*, 53; Wallace, *Psalms*, 24.

The selectivity [of connecting psalm to narrative] turned only on the limits of the narrative tradition itself, and the suitableness of matching the details of a specific psalm with the narrative presentation, neither overloading it artificially nor making merely superficial or word-association links, but seeking instead deeper theological penetration. The general tradition of David as author and singer of psalms was the warrant for this exploration.[18]

At the heart of the figure of David in the Psalter is this sense of "deeper theological penetration." Thomas Aquinas referred to this phenomenon as exceeding the historical meaning of the psalm. As I have argued throughout, the key to understanding the exploration into "something more" lies in the canonical shaping of the scriptural text; that is, in the relationship between Ps 3, its biographical title, and Pss 1–2.

4.1.2. Lexical and Thematic Links Between Pss 1–2 and Ps 3

Ps 3 shares several lexical and thematic links with Pss 1–2, which help us to read Ps 3 within the context of the Psalter.[19] The first of these holds together "the wicked" of Pss 1–2 with Absalom and his mutinous party in Ps 3. We can begin by observing the use of the preposition על ("upon, against") in 3:2, 7 and 2:2. While the use of a preposition on its own seems innocuous, its use here warrants its discussion. In Ps 3, the psalmist writes that "many are rising up against [על] me" (3:2) and that thousands of people have arrayed themselves all around him (3:7). This corresponds with the use of the preposition in 2:2, which says that the kings of the earth and rulers have stood up and conspired "against" (על) YHWH and his anointed.[20] The use of "wicked" (רשעים) in 3:8 makes this connection even more firm (cf. 1:1, 4, 5, 6). In this way, at a more thematic level, the people (עם) who surround the psalmist (3:7) can be compared with the nations (גוים) and peoples (לאמים) of Ps 2. Likewise, the psalmist's acknowledgment that YHWH has struck his enemies and shattered the teeth of the wicked (3:8) corresponds to the decree of YHWH in Ps 2:9, authorizing the Davidic king to break the nations with a rod of iron and dash them as a potter's vessel in order to establish his kingdom.

The characterization of the figures of Absalom and David are also developed through keyword links. This begins in the superscription of Ps 3, with the use of

---

[18] Christopher R. Seitz, "Psalm 34: Redaction, Inner-Biblical Exegesis and the Longer Psalm Superscriptions—'Mistake' Making and Theological Significance," in *The Bible as Christian Scripture: The Work of Brevard Childs*, ed. Christopher R. Seitz and Kent Harold Richards, BSNA 25 (Atlanta: SBL, 2013), 284–85.

[19] See Gianni Barbiero, *Das erste Psalmenbuch als Einheit: Eine synchrone Analyse von Psalm 1–41*, OBS 16 (Berlin: Peter Lang, 1999), 65–69; Botha and Weber, "'Killing Them Softly,'" 278–80.

[20] Robert L. Cole, "Psalm 3: Of Whom Does David Speak, of Himself or Another?" in *Text and Canon: Essays in Honor of John H. Sailhamer*, ed. Robert L. Cole and Paul J. Kissling (Eugene, OR: Pickwick, 2017), 141.

the word "son" (בֵּן). Given the tendency of terseness in Hebrew poetry, unnecessary or seemingly superfluous designations can be taken as signals to larger connections in the Psalter.[21] In this case, the use of "son," before we even enter the body of Ps 3, recalls the use of "son" only a few lines earlier in 2:12, "Kiss the son (בַּר), lest he be angry." Absalom, as David's son, was a potential heir to the promises and could have very well been the "son" of promise in 2:7, to whom the kings and rulers were to give fealty (2:11). Instead, he and his party played the part of the rebels, failing to give honor to the anointed of Yʜwʜ (David).[22] Here, the narrative of 2 Samuel informs our reading, as it speaks plainly about their destiny: the rebellion failed, and Absalom died in battle. In a final link, the use of the word ירא ("fear") in 2:11 and 3:7 adds to the characterization of David in Ps 3. In 2:11, the kings and judges of the earth are exhorted to serve Yʜwʜ with fear. David exemplifies this trait in Ps 3 as he confidently trusts in Yʜwʜ, determined not to fear the multitudes surrounding him (3:7).

Taken together, these observations paint a picture of development from Pss 1–2 into Ps 3. In an unexpected turn, it is not the nations of the world who are the first to rebel against the Davidic promises (2:1), but those within God's own people.[23] The Midrash offers an interesting reading at this point: "Why is the Psalm on Gog and Magog (Ps. 2) placed next to the Psalm on Absalom? To tell you that a wicked son works greater cruelty upon his father than will the wars of Gog and Magog."[24] More than this, however, we are not reading about just any son rebelling against his father, or that any Israelite would rebel against the Davidic king, but the potential heir in line for the Davidic promises!

Looking at the scope of the whole Psalter, the question about the heir of the promises and the apparent failure of the line of David continually emerges at the seams of the book (e.g., Pss 72, 89). If my reading of Ps 3 is correct, it is noteworthy that the question of the fulfillment of the Davidic promises does not wait until Ps 89 to be expressed but is already at work in the first psalm after the introduction. Indeed, there is a progression to consider: the heir who rebelled and failed (Ps 3), the heir of promise (Ps 72), and the apparent failure of the line

---

[21] See Andrew C. Witt, "Hearing Psalm 102 within the Context of the Hebrew Psalter," *VT* 62 (2012): 601–2.

[22] Botha and Weber, "Killing them Softly," 278. They noted: "The mighty, divinely protected king in Jerusalem who is announced to be the son of Yʜwʜ (Ps 2, cf. 2 Sam 7:14) is put to flight from Jerusalem by his own son (3:1)! Majesty (Ps 2) and modesty (Ps 3) are connected with one another."

[23] *Contra* Jean-Marie Auwers, "Le David des psaumes et les psaumes de David," in *Figures de David: A Travers la Bible*, ed. Louis Desrousseaux and Jacques Vermeylen (Paris: Cerf, 1999), 208–9. Note that in 2 Samuel this is not the case. David first establishes the kingdom against enemy nations before the narrative moves into the political repercussions of his personal life.

[24] William G. Braude, *The Midrash on Psalms* (New Haven: Yale University Press, 1959), 1:50.

of David (Ps 89). When we speak about the seams of the book, then, we should not jump straight from Ps 2 to Ps 72 to Ps 89. We need to think about how Ps 3's inclusion of Absalom fits into this picture. In my reading, Ps 3 introduces the theme of the apparent failure of the Davidic line at the very beginning of Book 1 proper, even before the death of David. In its context, this theme is united to Pss 1–2's sweeping vision of humanity's rebellion against the work and promises of God. This is significant in our understanding of the role Books 1–3 play in the Psalter: was there ever a time when the promises were not being threatened?[25]

At the same time, these psalms do not focus on the rebellion of Absalom as the end of the story. In my previous discussion of Pss 1–2, I noted how the enveloping use of אשרי in 1:1 and 2:12 showed that the blessings of "the Man" (1:2–3) were connected to the blessings of all who trust in him (2:12). The end of Pss 1–2 is not the rebellion and punishment of the wicked; they are invited to turn from their rebellion and join in the company of the righteous, that they too might receive the blessings of Yʜᴡʜ for those who take refuge in him. The same is true of Ps 3. As Auwers has demonstrated, there is a strong schematic correspondence between Ps 2 and Ps 3.[26] Both psalms begin with an evocation of the enemies who rise up against the king and Yʜᴡʜ (2:1–2; 3:2–3a), include discourse of the enemies (2:3; 3:3b) and the response of Yʜᴡʜ "in heaven"/"from his holy mountain" (2:6; 3:5), an affirmation of the privileged relationship between the king and Yʜᴡʜ (2:7–8; 3:6), and the destiny of the enemies who will be "shattered"/"broken" (2:9; 3:8). Auwers commented on 2:10–12 only in terms of its relationship to Ps 1, as purposely creating the structure of blessing. The schema, however, also continues in the final verses of Ps 3, as the warning to the enemies towards the fear of God (2:10–12a) and the promise of blessing for those who take refuge (2:12b) parallel the statement of salvation belonging to God (3:9a) and his blessing over his people (3:9b). Psalm 3, our first example of faithful *torah*-responsive prayer in the Psalter, is styled in the shape of Ps 2.

In both psalms, the place of hope is set on the one lexical link that I have yet to mention, Yʜᴡʜ's "holy hill" (2:6; 3:5). In Ps 2:6–7, the "holy hill" serves as the location where the anointed Son will be established as the co-regent of Yʜᴡʜ. The promises made to David in 2 Sam 7 serve as the theological background, allowing the kind of "deeper theological penetration" noted by Seitz. Though the historical David can look to Zion, where the Ark resides, he

---

[25] At this point, I wonder if this, too, helps to explain why the biographical superscriptions are not found in chronological order. The entirety of David's life, even when evading Saul's pursuit, has been subsumed within the larger and more important question of the fulfillment of God's promises (2 Sam 7). Indeed, even in the narrative of 1–2 Samuel the anointing of David by Samuel *precedes* any wrong David suffered at Saul's hands. This telescoping or collapsing of the Davidic promises back into 1 Sam 16 allows us to hear the psalms of David's deliverance as part of Yʜᴡʜ's providential purposes for David.

[26] Auwers, "Le David des psaumes," 208. See also Cole, "Psalm 3: Of Whom Does David Speak, of Himself or Another?"; Weber, "Psalm 1–3 als Ouvertüre des Psalters."

could also be speaking figurally, as a "voice without end." As a figure for future sons of promise (and ultimately, *the* son who would actualize the promises), David's experiences with Absalom are but one example of how the nations have rebelled against Yhwh and his anointed. The same is true of Absalom, as he becomes a figure of any who rebel against the Davidic promises—both within the confines of Israel and without.

4.1.3. *Historical-Critical Engagement with Ps 3*

Several suggestions for identifying the one praying have been articulated in the modern era. Gunkel, for instance, argued that we should understand the psalmist as a private citizen (and not a ruler), who uses grandiose metaphors to help capture the seriousness of his troubles and the extent of the danger in which he is caught.[27] Similarly, Kraus thought of Ps 3 in terms of a "performed liturgy" incorporating metaphors and conventionalized idea forms: the psalmist takes up the prayer formula that he might be "transposed to a 'kingly situation' which transcends his own individual fate and so encircles it that he can find a place for himself there."[28] A common feature of these reconstructions is that the petitioner prays within the temple grounds for justice after an accusation has been made against him (cf. 3:3). Seybold is representative of this view, and he summarized its key features well:

> The petitioner finds himself faced with an accusation. This, brought forward by "oppressors" and "enemies," has brought him to the sanctuary on Zion, in spite of contrary advice (3b), in order to find asylum protection and legal aid. The latter seems to have been given to him. The background, or course of a sacral process, determines the individual elements of the psalm, in which case it is possible to look back on what has already been experienced; namely, to the unrestrained overnight stay in the holy place, as well as a judgment which has already taken place.[29]

Complementing this reconstruction, Craigie argued that the psalm could have originally been used by Davidic kings in times of military crises, but over time was opened up for more general use: "The particular military crisis and the need for victory was analogous to the crisis and needs which may face any human being at any time; so the psalm entered the general resources of Israel's worship as a protective psalm, specifically as a psalm traditionally used during the morning worship."[30] Craigie helps to show how the original *Sitz im Leben* of the psalm could be adapted over time, allowing for a number of different contexts even before the psalm's inclusion as part of Scripture.

---

[27] See Kraus, *Psalms 1–59*, 137.

[28] Kraus, *Psalms 1–59*, 138.

[29] Klaus Seybold, *Die Psalmen*, HAT 1/15 (Tübingen: Mohr, 1996), 34–35. My own translation.

[30] Craigie, *Psalms 1–50*, 72.

Such historical-critical engagement is helpful for understanding the social dynamics at work in the psalm and may indeed be of aid for a canonical approach. Nevertheless, as it is by necessity fixated on the psalm independent of its canonical setting, its conclusions principally serve to illustrate the semantic transformation achieved by its scriptural setting (i.e., its superscription and literary context of Pss 1–2). Before this, however, dialogical analysis will help to lay out the speaking persona in greater detail.

4.1.4. Dialogical Analysis of Ps 3

In the first section (vv. 2–4), the psalmist uses first-person singular pronouns to describe his current situation with many enemies rising up against him (vv. 2–3), while also expressing his trust in YHWH to counteract their claims (v. 4). Throughout these verses the root רבב ("to grow, increase") plays an important role, used repeatedly in both its verbal and nominative forms, helping David to state both his past and present circumstances: "Not only have my enemies increased, but even now many are rising up against me!"[31] Rhetorically, there is an intensification in the enemies' position before David; they are both amassing soldiers and beginning to move against him.[32] These verses also include a quotation of his foes, who say: "There is no salvation for him in God" (v. 3). At stake for David is not simply his station as king over Israel or his physical life, but the entirety of who he is, his entire person (נפש). By speaking of God's support (ישע), the "many" (רב) are claiming that God will no longer sustain David's life or rescue him from trouble. In short, he has fallen out of favor with God.[33] Given the stature of David, such verbal abuse should be understood as a public declaration, aiding the growing popular support of Absalom.

Verse four, however, offers us a change of perspective.[34] David's enemies have placed their hope in Absalom, turning their trust away from him, but David continues to trust in YHWH, relying on his ongoing relationship and experiences with YHWH. In this verse, three images are used to describe David's special relationship with YHWH: YHWH is a shield (מגן) about him, to protect David and his ability to defend God's people; YHWH is his "glory" (כבד), giving David personal dignity before God and royal honor as YHWH's anointed;[35] and YHWH is the one who lifts up his head, emphasizing David's dignity or honor before

---

[31] See Franz Delitzsch, *A Commentary on the Book of Psalms*, trans. David Eaton and James E. Duguid (New York: Funk & Wagnalls, 1883), 62.

[32] See Kraus, *Psalms 1–59*, 139.

[33] Delitzsch, *Book of Psalms*, 62.

[34] The contrastive ואתה has led a number of psalm scholars to see a division in the text here. In my view, the contrast is not introducing a new topic, but is a single verse response to the view of his enemies and belongs with the first section. See Pierre Auffret, "Note sur la structure littéraire du psaume 3," *ZAW* 91 (1979): 93–106; John S. Kselman, "Psalm 3: A Structural and Literary Study," *CBQ* 49 (1987): 572–80.

[35] Kraus, *Psalms 1–59*, 140.

others.[36] Each of these images is personalized, offering a strong rebuttal to the enemies' claims in verse three: Yʜᴡʜ will indeed protect and deliver him, confirming his confidence and restoring his authority.

The addressee and pronouns switch in the second section, matching a shift in focus away from the enemies to David himself (vv. 5–7). First-person singular pronouns continue to be used, with references to Yʜᴡʜ in the third person. This indicates a shift in addressee from the first section, which was entirely addressed to Yʜᴡʜ. Now, he speaks to either the "many" (vv. 2–4), the reader, or perhaps even himself in a kind of inner dialogue. The content of these verses provides the grounds for David's confidence expressed in verse four. In verse five, David speaks of "his experience of a life rich in prayer,"[37] habitually calling out to Yʜᴡʜ and being answered from the place of Yʜᴡʜ's presence, "his holy hill" (הר קדשו). This is followed in verse six by the remembrance of divine aid as the proof that his prayers were indeed heard. The images of lying down, falling asleep, and reawakening are particularly striking, and will be used with similar force in the next psalm. Taken together, both lines outline David's past experience with the ישע ("deliverance") of Yʜᴡʜ: there has been and will continue to be salvation for David.

Verse seven switches from report to volitional forms, concluding the section with David asserting his confidence for any who are there to listen, "May I never be afraid of the myriads [מרבבות] of people." There is a pattern to his speech: he has twice recalled his situation before Yʜᴡʜ (vv. 2–3, 5–6), each time offering a confident response, the first to Yʜᴡʜ (v. 4) and the second to a generic audience (v. 7). By recalling the first line of verse two ("who set themselves against me all around"), this verse forms a kind of enveloping structure around the whole prayer. David has come full circle: instead of fearing his enemies and their denunciations of his hope, he will place his fear and faith in God, who shields him and has consistently sustained him.

We have a third switch in addressee in verse eight, as David finally makes his petition to Yʜᴡʜ.[38] The first two clauses are imperatives: "Rise up, O Yʜᴡʜ! Save me, my God!" Each has a direct connection to earlier verses in the psalm: to the enemies who are rising up against David (v. 2, קמים עלי), and to the quotation of the enemies in verse three (ישועתה). The earlier rebuttal of David (v. 4) similarly takes prayerful expression in this verse as David prays for Yʜᴡʜ to take decisive action in consonance with his previous experience (cf. Num 10:35). The second half of the verse further grounds these petitions through the image of his enemies as ferocious animals biting him with their sharp verbal abuse. As Kselman noted: "Since the hostile activity of the psalmist's foes included verbal attacks on him, their punishment will appropriately involve the destruction of the organs of speech."[39] God has vindicated David in the past from

---

[36] Artur Weiser, *The Psalms: A Commentary* (Philadelphia: Westminster, 1962), 117.
[37] Weiser, *The Psalms*, 117.
[38] Weiser, *The Psalms*, 118.
[39] Kselman, "Psalm 3," 579.

such verbal assaults, and he prays that God again would work to shut the mouths of his enemies.

And lastly, in verse nine, while no personal pronouns are used for the psalmist, we can detect two different addressees. In 3:9a, the psalmist refers to YHWH in the third person—suggesting an addressee who is not YHWH—while in 3:9b he refers to YHWH in the second person, asking for God's blessing to remain on his people. We have two main options for understanding the time frame of this petition. First, it could be in the future indicative, so that David is making a hopeful, prophetic announcement, "from YHWH *will be* salvation; your blessing will be on your people." Or second, the force of the prayer would be more emphatic in the present, "from YHWH *is this* deliverance; on your people is your blessing." With this option deliverance and blessing are found during the rebellion against David, and not simply at its conclusion. This is the final nail in his rebuttal against the speech of his enemies; their claim that there is no present support of God is met with a burst of confidence in YHWH's deliverance.

4.1.5. *The Figure of David in Ps 3*

In order to construct the figure of David in Ps 3, we must bear in mind each of the above analyses. In the historical-critical engagement with the psalm I observed that the focus rested not on the Davidic figure but a social situation which utilized grandiose royal imagery to add rhetorical force to a petitioner's prayer within a juridical context. While one could argue that this is the result of the psalm's democratization, the canonical editing of the Psalter moves us in a different direction. This happens on two levels. First, the biographical superscription provides a narrative context for the psalm specifically tied to Absalom's rebellion in 2 Sam 15–18. This sets up a Davidic persona that I will call the "Biographical David." At its most basic level, the psalm can be heard as a prayer from the lips of this David during his flight from Absalom. Interpreters are invited to compare the psalm to the narrative to fill out the full contours of David's prayer, as will be done later in this chapter.

Second, I have also noted the importance of hearing Pss 1–2 as a preface to the book of Psalms, which is heightened by their immediate juxtaposition with Ps 3. This literary context introduces a second level of configuration to the Davidic persona. He is not simply the "Biographical David" but has been joined together with the Davidic figure from Pss 1–2 to become a figure of the ideal Davidic king. Within this persona, the Biographical David has been extended into two directions: first as a typical figure whom the righteous imitate (Ps 1), and second, as a typological figure in his alignment with the Davidic heir, who would one day actualize YHWH's promises to David (Ps 2). In the former case, the reader is challenged to join with those who take refuge in YHWH, associating with David in his flight from Absalom, and praying that YHWH would bring justice to those who rebel against his anointed. Like David, readers can look back upon former times of divine aid and pray for YHWH's continued support in times of accusation and doubt.

In the latter, within David himself is embodied the destiny of his progeny; just as he experiences his own kind of "exile," with the Davidic promises hanging on by a thread, so too will his line seemingly end in Ps 89. Hope, then, remains. Just as David was delivered by Yнwн in the revolt of Absalom, so would the Davidic line from the threat of exile, and David's heir from further rebellions of future "Absalom" figures. Thus, David embodies both the hope of the people in establishing a just kingdom and the penitent humility necessary for a right relationship with God. Through its careful construction of the Davidic figure, Pss 1–2 and the superscription to Ps 3 allow the reader to behold the hope of the future in the Davidic heir (the Typological David), as well as the way of hope in the ideal royal figure (the Typical David), that they may look to Yнwн to bring about the consummation of his work amongst his people.

Such an understanding of the configuration of the Davidic voice helps to make sense of the history of interpretation, surveyed earlier. As we saw, Christian interpreters worked with an understanding that the Davidic heir should be identified as Jesus of Nazareth. As such, the Typological David, now identified as Jesus the Messiah, moves us beyond the threats found in Israel's history against the Davidic line to the threats and ultimate deliverance experienced by the Son of God in his earthly ministry (as told in the Gospels). If the editors of the Psalter are only pointing us to the "David of Samuel" in order to reconstruct a fuller portrait of the historical David, then such wider readings run against the grain of the Psalter's own theological grammar. My argument, however, has been the opposite: the editors are constructing their own figure of David by means of Pss 1–2 and the superscription to Ps 3, a Davidic figure which has a built-in typological extension between David and his heir.

4.2. An Analysis of Psalms 4–6 in the Context of Psalm 3

4.2.1. The Superscriptions of Pss 4–6

In my discussion of the superscription of Ps 3, I argued that the biographical notice asks its readers to understand the psalm within an inner-biblical relationship with the episode of Absalom's rebellion (2 Sam 15–18). While the superscriptions in Pss 4–6 do not include this biographical information, my discussion will show that the same episode in David's life can stand as the contextual setting for Pss 4–6.[40]

Psalms 4–6 share a uniform heading with little variation: the rubric for the leader of music (למנצח), musical elements (בנגינות ;אל־הנחילות ;בנגינות על־ השמינית), indication of ancient literary type (מזמור), and an association with David (לדוד). Syntactically, while the superscription to Ps 3 used an infinitive clause to express contemporaneity with the biographical element, the superscriptions in Pss 4–6 contain only brief nominal clauses. Each can be understood as coming from the hand of an editor, giving basic background information to the psalm.

---

40 See Weber, "Psalm 1–3 als Ouvertüre des Psalters," 242–43.

At the end of the previous chapter I argued that within the final form of the Psalter these superscription elements may have taken on new signification within their canonical context. In this respect, the difference between Ps 3 and Pss 4–6 is important. For Ps 3, I suggested that the superscription (לדוד + מזמור + biographical setting) contextualized the psalm as a song of worship offered to Yhwh, spoken by the figure of David within the context of Absalom's rebellion in 2 Sam 15–18. For Pss 4–6, the absence of the biographical note and the additions of למנצח and further musical elements alter their contextualization.

I have hypothesized that למנצח indicated a psalm should be "put into the mouth" of the reader, democratizing the psalm for any individual worshipper, and prompting her towards the completion of God's work. In the context of Pss 1–2, such democratization also connects readers closely with the way the "Blessed Congregation" are to imitate the "Blessed Man," inviting them to join with "those who take refuge in him" (2:12). In this way, they recommend a psalm for encouragement and support. Importantly, when used in conjunction with לדוד, the prayers spoken by the figure of David are also to be spoken by the readers themselves. In this context, the additional musical elements present a more difficult case: Ps 4, בנגינות ("with strings"); Ps 5, אל־הנחילות; ("for the flutes"); and Ps 6, בנגינות על־השמינית ("with strings, upon the *sheminith*"). Both Jewish and Christian premodern interpreters attempted to understand these musical terms through complex etymologies, which in the Christian context occurred even using Greek and Latin translations. Their attempts, while rightly dismissed by contemporary scholarship, nevertheless bear witness to the hermeneutical role they assumed for the superscriptions. Even though the new significations of these performative notes are difficult to ascertain, they may indicate the actualization of the psalm in various personal situations by aligning with the way of the righteous.[41] If that be the case, then the addition of למנצח + musical performance notes would indicate that the psalm is an aid to align one's life with God's work in the world.

For Pss 3–6, this sets up Ps 3 as the head of the cluster, functioning as a scene-setting psalm and helping develop the figure of David. Psalms 4–6 continue to use this same figure of David as their speaking persona, but also indicate that these psalms are to be learned and actualized by readers as songs of worship to Yhwh, and in imitation of the Davidic figure. As such, Ps 3 plays a key role in helping orient readers towards their reading of Pss 4–6.

The following table summarizes the superscriptions of Pss 3–6:

---

[41] Each musical element would need to be investigated individually in order to see if there is any further hermeneutical significance.

Ps 3	Ps 4	Ps 5	Ps 6
A Psalm of David. When he fled from Absalom his son.	For the leader. With strings. A Psalm of David.	For the leader. For the flutes. A Psalm of David.	For the leader. With strings. Upon the *sheminith.* A Psalm of David.
A song of worship offered to YHWH, spoken by the figure of David within the context of Absalom's rebellion in 2 Sam 15–18	*Recommended for encouragement and support, that one's life might be aligned with God's work in the world; a song of worship offered to YHWH, related to the figure of David*		

4.2.2. Dialogical Analyses of Pss 4–6

The following dialogic analyses of Pss 4–6 demonstrate that the figure of David continues to speak in the remaining psalms of the opening psalm cluster.

4.2.2.1. Dialogical analysis of Ps 4.　　The dialogical analysis of Ps 4 has several more twists and turns than were observed in Ps 3. The psalm can easily be split up into three different sections based on who is being addressed: YHWH (v. 2), the "sons of man" (vv. 3–6), and YHWH (vv. 7–9). Starting with verse two, the psalmist uses first-person singular references throughout, addressing his prayer explicitly to God using second-person reference. He describes his enemies as putting him "in distress [בצר]," using the same root for the adversaries themselves in 3:2 (צרי). Thematically, this has the result of picturing the psalmist as surrounded or boxed in (cf. 3:7). As in Ps 3, he seeks shelter from them by calling upon YHWH and expecting YHWH to answer him.

This dialogical situation changes in the second section (vv. 3–6). While the psalmist continues to use the first-person singular in reference to himself, YHWH is now referred to in the third person, and a group of people named the "sons of man" (בני איש) is addressed directly.[42] This locution is rare in the Old Testament, occurring only three other times (Ps 49:3; 62:10; Lam 3:33).[43] A clue to its meaning comes in Ps 49:2–3: "Hear this, all people! Give ear, all inhabitants of the world, the *sons of humanity* (בני אדם) and the *sons of man* (בני־איש), together the rich (עשיר) and the poor (אביון)." In this verse, there is a chiastic contrast between two groups of people: the "sons of humanity" paralleling "the poor" and "sons of man" paralleling the "rich." Independently, these groups are

---

[42] For another view, see Carleen Mandalfo, *God in the Dock: Dialogic Tension in the Psalms of Lament*, JSOTSup 357 (Sheffield: Sheffield Academic, 2002), 31–32. She has argued that verse three might be the voice of either the deity or the petitioner. In her view, there is a difference in didactic speeches referring to God in the third person (vv. 4a, 5–6) and the challenge given to the opponents.

[43] In contrast, the more common "sons of humanity" (בני אדם) occurs sixty-two times in the Psalter alone.

contrasted elsewhere (cf. Ps 62:10; Prov 8:4; Isa 2:9). Proverbs 8:4 proves to be especially helpful, showing that איש refers to a particular group of people, while אדם indicates broader humanity: "Unto you, O men (אישים), I will call, while my voice is to all humanity (בני אדם)." From this evidence, modern translations and commentaries agree that בני־איש is a specific reference to persons of "elevated social rank and position," the "influential members of society...who wield the power to affect the nature of communal life that the [בני אדם] must simply accept or endure."[44] The psalmist, then, is addressing those who have a certain power of influence over him, perhaps the wealthy who could accuse and condemn him before the people. This raises a question about our identification of the psalmist: if he is the figure of David, then in what sense might these "sons of man" have a status more elevated than the anointed king? I will return to this question later in the chapter.

The most difficult verse for dialogical analysis occurs in the final section (vv. 7–9), as a quotation is introduced in verse seven: "Many [רבים] are saying, 'Who will show us good [מי־יראנו טוב]? Lift upon us the light of your face, O Yʜᴡʜ!'" There are two issues with this quotation. First, it is attributed to "many" (רבים), so we need to identify whom is being referenced. Second, we need to determine the extent of the quotation. Does it include only one clause (v. 7b) or both remaining clauses in the verse (v. 7b–c)? In favor of the former view, the final clause maintains a first-person plural pronoun whereas verses eight and nine, which clearly belong to the psalmist, switch back to the first-person singular. On the other hand, one could imagine the psalmist picking up the first-person plural as a response to the first line of the quotation, especially if the "many" are considered his allies. Their identification, then, is critical.

In most studies, the "many" have been understood as either a group of people allied with the psalmist, but who are losing hope in their present situation, or as the same group of the "sons of man" addressed in verses 3–6.[45] The only clue in the text comes in verse eight, as the psalmist includes a plural pronominal suffix in describing "their corn and wine" (דגנם ותירושם). As Tremper Longman noted, the only masculine plural antecedent available is the "many" of verse seven.[46] Since the pronominal suffix in verse eight refers to the psalmist's enemies, the "many" must also refer to his enemies. Given this identification, we are also able to determine the extent of the quotation in verse seven, which naturally extends to the end of the verse based on the use of the plural pro-

---

[44] Gerald H. Wilson, *Psalms: Volume 1*, NIVAC (Grand Rapids: Zondervan, 2002), 152–53. See also Delitzsch, *Book of Psalms*, 113; C. A. Briggs and E. G. Briggs, *A Critical and Exegetical Commentary on the Book of Psalms*, ICC (Edinburgh: T&T Clark, 1906), 1:33; Kraus, *Psalms 1–59*, 148; Craigie, *Psalms 1–50*, 80.

[45] See, for instance, Craigie, *Psalms 1–50*, 81; Mays, *Psalms*, 56.

[46] Tremper Longman III, *Psalms*, TOTC (Downers Grove: InterVarsity, 2014), 68–69.

nouns. These "many" speak using a collective voice (first-person plural), petitioning YHWH for his blessings using phrases reminiscent of the priestly blessing from Num 6:24–26.[47]

In the remaining two verses (vv. 8–9), the psalmist begins to speak again, returning to first-person singular pronouns, and referring to YHWH using second-person pronouns. He uses the third-person plural once in verse eight, referring to his enemies.

4.2.2.2. Dialogical analysis of Ps 5.   Throughout Ps 5, the psalmist uses only the first-person singular to refer to himself and uses second- and third-person pronouns throughout the psalm to refer to YHWH and to other groups of people. A description of the nature of the wicked and the righteous is more pronounced in this psalm, bringing it into closer affiliation to Pss 1–2 than Pss 3–4.[48]

In the first section (vv. 2–3), he only refers to himself in the first-person singular, referring to God with second-person pronouns. No other groups of people are referred to in this opening section; rather, the psalmist uses imperatives and vocatives, pleading with YHWH to hear his prayer. The second section (vv. 4–8) follows suit, but here the psalmist refers to his opponents using the third-person: the "evil man" (v. 5), "the boastful" (v. 6), "workers of iniquity" (v. 6), "speakers of lies" (v. 7), and a "man of blood and deceit" (v. 7). Complementing this negative imagery, the speaker prays that YHWH would act in judgment against his enemies. Further, he prays that he would be able to enter the house of YHWH and worship in the fear of YHWH (v. 8). In the final section (vv. 9–13), he begins by mentioning the "waiting watchers" (v. 9), referring to them with third-person plural pronouns in the following verses (vv. 10–11). A second group of people is introduced in verse twelve, who rejoice in YHWH. They are also the referents of third-person pronouns throughout verses twelve and thirteen.

4.2.2.3. Dialogical analysis of Ps 6.   In Ps 6, the psalmist consistently uses first-person singular pronouns to refer to himself alone, and for most of the psalm uses second-person pronouns and vocatives to address YHWH. In the first section (vv. 2–4), he uses seven first-person singular pronouns to refer to himself, and a combination of four vocatives and three second-person singular pronouns to address his prayer to YHWH, at the same time using volitional verbs (with two negated and two positive imperatives). There are no third-person pronouns, and the closing question is very personal. It is clear, then, that this section is addressed to YHWH as prayer, and the psalmist is praying individualistically.

In the second section (vv. 5–6), while the pronouns remain largely the same, the rhetorical force changes, opening the psalm to broader reflection. In verse

---

[47] It re-uses the root "to lift" (נשׂא/נסה), shares a locative use of the preposition (אליך/עלינו), has a nominal form of the verbal root אור, and references the face (פנה) of YHWH.

[48] See Nancy L. deClaissé-Walford, Rolf A. Jacobson, and Beth LaNeel Tanner, *The Book of Psalms*, NICOT (Grand Rapids: Eerdmans, 2014), 92.

five, the dialogical situation is identical to the first section, but in verse six we can observe not only a topical change, but also a change in rhetoric. Still addressing Yʜᴡʜ with second-person pronouns, the speaker no longer uses the first person but indirectly speaks of his situation with a more generic view to the nature of humanity's relationship to Yʜᴡʜ. Importantly, the closing question includes a third-person reference to humanity at large (מִי), which matches a turn in the psalm towards addressing others.

In the third section (vv. 7–8), there are no second-person references, with only first-person pronouns. Thus, the addressees of this descriptive section are less clear. Is the psalmist continuing to describe his condition to Yʜᴡʜ, or has it changed to the "workers of iniquity," who become the addressees starting in verse nine? My inclination is to understand Yʜᴡʜ as the principal addressee, but the reference to "my adversaries" (צוֹרְרָי) at the end of verse eight shows that he may have more than Yʜᴡʜ in his mind. Perhaps his adversaries are present, indirectly addressed as they overhear his prayer to Yʜᴡʜ.

The final section (vv. 9–11) gives us a definite change in dialogical situation, signaled by a switch in vocative address, "Depart from me, all you workers of iniquity" (v. 9). Throughout verses nine and ten the speaker makes third-person references to Yʜᴡʜ, summarizing how Yʜᴡʜ has acted on his behalf, using first-person singular references for himself. In verse eleven, he switches the addressee back to the more ambiguous situation of verses seven and eight, using first-person singular pronouns for himself and no second-person pronouns. Notably, every third-person reference is made to his enemies. That Yʜᴡʜ is still being addressed is implied by Yʜᴡʜ being the primary actor to bring about what the psalmist prays for; but again, it could also be a rhetorical strategy in order to convince his enemies to also turn aside from him (v. 9).

In sum, Ps 6 is a strategically organized prayer which addresses both Yʜᴡʜ and the psalmist's enemies. His current situation is first described in terms of his relationship with Yʜᴡʜ, and the description of his weariness can be heard in relationship to this (vv. 7–8). At the same time, verses nine to eleven could indicate that his weariness (vv. 7–8) was brought about or escalated by the continued pressure of his enemies.

4.2.2.4. Dialogical analysis of the entire Pss 3–6 cluster. Given the consistent association with David in the psalm titles and first-person singular prayer throughout each psalm, I identify the speaking persona of the cluster with the same figure of David who speaks in Ps 3. Bringing the above dialogical analyses together, in this section I want to take note of how Pss 3–6 present the laments of David before Yʜᴡʜ and the third parties involved (whether they be friends, opponents, or simply onlookers).[49] Adding to the preceding discussion, I will build a profile

---

[49] See Gerald T. Sheppard, "Theology and the Book Psalms," *Int* 46 (1992): 145–47.

for the figure of David and the others by looking at the motivations underlying their sayings.[50]

In all four psalms, the figure of David is the only speaker, though at a few points he quotes speech made by others (3:3; 4:7). These quotations occur as David addresses Yʜᴡʜ, bringing to Yʜᴡʜ's attention the statements of his opponents. When he speaks in his own voice, he uses first-person singular pronouns. In most of the verses in Pss 3–6, David is speaking to Yʜᴡʜ directly in prayer, often using imperatives and vocative address (3:2–4, 8, 9b; 4:2, 7–9; 5:2–13; 6:2–6). For David, Yʜᴡʜ is a personal God (3:4, 8; 4:2, 4, 8, 9; 5:3, 4), hearing the prayers of his servants and answering them (3:5; 4:4; 5:4; 6:9–10), and providing safety and deliverance (3:6–7, 8–9; 4:2, 9; 5:12–13; 6:5). Yʜᴡʜ does not delight in wickedness of any kind (5:5–7), but leads his people in the way of righteousness (5:9). Yʜᴡʜ is the true king (5:3), a Judge (4:2; 5:11) who punishes the wicked (5:11) but blesses or grants favor to the righteous (3:9; 4:9; 5:12–13). He can discipline his servants (6:2–4) yet is sympathetic to their cries and anguish (4:2; 6:3, 10), perhaps even willing to change course for them (6:2–6). The steadfast love (חסד) of Yʜᴡʜ plays a significant role in these psalms (5:8; 6:5), even if Yʜᴡʜ does not act in accordance with the timing his people desire (6:4). These attributes and characteristics of Yʜᴡʜ fit well within the scope of Pss 1–2, affirming Yʜᴡʜ as one beyond the thoughts of his people as their King and Judge, yet as one who engages with them individually in personal terms, providing for them and hearing their prayers.

At several junctures, however, David addresses an audience other than Yʜᴡʜ. This should remind us that psalms of lament are not simply prayers directed by someone towards God but have a wider audience in mind. At times this audience is unclear or unnamed (3:5–7, 9a; 6:7–8, 11), but at other points particular groups of people are addressed with vocatives and imperatives (4:3–6; 6:9–10). In these latter cases, David identifies his opponents as the "sons of man" (בני איש; 4:3–6) and "all workers of iniquity" (כל־פעלי און; 6:9–10). Even though neither group is directly addressed in Pss 3 or 5, I have argued that the words of the "many" (רבים) in 4:7 can be identified with the "sons of man." Given the close connection between Pss 3–4, perhaps the "many" (רבים) who speak in 3:3 belong to the same group. Likewise, the "workers of iniquity" are also referred to in 5:6, providing a close connection between Pss 5–6.

Having summarized the speakers and addressees in Pss 3–6, I will now turn to how the various parties are described. Starting with the psalmist himself, throughout Pss 3–6 we are given a better glimpse of the ideal Davidic figure we were introduced to in Pss 1–2. The speaker is presented as a meditative and introspective man: he recalls his past relationship with Yʜᴡʜ (3:5; 5:2; 6:9–10), and

---

[50] For a similar investigation, see Friedhelm Hartenstein, "'Schaffe Mir Recht, JHWH!' (Psalm 7, 9): Zum Theologischen und Anthropologischen Profil der Teilkomposition Psalm 3–14," in *The Composition of the Book of Psalms*, ed. Erich Zenger, BETL 238 (Leuven: Peeters, 2010), 229–58 (esp. 242–47). See also Rendtorff, "The Psalms of David," 55–56.

he calls upon YHWH, expecting YHWH to answer him and act on his behalf (3:5; 4:2, 4; 5:2–4, 13; 6:2–6). He is not self-sufficient or self-reliant, but admits his weakness (6:2–4, 7–8), and is thoroughly dependent on the mercy of YHWH (4:2; 5:8; 6:5). Using a variety of images, he trusts in YHWH as his protector and sustainer (3:4, 6–7; 4:2, 9), as upholding his glory/honor (3:4; 4:3), as the one who lifts his head out of despair (3:4; 6:2–8), and as the one who is able to defeat his enemies and deliver him from his troubles (3:8–9; 4:2; 5:11–12; 6:4). Such faith places him in the company of the righteous (5:12–13), as he expresses his desire to walk in the righteous way of YHWH (5:9; cf. 4:5–6), worshipping YHWH with fear (5:8, 12; 6:5–6), and praying in concert with the Two Ways of Pss 1–2 (5:5–12). Moreover, throughout Pss 3–6 his social standing among his peers and before God reflects his leadership amongst his people. In 3:9, this is manifest in the direct connection between his deliverance from the multitude and the blessings poured out on God's people. It is also expressed in 4:4, as he refers to himself as a חסיד, a "holy one" whom God has especially set apart (פלה) for himself. The nature of his troubles, particularly in Ps 3, set up him up as an important leader within Israel.

Not much is made of David's allies, friends, or supporters in Pss 3–6. In fact, there is only one passage in these psalms that directly refers to them. In 5:12–13 we are introduced to a group of people called the "trusters" (כל־חוסי בך, cf. 2:12), who are mentioned in immediate contrast to the opponents of David (5:5–11). The fall of the wicked will cause this group to rejoice in YHWH, and David prays that YHWH would protect them (5:12). In 5:13, they are referred to as the righteous (צדיק), and David has confidence that YHWH will bless them (ברך), protecting them with favor (רצון) as a shield (כצנה; cf. 3:4, מגן). The only other possible reference to this group is in 3:9, when David prays that YHWH's blessing (ברכה) would be on his people (עם).

In contradistinction to David and the righteous are their opponents, who are given a variety of names in Pss 3–6. In Ps 3, they are referred to as "adversaries" (צרר), "people" (עם), "enemies" (איב), and "wicked ones" (רשעים). They have arisen against David in battle array (3:2, 7). In 3:3, the "many" (רבים) are quoted as saying, "There is no salvation for him in God." This statement is addressed to a public audience with the goal of discrediting and deriding David, boosting the growing popular support for those against him—Absalom and his party—with the hope that David would fold under social pressure.

In Ps 4, the specific group addressed is the "sons of man" (4:3–7). As discussed earlier, this group consisted of persons of high standing in Israelite society, likely in the ruling class and having both power and influence. They are criticized for treachery, not only for what they have said, but also for how they plot against David: "How long is my honor for shame? How long will you love an empty thing? How long will you seek a lie?" (4:3). Unafraid of YHWH, they give themselves license to sin more easily, plotting and scheming even in their beds (v. 5). If they sacrifice, their sacrifices are not made with an underlying trust in YHWH, but from a desire for gain and success (v. 6). Such an attitude is evident in the quotation of the "many" (רבים) in 4:7: "Who will show us some good? Lift up on us the light of your face, O YHWH!" Speaking as a collective whole ("us"), they make an appeal to YHWH recalling a variation of the priestly blessing from Num 6, as noted earlier. In their delusion, they expect that YHWH will provide for them. Given their depiction in 4:3–6, though, we are led to see their words in a negative connotation. Their pattern of life proves their intentions are not honorable, and the invocation of the priestly blessing is only made as if it were a magic. That they have success adds to David's anxiety about them (4:8): has YHWH, in fact, given them support?

In Ps 5, we have both generic descriptions of the wicked as well as mention of a specific group called the "watchers" (שוררי; 5:9). Their description is presented in the context of David referring to YHWH as a God who "does not delight in wickedness" (לא אל־חפץ רשע, v. 5). He labels the wicked as "evil" (רע), "boastful" (הוללים), "workers of iniquity" (פעלי און), "speakers of lies" (דברי כזב), and "men of blood and deceit" (איש־דמים ומרמה). As a whole, they are presented as the kinds of people with whom the presence of YHWH does not reside. The most developed picture of the wicked in Ps 5 is of those labeled "watchers" (5:9–11), who are presumably those waiting for him to slip up so that they can pounce on him. In 5:10 he demurs the nature of their speech: their mouths are unstable and full of destruction, like an opened grave (with death, rotting, and stinking), yet "smooth," making them all the more dangerous. In David's view they are guilty, and their transgressions are many, since they have rebelled against God (v. 11). As in Pss 3–4, David prays according to the Two Ways ideology of Pss 1–2. In the foreground of his prayers are the vocal aspects of their wickedness: deceitful speech and verbal abuse. In contrast, the righteous are described principally by their laudable verbal actions: David's own voice in prayer and praise (5:2–4, 8), and the rejoicing exultation of the righteous (5:12).

In Ps 6, we learn that YHWH's reproof and chastisement of David were felt principally through the provocation of his adversaries (בכל־צוררי; 6:8). He further identifies them in 6:9 as "all workers of iniquity" (כל־פעלי און; cf. 5:6) and "all my enemies" (כל־איבי; cf. 3:8). The nature of their provocation is not stated, but the intense impact it had on David shows that it must have been quite fierce and personal. In this psalm David does not call for their just punishment or destruction, but instead warns them of God's continued support of him (vv. 9b–10) and urges them to change their course (v. 11). This leads us to a surprising tendency in Pss 3–6 which is rarely recognized: while severe words are spoken about the destruction awaiting the wicked in 3:8 and 5:6b–7, we also have fervent calls of warning (5:5–6a; 6:9–10), that they might change their ways (4:3–6; 6:11). In fact, the punitive words of 5:6b–7 are qualified in 5:11 so that their punishment appears more as a coincidence of divine providence: the wicked falling into the traps of their own plotting and counsels. Like Pss 1–2, the actions of humanity can arouse both the rod of divine chastisement (2:9) and the rod of divine fury (2:11–12). The wicked, however, need not face divine punishment if they turn from their ways (2:10).

In addition to the foregoing analysis, we need to recognize that onlookers were present as these psalms would have been performed in ancient Israel. As

Derek Suderman noted, "Raising one's voice in lament not only calls on God to act but also invites social discernment and the response of the social 'other' to the speaker's claim.... Biblical lament frequently moves beyond an implicit sociological critique to an open social accusation and broader social appeal."[51] As such, laments "function rhetorically as warnings, threats, accusations, and appeals for empathy and support," and require "the attentive, discerning ear of those who hear or hear about these pained cries."[52] The onlookers, then, who are not directly addressed in these psalms, need to be recognized in how the psalms are communicated. Indeed, as readers of these texts, you and I are not simply innocent bystanders, but are also confronted by the language of the psalmist. Like the audiences who would have heard these psalms in ancient Israel and throughout the history of the synagogue and church, we too are called upon to choose sides, using our "discerning" hearts to help bring about the justice called for in the laments (or not, if that be our choice).

4.2.3. The Contextual Setting of Pss 4–6

Having made the case for a Davidic speaking persona in Pss 3–6, I will now use the superscription of Ps 3 to consider how they can be heard together as a complete unit connected by a shared biographical setting, Absalom's rebellion (2 Sam 15–18). Beyond their formal categorization as psalms of individual lament, or the possibility of a sequential day-night pattern anticipated by Ps 1:2,[53] each psalm has been linked together by an unbroken series of "hook-words" (*mots crochets*) or concatenation (*concatenatio*).[54] This creates continuity between the psalms and indicates that they were meant to be read in sequential order. This does not mean that their sequence should be understood as analogous to a narrative, as if each psalm were progressing through a story; rather, individual psalms have been juxtaposed to create a kind of clustered, prolonged reflection—a parallelism of sorts in which similar prayers are repeated with shared lexicons and themes. The aim of this "progression by psalm cluster" is to allow the reader an extended meditation on the kinds of prayers being offered. As will be seen, the assemblage of discrete psalms with a prior history betrays interests that were not necessarily against their original settings, but have now been allied with the larger concerns of their present canonical context—a context not

---

[51] Suderman, "The Cost of Losing Lament," 209.

[52] Suderman, "The Cost of Losing Lament," 209.

[53] See Barbiero, *Das Erste Psalmenbuch*, 68. Alongside many others, he notes that the theme of meditating on the Torah night and day finds implicit connection in the repetition of day-night psalms: day/morning (3:6), night/evening (4:9), day/morning (5:4), and night (6:7).

[54] Auwers, "Le David des psaumes," 207–8. See also Christoph Barth, "Concatenatio im ersten Buch des Psalters," in *Wort und Wirklichkeit: Studien zur Afrikanistik und Orientalistik*, ed. Brigitta Benzing (Meisenheim am Glan: Hain, 1976), 30–40; J. P. Brennan, "Psalms 1–8: Some Hidden Harmonies," *BTB* 10 (1980): 25–29.

interested in the cult for the sake of the cult, but in the construction of the figure of David.

4.2.3.1. The contextual setting of Ps 4.   Modern engagement with Ps 4 almost entirely hangs on our identification of the "sons of man" (vv. 3–6), the "holy one" (v. 4), and the "many" (v. 7). In the opinion of most, the language of the psalm indicates some form of false accusation against the speaking persona, and several iterations of the *Sitz im Leben* have been offered.

For Kraus, Ps 4 is concerned with an innocent, poor, and uninfluential person who has been "persecuted and accused," but "has had his rights restored through a divine verdict in the temple."[55] References to the act of sacrifice, the unwillingness of other parties to recognize God's verdict, and peaceful sleep all point to the scene of a divine court procedure within the precincts of the temple. Kraus considered it important that the psalm be heard after the divine verdict had been given, as the verdict itself was being attacked by those against the psalmist. Seybold, on the other hand, argued that the psalm had been borne out of individual living conditions (*individuellen Lebensverhältnissen*), and offers a glimpse at a personal healing experience (*persönlichen Heilserfahrung*). He thought it was offered by an asylum seeker who had taken up protection in the sanctuary in expectation of a verdict, rather than after (*contra* Kraus).[56] Against a juristic setting, Gerstenberger argued that we should read the psalm more in terms of its liturgical context. For him, the psalm was part of a complaint liturgy which attempted to counteract those who threatened the afflicted person (vv. 3–6).[57] The ceremony could be understood as a last-ditch effort for protection or for restoring an ill-fated member of the community.[58]

As we read the psalm, these theories can be quite helpful, especially in terms of its dialogical and social interactions. At the same time, Jacobson rightly warned against fixing a precise original setting based on nuanced interpretations of individual words or phrases.[59] Support for a generic juridical situation for the psalm, however, is supported by my foregoing analyses of the psalm. As I argued, the "sons of man" should be identified as persons of means and influence in Israelite society who are attempting to shame David's calling and its associated honor (כבוד; cf. 3:4; 4:3). The "honor" mentioned here is not simply the dignity afforded the psalmist as a human being or even the elevated dignity one might claim as part of the people of Israel; the psalmist is a particular חסיד with a unique (פלה) election (4:4). The speaking persona, then, cannot be just any Israelite. One of the only positions in ancient Israel which encompasses his standing in the community and special calling from Yhwh is that of kingship.

---

[55] Kraus, *Psalms 1–59*, 146–47; Frank-Lothar Hossfeld and Erich Zenger, *Die Psalmen, Vol. 1: Psalmen 1–50*, NechtB (Würzburg: Echter Verlag, 1993), 59.

[56] Seybold, *Die Psalmen*, 37–38.

[57] Gerstenberger, *Psalms: Part 1*, 56.

[58] Gerstenberger, *Psalms: Part 1*, 56–57.

[59] deClaissé-Walford, et al., *Book of Psalms*, 79. See also Craigie, *Psalms 1–50*, 79.

Not only are the obligations of kingship different from that of normal citizens within the covenant community (cf. Deut 17:14–20), but David alone is best suited to fit that role; he alone entered into a second covenant agreement with YHWH concerning the legacy of his line on the throne of Israel (cf. 2 Sam 7).

Given Ps 4's Davidic association and context immediately subsequent to Ps 3, it is worth considering whether Ps 3's biographical setting could also be at work in Ps 4. Beyond Absalom's position as son of the king, what stands out about the rebellion of Absalom is that he had both won over the hearts of the general population (2 Sam 14:28–15:6) and had surrounded himself with people of political significance. Perfectly suited to be called "sons of man," Absalom and his party not only attacked David's personal honor but also his royal and divine dignity as the anointed of YHWH. Moreover, there are several parallels between Pss 3–4. In Ps 3, we saw that the words of the "many" who had risen against David put YHWH's support of David into question (3:2–3), which cast doubt on the dignity or honor (כבוד) bestowed on him (3:4). Returning to my earlier question, who but the king's son, potentially next in line for the throne, could claim equal or higher status than his father, who was being derided as having lost favor with YHWH? Similarly, both psalms are concerned with an increase of his opponents, building off the root רבב (3:2; 4:8), and identify YHWH as the source of all deliverance and blessing (3:9), of one's safety and support (4:9). Indeed, amid his distress the speaker is able to experience the providential protection of YHWH (3:4) and can sleep easy (3:6; 4:9) in the joy and peace of YHWH (4:8–9). While his adversaries may petition YHWH to lift up his face upon them (4:7), the psalmist is the one whose head is raised up by YHWH (3:4) and, instead of lifting up his face on his enemies, YHWH strikes their faces in judgment (3:8).

Additionally, if David is identified with the הסיד of verse four, then we can make better sense of the previous verses in the psalm. As Mays observed:

> The psalm suggests a situation in which the psalmist has already appealed to God and been answered, probably in sacral proceedings, by a word or sign that God has identified and claimed the psalmist as one of the faithful (v. [4]) and by doing so has freed the one who prays from the constraints of distress (second line of v. [2]).[60]

Reviewing David's life in 2 Samuel, after his rapacious encounter with Bathsheba and subsequent murder of Uriah (2 Sam 11), the prophet Nathan put him on trial at the behest of YHWH (2 Sam 12:1). David admitted his guilt, and Nathan reported that YHWH had put away his sin (2 Sam 12:13). Yet the consequences of David's actions would have drastic effects on his family life, with Nathan's prophecy coming to fruition, in part, with the revolt of Absalom: "I will raise trouble against you from within your own house" (12:11; cf. 16:21–22). While Kraus was unwilling to apply his own observations to David, what he noted about the psalm fits this incident quite well:

---

[60] Mays, *Psalms*, 55.

Voice Without End

> As the "Sitz im Leben" we easily assume an experience in the tem-
> ple... an innocent person who has been persecuted and accused has
> had his rights restored through a divine verdict in the temple.... We
> must be dealing with highly placed, influential persons (v. [3]) who,
> even after the intervention of Yahweh has already taken place, do not
> cease to present their accusations (v. [3]) and probably also invent
> new arguments (v. [5]).[61]

Having already received the righteous verdict from Nathan, David was poised to
again lead Israel as their king, though numerous familial tragedies would come.

Even so, while one can coordinate much of the psalm to what we know of
David's life in 2 Samuel, there is not a full correspondence. In the narrative, Absalom's partisans show little concern that YHWH bless their pursuits (4:7), nor
does the narrative describe David experiencing the joy and peace described in
4:8–9 during the time of the revolt. Rather, we meet a downcast and dejected
David, a David resigned to whatever decision YHWH would make concerning his
destiny (2 Sam 16:11–12).[62] In my view this is a clue to understanding the role of
the Davidic figure in the psalm, and not an indication that the Absalom episode
is far from the words of the psalmist. The incongruences help to show that the
psalm is not meant to fill up a *lacuna* in the Davidic narratives, nor give us an
insight into David's mind during certain narrative episodes, but is making reference to the earlier narrative for its own configuring purposes. Semantic transformation, grounded in the biographical situation referenced in the superscription of Ps 3, allows the Davidic figure in Ps 4 to take on similar typical and typological extensions.

4.2.3.2. The contextual setting of Ps 5.   Psalm 5 has offered modern scholars much
in terms of intriguing details, so that speculation concerning its *Sitz im Leben* has
reached a closer consensus than in many other psalms. It bears a strong resemblance to that posited for Ps 4, and has been summarized well by Mays:

> The psalm may have been written for a person who was falsely ac-
> cused or slandered in a way that destroyed standing or rights in the
> community. The psalm would be prayed in the temple as a last resort
> to appeal to God as the final administrator of justice, looking for a
> vindicating answer through oracle or sign or event.[63]

In the opinion of most commentators, the psalmist has already gained access to
the temple court, and is ready to bring his sacrifice and await the judgment of
YHWH.[64] As several commentators have pointed out, though, caution should be
used even against the strong scholarly support of this view.

---

[61] Kraus, *Psalms 1–59*, 146.
[62] See Rendtorff, "The Psalms of David," 56.
[63] Mays, *Psalms*, 58.
[64] See Delitzsch, *Book of Psalms*, 122; Briggs, *Psalms Volume I*, 38; Weiser, *Psalms*, 123;
Kraus, *Psalms 1–59*, 153; Seybold, *Die Psalmen*, 39.

Gerstenberger, for instance, observed that the temple in Jerusalem could not have served as the only juridical location in ancient Israel: "In reality, particular services supported by primary groups and special cult officials (priests; men of God; prophets) must have been conducted in many places throughout ancient Israel (cf. 1 Sam 1; 2 Kgs 23:8–13)."[65] Likewise, Craigie observed that the future indicative verb sequence in 5:8 does not assume that the speaker was already at the temple but expresses his confidence that he would be able to worship in the future. This, too, would alter one's conception of the original situation. Moreover, while the psalmist does describe the wicked as liars (v. 7) and as having no truth in their mouths (v. 10), he "never claims to have been accused or to be innocent" but "simply asserts that the wicked speak lies."[66] Jacobson suggested cautiously—following Broyles's idea that the wicked are described not as using accusatory words but "enticing and tempting" ones—that we forego the attempt to describe an original setting and read the psalm as a "prayer counterpart" to Pss 1, 15, and 24.[67] This suggestion complements my own concern to show how Pss 3–6 resonate Pss 1–2, but goes too far by completely disengaging with the modern discussion of the psalm's pre-history. Again, I call your attention to semantic transformation, as the pre-scriptural use of the psalm has been reconfigured under a Davidic persona in the canonical text. The life of David, and not the cultic traditions of ancient Israel, have been utilized by the editors of the Psalms to provide the means for later generations of God's people to plead with YHWH for his providential justice. For the editors, the presence of YHWH manifest within David's life is a beneficent well of life and healing. By uniting David's story with the psalm, they make room for fruitful imitation of the figure of David.

Among those who see a link between Ps 5 and the life of David, Franz Delitzsch argued that the psalm must have been written prior to the rebellion of Absalom, when the "fire which afterwards broke forth was already smoldering in secret."[68] This would place the context at the beginning of 2 Sam 15. Alternatively, Michael Wilcock has taken seriously the sequence of morning and evening in Pss 3–5, arguing that in Ps 5 David awakes for a second time during the rebellion, but now with a better and larger perspective on the matter. For him, the intrigues of Absalom (2 Sam 15:1–12) and the destruction proposed by Ahithophel (2 Sam 16:23–17:4) are enough to show how the words of the wicked can be used to destroy the righteous.[69] While these suggestions are thought-provoking, a better biographical setting can be found by considering the juristic context proposed in the historical-critical discussion. The scene in 2 Sam 16:5–

---

[65] Gerstenberger, *Psalms: Part 1*, 60. To this, we can add from the Absalom narrative (2 Sam 15) and elsewhere that city gates were prominent places to hear cases.

[66] deClaissé-Walford, et al., *Book of Psalms*, 90–91.

[67] deClaissé-Walford, et al., *Book of Psalms*, 91–92.

[68] Delitzsch, *Book of Psalms*, 119.

[69] Michael Wilcock, *The Message of Psalms 1–72: Songs for the People of God* (Downers Grove: InterVarsity, 2001), 30. See also Millard, *Die Kompositions des Psalters*, 131–32.

13 would work, provided one allows for an adaptation of the typical juristic setting at the temple (cf. 1 Kgs 8:31–32) into a broader narrative setting as an example of semantic transformation.

In this well-known scene, David and his partisans are fleeing Jerusalem
when Shimei approaches them, cursing and throwing stones (16:6). He shouts
that David should be driven out of the city, believing him to be a murderer,
scoundrel, and usurper (16:7–8). Connecting the narrative to the psalm, Shimei
uses the phrase "man of blood" (אישׁ דמים), which occurs in only these two places
in the Old Testament (Ps 5:7; 2 Sam 16:8). And, at the pivotal moment, while his
men almost prove the charge to be true, David forces restraint: "My own son
seeks my life; how much more now may this Benjaminite! Let him alone, and let
him curse; for Yhwh has bidden him. It may be that Yhwh will look on my distress, and Yhwh will repay me with good for this cursing of me today" (16:11–
12). If Yhwh looks upon his distress and gives him victory, then Shimei's curse
will prove untrue and David will be vindicated; but, if the opposite occurs, then
perhaps Yhwh did indeed bid Shimei to curse him. In this case, David does not
view Yhwh's courtroom as the temple precincts or even the city gates (cf. 2 Sam
15:1–6), but the outcome of the rebellion itself: "Hold them accountable, O God!
Let their own plans be their downfall; because of their many transgressions
drive them out, for they have rebelled against you" (Ps 5:11). As such, the psalm's
biographical context has opened it up for a much broader application than a
historical-critical *Sitz im Leben* supposes, and may offer clues as to how psalms
could be adapted for secondary use.

The major impediment to this understanding of the psalm's setting, however, is the reference to worship at Yhwh's house (בית) and holy temple (היכל-
קדשׁך) in Ps 5:8.[70] In the narrative, even though David was vindicated by his victory over Absalom, he never returned to Jerusalem to worship Yhwh. Instead,
he took his place at the gates of Mahanaim and grieved the death of his son (2
Sam 19:1–8). Moreover, even after his return to Jerusalem, there is never a word
about worshipping Yhwh in the context of Absalom's rebellion; the next time
David seeks the presence of Yhwh is within the context of famine (2 Sam 21:1).
Such incongruences again show us that the intertextual link is not meant to give
us a privileged glimpse into David's mind, but further configure the voice of the
Davidic figure in typical and typological directions.

4.2.3.3. The contextual setting of Ps 6.   Within the history of interpretation, we find
two very different readings of Ps 6. As representative of the premodern period,
we can look to Theodore of Mopsuestia and John Calvin. Theodore thought of Ps
6 as David's confession of his sins against Bathsheba and Uriah, especially in

---

[70] See Delitzsch, *Book of Psalms*, 122–25. These terms would only be anachronistic if
used for the permanent temple complex built by Solomon. However, within the narrative of 2 Samuel, David sacrifices at the tent of meeting (2 Sam 6:17–18), which the nar-
rator calls the בית יהוה (2 Sam 12:20). At stake, then, is not the terminology used, but the
referent and the narrative setting.

view of the misfortunes which arose because of them, including Absalom's rebellion. He wrote: "Blessed David confesses to God his own sin, committed when he slept with Bathsheba. He recites it when in difficulties, by which he was also tested on account of his sin."[71] Likewise, over a millennium later, Calvin understood the psalm within the context of David's life: "David, being afflicted by the hand of God, acknowledges that he had provoked the Divine wrath by his sins, and, therefore, in order to obtain relief, he prays for forgiveness."[72] This is followed by a longer reflection on what in David's life would have led to this kind of psalm:

> The life of David was in the utmost danger, but it may have been some other kind of affliction than bodily sickness under which he labored. We may, therefore, adopt this as the more certain interpretation, that he had been stricken by some severe calamity, or that some punishment had been inflicted upon him, which presented to his view on every side only the shadow of death.[73]

For both Theodore and Calvin, the crucial point is that Ps 6 is a psalm of confession for sins committed in the face of imminent danger and affliction.

Despite the longstanding Christian tradition of reading Ps 6 as a penitential psalm, most modern commentators have pointed out that there is no explicit confession of sin; rather, the psalm should be understood as a prayer used by a sick person for healing.[74] The temple in Jerusalem is taken as the setting, where the supplicant would have come to recite the psalm in order to obtain some kind of assurance that his prayer had been answered.[75] Gerstenberger gave a description representative of this modern view:

> We can easily picture the circumstances in which the prayer was used. A man had fallen ill. He and his family tried all sorts of remedies, to no avail. Finally, they turned to the ritual expert, the liturgist, who knew and owned the proper prayers and rites to heal a sick man. He would prepare and conduct a service or incantation for the ailing person, and the immediate family of the patient would participate in

---

[71] Theodore of Mopsuestia, *Commentary on Psalms 1-81*, trans. Robert C. Hill, SBLWGRW 5 (Atlanta: SBL, 2006), 63. See also Diodore of Tarsus, *Commentary on Psalms 1-51*, trans. Robert C. Hill, SBLWGRW 9 (Atlanta: SBL, 2005), 19; Theodoret of Cyrus, *Commentary on the Psalms: Psalms 1-72*, trans. Robert C. Hill, FOC 101 (Washington, DC: Catholic University of America Press, 2000), 74.

[72] John Calvin, *Commentary on the Book of Psalms*, trans. J. Anderson, 5 vols (Edinburgh: Calvin Translation Society, 1845), 1:65.

[73] Calvin, *Commentary on the Book of Psalms*, 1:65.

[74] See Mays, *Psalms*, 59; Kraus, *Psalms 1-59*, 161; Hossfeld and Zenger, *Psalmen 1-50*, 56.

[75] See Weiser, *Psalms*, 130, 133.

> it. The healing ritual probably consisted of a sacrifice or offering...
> and, most important, a prayer to be recited by the patient himself.[76]

After becoming part of the collection of written psalms, Gerstenberger surmised, the psalm could be used in more situations than formal worship.

Notwithstanding the speaker's complaint about his spiritual and physical anguish, this reconstruction of the *Sitz im Leben* does not account for the role played by his enemies in verses nine through eleven, who are at least partially the source of his grief. Their presence in the psalm brings it closer to what we have seen in Pss 3–5.[77] As such, we must seek to understand the psalm as a whole, not merely one part (vv. 1–6) or the other (vv. 9–11). Given the superscription's association with the figure of David and its grouping within Pss 3–6, the canonical context provides a middle way between premodern and modern interpretations, focusing on the sins of David against Bathsheba and Uriah, while also making room for David's enemies within the rebellion of Absalom.[78]

Wilcock has made this argument most explicitly.[79] He began by noting certain interlocking tensions in the psalm as underlying the speaker's anguish, the first concerning his sin (vv. 2, 3, 10) and the second concerning the malice of his enemies (vv. 8, 9–11). Additionally, the speaker is threatened with death (v. 6) and undergoes emotional turmoil (vv. 7–8) but is suddenly renewed with confidence (vv. 9–11). For him, these puzzle pieces fall into place by considering the heading of Ps 3 as it applies across Pss 3–6. The contribution of Ps 6 in the sequence is that it allows the reader into the mind of David, who understands his son's rebellion as a result of his own "sinful mismanagement of his family and his kingdom."[80] At issue is not whether David was the actual author of the psalm, but that the title of Ps 6 "puts into words the traumatic experience of one servant of God, and it has been preserved for others to make it their own."[81] Semantic transformation is again operative, allowing the figure of David to take on more than a biographical profile.

For such a reading to hold, one must offer more than thematic resemblance to connect the psalm to this specific episode of David's life. In my opinion, we have evidence for this setting by tracing out some lexical connections, but most are common words. As such, they must be weighed as a whole. First, the root חנן is used in Ps 6 as David both prays for and acknowledges receiving mercy (vv. 3, 10). While a very common root in the Old Testament, it is used only twice in the Davidic narratives of Samuel: in the context of the death of his first son with

---

[76] Gerstenberger, *Psalms: Part 1*, 62.

[77] See Goldingay, *Psalms 1–41*, 135; Delitzsch, *Book of Psalms*, 130.

[78] Even in the Deuteronomistic History itself, the only sin of David mentioned is concerned with Bathsheba and Uriah: "David did what was right in the sight of the Lord, and did not turn aside from anything that he commanded him all the days of his life, except in the matter of Uriah the Hittite" (1 Kgs 15:5).

[79] Wilcock, *Psalms 1–72*, 31–34.

[80] Wilcock, *Psalms 1–72*, 32–33.

[81] Wilcock, *Psalms 1–72*, 34.

Bathsheba (2 Sam 12:22); and within Absalom's rebellion, as David expresses his
hope of returning to Jerusalem and worshipping before the ark of the covenant:
"If I find favor (חֵן) in Yʜᴡʜ's sight, he will bring me back and enable me to see
both it and his dwelling place again" (2 Sam 15:25). Second, in Ps 6:7 David expresses his weariness (יגע), a weariness which is anticipated by the advice of
Ahithophel to Absalom during the rebellion (2 Sam 17:1–3):

> I will set out and pursue David tonight. I will come upon him while
> he is weary (יגע) and discouraged, and throw him into a panic; and all
> the people who are with him will flee. I will strike down only the king,
> and I will bring all the people back to you as a bride comes home to
> her husband. You seek the life of only one man, and all the people
> will be at peace.

This connection is not only fitting for the speaker's weariness and inner turmoil
in the psalm, but also the fault attributed to his enemies (vv. 8, 9–11). In fact, the
weary tears poured out nightly on his bed (Ps 6:7) are manifest at a number of
points throughout the story of Absalom's rebellion, such as when David flees
from Jerusalem (2 Sam 15:30) and as he mourns for Absalom after his death
(19:1). Finally, a third lexical connection occurs during the scene where Shimei
curses David, which we already highlighted above for Ps 5. During this scene
David remarks, "Perhaps Yʜᴡʜ will look upon my punishment (עָוֺן) and recom-
pense me (שׁוּב)." In the psalm, I would point to the speaker's concern over the
nature of God's chastisement and discipline (6:2), as well as the use of שׁוּב in
respect to Yʜᴡʜ (6:5).

Given these links, it is intriguing to hear the psalm with the sinful episode
against Bathsheba in the background, as well as the fact that David's opponents
might still be hounding him because of it. The plotting of Ahithophel and cursing of Shimei hold much of the psalm together. Yet, Shimei's criticism against
David is not related to the episode with Bathsheba in 2 Sam 11–12, but to the
taking away of the throne from Ishboseth in 2 Sam 5 (cf. 16:7–8). There are, then,
two perspectives to keep in mind. The first is David's, in which his current falling
away from favor has to do with the consequences of his sins, even though it had
been "put away" through Nathan's pronouncement (12:13); and the other, the
populace, who view his entire political career as one of murder and scandal, un-
doubtedly including Uriah. In Ps 6, then, we find a David who has no need to
continue to plead his innocence, but to plead for his rescue and deliverance. He
asks that Yʜᴡʜ's righteous chastisement—which was prophesied by Nathan—be
turned into healing for him, his family, and his kingdom; and that the faction of
iniquity-workers be turned away from him, recognizing the agony and weight
his sins have wrought upon them all, in submission to the rule of Yʜᴡʜ.

Even so, the psalm and the narrative are not completely congruous. In the
narrative, the rising up of Absalom and his party is rather sudden, leaving little
time for David to prepare for his flight from Jerusalem. In the psalm, however,
the speaker is troubled by a chastisement that seems to have lasted for quite
some time: "But you, O Yʜᴡʜ—how long?" (6:4). As before, incongruences are

not signs that the narrative background is meaningless, but that the Psalter is using the narrative for its configuration of the Davidic figure.

4.2.4. *Summative Remarks on Pss 3–6*

In my analyses of all four psalms I have argued that the context of Absalom's rebellion (2 Sam 15–18), especially connected with Nathan's oracle following David's trial (2 Sam 12:7–15), provides ample narrative space in which to hear a Davidic persona speaking. At the same time, I have also pointed out that while there are numerous correspondences between a psalm and this narrative, incongruences are present. Rather than throwing out the Davidic association, I have argued that the incongruences lead us into a deeper theological reflection.

Taken together, Pss 3–6 give us a "clustered" reflection on the figure of David within this biographical setting, allowing the reader an extended meditation on the kinds of prayers being offered. Indeed, as Auwers has observed: "The words of such-and-such psalm hear an echo in the next and the impression is created that it is the same voice that is expressed throughout the psalms."[82] We have discovered that the sequential movement through the cluster is not organized chronologically, but in a kind of parallelism. Ps 3 provides the "rule" or organizing principle, orienting the reader for what to expect in the remaining psalms. The biographical superscription sets the agenda, asking its readers to consider these psalms through the lens of David's flight from Absalom in 2 Sam 15–18. Psalms 4–6, for their part, work in parallel with Ps 3, inviting readers to ponder David's response to these situations in his life, that they might place these prayers upon their own lips, appropriating them in their own lives.

Methodologically, reading and praying psalms in this way requires a recognition of the editorial work lying behind the final form of the Psalter. While the prior use of a psalm in its original cultic setting lies in the background, and may even have played an important part in connecting the psalm to the life of David, as it stands in the text of the Psalter, it has taken on a Davidic lens as a consequence of its canonical placement. In other words, whatever may have been true of Pss 3–6 in their original situation, they have now been given an intended Davidic voice through their sequence and juxtaposition, as well as their literary setting under the biographical superscription of Ps 3 and within the Psalter's introduction (Pss 1–2). In this light, the lack of congruence between a psalm and the narrative is due to this changing of context, from *cult* to *canon*. Psalms with an originally generic or cultically confined character have been reassessed and semantically transformed by means of arrangement and superscripting as coming principally from the voice of the figure of David. While this leaves Pss 3–6 with a somewhat untidy fit to the narratives of 2 Samuel, they fit tightly with the developing portrait of the Davidic figure under the pressure of Pss 1–2. In fact, the untidiness itself has allowed for a figural extension of the Biographical David into typical and typological directions.

---

[82] Auwers, "Le David des psaumes," 208. My own translation.

4.3. The Development of the Figure of David in Psalms 3–6

My earlier survey of the history of interpretation discussed how premodern interpreters understood the role of David in several different ways. Within prosopological approaches, David was understood prophetically, authoring psalms which would be spoken and actualized by later figures in history without any need for correspondence in David's own life. Typological approaches, on the other hand, found correspondence between the person of David and the person of Jesus Christ, so that both David and Christ could be heard speaking at the same time. In the contemporary recovery of the Davidic voice in the Psalms, constructions of the figure of David have incorporated insights from prosopological and typological exegesis. My own proposal for the construction of the Davidic figure is both similar and different, illustrated well by the models proposed by Alan Cooper and James Mays.[83] Both have identified a threefold voice for David, from Jewish and Christian perspectives, respectively.

For Cooper, the Davidic persona is "malleable" and can be summarized in three general types which align temporally with past, present, and future constructions. He wrote:

> The "David" of the Psalms is both a king of yore and the longed-for Messiah, signifying past and future orientations that are reified in historical/biographical readings and prophetic/eschatological interpretations, respectively. In addition, "David" comes to signify the Everyman of the present. The vicissitudes and triumphs of this third "David," then, represent the life experiences of any reader who chooses to identify with them. Sometimes... David's experience is exemplary for the reader, and sometimes the reader's identity effectively substitutes for David's.[84]

In this understanding of the Davidic persona, one can observe typical and typological nuances. Typologically, the past and future royal voices are connected as one pairs biographical readings with prophetic or eschatological interpretations. Similarly, the Davidic voice is understood typically as an "Everyman" of the present, through which David's biographical experience is exemplary for anyone who reads and prays the Psalms.

Mays has also argued for a threefold function of David in the Psalms, but emphasized that this was not a product of later interpretation. The Psalter itself creates a composite identity using the figure of David which, when combined with poetic idioms and typical features, creates "a persona intentionally open

---

[83] Alan Cooper, "On the Typology of Jewish Psalms Interpretation," in *Biblical Interpretation in Judaism and Christianity*, ed. Isaac Kalimi and Peter J. Haas, LHBOTS 439 (London: T&T Clark, 2006), 79–90; James L. Mays, *The Lord Reigns: A Theological Handbook to the Psalms* (Louisville: Westminster John Knox, 1994), 46–54.

[84] Cooper, "On the Typology of Jewish Psalms Interpretation," 80.

to use by different and successive persons."[85] He explained the threefold voice of David as three different ways of prayer: (1) as Christological and not just autobiographical, in that the words of the psalms "witness to the identification of Christ with our humanity"; (2) as corporate and not just individual, using the psalms "as the voice of the community and of others in it in vicarious representative supplication"; and (3) as typical instead of subjective, using the psalm to "create a consciousness of who and what we are, rather than as expressions of a consciousness already there."[86] In contrast to Cooper's "malleable" David, Mays has argued for a construal of David which begins with a Christological voice and then moves towards both corporate and typical voices.

My own contribution towards conceptualizing the Davidic identity of the speaking persona, then, is not by any means "new." Indeed, one of my aims in reviewing the history of interpretation was to show that the pressure of the canonical text has consistently been felt throughout history. What originality there might be comes in locating the configuration of the Davidic figure as part of the stage-setting role of Pss 1–2 in conjunction with the biographical superscriptions. With Mays, my own understanding of the Davidic persona in Pss 3–6 is built by paying attention to how the Psalter itself has sought to construct and develop the function and role of the figure of David. I differ from his model in that my Davidic figure is constructed primarily using Pss 1–2. They put forward the images of the "Blessed Man" (1:1), the Anointed of Yhwh (2:3), and the Son enthroned on Mount Zion (2:6–7) as joint figures united under the same Davidic persona. This "David" can speak with a threefold voice: (1) typically as the ideal, exemplary king of Israel (1:1–3); (2) historically as the anointed king of Yhwh (Ps 2); and (3) typologically, as David himself finds correspondence with his promised heir (Ps 2:7; 2 Sam 7). Likewise, with Cooper I will argue for a threefold understanding of the Davidic persona in Pss 3–6 along similar past, present, and future orientations. I differ in that my proposal is not temporal, but results from the introduction of the biographical superscription in Ps 3. This further links the historical David to certain episodes in his life, on which the typical and typological voices can be mapped in a more focused direction. The resulting figure of David can be understood in a threefold model: (1) a Biographical David, (2) a Typical David, and (3) a Typological David.

4.3.1. *The Biographical David*

The first "David" we encounter in Pss 3–6 is the David introduced by the biographical superscription to Ps 3, the "David" we know from 2 Sam 15–18 who fled Jerusalem when his son Absalom rebelled against him. As Michael Fishbane explained, this kind of superscripting brings into association two disparate contexts, a process which coordinates "distinct traditions" in a manner that does

---

[85] Mays, *The Lord Reigns*, 49.
[86] Mays, *The Lord Reigns*, 50.

not "harmonize, transform, or otherwise obscure them."[87] The result is that the voice of David can be heard inner-biblically, and, for some, may help fill in *lacunae* of the narrative traditions.[88] In this vein, as Childs noted, by creating this biographical link readers are "given access to previously unknown information," hearing David's "intimate thoughts and reflections."[89] In terms of Pss 3–6, the link to 2 Sam 15–18 allows these psalms to be heard as "a Midrash to an important chapter of David's history: a chapter of persecution and danger, but also of final divine help."[90] As I showed during my contextual analyses, each the four psalms finds strong correspondence with the narrative account of Absalom's rebellion, allowing the psalm to be read with that narrative context.[91] Nevertheless, incongruences led me to propose that the intertextual link is not meant to provide missing details in the narrative but functions to sharpen the Davidic profile in the Psalter.

Gerald Wilson, for instance, highlights one of the problems with a purely historical reading. He argued that the biographical superscriptions inhibited the application of psalms into one's personal life by so fixing the setting that they further distanced readers from the text.[92] In fact, he went so far as to say that the psalms "included in the canonical collection were chosen (for the most part) precisely *because* they were not so tied to specific historical situations as to inhibit their appropriation and application in any day and age."[93] The shape of the final form, then, would speak against the appropriation of these psalms, at least the ones with biographical details. Such a view is only accurate, however, if the only reason for the superscriptions was to historicize a psalm within the life of David. Indeed, Karl-Heinz Bernhardt has commented, "The editor is obviously not so much concerned about giving the impression of an exact historical fact by means of a historicizing title; rather, he wants to find a situation taken from the history of his people, a place in the history of election, from which the psalm may always be understood."[94] In this perspective, the concrete setting was only one of many which illustrated how this psalm could have been heard. But again, if the editor(s) of the Psalter could have supplied *any* setting within the narrative traditions of Israel, then why did they only choose settings within the life

---

[87] Michael Fishbane, *Biblical Interpretation in Ancient Israel* (Oxford: Clarendon, 1985), 404–7.

[88] See also Vivian L. Johnson, *David in Distress: His Portrait in the Historical Psalms*, LHBOTS 505 (London: T&T Clark, 2009); N. H. Tur-Sinai, "The Literary Character of the Book of Psalms," in *Oudtestamentische Studiën VIII*, ed. P. A. H. de Boer (Leiden: Brill, 1950), 263–81.

[89] Childs, "Psalm Titles," 150.

[90] Rendtorff, "The Psalms of David," 55.

[91] See also Brennan, "Psalms 1–8," 28.

[92] Wilson, *Psalms: Volume 1*, 128.

[93] Wilson, *Psalms: Volume 1*, 128.

[94] Karl-Heinz Bernhardt, *Das Problem der altorientalischen Königsideologie im Alten Testament*, VTSup 8 (Leiden: Brill, 1961), 11. [quoted in Kraus, *Psalms 1–59*, 139.]

of David? And why select so few with this purpose in mind? This suggests that for the editor(s) of the Psalter, no other biographical setting besides a Davidic one would have been appropriate for their purpose of including them.

At an initial level, then, it is important to tease out the significance of a biographical Davidic voice in Pss 3–6. According to Mays, one of the main reasons is that in David we meet not only the up-and-coming figure who must fight the powers that be to fulfill his calling, but also a David who fails magnificently, displaying penitence before YHWH and his people. He wrote:

> [These] psalms cumulatively identify and elaborate one dimension of his story. They all concern situations of need and the deliverance of the Lord as its resolution. They are either prayers for salvation or praise for salvation from trouble or songs of trust on the part of one who must and can live in the face of trouble in reliance on God.[95]

The Biographical David, then, provides readers with a rich understanding of the speaking persona in Pss 3–6. At a ground level, hearing these psalms inner-biblically with 2 Sam 15–18 provides readers a context to hear the psalm within a concrete narrative setting. Botha and Weber describe this effect well: "David is depicted as the person after the heart of God whose prayer and trust become exemplary."[96] More, he is depicted "as someone who prayed with great fervour and who was sure of the answer of YHWH," "as someone who could draw from his earlier experiences of triumph and consequently put his trust in YHWH."[97] Again, the goal is not to fill up something missing in the narrative, but to allow David's portrait from the narrative to provide depth to the profile of the Davidic figure in the Psalter.

This aspect of the Davidic persona might help to make sense of the larger concerns of the book. As I noted in the first chapter, Gerald Wilson's seminal work *The Editing of the Hebrew Psalter* set off a storm of psalm scholarship which sought to comprehend the editorial purpose which underlies the final form of the book. Wilson argued that the Davidic promises come to the fore of the discussion when we look at the so-called "seams" or divisions of Books 1–3, where royal psalms are found (Pss 2, 41, 72, 89). Moreover, he observed that they move through a progression of thought regarding kingship and the Davidic covenant. Ps 2 introduces the idea of covenant and finds resonances with Pss 41 and 72: "The covenant which YHWH made with David (Ps 2) and in whose promises David rested secure (Ps 41) is now passed on to his descendants in this series of petitions on behalf of 'the king's son' (Ps 72)."[98] Ps 89, however, introduces a new perspective. While admitting that hope remained alive for David's dynasty in view of YHWH's steadfast love, Wilson concluded that Ps 89 effectively declares

---

[95] James L. Mays, "The David of the Psalms," *Int* 40 (1986): 151.
[96] Botha and Weber, "Killing Them Softly," 287.
[97] Botha and Weber, "Killing Them Softly," 295.
[98] Wilson, *The Editing of the Hebrew Psalter*, 211.

that the vision of David in Ps 2 has "come to nothing"; it is "a covenant failed."[99] From here, as the Psalter progresses into Books 4–5 a new vision for the future of Israel is unveiled, one which rests resolutely on the mercy of YHWH. Book 4 never pleads for YHWH to live up to his covenant obligations concerning David, but instead turns the table on the Israelites themselves, closing with a plea for the restoration of the exilic community (Ps 106). This central turn is carried into Book 5, which tells those in the *diaspora* that deliverance is dependent on an attitude of reliance and trust in YHWH.[100] In Wilson's understanding of the book, the Psalter envisions a future ambivalent to a Davidic king and encourages Israel to look to YHWH alone.

While Wilson's view has won wide support, some scholars have argued for a different understanding of this movement throughout the book.[101] In their view, the answers given in Books 4–5 to the questions posed in Ps 89 affirm a future for David. Jamie Grant's summary of his position can be considered representative:

> The intent of the editors of the final form of the Psalms was not that readers should reject the Davidic king and the centrality of Zion, in favour of commitment to the rule of Yahweh and hope of his eschatological kingdom. Rather, they were pointing the reader towards the *reinterpretation* of the concepts of kingship and Zion in the light of a future realisation of Yahweh's rule and plan in the figure of a restored Davidic leader. If there is any degree of corrective going on, it is for those who despair at the loss of the Davidic monarchy—Book IV assures them that Yahweh's reign continues, and Books IV and V point towards a new Davidic reign and a restored Zion.[102]

Within this larger question of the Davidic promises, the bulk of Books 1–2 have been largely neglected. Psalms 3–6, in my opinion, offer a great deal more insight into this issue than previous scholarship has led us to think: the rebellion of the sons of David—not just his dynasty, but his very own son—is a central concern from the beginning of the book. The prayer expressed at the end of Book 3 could easily be prayed by David in the context of Absalom's rebellion: "Remember, O Lord, the reproach of your servants, my bearing in my bosom all the multitudinous peoples, with which your enemies have reproached, O YHWH,

---

[99] Wilson, *The Editing of the Hebrew Psalter*, 213.

[100] Wilson, *The Editing of the Hebrew Psalter*, 227.

[101] See David C. Mitchell, *The Message of the Psalter: An Eschatological Programme in the Book of Psalms*, JSOTSup 252 (Sheffield: Sheffield Academic, 1997); Mitchell, "Lord, Remember David: G. H. Wilson and the Message of the Psalter," *VT* 56 (2006): 526–48; David M. Howard, *The Structure of Psalms 93–100* (Winona Lake: Eisenbrauns, 1997), 200–7; Mays, *The Lord Reigns*, 125; Jamie A. Grant, *The King as Exemplar: The Function of Deuteronomy's Kingship Law in the Shaping of the Book of Psalms*, AcBib 17 (Atlanta: SBL, 2004), 33; Witt, "Hearing Psalm 102 within the Context of the Hebrew Psalter," 582–606.

[102] Grant, *King as Exemplar*, 36.

with which they reproached the footsteps of your anointed" (Ps 89:51–52). Perhaps we are not meant to wait until Book 4 to receive instruction on the status of the Davidic covenant. It may be that the figure of David is already giving us the perspective of the book's editors, to continue to trust in Yʜᴡʜ for the deliverance of his anointed, perhaps even the resuscitation of the Davidic dynasty from its death at the hands of Babylon. The pairing of Absalom at the beginning of Book 1 (Ps 3) with Solomon at the end of Book 2 (Ps 72) shows that the promises made to David, and the responses of his heirs, are critical to the concern of these books. Moreover, the prayer of David in Ps 72, echoing the concerns of Ps 2, invites a sharp contrast regarding the two sons of David: one is a rebel and a threat to the dynastic promises, while the other embodies dynastic hope.

As I have recognized throughout this chapter, while there are certain degrees of correspondence between the psalm and the story, the incongruities remind us that the purpose of inner-biblical coordination is to bring the narratives of 1–2 Samuel to bear on the development of the figure of David in the Psalms. That is, the incongruities are signs that the biographical link is to be heard within the broader concerns of Pss 1–2. My proposal is that this presses the Davidic voice in two further directions. First, David is extended as a typical, representative figure to be identified with by the reader such that one is "held in continuity with David and in relation to David's God."[103] And second, David is extended typologically in connection with Ps 2, such that the biographical connection to 2 Sam 15–18 can be read typologically as what would also be experienced by this future heir.

4.3.2. *The Typical David*

In Pss 3–6 the first way in which the Davidic persona has been extended is as the Typical David. In contemporary studies, this way of understanding the role of David within the Psalms has been increasingly common since the work of Childs. In my view, it is constructed on top of the image of the Davidic figure already in place within Pss 1–2. There, just as David represented the benchmark and touchstone for all future kings of Israel, so too he represented the ideal, exemplary Israelite. Typically, the figure of David encompasses all facets of the prayers repeated century after century by the people of God. The point is that threats to the promises and to the community of Yʜᴡʜ's people were not lost on David; he suffers alongside them, patiently waiting for Yʜᴡʜ to overcome his enemies and theirs. We saw this throughout Pss 3–6 in our review of the reconstructed *Sitz im Leben*. Rather than pointing to these situations, the titles unite the psalm with David and his story, so that David, *and not historical use in the cult,* provides a context in which the paragon meets the parishioner. The canonical text has replaced the original cultic situation (as much as we can reconstruct it) with the life of David, allowing us to hear the Psalms as David used them *outside* the cult,

---

[103] Mays, "The David of the Psalms," 152.

that they might continue to be used in a variety of situations after the ancient Israelite cult has disappeared.

As an extension of the biographical link to 2 Sam 15–18 in Ps 3, the typical nature of David can be further nuanced. For instance, Rolf Rendtorff has argued that in the opening laments of the Psalter David has been characterized as the righteous individual *par excellence*, suffering at the hands of the wicked: "In this cluster of psalms David appears as a suffering and lamenting individual, far from the heights of kingship, dependent on the help and mercy of God."[104] This characterization of David begins in Ps 3, the first of a series of psalms in which David cries out to YHWH for deliverance (3:3). Situated within the Samuel narrative, David's faith is quite the opposite of his enemies, and he submits to the rule of God over his life, whether for good or for ill (2 Sam 15:25–26). In the psalm, this confidence is expressed by acknowledging YHWH as his shield and glory (3:4). David trusts that God will answer him from Zion, the home of the Ark of the Covenant (2 Sam 15), enabling him to sleep peacefully in the midst of his distress (3:6–7). In the final section of the psalm, David cries out for YHWH to rise up and save him by shattering the teeth of those hostile to him (3:8). As part of his typical character, David prays within the paradigm of Ps 2, where the anointed Son has been granted the authority from YHWH to rule the nations, dashing them as a potter's vessel (2:9). He is also aligning himself as one who trusts YHWH (2:12), and by serving as a representative of that group, gives readers the option to pray with him.[105]

To pray these psalms is to pray alongside David, identifying with his struggles and continued hope in YHWH to rescue him out of his distresses.[106] This is true even as we realize that our own struggles and trials are not the same as David's. As Harry Nasuti stated: "We are able to 'identify' with David, even as we realize that we are not identical with him. The magnified example of David helps us to realize our own shortcomings and our own neediness."[107] He continued:

> While our human situation may well mirror David's, it is not necessarily the case that our response will be the same as his. Indeed, it is only through the psalm that we are able to make David's response our own. The psalm does this first of all by providing a "model" of what the proper response should be. Even more significantly, however, the psalm is what "enables" us to respond as David did.... The psalm functions as a means of transformation.[108]

---

[104] Rendtorff, "The Psalms of David," 56.

[105] See Brennan, "Psalms 1–8," 26.

[106] See Howard N. Wallace, "King and Community: Joining with David in Prayer," in *Psalms and Prayers*, ed. Bob Becking and Eric Peels, OTS 55 (Leiden: Brill, 2007), 270.

[107] Harry P. Nasuti, *Defining the Sacred Songs: Genre, Tradition and the Post-Critical Interpretation of the Psalms*, JSOTSup 218 (Sheffield: Sheffield Academic, 1999), 144.

[108] Nasuti, *Defining the Sacred Songs*, 144.

Praying in this way also urges the reader to recognize that she, now alongside David, is part of a group of people who trust in YHWH.[109] This personal connection between the reader and David becomes a vehicle for the community to pray with David as a means of transformation. At the same time, Sheppard made an important qualification on the nature of David's typical function:

> One encounters a resistance to any glorification of David as a human being or to any treatment that might view him as an unhistorical, ideal, or typological figure, an "everyman," as Job might appear. We are invited by the biblical portrayal more to identify with some of David's ordinary actions and feelings than to compare our experiences with his. David's life strikes in all of us some familiar notes not because it is so typical but because it is so thoroughly human, not because it provides a universal pattern of human distress but because of its psychological depth. David's life attests to the profundity, particularity, and even the mystery of being human, a whole truth that only God can fully know.[110]

The figure of David, then, should not be construed as an "Everyman." The uniqueness of his persona is that it reveals realities faced by any worshiper through the vehicle of the biographical element.[111]

Along similar lines, the Typical David also teaches the reader how to continue to hope in God's promises concerning his anointed heir.[112] Pss 3–6 encapsulate the struggle of David and later Israel to understand YHWH's purposes for his dynasty. Since David's own son is rebelling against him, in what sense is YHWH being faithful? These psalms teach their readers that David continued to have confidence in YHWH even though obstacles to the fulfillment of the covenant were already beginning to take place. Moreover, these threatening elements would not remain the final word, even if due to David's sin. His own deliverances, time after time reported in 1–2 Samuel, was understood as a sign that the promises were sure, and that YHWH provided security against any and all rebellion (cf. 2:4–6).

In sum, the typical voice of David has a critical role in connecting the reader of the Psalms to the Davidic figure. Suffering alongside his people, generation after generation, the figure of David waits patiently for YHWH to overcome his and their enemies. While this aspect will be foregrounded more strongly in Pss 7–14, we are already prodded to pray with David, "O YHWH, how long?" (6:3).

---

[109] See Mays, *The Lord Reigns*, 49.

[110] Gerald T. Sheppard, "Theology and the Book Psalms," *Int* 46 (1992): 148. Though he clearly is against the use of the term "typical," I still think it is appropriate with his stated qualification.

[111] See Nasuti, *Defining the Sacred Songs*, 143–47. For him, there is an important distinction between this way of identifying with David than the appeal to universal human experience, as found in the work of Brueggemann.

[112] See John H. Sailhamer, *NIV Compact Commentary* (Grand Rapids: Zondervan, 1994), 316.

4.3.3. The Typological David

The Biographical David of Pss 3–6 has also been extended in a second figural direction, in what I have called the "Typological David." This David, like the Typical David, has been developed using the Biographical David in conjunction with figure of David who emerges from Pss 1–2. Differing from the Typical David, the Typological David holds in tension the ideal, exemplary "Blessed Man" (1:1) and anointed Son (2:7), with the expectation of a future Davidic heir who would actualize the promises made to David (2 Sam 7) and rule over the nations in accordance with Ps 2:7–9 (and the other royal psalms). In theory, this David functions almost identically to the way typological exegesis had been used throughout the history of interpretation. We saw this at work principally in the exegetical tendencies of both Thomas Aquinas and John Calvin. Pitkin summarized their views well: "Under the description of a present situation, David provides a 'type' of Christ's future kingdom; in his own person David represents Christ; and, in fact, David says some things about himself and his reign that are most appropriately applied to Christ."[113] In constructing my own model, I have shown that their typological intuition is grounded within the editorial structure of the Psalter itself.

I argued earlier that the superscription introduces a biographical function for the figure of David, allowing the reader to hear the psalm with a sharpened Davidic background. At the same time, the broader theological concerns of Pss 1–2 recast this entire event as a *type*, not only of what has happened throughout Israel's history, but what will ultimately happen to the heir of David, when YHWH establishes his anointed on Zion as ruler over the world (Ps 2; cf. Acts 13:32–33; Rom 1:4; Rev 2:26–27). Moving directly from Ps 2 into Ps 3, we would not likely expect David to be found in trouble. Yet, instead of finding the Anointed One established on Mount Zion, enjoying his worldwide inheritance, we find king David fleeing the city. We do not find a renowned warrior slaying thousands and breaking his enemies with a rod of iron, but a helpless, powerless, and downcast ruler, who is content to be humiliated, to be hit with stones and cursed publicly.[114] Like the rebellious nations and peoples of 2:1–3, Absalom seeks to cast off the rule of YHWH and David. Rather than serving YHWH with fear, rejoicing with trembling, or showing fealty, Absalom seeks after David's life in order to usurp the throne.[115]

When we move beyond the superscription and into Pss 3–6, we also find that while there is much correspondence with this setting, there are also incongruities. Throughout, I have argued that this pushes us deeper into the figure of David. The historical psalm titles set up for us "a dialectical movement, which allows the ancient text to address the changing context of the community, and

---

[113] Barbara Pitkin, "Imitation of David: David as a Paradigm for Faith in Calvin's Exegesis of the Psalms," *SCJ* 24 (1993): 858–59.

[114] Rendtorff, "The Psalms of David," 56.

[115] Picking up this typological extension, the early Christian community applied these words to Christ's and their own present persecution (cf. Acts 4:23–31).

conversely permits the new conditions of life dynamically to reinterpret the past."[116] In Pss 3–6, the discordance between psalm and story has opened up the figure of David to become something *more* than the biographical David. The story of Absalom's rebellion and the figure of David have been used to re-present, re-pattern, and reconfigure the past.

In the wider canon of the Old Testament, the reader already knows how the story ends: Absalom is killed in battle and the heir to the throne is Solomon. The juxtaposition of Absalom with Ps 2, then, is curious. More than offering readers a lesson about the potential faithlessness of those closest to us, David and Absalom become types of larger concerns related to the promises of the Davidic heir (Ps 2). Thomas Aquinas illustrates well how the types work. After describing the historical sense in the biographical account, he wrote that it "prefigured the persecution which Christ suffered from his child Judas."[117] Those familiar with the history of interpretation know that this reading of Ps 3 has its roots in the prosopological reading of Augustine, but Thomas builds it rather on typological grounds: whereas Augustine used the biographical superscription to point to Christ allegorically *without any need for David*, for Thomas David's role in the psalm was absolutely necessary. My own proposal endorses this Christological dimension, yet also stresses that the Psalter itself never makes this identification. This is important because it allows us to build a larger typological profile for David than that expressly practiced in the New Testament.[118] For instance, Mays noted the following typological role for David in Ps 3:

> The king identified as the son of God once had to flee from Absalom, his own son. Moreover, he was surrounded by many who said that there was no salvation for him in God, an even higher irony. He prays for the salvation of God.... The blessing of the people of God depends on and is given through his salvation. The Messiah in the Psalms... is a quite human figure, vulnerable to the hostility of his own family and the multitudes. His way is the way of prayer and trust.[119]

In this account, the identification of Jesus as the Messiah would not only look to the betrayal of Judas as anti-type, but also leave room for other gospel stories to inform our typological picture, such as his escape from the throng of persecutors at Nazareth (Luke 4:28–30). The Passion does not exhaust typological extension.

In turn, Absalom and his followers have been set up as a type of those who plot against YHWH and his anointed (2:1–3). Using the language of Pss 1–2, they represent the "wicked," who neglect to ruminate on Torah (1:2) and must be

---

[116] Childs, "Psalm Titles," 151.

[117] Thomas D'Aquin, *Commentaire sur les Psaumes* (Paris: Cerf, 1996), 55.

[118] See Brevard Childs, "Psalm 8 in the Context of the Christian Canon," *Int* 23 (1969): 20–31; Christopher R. Seitz, *The Character of Christian Scripture: The Significance of a Two-Testament Bible* (Grand Rapids: Baker Academic, 2011), 147–54.

[119] Mays, *The Lord Reigns*, 102.

convinced through threats of judgment to serve YHWH (2:10–12). Patrick Miller summarized how this type is developed in Pss 3–6:

> Psalm 3 is understood easily, if not preferably, as the voice of the king surrounded by his foes and praying for God's deliverance and blessing on the people or nation. But Psalms 4 and 5 also make sense as prayers of the king beset by enemies. In fact, one of the primary moves made in the hermeneutics of reading—created by adding Psalm 2 to Psalm 1 in the introduction—is a setting of the category of the wicked under the rubric of "enemies." The wicked are present in Psalm 3, for example, but they are there in the form of the enemies of the one who prays—David, the king. The enemies who oppose the anointed of the Lord are comparable to, and a part of, the wicked who oppose God's way as found in the Torah.[120]

The figure of David has been used as part of a larger typological movement that has recast the rebellion of Absalom as oriented towards the future struggles and deliverance of David's heir. The concerns of Pss 3–6 are not exclusively biographical or sapiential, but typical and typological.

4.4. Conclusion

To draw from the title of this book, the "voice without end" is not a "David" who simply reminds the reader what life was like under the Davidic covenant, nor is he simply a window into the inner life of the David we know from 1–2 Samuel or 1–2 Chronicles. Rather, Pss 3–6 help the reader voice her lament to YHWH by using the identity of the biographical David from 2 Sam 15–18 and extending it figurally in both typical and typological directions. In this way, the threefold voice of David in Pss 3–6 allows David to speak historically (the Biographical David), as a representative exemplar (the Typical David), and eschatologically, anticipating the actualization of the Davidic promises by his future messianic heir (the Typological David). Importantly, I want to reiterate that this account of the Davidic voice is not programmatic for the entirety of the Psalms. Previous attempts to define the literary persona upon strict categories have not done justice to the breadth of the Davidic voice at different positions in the Psalter. While a similar function for the Davidic figure may be found in other psalm clusters, that need not be the case. As a case in point, Pss 7–14 move in a different figural direction than Pss 3–6.

---

[120] Patrick D. Miller, "The Beginning of the Psalter," in *The Shape and Shaping of the Psalter*, ed. J. Clinton McCann, JSOTSup 159 (Sheffield: JSOT Press, 1993), 88–89.

5

The Figure of David in Psalms 7–14

In the opening chapter I argued that we should take Pss 3–6 and 7–14 as two sets of psalm clusters (or sub-groupings) within Pss 3–14. The two biographical superscriptions orient the reader to grasp the role of the Davidic voice in subsequent psalms as well as the thematic development of the book. Building off that argument, in the previous chapter I applied a canonical approach to Pss 3–6. Psalm 3 oriented the cluster as contextually situated within the rebellion of Absalom (Ps 3:1; 2 Sam 15–18). At the same time, juxtaposition with Pss 1–2 helped to construct the voice of the figure of David, who speaks through the Absalom narrative typically and typologically. In this chapter, I will turn my attention toward Pss 7–14 with the same aim, to trace the continued development of the figure of David from Pss 1–6 onward.

I will argue that Ps 7 functions much like Ps 3, to orient the reader towards a certain profile for the Davidic figure in Pss 7–14. In Pss 3–6, that profile took on three different configurations: a Biographical David, a Typical David, and a Typological David. With its own biographical superscription, Ps 7 orients the reader towards David's life, but does so differently than Ps 3. Here, the literary persona is not speaking in the midst of activity but retrospectively, over David's entire career. This results in a figural extension of the Biographical David along didactic and typical lines, instead of typical and typological ones. The figure of David, then, is both a representative and teacher: instructing the reader to pray for divine justice and pursue the way of Yhwh within a hostile environment. A thematic focus on the poor and afflicted in society also comes to the fore (cf. 8:3), in the recognition that humanity has failed in its responsibility to care for Yhwh's creatures, both human and animal (Pss 8–14).

5.1. A Changing Literary Context: The Superscription of Ps 7

I will begin by attending to the changing literary context offered by a second biographical superscription in Ps 7. Like Ps 3, Ps 7 functions to orient the reader towards the thematic concerns present in Pss 7–14, as well as cluing in the reader to the role of the figure of David.

5.1.1. The Interpretive Challenge of the Heading to Ps 7

The superscription of Ps 7 reads, "A *shiggaion* of David, which he sang to Y<small>HWH</small> on account of the words of Cush, a Benjaminite." It includes three elements: ancient genre designation (*shiggaion*),[1] an association with David ("of David"), and a biographical element ("which he sang to Y<small>HWH</small> on account of the words of Cush, a Benjaminite"). This structuring of elements follows the same basic pattern we saw in Ps 3 (*genre + biblical figure + biographical setting*), but differs from the patterns used in both Pss 4–6 and 8–14 (*liturgical notes + biblical figure*). Moreover, the only two psalms lacking למנצח in Pss 3–14 are Ps 3 and Ps 7, both containing biographical elements. Based on this and other likenesses, Ps 7 shares a similar hermeneutical function as Ps 3; namely, to orient the reader towards a certain way of understanding the figure of David within the contextual setting supplied by the biographical element. At the same time, the hermeneutical significance of this title differs from what we find in Ps 3. In that psalm, the superscription was connected to a specific episode in David's life—the rebellion of Absalom (2 Sam 15–18)—while here the superscription is more broadly construed.

The title's changing significance is indicated in part by its different syntax. In Ps 3, the biographical data was introduced using an infinitive clause ("when he fled…"), which indicates contemporaneity with the psalm itself. It tells us to read the psalm as if David were praying during the inscribed incident, *as he was fleeing from Absalom*. In Ps 7, however, a perfect verb form is used, introduced by the relative pronoun אשר. This kind of clause (*x-qatal*) does not indicate contemporaneity, but recalls an antecedent event. As such, instead of taking place at the time of the event, Ps 7 should be read as a meditation on a past event or series of events. There is an implied distance between the psalm and the setting that we do not find in Ps 3, suggesting that the role of David in this context might also be different than his role in Ps 3. In Ps 3, we meet a David in the midst of activity (fleeing, surrounded, and assailed); in Ps 7, we meet a David reflecting on previous incidents and his involvement in them. Whereas Ps 3 is sung *during the flight*, Ps 7 is sung on account of previous words spoken against David by Cush, a Benjaminite.[2]

---

[1] Every other psalm in our group (except Ps 10, which is included with Ps 9) is designated מזמור ("psalm"). שגיון ("*shiggaion*") is a rare term, only found elsewhere in Hab 3:1. See my earlier discussion in chapter three.

[2] *Contra* Brevard S. Childs, "Psalm Titles and Midrashic Exegesis," *JSS* 16 (1971): 151. He argued that the title in Ps 7 did not follow the basic form in most of the other biographical psalm headings, which use the infinitive construct introduced by the preposition ב, usually followed by a coordinate or subordinate clause with a finite verb. Moreover, the use of על instead of ב suggests the superscription should be understood as liturgical directions rather than a reference to a historical episode. While the rest of Childs's argument on the role of biographical superscriptions has gained widespread support, few

The longstanding interest in the superscription of Ps 7 does not rest on its syntax, however. The issues are twofold. First, what is one to make of the ancient genre description, *shiggaion* (שִׁגָּיוֹן)? And second, what is one to make of the referent of the biographical element, "which he sang to Yʜwʜ on account of the words of Cush, a Benjaminite"? The former is difficult to answer with any confidence given the rarity of the Hebrew term and the uncertainty in scholarship on the root being used. This is a problem shared by all ancient versions and modern translations, which often transliterate the term. The second issue, however, is more challenging. In short, there are no episodes in David's life (1–2 Samuel, 1–2 Chronicles) or any other biblical narrative, nor any extra-biblical tradition that we are aware of, that refers to a Benjaminite named "Cush" (כּוּשׁ בֶּן־יְמִינִי). How, then, should we understand the reference?

The word כּוּשׁ is a proper name, "Cush" (Gk: Χους; Lat: *Chus*), referring first in the Old Testament to one of the sons of Ham (Gen 10:6–8; cf. 1 Chr 1:8–10), the father of a people who lived south of Egypt in Cush (or Ethiopia; Αφιθιοπία, Αφιθίοπες).[3] Related, an adjectival form of כּוּשׁ is used, inflected for both gender and number (כּוּשִׁי, בְּשִׁית כּוּשִׁים, בְּשִׁים, or בְּשִׁיִּים), and can refer to an entire people or individuals ("Cushite" or "Ethiopian" or "Nubian").[4] Like the form we have in Ps 7:1, though, it is also used as a personal name for several individuals.[5] The relationship between the personal name כּוּשׁ and the tribe of Benjamin remains a mystery, and has been the cause of significant comment throughout the history of interpretation. Most have understood the referent in terms of David's experiences with the Benjaminites, but have disagreed as to whether the referent should be identified with the narrative accounts of the Benjaminite Saul (1 Sam 24–26) or with Benjaminites involved in Absalom's rebellion and its

---

have followed him on this particular point. In part, this is because Childs had not adequately studied the order of elements within psalm headings. In all twenty-nine psalms with musical directions, each is preceded by the element לַמְנַצֵּחַ; that is, there are no examples of psalms that have musical directions without reference to the director of music. Further, in all examples given except one (Ps 46), the musical directions follow immediately after לַמְנַצֵּחַ. Psalm 7 not only lacks the reference לַמְנַצֵּחַ, but it also would have placed the musical directions in an unprecedented position, after both the biblical association ("of David") and ancient genre ("*shiggaion*"). Given the musical nature of the other liturgical directions (e.g., Pss 6, 8, 12), this suggests that the preposition עַל further nuances the biographical setting, "on account of."

[3] See Gen 2:13; 2 Kgs 19:9; Est 1:1; 8:9; Job 28:19; Pss 68:32; 87:4; Isa 11:11; 18:1; 20:3, 4, 5; 37:9; 43:3; 45:14; Jer 46:9; Ezek 29:10; 30:4, 5, 9; 38:5; Nah 3:9; Zeph 3:10.

[4] See Num 12:1; Jer 13:23; 38:7, 10, 12; 39:16; 2 Chr 14:8; 2 Sam 18:21–23, 31–32; Zeph 2:12; 2 Chr 12:3; 14:11, 12; 16:8; 21:16; Dan 11:43; Amos 9:7. As a description for individuals: a servant (?) of Joab (2 Sam 18:21–23, 31–32), a servant of a king (Jer 38:7, 10, 12; 39:16), a Cushite prince (2 Chr 14:8), and the wife of Moses (Num 12:1).

[5] The father of Shelemyahu (Jer 36:14), the father of the prophet Zephaniah (Zeph 1:1), and the father of a messenger sent to Baruch (Jer 43:14).

aftermath (2 Sam 15–20).[6] There was a commitment, then, to attempt to find a referent within the biblical narratives connected with David.

Beginning with Abraham Ibn Ezra and John Calvin, however, interpreters have argued that "Cush" need not refer to a known character in the Old Testament, but could refer to an otherwise unknown servant or ally of Saul.[7] In this case, כוש is understood as a personal name ("Cush"), and, even though there is no record of him in the biblical narratives, one can envision a context similar to when David was verbally and physically attacked (e.g., 1 Sam 24:10; 26:19).[8] This interpretation of the title is appealing since it upholds a biographical context for the psalm even though it is an episode of David's life of which we are ignorant.

Given the complexities involved in many of these theories, recent commentators have typically concluded that we are at a loss and should simply not worry about the title for our exegetical purposes.[9] The difficulty with this view is that every other biographical superscription has a clear reference to an episode in the life of David.[10] The working assumption—unless proven otherwise—is that the referent attempts to bring a narrative episode of David's life to bear on our reading of the psalm.[11] The problem, in my opinion, is that

---

[6] For a detailed treatment of the exegetical possibilities, which are numerous and often complex, see Rodney R. Hutton, "Cush the Benjaminite and Psalm Midrash," *HAR* 10 (1986): 123–37; Vivian L. Johnson, *David in Distress: His Portrait Through the Historical Psalms*, LHBOTS 505 (London: T&T Clark, 2009), 131–39; and Yitzhak Berger, "The David-Benjaminite Conflict and the Intertextual Field of Psalm 7," *JSOT* 38 (2014): 279–96.

[7] See Abraham Ibn Ezra, *Commentary on the First Book of Psalms: Chapters 1–41*, trans. H. Norman Strickman (Boston: Academic Studies, 2009), 61; John Calvin, *Commentary on the Book of Psalms*, trans. James Anderson, 5 vols (Edinburgh: Calvin Translation Society, 1845), 1:75–76.

[8] Heinrich A. von Ewald, *Commentary on the Psalms*, trans. E. Johnson, vol. 1 (London: Williams & Northgate, 1880), 74; Franz Delitzsch, *A Commentary on the Book of Psalms*, trans. David Eaton and James E. Duguid (New York: Funk & Wagnalls, 1883), 137–38; C. A. Briggs and E. G. Briggs, *A Critical and Exegetical Commentary on the Book of Psalms*, ICC (Edinburgh: T&T Clark, 1906), 52. See also F. F. Bruce, "The Earliest Old Testament Interpretation," in *The Witness of Tradition: Papers Read at the Joint British-Dutch Old Testament Conference held at Wouschoten, 1970*, ed. A. S. Van Der Woude, OTS 17 (Leiden: Brill, 1972), 48–49; Peter C. Craigie *Psalms 1–50*, 2nd ed, WBC 19 (Dallas: Thomas Nelson, 2004), 99; Matthias Millard, *Die Komposition des Psalters*, FAT 9 (Tübingen: Mohr, 1994), 131. In a similar vein, it has been argued that "Cush" is substituted for "Kish," such that "Kish, a Benjaminite" refers to another person within the same family/clan as Saul, perhaps even Saul himself. See E. W. Hengstenberg, *Commentary on the Psalms*, trans. P. Fairbairn and J. Thomson (Edinburgh: T&T Clark, 1866), 106.

[9] See Artur Weiser, *The Psalms: A Commentary*, trans. Herbert Hartwell, OTL (Philadelphia: Westminster, 1962), 135; Hans-Joachim Kraus, *Psalms 1–59: A Commentary*, trans. Hilton C. Oswald (Minneapolis: Augsburg, 1988), 169; James L. Mays, *Psalms*, IBC (Louisville: Westminster John Knox, 1994), 64–65.

[10] Hutton, "Cush the Benjaminite," 125.

[11] Hutton, "Cush the Benjaminite," 127.

scholars have so focused on connecting the superscription to *one particular narrative moment* that they have lost sight of its ongoing function: to refer to several possible episodes in David's career.[12] While the original referent may have been to a particular known episode, its canonical ambiguity opens the psalm for a wider context within the life of David.

5.1.2. The Narratives of 1–2 Samuel and the Context of Ps 7

When we trace out the lexical connections between Ps 7 and the narratives of David in 1–2 Samuel, several scenes from both the time of Saul and the time of Absalom find strong resonance. Rather appropriately, in the opening section of the psalm (vv. 2–3) this pan-episodic approach finds support when David calls on Yhwh to deliver and rescue him from "all my pursuers" (מכל־רדפי; 7:2). Working through the narratives we find two people who had pursued (רדף) David: Saul (1 Sam 23:24, 28; 24:15; 26:18–20) and Absalom (*via* Ahithophel, 2 Sam 17:1).[13] Since the psalm is not prayed in the moment but in retrospect, David's prayer could be referring to Saul and Absalom inclusively, "all my pursuers."[14]

Moving into the second section (vv. 4–6), we continue to find lexical links to both narratives. With Saul, the language of "in my hands" (בידי;בכפי) finds very strong parallels in multiple encounters where David spares Saul's life (1 Sam 24:6, 11, 12; 26:18), as does the language of repaying (גמל) evil (רע) for good (1 Sam 24:18). Moreover, Saul is the quintessential "enemy" (אויב) of David throughout 1–2 Samuel (1 Sam 18:29; 19:17; 24:5, 20; 26:8; 2 Sam 4:8).[15] At the same time, Absalom can be referred to as an אויב of David (2 Sam 18:19, 32). Other lexical links only correspond to Absalom narratives. For example, Absalom is the only enemy who might "overtake" (ישג) David (2 Sam 15:14), and as David flees Jerusalem, Shimei humiliates him by covering him with "dust" (עפר; 2 Sam 16:13).[16]

---

[12] See Robert Bellarmine, *A Commentary on the Book of Psalms*, trans. John O'Sullivan (Dublin: James Duffy, 1866), 12–15; John Goldingay, *Psalms, Volume 1: Psalms 1–41*, BCOT (Grand Rapids: Baker Academic, 2006), 144–45. Outside of Bellarmine's 1611 work, Goldingay was the first commentator I read who argued for multiple referents, though he only sees a connection to the Absalom narratives and their aftermath. My view, drawing on Bellarmine, also includes the narratives of Saul's pursuit in 1 Sam 24–26.

[13] Another comment about pursuers is given by Abigail (1 Sam 25:29).

[14] See Bellarmine, *Commentary on the Psalms*, 13. He paraphrased verse one: "Because nearly all have deserted me, so that my very son Absalom, and my father-in-law Saul, seek to put me to death. I have no one to trust in but you, my God." He continued: "Numerous were his persecutors—some by their advice, some by their maledictions, some by wars and arms" (13).

[15] Other named "enemies" of David include the Philistines and Amalakites (1 Sam 30:26; 2 Sam 5:20; 19:10; cf. 2 Sam 7:1, 9, 11), as well as generic references (1 Sam 20:15–16; 25:26, 29).

[16] There may also be a clever wordplay connected to Absalom in the use of the rare term שולמי used in verse five, "my ally," or more woodenly, "my peaceful one."

Sections three (vv. 7–11) and four (vv. 12–14) do not contain many lexical links to the Samuel narratives, but what links do exist connect the psalm again to both Saul and Absalom. We find the main points of connection in verses nine and ten. In verse nine, David calls upon YHWH to "judge" (דין) the peoples, but then also to "judge" (שפט) himself, according to his own righteousness (צדיק) and integrity (תם). The root דין is only used three times in 1–2 Samuel, and is used very similarly in 1 Samuel 24:16, when David confronts Saul. In the same sentence, David also uses the root שפט to ask for YHWH's judgment between himself and Saul: "May YHWH be for a judge (לדין), and make judgment (ושפט) between me and you; may he see to it, and plead my cause, and vindicate me against you."[17] Similarly, the root שפט is used in the Absalom narrative, when the Cushite messenger is reporting the news of Absalom's death to David: "Let good tidings be made for my Lord, the king; for YHWH has vindicated you (שפטך) this day, from all the ones raised up against you" (2 Sam 18:31).[18]

Verse ten opens with David's plea that God "let the evil (רע) of the wicked (רשעים) come to end." Even though these are common terms in the Psalter, one of the few references to רשעים in Samuel comes in 1 Sam 24:14, "As the proverb of the ancients says, 'Out of the wicked (מרשעים) comes wickedness (רשע),' but my hand is not against you." Similarly, though the root רע is common, only four people are referred to in some sense as "evil" in Samuel: Saul (1 Sam 15:19), Nabal (1 Sam 25:3), David (2 Sam 12:9), and Absalom (2 Sam 12:11). More positively, verse ten also refers to the "establishing" (כון) of the righteous, and verse eleven to the "upright of heart" (ישרי־לב). Throughout 1–2 Samuel, David is one of the only people called upright (1 Sam 29:6), with the establishing of his kingdom being one of the only uses of כון in that sense (cf. 2 Sam 5:12; 7:12, 13, 16, 32).

Finally, in the last section (vv. 15–18) we find more correspondence to the Absalom narratives. The most direct connection is made to Shimei, whose death is sealed by Solomon in ways strikingly similar to verse seventeen: "You know in your own heart all the evil (כל־הרעה) that you did to my father David; so YHWH will return (שוב) your evil (רעתך) on your own head (בראשך)" (1 Kgs 2:44). While the term for evil (רע) is different in 7:17 (עמל, "mischief"), we have both the verb שוב and the phrase בראש (with a different pronoun). Moreover, in Shimei's encounter with David (2 Sam 16), his cursing turns out to be false (cf. Ps 7:15) and, anticipating his death, Abishai threatens to behead him (16:9). While these verbal links have caused some to view Shimei as the "Cush" of the superscription (he *is* a Benjaminite; cf. 2 Sam 16:11), several people connected with the Absalom narrative have "head" problems: Sheba the Benjaminite (2 Sam 20:21–22), Joab (1 Kgs 2:30–33), and even Absalom himself (2 Sam 18:9). Moreover, the only other use of קדקד ("crown of the head"; Ps 7:17) in the David

---

[17] This almost repeats verbatim David's words to Saul in 24:13, "May YHWH judge (ישפט) between me and you."

[18] See 2 Sam 18:19, "And Ahimaaz son of Zadok said, 'Let me run and bring good tidings to the king, that YHWH has vindicated him (שפטו) from the hand of his enemies.'"

narratives is in reference to Absalom (2 Sam 14:25). Turning to the Saul narratives, there is no direct link to Saul himself, but enveloped in 1 Sam 24–26 is the story of Nabal. In reference to his death David is quoted as saying, "Yнwн has returned (השיב) the evil (רעה) of Nabal on his head (בראשו)" (1 Sam 25:39). In sum, both the narratives of Saul's pursuit of David (1 Sam 24–26) and Absalom's rebellion (2 Sam 15–18) find strong parallels with this section.

5.1.3. The Role of the Superscription of Ps 7

Bringing these observations together, what then can we say about the function of the superscription to Ps 7? Even though there are many different interpretive options for identifying the enigmatic "Cush, a Benjaminite," the simplest reading is preferred: כוש is a personal name (cf. Gen 10), and בן־ימיני further describes him as a Benjaminite (cf. 1 Sam 9:21). Whoever this person was, the story relating the specific words he spoke to David is nowhere to be found in the biblical text. This does not mean that we should ignore the superscription or throw our hands up in frustration; rather, it allows us to place Cush's accusation of David as potentially taking place during key events in David's life, fitting both the time of Saul's pursuit (1 Sam 24–26) and Absalom's rebellion (2 Sam 15–18).

Along these lines, we might take a clue from 2 Sam 22 on the interpretative role that Ps 7 plays in the structure of Pss 3–14. As Rodney Hutton noted about the version of Ps 18 in 2 Sam 22, "[It] was intended to serve as a fitting conclusion to David's career. The title was not intended to refer to any specific event in David's life but rather to serve as a comprehensive theological commentary on the entire history of David."[19] Analogously, the biographical heading of Ps 7 serves a similar function.[20] First, it is not meant to connect us to any *particular* episode in David's career, but could connect us to several of them. Second, instead of introducing the psalm as a theological commentary, as in Ps 18, the rhetorical effect for Ps 7 would be to transform David's personal experiences of verbal accusation and generalize them as an example of any number of experiences. David's unique experiences take on an illustrative quality, and since this psalm *could* be applied equally in several specific experiences, its words have a more universal appeal.[21] As Yitzhak Berger concluded:

> The heading does not focus narrowly on the immediate context of Cush's remarks. Rather, when considering the Psalm in light of the experiences of David, the author of our superscription would have perceived Cush's allegation, leveled at an early stage of the young Judean's travails, as a fitting expression of what became a sustained

---

[19] Hutton, "Cush the Benjaminite," 126.

[20] See Berger, "The David-Benjaminite Conflict," 290–91.

[21] One is tempted to see "Cush" as a fictional character who represents the entire Benjaminite and Davidic conflict throughout 1–2 Samuel. Such a construal of Cush would allow us to rightly make connections between the psalm and other actual characters in the stories (e.g., Saul, Absalom, Shimei, Sheba), while also holding up the illustrative quality and didactic function of the psalm.

accusation of betrayal, one which dogged David throughout his conflict with Saul's supporters—as for example, in the Shimei episode—and against which the text of Samuel provides consistent resistance.[22]

As I will discuss further below, it is striking that, just at this particular point in the book of Psalms, David begins to speak in terms of *all* his experiences (7:2, "deliver me from all my pursuers"), looking towards the God who judges in a divine council (7:8b) over *all* of the wicked and righteous (7:10), in front of *all* peoples (7:8a), and describes in general, unspecified terms the punishment of the unrepentant (7:13–17). By leaving the superscription specified but not determinable, the psalm opens itself up for a wider thematic understanding of Yhwh's judgment, which will be further expanded in subsequent psalms. In one hand, the Saul narratives help us see the vindication of the innocent and righteous David; in the other, the Absalom narratives help us to navigate a more morally ambiguous David.

5.2. Psalm 7 and the Development of the Figure of David

I have argued in the first two sections of this chapter that Ps 7 functions in a similar fashion as Ps 3, orienting the reader in both thematic content and the role of the figure of David. To better nuance the persona played by the Davidic figure in Pss 7–14, in this section I want to undertake a fuller analysis of Ps 7.

5.2.1. Dialogical Analysis of Ps 7

In Ps 7, we find an interesting mix of speaking persona and changes of audience that must be understood to properly hear the psalm. In the first two sections (vv. 2–3, 4–6), the speaking voice consistently uses first-person singular pronouns and addresses his words to Yhwh using vocatives and volitional verbs. Using third-person pronouns, the psalmist refers several times to his accusers. Outside of his use of the plural "all my pursuers" (כל־רדפי; 7:2), only singular nouns are used in verses 3–6 (אויב, צוררי, שולמי). From these enemies he seeks both deliverance and vindication.

The situation is more complicated in the third section (vv. 7–11):

קומה יהוה באפך	[7] Rise up, O Yhwh, in your anger!
הנשא בעברות צוררי	Lift yourself against the fury of my foes,
ועורה אלי משפט צוית	and awake, O my God! Judgment you have appointed.
ועדת לאמים תסובבך	[8] So the assembly of the peoples will be gathered to you;
ועליה למרום שובה	and over it return on high!
יהוה ידין עמים	[9] Yhwh will judge the peoples;
שפטני יהוה כצדקי	judge me, O Yhwh, according to my righteousness,
וכתמי עלי	and according to my integrity within me.

---

[22] Berger, "The David-Benjaminite Conflict," 291–92.

יגמר־נא רע רשעים	[10] May the evil of the wicked be ended,
ותכונן צדיק	but establish the righteous;
ובחן לבות וכליות אלהים צדיק	yes, he who examines hearts and loins is the righteous God.
מגני על־אלהים	[11] My shield is upon God,
מושיע ישרי־לב	the deliverer of the upright in heart.

In the first two verses (vv. 7–8), the speaker continues to use first-person pronouns and addresses YHWH in the second person, using vocatives and volitional verbs. An addressee change happens in 7:9a, however, as YHWH is referred to in the third person. There is no identification of the new audience, whom I have simply labeled "others." In 7:9b-c, the addressee reverts back to YHWH, using vocatives and first-person pronouns. In verses ten and eleven, while I am more certain that the audience in verses 10c and 11 should be the "others," the jussive clauses in verse 10ab are harder to determine, as they could be speaking to either the others or YHWH, or even both. From this point forward, though, the rest of the psalm is easier to analyze. The "others" continue to be addressed from verses twelve to sixteen, with volitional verbs creating another ambiguous context in verses seventeen and eighteen. Given that that the speaker does not use first-person pronouns from verses twelve to seventeen, some have also questioned who might be speaking in these verses.

In her dialogical analysis, Carleen Mandalfo has argued that instead of one speaker throughout the psalm, an ongoing dialogue occurs between the accused petitioner and a didactic speaker, to whom the accused responds.[23] The change of audience from second-person to third-person speech in verse nine "signals a new voice" who "makes a general claim about YHWH's attributes."[24] Responding directly to this general claim, the accused speaks again in 7:9b-c, "requesting that YHWH act in a way consistent with that attribute."[25] This analysis leads her to understand 7:10a–b as a continuation of the petitioner's voice, verse 10c as another response of the didactic voice (using third-person pronouns), and verse eleven as the petitioner's response to verse 10c. Verses 12–17 are again heard as the didactic speaker's response to the petitioner in verse eleven, with a final vow of praise spoken by the petitioner in verse eighteen.

While her analysis has been accepted in at least one recent commentary, it is not without problems.[26] First, she has not paid careful attention to verbal

---

[23] Carleen Mandalfo, *God in the Dock: Dialogic Tension in the Psalms of Lament*, JSOTSup 357 (Sheffield: Sheffield Academic, 2002), 36–41.

[24] Mandalfo, *God in the Dock*, 36, 37.

[25] Mandalfo, *God in the Dock*, 37.

[26] See Walter Brueggemann and William H. Bellinger, Jr., *Psalms*, NCBC (New York: Cambridge University Press, 2014), 56. For recent criticism which complements my own, see W. Derek Suderman, "From Dialogic Tension to Social Address: Reconsidering Mandolfo's Proposed Didactic Voice in Lament Psalms," *JHS* 17 (2017): 6–11.

forms, ignoring the use of *waw* at the beginning of lines.[27] For instance, her argument for a new voice in 7:10c ignores the *waw* which occurs at the beginning of the line.[28] With the *waw*, this line is better heard as a continuation of the voice from 7:10a–b. Second, her argument for a different didactic voice in verses thirteen to seventeen is not based on anything in the text, but is her opinion on what is appropriate for someone to pray during a time of crisis.[29]

A more sensitive reading is given by Ellen Charry.[30] For her, the psalm "presents us with a protagonist crying out to God for vindication against enemies in pursuit, but it moves on quickly to address and shape Israel's understanding of God and the standards of moral conduct that flow from that understanding."[31] Instead of hearing multiple voices, she thinks the first half of the psalm addresses God directly in the first person, followed in the latter half with the speaker addressing a human audience with descriptions about God. The dialogue, then, is not between a didactic voice and the petitioner, but first between the petitioner and God, and second between the petitioner and those listening in on the prayer. She wrote: "This psalm shows the praying community both watching the intimate relationship between God and the speaker and seeing into the speaker's inmost being."[32] Moreover, with Mandalfo, Charry recognizes the didactic quality of the second half of the psalm. She understands the change in audience signaled in verse 9a and continued in verses eleven to seventeen as speaking "about God to the worshipping community in light of what has just transpired. *The change of audience suggests that the personal lament is designed as a teaching tool.*"[33] The speaker both prays for justice and instructs his audience about judgment. In the end, she interprets Ps 7 as an attempt to persuade later singers and petitioners that Yhwh is "to be thanked and praised as a righteous judge who will vindicate the straight-hearted against those who give birth to lies."[34]

From my point of view, then, while there is no change of speaker throughout the entire psalm, we do have important changes in audience and tone: the speaker petitions Yhwh to give him justice against those who pursue him (7:2–8, 9b–10:b, 11), instructs all who listen about the just judgment of God

---

[27] See Mandalfo, *God in the Dock*, 37. In verse ten, she claims that imperatives have been used, but these are third-person jussives, which rhetorically express the petitioner's desires rather than directing God's actions.

[28] Mandalfo, *God in the Dock*, 37.

[29] Mandalfo, *God in the Dock*, 39.

[30] Ellen T. Charry, *Psalms 1–50: Sighs and Songs of Israel* (Grand Rapids: Brazos, 2015).

[31] Charry, *Psalms 1–50*, 35.

[32] Charry, *Psalms 1–50*, 36.

[33] Charry, *Psalms 1–50*, 37. Emphasis my own.

[34] Charry, *Psalms 1–50*, 39. Much earlier in the history of interpretation, John Chrysostom made similar observations about this dual rhetoric, "instruction is at every point mingled with supplications." See John Chrysostom, *Commentary on the Psalms*, trans. Robert C. Hill, 2 vols. (Brookline, MA: Holy Cross Orthodox Press, 1998), 1:126.

against the unrepentant (7:9a, 10c, 12–17), and expresses a final desire to praise Yhwh (7:18).[35] We have also seen that the rhetoric of the psalmist has transformed the prayer to be instructive, teaching both the unrepentant about God's judgment and the penitent about how to pray for God's vindication. One must not simply call down judgment on one's enemies, but also ask that judgment be made against oneself; the petitioner must also heed the didactic words of the latter half of the psalm.[36] While connected to the Benjaminites during the episodes with Saul and Absalom, such rhetoric also speaks beyond it.

On this point, John Chrysostom commented on the rhetorical effect of the instructive nature of the psalm. After quoting Ps 78 and its didactic review of history, he wrote: "Speaking of future things... he provided proof of them also from past examples, bringing to notice the very ones who had been punished, some from snakes, some from the destroyer. That is exactly what David is doing here, too, speaking either of Absalom or of Ahithophel."[37] For Chrysostom, David is looking back upon his experiences and uses past examples to give instruction concerning divine judgment. Concerning the figure of David, he pointed out that the David who appears in the story is "not the same man as these words now." For example, the David of the narrative spoke about sparing Absalom (2 Sam 18:5) and even trading places with him in death (2 Sam 18:33), whereas in the psalm, looking back on that story or experience, and inspired by the Spirit, David says something different (cf. 7:18). For Chrysostom, this helps us to see that the meaning of the psalm goes beyond any particular story or characters: "Whether he spoke about Absalom or about Ahithophel, what he said deserves attention; in my view the significance has little to do with the characters."[38] Indeed, as I argued above, the psalm recalls not just one episode for its construction of the Davidic figure, but multiple episodes in which David was pursued by Benjaminites. This certainly applies to episodes with Saul, but it equally applies to David's experiences with Absalom's rebellion and its aftermath. Reflecting on past crises, the figure of David teaches the penitent how to pray for the just judgment of God. As we will shortly see, the context of the Psalms has again allowed for a semantic transformation of the psalm in its secondary setting within sacred Scripture.

5.2.2. Historical-Critical Engagement with Ps 7

In large measure, modern understanding of Ps 7 has been straightforward, connecting the psalm to some sort of judgment ritual that took place at the

---

[35] Verses 9–11 are complicated. As I have understood them, the instructive voice bookends verse nine and ten, and then picks up again in verse twelve. The praying voice continues in 9b–10b and verse eleven, making a final, more instructive appeal in verse eighteen.

[36] See Delitzsch, *Book of Psalms*, 143. He wrote, "This Psalm is the key to all Psalms which contain prayers against one's enemies."

[37] Chrysostom, *Commentary on the Psalms*, 1:138–39.

[38] Chrysostom, *Commentary on the Psalms*, 1:139.

temple in Jerusalem.[39] While several texts have been put forward as supplying the its cultic background (e.g., Num 5:11–28; Deut 17:8–13), the most striking is 1 Kgs 8:31–32. It reads:

> If someone sins against a neighbor and is given an oath to swear, and comes and swears before your altar in this house, then hear in heaven, and act, and judge your servants, condemning the guilty by bringing their conduct on their own head and to declare righteous the righteous, to give him according to his righteousness.

The parallels with Ps 7 are remarkable. For instance, the accusation of sin against a neighbor is present (7:5), as is the oath of self-imprecation (7:4–6), which may have even taken place at the temple (7:2; 18). Moreover, the psalmist prays that God would return on high and judge between the two parties (7:7–10), with a call for the mischief and violence of the wicked to come back upon his own head (7:17).

The connection is so strong, in fact, that Kraus called Ps 7 *the* formulary used for the ritual described there.[40] While we can never have certainty in the matter, Gerstenberger noted that its closeness to 1 Kgs 8:31–32 enables Ps 7 to represent "an accumulation of the agonies of generations of supplicants facing unfounded charges of various types."[41] What I find most interesting about these contexts is that the superscription to the psalm actualizes the same kind of divine courtroom setting by directing readers not to the ritual itself (e.g., 1 Kgs 8:31–32)—which it could have—but to David's experiences with the Benjaminites throughout his career. Notably, none of those experiences are located within Jerusalem at the sanctuary. This parallels my earlier discussion of Ps 5, where I observed how the psalm could be read in connection with Shimei's cursing of David instead of the temple. In that situation, Absalom's success, or lack thereof, was understood *as* the divine verdict.

The superscription gives the psalm a new significance that has been separated from what may have been its original cultic setting. Childs is correct here: "Within late Israel, the psalms have been loosened from their original cultic context and the words assigned a new significance as Sacred Scripture for a new and different function."[42] For him, "the most far reaching alteration with

---

[39] Kraus, *Psalms 1–59*, 169; Weiser, *Psalms*, 135–136; Frank-Lothar Hossfeld and Erich Zenger, *Die Psalmen, Vol. 1: Psalmen 1–50*, NechtB (Würzburg: Echter Verlag, 1993), 72; Klaus Seybold, *Die Psalmen*, HAT 1/15 (Tübingen: Mohr, 1996), 46. The various views are summarized well by Nancy L. deClaissé-Walford, Rolf A. Jacobson, and Beth LaNeel Tanner, *The Book of Psalms*, NICOT (Grand Rapids: Eerdmans, 2014), 109.

[40] Kraus, *Psalms 1–59*, 169.

[41] Erhard S. Gerstenberger, *Psalms: Part 1 with an Introduction to Cultic Poetry*, FOTL 14 (Grand Rapids: Eerdmans, 1988), 64.

[42] Brevard S. Childs, "Reflections on the Modern Study of the Psalms," in *Magnalia Dei: The Mighty Acts of God; Essays on the Bible and Archaeology in Memory of G. Ernest Wright*, ed. Frank Moore Cross, Werner E. Lemke, and Patrick D. Miller (Garden City, NY: Doubleday, 1976), 383.

which the collector shaped the canonical psalter was in his use of superscriptions," which "represent an important reflection on how the psalms as a collection of sacred literature were understood and how this secondary setting became normative for the canonical tradition."[43] By connecting the psalm to David's ongoing troubles with the Benjaminites, the superscription has broadened the appeal of the psalm to any who are accused, while at the same time using the figure of David to stand in as their representative model, a "voice without end."

5.2.3. The Figure of David in Ps 7

As my above analyses have shown, Ps 7 introduces the figure of David with several important developments which extend beyond the concerns of Pss 3–6. Showing some continuity with Pss 3–6, the superscription allows the voice of David to be heard within the rebellion of Absalom; yet, it has lifted us out of that specific narrative world to reflect on the entirety of David's experience with the tribe of Benjamin. The same is true when we compare the use of key terms and themes in Pss 1–2 and 3–6.

In the opening section (vv. 2–3), David continues in a typical role by praying that he has taken refuge in YHWH (בך חסיתי), building on his earlier prayer for "all who take refuge" in YHWH (כל חוסי בך; 5:12).[44] In like manner, the motif of deliverance (3:8; 6:5; 7:2) and focus on the נפש of David (3:3; 6:4, 5; 7:3, 6) show continuity between Ps 7 and these earlier psalms. Such continuity remains in the second section (vv. 4–6), where terms of distress (צר; צוררי; 3:2; 4:2; 6:8; 7:5, 7), enemy (איוב; 3:8; 6:11; 7:6), honor/glory (כבוד; 3:4; 4:3; 7:6), and vanity (ריק; 4:3; 7:5) reappear. In the latter half of the psalm (vv. 7–11, 12–18), elements of continuity include the command of YHWH to arise (3:8; 7:7), the concept of uprightness before YHWH (5:9; 7:11), the image of YHWH as a shield (3:4; 7:11), and the motif of working iniquity (5:6; 6:9; 7:15–16) alongside self-retribution (5:11; 7:15–17).[45]

These continuities, however, should not mask the notes of discordance. For instance, 7:4 is one of the most important verses in the psalm connecting it to the Saul narratives, but it shares no lexical terms with Pss 3–6. Further notes of discontinuity reintroduce other themes and motifs from Pss 1–2 that were not picked up in Pss 3–6.[46] For instance, neither the verb nor noun for the root שפט ("to judge") occur in Pss 3–6, but each is used in Pss 1–2 (1:5; 2:10) and are reintroduced by Ps 7 (7:7, 9, 12) into the landscape of Pss 8–14 (9:5, 8, 9, 17, 20; 10:5, 18). We also find examples of extension, such as with the term עם

---

[43] Childs, "Reflections on the Modern Study of the Psalms," 383–84.

[44] Both verses show affiliation with the motif of refuge in Ps 2:12.

[45] Other elements of concordance include the terms צדיק (1:5, 6; 4:2; 5:13; 7:9, 10, 12, 18), רשעים (1:1, 5, 6; 3:8; 7:10), and שוב (6:11; 7:13), but these are not limited to Pss 3–6, sharing in the vocabulary and themes of Pss 1–2.

[46] See Howard N. Wallace, "King and Community: Joining with David in Prayer," in *Psalms and Prayers*, ed. Bob Becking and Eric Peels, OTS 55 (Leiden: Brill, 2007), 274n21.

("people"). It is used in 3:7, 9 to refer to those in Israel who had joined Absalom in his rebellion against David, but in its plural form (7:9) to refer to all nations.[47] This extension corresponds with the use of לאם ("peoples") in Ps 2:1, and thus reintroduces the broader literary concerns of the introductory psalms.[48]

In tracing these elements of continuity, discontinuity, and development between Ps 7 and Pss 1–6, I am not making any claims about the diachronic shaping of the book. It is difficult to determine where and/or how these psalms came together in their final canonical context, or whether redactional moves were made to bring terminology into closer uniformity. In the sequence of the psalms set before us, however, there is a sense of both continuity and development, and it is striking that this development occurs precisely where we also have a second biographical superscription that extends the concerns of the figure of David in Pss 3–6 from a particularized context (in Absalom's rebellion) to a more general context linked to the verbal abuse of the Benjaminites throughout David's life. Psalms 8–14 will use this broader context to address the exploitation of the poor in needy in society.

Psalm 7's continuity with and development of Pss 3–6 is also reflected in its construction of the figure of David. While my full argument will come at the end of the chapter, I want to note a few points here to set up my analysis of Pss 8–14. For Pss 3–6, I argued for three different configurations of David: Biographical David, Typical David, and Typological David. In Ps 7, I have spent much time arguing that the Biographical David can still be heard through the referents both within the superscription and in the psalm itself. At the same time, this Biographical David has been set up in a different relationship to the episodes it engages. Spoken retrospectively, instead of building figural extensions from Biographical David to Typical and Typological David, the figural extensions are constructed primarily on typical and didactic lines. The David who speaks in Ps 7 can be understood as representative in the way he prays for justice, and by extension of his didactic role he instructs the people about the nature of God's righteous judgment. The typological role is not developed in the same way. Rather, considering the messianic concerns of the Psalter, the figure of David's promised heir is more closely related the poor and oppressed, who come to the fore in Pss 8–14, and for whom David offers prayer.

---

[47] See Goldingay, *Psalms 1–41*, 147. He took the reference to peoples as "all the nations of the earth." See also Weiser, *Psalms*, 137; Craigie, *Psalms 1–50*, 98; Samuel Terrien, *The Psalms: Strophic Structure and Theological Commentary* (Grand Rapids: Eerdmans, 2003), 120–21.

[48] See Charry, *Psalms 1–50*, 35. She noted how Ps 7 "exemplifies Ps. 1's stark division of people into two categories: the faithful who follow God's torah-given way of life and the wicked who do not and trouble and scoff at those who do."

5.3. An Analysis of Pss 8–14 in the Context of Ps 7

5.3.1. The Superscriptions of Pss 8–14

Since we do not find any further biographical settings in Pss 8–14, the heading of Ps 7 stands as the contextual setting for the entire cluster.[49] Each psalm begins with liturgical direction (למנצח + על + melody/ instrument), most have ancient genre descriptions (מזמור), and all are associated with the figure of David (לדוד). While we find more variety in these superscription patterns than in Pss 3–6, they function in much the same way: to orient the reader in light of the biographical setting of Ps 7. In terms of the canonical meaning of the elements in the titles, I will defer to my argument in the chapter three, but have included summaries here:

Ps 7	Ps 8	Ps 9/10
A *shiggaion* of David, which he sang to Y<small>HWH</small> concerning the words of Cush, a Benjaminite.	For the leader. Upon the *gittith*. A psalm of David.	For the leader. Upon 'Death of the Son' A psalm of David.
An expression of the chaotic reversal of expected blessings, spoken by the figure of David, of his trust in Y<small>HWH</small> despite lifelong verbal accusations and attacks from the Benjaminites.	*Recommended for encouragement and support, that one's life might be aligned with God's work in the world; a song of worship offered to Y<small>HWH</small>, related to the figure of David.*	

Ps 11	Ps 12	Ps 13	Ps 14
For the leader. Of David.	For the leader. Upon the flutes. A psalm of David.	For the leader. A psalm of David.	For the leader. Of David.
Recommended for encouragement and support, related to the figure of David.	*Recommended for encouragement and support, that one's life might be aligned with God's work in the world; a song of worship offered to Y<small>HWH</small>, related to the figure of David.*	*Recommended for encouragement and support, a song of worship offered to Y<small>HWH</small>, related to the figure of David.*	*Recommended for encouragement and support, related to the figure of David.*

---

[49] There are some who understand Ps 9 as another biographical element (e.g., Millard, *Die Komposition des Psalters*, 133), but this does not follow any pattern of biographical superscriptions; it refers to the name of an ancient melody. I have rendered it in the table as "Upon 'Death of a Son.'" See Robert D. Wilson, "The Headings of the Psalms," *PTR* 24 (1926): 364–65; Herbert Gordon May, "'Al...' in the Superscriptions of the Psalms," *AJSL* 58 (1941): 77–78; Gerstenberger, *Psalms: Part 1*, 73.

5.3.2. Hearing Ps 8 in the Context of Ps 7

On its own, there is a strong consensus categorizing Ps 8 as a hymn. Structurally, the psalm has proved to be difficult throughout the history of interpretation.[50] After the superscription, the opening and closing verses are a refrain that acts as a bookend (8:2, 10). In them, the psalmist speaks for the first time in the Psalter using a first-person plural pronoun, "Yнwн, *our* Lord, how majestic is your name in all the earth!" One may be led to think that we are hearing the voice of a group rather than an individual, but the only other indication of speaking voice in the psalm is singular: "For I see your heavens, the work of your fingers, the moon and stars that you have established" (8:4). The voice we hear, then, is one speaking on behalf of many (a cultic leader of some sort), or perhaps one speaking *as* many (the Davidic king). Yнwн is addressed in the second person and with vocatives throughout the whole psalm.

The refrain lifts up the majestic "name" (שֵׁם) of Yнwн as the psalm's overarching theme.[51] For the psalmist, the name of Yнwн connotes both magnitude and power, displayed in how Yнwн both exercises his kingship over the earth and sets his glory in the heavens (8:2). The refrain also serves as an important structural link, creating a hymnic bridge across Pss 7–8–9 centering on the "name" of Yнwн.[52] In 7:18 we read, "I will praise Yнwн [אודה יהוה] according to his righteousness, and make music [ואזמרה] to the name of Yнwн, Most High [שֵׁם־יהוה עליון]." Similarly, we read in 9:2–3, "I will praise Yнwн [אודה יהוה] with my whole heart, I will tell of all your wonderful deeds; I will be glad and exult in you, I will make music to your name, O Most High [אזמרה שמך עליון]." Within the frame of Pss 7 and 9/10, the refrain of Ps 8 has been perfectly situated. This means, in part, that Ps 8 is the very expression of praise and thanksgiving the figure of David had desired to sing coming out of his reflections on the just judgment of Yнwн (7:18). Bridged together with Ps 9/10, the majesty of Yнwн's name found in Ps 8 is not only accounted for in David's awe of creation and the role granted to humanity within it, but also in the wonderful deeds of Yнwн, which look towards the execution of his justice.

Indeed, in 8:3 the psalmist reflects on how the strength of Yнwн is related to the weakest and most vulnerable people in society, who will feature prominently in Pss 9–14. We read: "From the mouths of infants and sucklings you have founded strength for the sake of your adversaries, in order to remove the enemy and self-avenger." As Hossfeld and Zenger argued, the psalmist proclaims that Yнwн has the power not only to protect the most weak and vulnerable group of people, but to do so in the midst of a hostile environment.[53]

---

[50] See Pierre Auffret, "Essai sur la structure littéraire du Psaume viii," *VT* 34 (1984): 257–69; Judah Kraut, "The Birds and the Babes: The Structure and Meaning of Psalm 8," *JQR* 100 (2010): 10–24.

[51] Hossfeld and Zenger, *Die Psalmen 1–50*, 78–79.

[52] Patrick D. Miller, "The Beginning of the Psalter," in *The Shape and Shaping of the Psalter*, ed. J. Clinton McCann, JSOTSup 159 (Sheffield: JSOT Press, 1993), 90.

[53] Hossfeld and Zenger, *Die Psalmen 1–50*, 79.

Here, the establishing of strength is not located in the cry itself, but in the fact that the helpless have been protected in such a way that they are still able to praise him in response to persecution and oppression. In light of the other occurrences of "infants and sucklings" in the Old Testament (1 Sam 15:3; 22:19; Jer 44:7; Lam 2:11), it becomes clear that they are not to be understood literally but as a metaphor for those weakest and helpless in society (exemplified by the helplessness of the newly born). For the psalmist, the name of Yʜᴡʜ provides the defenseless with protection; he is a bulwark in the midst of enemies.[54]

Given this divine commitment to the helpless, we can note some striking parallels between Pss 7–8. First, two of the ascriptions given to the opponents of the psalmist in 8:3—צורר ("foe") and אויב ("enemy")—form the core of the oath formula used by David in 7:4-6: "If I have repaid my friend with evil, or plundered my foe [צוררי] without cause, then let the enemy [אויב] pursue me." The "foe" also figures in David's call for justice in 7:7, "Lift yourself against the fury of my foes [צוררי]."[55] In light of Ps 7, the opponents mentioned in 8:3 are not some unknown entity, but are already known by David through his experience of their pursuit in his own life. The claims of 8:3 do not function in the psalm merely as part of David's praise, but give instruction for those who pray for justice and for those who are acting unjustly. Reading the psalms together, we can see that David prays in Ps 7 according to the faith claims expressed in 8:3. On the one hand, he calls for God to deliver him from those who pursue him, to let his enemies be silenced or stilled; yet, on the other hand, if he is not innocent in these matters, then let his enemies overtake him instead. In Ps 7, David illustrates what it means to pray as one of the "infants," petitioning God to act in strength on his behalf. As we will see, the claim of Ps 8:3 will act as a kind of "rule of faith" that undergirds the prayers and petitions of Pss 9–14.

The latter half of the psalm (vv. 4–9) enters new territory for the Psalter. The psalmist looks up from the weakest and most vulnerable parts of creation to behold the grandeur of the universe (8:4). Sharing synonyms for "establishing," 8:3-4 suggest a merism: Yʜᴡʜ establishes his strength to bring justice to the weak (יסד; 8:3) and sets in place the heavenly bodies (כון; 8:4). The psalmist's reflections center on the personal care Yʜᴡʜ took to set the heavenly bodies in order, and he has trouble understanding how Yʜᴡʜ could give attention to and care for humankind: *why* has Yʜᴡʜ founded this strength to remove the enemy? Or, "What is humankind [אנוש] that you remember him; and a son of man [בן־אדם] that you attend to him" (8:5)? To answer such questions, the psalmist takes some cues from Gen 1, contemplating the great honor and privileges bestowed on humanity. God not only remembers them and cares for

---

[54] See Goldingay, *Psalms 1-41*, 156–57.

[55] These terms also appear in 6:8 (צורר), and 3:8; 6:11 (אויב).

them (8:5), but has crowned them with glory and honor,[56] and has given them dominion over the works of his hands.[57]

The remaining verses (vv. 7–9) describe the breadth of humanity's commission, listing each of the creatures under their care. As in Gen 1–2, they are given dominion over domestic and wild animals, birds, and various kinds of fish and sea creatures. It would be a mistake, however, to limit humanity's responsibility to only these creatures. The association of human and animal dominion in Ps 8 resembles the eschatological state in texts like Isa 11, where the Branch of Jesse, in the power of the Spirit of YHWH, establishes the world so that wild and domestic animals, along with nursing and weaned children, can co-exist without hurting or destroying one another.[58] In imitation of YHWH, humanity must also help provide protective barriers for the vulnerable (8:3) and be mindful of them (8:5).[59] Humanity, then, shares in God's sovereign rule, having been commissioned to maintain justice in defense of the weak and oppressed. The Psalter's primary reflection on humanity's dominion, in fact, is on how it relates to society's most vulnerable. For instance, the prayer of Ps 72:12-14 reads: "For [the king] delivers the needy when they call, the poor and those who have no helper. He has pity on the weak and the needy, and saves the lives of the needy. From oppression and violence he redeems their life; and precious is their blood in his sight." Psalm 8, then, continues Ps 7's more generic reflections on—and calls for—a just society. We have entirely left behind the specific episodic realm of Pss 3–6, where notions of worldwide domination and human sovereignty are not at work. Indeed, until this point in the Psalter, the only passage which remotely resembles such dominion is the promises of Ps 2:8: "Ask of me, and I will make the nations your heritage, and the ends of the earth your possession."

As I have discussed, one of the purposes of Pss 1–2 is to make a connection between the blessings of those who trust in YHWH (2:12) and the blessings of the "Man" (1:1). He is blessed because of his ruminations on the *torah* of YHWH (1:2) and his ability to walk in the way of YHWH while living in the midst of wicked people (1:1). His blessings consist of his own stable and thriving life in the presence of YHWH, as well as fruit of these blessings that he can bring into his community (1:3). The righteous of 1:6, likewise, are set in parallel with those who trust in YHWH (2:12b), who are said to receive their blessings in connection with the establishment of the anointed king upon Zion and his worldwide

---

[56] Note the similar use of כבוד in both 7:6 and 8:6.

[57] Humanity has not achieved this status on their own; it is something that only God could have bestowed on them. See Weiser, *Psalms*, 144–45. He wrote: "It is God's will that all things be subject to man, and it is by virtue of God's might that all things are subject to man."

[58] Goldingay, *Psalms 1-41*, 160.

[59] See Mays, *Psalms*, 67. He wrote: "God has established dominion over chaos and brought forth creation; humankind is given capacity and vocation to master other animals and bring forth civilization."

kingdom (2:7–12a). If the dominion indicated by Ps 8 is connected to the establishment of the king in Ps 2, then the blessings received by those trusting in YHWH can also be included in the same vision; the blessings of the people of God will resemble the blessings of the anointed king. Within this context, the reconciliation between the world as it now is (Ps 7) and the world as it should be (Ps 8) can only take place when the anointed king of Ps 2 begins his worldwide rule, reigning in the rebellion of the nations with his rod of iron and requiring the fealty of human rulers (2:7–12a). The importance of Ps 8, then, lies in its further exploration of the themes of Ps 7 within the context of Pss 1–2.

Recalling the Davidic voice of Ps 7, we can hear Ps 8 in similar ways. On the one hand, the psalm has been contextualized within the canonical setting of Ps 7 as the expression of David's thanksgiving and praise concerning the just judgment of YHWH (7:18; 8:2, 10). The words of Ps 8 are words that the wicked would not and could not ever utter, since they are busy conceiving evil, becoming pregnant with mischief, and giving birth to lies (7:14). David, refusing to yield to the state of the world around him, turns to God in praise and exaltation. His words of praise, however, are not simply hymnic, but ruminating. His prayer is both typical and instructive. As a didactic speaker, David's meditations on divine sovereignty and human dominion—that is, the status afforded to humanity and the care God provides for those who bear his image— give the reader wisdom on how to pray and understand the world around them.

5.3.3. Hearing Pss 9–14 with Pss 7–8

Within the orienting role that Pss 7–8 play, Pss 9–14 can be heard as maintaining the didactic function of teaching the reader how to pray for divine justice and pursue the way of YHWH within an unbelieving generation (cf. 1:1). Hope is held out for the poor and afflicted within society under YHWH's providential care (Ps 7; 8:3), while at the same time the cluster recognizes the failure of humanity to uphold its creative purpose over YHWH's creatures, human and animal (Ps 8). In this section, I will focus my attention on how Pss 9–14 engage with these key motifs in Pss 7–8, adding further dimensions to notable theological themes in Pss 3–14 as a whole.

5.3.3.1. Psalms 9/10.[60]
According to the redactional model of Hossfeld and Zenger, Ps 9/10 is the latest addition to Pss 3–14. It was consciously included

---

[60] There has been a longstanding debate whether this should be read as a single, unified psalm (Ps 9/10), or as two separate psalms (Ps 9, Ps 10). Previous scholarship has gone into great detail on both sides of the discussion, and there is no need to recapitulate it here. I will proceed with the understanding that Ps 9/10 form a unified psalm, as witnessed by the LXX, by its acrostic pattern (though incomplete), through shared lexicon and themes, and in the absence of a superscription to Ps 10 where one would be expected. I will continue to use the MT verse enumeration of the psalms individually, but I will use the designation "Ps 9/10" to refer to the unity of the psalm. See Kraus, *Psalms 1–59*, 191–

after Ps 8 in order to transform our understanding of Pss 11–14 by identifying "all Israel" with "the poor."[61] While it is nearly impossible to determine the accuracy of their reconstruction of redaction history, their observations concerning the rhetorical effect of the placement of Ps 9/10 are correct, as it contains lexical and thematic links to Pss 3–14 in nearly every verse. In my final-form reading, this psalm both reiterates the Psalter's vision for YHWH's justice and commitments to his people (Pss 1–2, 7–8), and goes into greater depth describing the nature of the wicked and what is demanded in the call to seek after God (Pss 3–6, 11–14).

Beyond the concerns of Pss 3–14, however, Ps 9/10 is significant because it engages nearly every key theological and sociological issue in the entire Psalter. Patrick Miller has observed: "No other psalm so fully joins the basic themes of the Psalter—the rule of God, the representative rule of the king, the plea for help in time of trouble, the ways of the wicked and the righteous, and the justice of God on behalf of the weak and the poor." [62] At the heart of the psalm is the commitment of YHWH to the poor and oppressed (9:10, 19; 10:17–18). This is built upon two theological realities: (1) YHWH is the eternal King (9:8a; 10:16a), who rules the nations from Zion (9:12, 15); and, (2) YHWH is the Judge of all peoples (9:16, 18, 20–21), whose judgment is declared from on high (10:5).[63] As 9:8–9 state: "YHWH is enthroned forever! He has established his throne for judgment (מִשְׁפָּט), and he will judge (שָׁפַט) the world with righteousness; he will judge (דִּין) the peoples with equity." Significantly, the psalmist does not conceive of YHWH's rule and justice as mere ideals, but an actuality to be experienced in his active judgment towards an oppressive enemy (9:4–7, 16–17; 10:14, 16b) and in the salvation of the righteous (9:5a, 10–11, 13, 14–15, 19; 10:12, 14, 17–18).

The expectations of the psalmist, however, have not been met in the on-the-ground reality of his life: "Why, O YHWH, do you stand far off? Why do you hide yourself in times of trouble?" (10:1). The rare phrase "in times of trouble" (לְעִתּוֹת בַּצָּרָה), used in both 9:10 and 10:1, emphasizes the centrality of this question. If YHWH is so concerned about the poor and needy, then how is it that he stands idly by when he is needed most?[64] Raising this question, the psalmist goes into great detail highlighting the thought life, deeds, and speech of the wicked (10:2–11, 13). For him, the wicked act in arrogance (10:2a), and in four

---

93; Svend Holm-Nielsen, "The Importance of Late Jewish Psalmody for the Understanding of Old Testament Psalmodic Tradition," *STNJT* 14 (1960): 50–53.

[61] Hossfeld and Zenger, *Die Psalmen 1–50*, 83. See Seybold, *Die Psalmen*, 55. He likewise argues that Ps 9/10 was combined and put into parallel with Ps 8 through its close connection to 7:18, where the initial *toda* was announced.

[62] Patrick D. Miller, "The Ruler in Zion and the Hope of the Poor: Psalms 9–10 in the Context of the Psalter," in *David and Zion: Biblical Studies in Honor of J. J. M. Roberts*, ed. Bernard F. Batto and Kathryn L. Roberts (Winona Lake: Eisenbrauns, 2004), 188–89.

[63] See Kraus, *Psalms 1–59*, 192, 198; Miller, "Psalms 9–10," 190–91.

[64] See Craigie, *Psalms 1–50*, 127.

places he notes how they think (10:4, 6, 11, 13).[65] In 10:4, the psalmist claims that every plan concocted by the wicked works from the principle that "there is no God" (אֵין אֱלֹהִים). This most directly contrasts with the psalmist, who delights in Yнwн's existence and deeds (9:2–3), calling on others to do the same (9:12). In 10:6, the wicked claim that they are impervious to calamity: "I shall not be moved; throughout all generations I will not meet adversity." Not only does this contradict the claim of the psalmist in 9:7, but it also works against the Davidic commitments to Yнwн in 7:11: "My shield is upon God." In David's view, the evil of the wicked will come to an end, while the righteous will be established (7:10). In 10:11, the wicked claim that God has forgotten the poor and hidden his face, and that God will never see their acts of persecution and exploitation. This verse expresses the deep worry of the psalmist.[66] It counters explicitly the claims made by him in 9:13 ("He has not forgotten the cry of the afflicted") and overturns the reality of judgment in 9:18–19 ("May the wicked depart to Sheol, all the nations forgetful of God; for the needy will not always be forgotten, the hope of the poor will never perish"). And finally, in 10:13, though the wicked never think they will be called to account, Ps 9/10 affirms that God sees all and examines all (10:14–15; cf. 7:10).

Turning to the deeds of the wicked, we can recognize that their basic claims manifest oppressive and destructive behavior in both speech and action. Of their speech: they boast of their own desires (v. 3); they curse and renounce God (vv. 3, 13); their "mouth" is marked with cursing, deceit, and oppression (v. 7), contrasting the cries of the "mouth" in 8:3; and the movement of their tongue works mischief and iniquity (v. 7), comparable to the unrepentant in 7:15, 17. The same is true of their actions: they are greedy for gain (v. 3); they do not seek out God (v. 4; note the contrast with 9:11); and they sit in ambush to harm and exploit the poor (vv. 2, 8–10). Simply stated, "anything goes" for the wicked.[67] Nevertheless, the psalmist repeats his hope while also bringing his question to God's attention, using key terms from earlier: though they lurk "like a lion" (כְּאַרְיֵה) to seize the poor, they will be judged (10:9; 7:3); while they lay a net (רֶשֶׁת) to capture the poor (v. 9), they instead capture their own foot in it (9:16); they hope to make the helpless "fall" (נפל) by the brute force of their strength (v. 10), but they fall into the pits they have made (7:16; cf. 9:16). And most

---

[65] The patterns of life described here are the most detailed we find for understanding the "way of the wicked" (1:1). The "way of the righteous," on the other hand, is not only exemplified by the psalmist in the way he prays throughout the Psalter, but is explicated in several places (Pss 1; 15; 24; etc.) and can be seen in the ideal set forth for the Davidic king (e.g., Pss 72; 101).

[66] See deClaissé-Walford, et al., *Book of Psalms*, 141–42.

[67] Craigie, *Psalms 1–50*, 127.

illustratively, while they "sit" (ישׁב) in ambush in the villages (v. 8), Yʜᴡʜ "sits" enthroned in Zion on a seat of righteous judgment (9:5, 8, 12).[68]

While this description of the wicked dominates nearly half of Ps 10, it is important to see that the description itself is framed by the psalmist's prayer for the oppressed (10:2, 12). The point is that the present prosperity of the wicked and the apparent idleness of Yʜᴡʜ's judgment does not lead the psalmist to give up hope and himself forget God, but deeper into prayer and trust. The repetition of the prayer for Yʜᴡʜ to "rise up" (9:20; 10:12) makes it the dominant petition in the psalm.[69] In militaristic terms (cf. 7:7; 8:3), this is a cry for God to arise in judgment and act in protection of the vulnerable and weak. Again, these prayers are grounded in Yʜᴡʜ's eternal kingship over the nations and in his capacity as Judge (9:4–9; 10:16–18; cf. Ps 7). The psalmist has in mind national enemies (9:6–7, 16, 20) as well as enemies and oppressors who have risen up in the ranks of Israel and threaten him personally (9:4–5, 14–15). By including both, Ps 9/10 can be used by someone in either situation; the promises of 9:10–13 apply regardless of how one's enemy is defined.[70]

Coming out of these discussions, the questions of setting and context are important. Viewed within purely historical terms, scholars have made a good case that the psalm has a post-exilic setting, when Jews would have faced opposition from external national powers and internal societal injustices.[71] This would help make sense of the variety of singular and plural references to enemies and oppressors, which fit both personal (9:14–15) and national (9:16–17) interests. But within the context of the Psalter, this potential historical setting has been reassessed and placed under the introductory setting of Pss 1–2 and the orienting work of the superscription of Ps 7. Dialogically, we hear the words of Ps 9/10 as coming from the lips of the figure of David in retrospective rumination.[72] Like Pss 7–8, David speaks in Ps 9/10 having faced lifelong trouble with the Benjaminites. Though he experienced important victories, Yʜᴡʜ's judgment was anything but swift. With hindsight, David allows his former

---

[68] This is the same contrast we saw earlier in Pss 1–2. There, the characteristics of the wicked were recalled in Ps 1:1, which included a reference to the "seat (מושׁב) of scoffers." This contrasted with Yʜᴡʜ's response to the schemes of the nations, who derides them as "one who sits (ישׁב) in the heavens" (2:4).

[69] See Miller, "Psalms 9–10," 189.

[70] See Steven J. L. Croft, *The Identity of the Individual in the Psalms*, JSOTSup 44 (Sheffield: Sheffield Academic, 1987), 68. The final verses of each part of the psalm capture this dual sense of the enemy well (9:20–21; 10:14–18).

[71] See Gerstenberger, *Psalms: Part 1*, 75; Seybold, *Die Psalmen*, 55.

[72] Dialogically, only first-person pronouns are used by the speaker (9:2–7, 14–15), but for most of Ps 9/10 no personal pronouns are used (9:8–13, 16–21; 10:1–18). Since there are no strong reasons to argue for a change of speaker, I assume the same voice speaks throughout. There is, however, a change of addressee between Yʜᴡʜ (9:2–7, 11, 14–15, 18–21; 10:1, 12–15, 17–18) and "others" (9:8–10, 12–13, 16–17; 10:2–11, 16). See Miller, "Psalms 9–10," 191–92.

experiences to shape his typical role as one of the "afflicted,"[73] while at the same time utilizing his abiding hope in YHWH didactically. His experience with the Benjaminites gives us a window into his own response to situations in which God is seemingly inactive in his help for and deliverance of the faithful.

I should also reiterate John Chrysostom's earlier point with Ps 7, that the figure of David in Ps 9/10 is different than the David we read about in the narratives of 1–2 Samuel. The superscription of Ps 7 orients this cluster of psalms for rumination on the broader themes of YHWH's justice and the characteristics of the wicked and the righteous. It does so without the need to find direct correspondence between the psalm and a specific situation in the life of David, as we had in Pss 3–6. In Ps 9/10, we meet a David who prays—and teaches us to pray—according to the principles of divine justice outlined in Ps 7 and YHWH's commitment to the vulnerable in Ps 8. He calls upon YHWH to act against those who are abusing the role that YHWH has given humanity in the created order (8:4–9). While the wicked renounce YHWH and imagine him as not caring about the actions of humanity, David takes the opposite stance: "You do see! For you note mischief and vexation, that you may take it into your hands" (10:14). He longs for God to "do justice to the fatherless and the oppressed, so that man who is of the earth may strike terror no more" (10:17–18), and is careful to remind humanity that they are not gods; the proud stand in a precarious relationship to their Creator: "Rise up, O YHWH! Let not mortals (אנוש) prevail; let the nations be judged before you. Put them in terror, O YHWH! Let the nations know that they are only humans (אנוש)" (9:20–21). But most important in Ps 9/10, the psalmist ultimately sets out to praise YHWH for his deeds (9:2–3), calling on his readers to do the same (9:12–13). He anticipates such praise following his deliverance (9:15) and sings of it to all who have the ears to hear (10:16–18). As I noted earlier, the opening vow of praise (9:2–3) is lexically connected to 7:18, as well as the refrain of Ps 8 (vv. 2, 10). This suggests that the prevailing themes of justice and righteousness of Ps 7, erupting in the praise of Ps 8, continue to have their place in Ps 9/10 in the hope expressed for the poor and afflicted (cf. 9:9–10, 17–18). As in Ps 7, Ps 9/10 depicts the judgment of God over both the nations (7:7–12) and the wicked (7:13–17).[74] The irony of divine providence in executing this justice is summarized perfectly by 9:17: "YHWH has made himself known; he has executed judgment; in the work of their hands the wicked are snared."

5.3.3.2. Psalm 11. As was noted at the beginning of Ps 9/10, Hossfeld and Zenger view Pss 11–14 as a collection of prayers that allow one to think through the reality that YHWH is the God of the "poor."[75] These psalms pick up on central concerns already stated in Pss 7–10, such as the oppression of the poor and weak, the immorality of the wicked, and the related sovereignty, providence, and

---

[73] See Wallace, "King and Community," 276.
[74] See Charry, *Psalms 1–50*, 46.
[75] Hossfeld and Zenger, *Die Psalmen 1–50*, 100.

justice of Yʜᴡʜ. Like Ps 9/10, these psalms illustrate for the reader how to pray for the restitution of God's people from both the threat of outside enemies and the ever-present social fracture which is internal to the community of Israel.[76]

In its voicing, Ps 11 is different from any other psalm we have come across thus far. While it continues to use a first-person singular voice throughout, the speaker consistently addresses a plural group of counselors who are never explicitly identified.[77] As we will see, the situation in which the psalmist finds himself is quite similar to what we have discussed in Pss 7–10. Here, instead of praying for his own deliverance from oppressors, he expounds on the nature of his trust in Yʜᴡʜ to those offering ill-founded advice. The psalm itself can be split into two main sections. In the first, the psalmist responds disdainfully to the advice of his counselors (11:1–3), and in the second he explains how Yʜᴡʜ figures into his perilous situation (11:4–7).

In the first section, the psalmist begins by offering his response to his counselors (vv. 1b–c), whose advice is quoted afterwards. The response opens with a simple declaration of his trust in Yʜᴡʜ, "In Yʜᴡʜ I have sought refuge" (11:1b), paralleling the opening prayer of Ps 7. The verb חסה denotes a search for shelter by those being persecuted, and is a fitting opening statement in a psalm thematically focused on faith in Yʜᴡʜ in the midst of opposition.[78] The second line of his response also echoes the earlier Ps 3:3, "How could you say of my soul...?" More than a simple rejection of their counsel, it signifies that their counsel has been heard as a reproach or insult against his very person. It is an attempt to lessen his trust in Yʜᴡʜ.

On the surface the advice (11:1d–3) does not seem altogether inappropriate: "Flee to your mountain *as a* bird" (v. 1d).[79] The imperative and possessive pronoun with "mountain" are plural, indicating the advice is given to the entire group in which the psalmist belongs, who are identified as the "upright in heart" (ישרי־לב) in 11:2 ("to shoot in darkness at the upright in heart") and 11:7 ("the upright will behold his face"). From this identification, we have further correspondence with Ps 7, as there the figure of David also aligns with this group: "My shield is upon God, a deliverer of the upright of heart" (7:11). The advice, then, is not offered by the psalmist's opponents, nor those with whom he is aligned, but from a group of fainthearted counselors who, while not in the psalmist's inner circle, advise him and his close associates to escape the peril at

---

[76] See Seybold, *Die Psalmen*, 60. While these concerns are particularly potent in the Hellenistic period, the editors of the Psalter situate them as coming from the mouth of David in retrospective rumination. They see in Yʜᴡʜ's support of David throughout his life the grounds for their own hope. In their construction of the figure of David, they put before God's people a teacher and representative, that they might continue to take refuge in Yʜᴡʜ as David had.

[77] Yʜᴡʜ is never addressed in Ps 11.

[78] See Kraus, *Psalms 1–59*, 202.

[79] See Delitzsch, *Book of Psalms*, 187, who makes a good case to follow the *kethib*. For a strong argument in favor of the *qere*, see Craigie, *Psalms 1–50*, 132–33.

hand.[80] Using the same imagery from Ps 7:13–14, they advise an escape from the predatory nature of the wicked into mountain safety. While in Ps 7 the imagery is used for the preparations of Yhwh's judgment of the unrepentant, it is here used to describe the preparations of the wicked in their hunting of the upright (v. 2). We find the same imagery and conceptual understanding of the wicked in Ps 9/10. In 9:16 the nations and the wicked have dug pits and laid nets to trap the righteous, further portrayed in 10:2–11 as devising schemes (v. 2), hiding out in ambush to attack the innocent (v. 8), and lurking in secret like lions on the hunt for the poor (v. 9). They are described in Ps 11 as a collective whole, unified in their attack on the upright.[81] The advice, then, is not trivial; the danger is both real and present.

An important distinction from Pss 7 and 9/10, however, is that the wicked are not described as enemies of the psalmist *per se*, but the upright more generally.[82] The work of the wicked threatens to destroy the very foundations of society (v. 3). At stake is the "disintegration of those institutions that maintain social order, protect virtue, and fend off evil."[83] For the faint-hearted counselors, the aim of the wicked is to turn the world upside-down, subverting justice and allowing violence to reign. In such a social situation, they ask, "What could the righteous have done?" (v. 3). Their only option must be to flee for safety. The psalmist, however, will have none of it. Instead, he "returns question for question, faith and trust for unfaith and mistrust."[84] He declares that his trust lies in the security of Yhwh and is offended that the faint-hearted would suggest any other place of refuge.

In the remaining verses of the psalm, the speaker goes into detail responding to each of these pieces of advice. Yhwh is the direct or indirect object of all but one line and is named in a syntactically emphatic position three times. The psalmist puts focus on how Yhwh is present for the upright, something that his counselors had refused to mention. Unlike the wicked who are positioned in secret ambush, Yhwh is both present amongst his people in his holy temple and enthroned in heaven, seeing all (v. 4). Though he resides upon a transcendent and lofty throne, above human affairs, he is not indifferent to what transpires on earth. Corresponding to David in Ps 8, who looks to the heavens to better understand Yhwh's call and commitment to humanity, in Ps 11 we find Yhwh gazing back at creation. In his sight, the efforts of the wicked rebound back upon themselves, recalling the motif of providential (self-)retribution (cf. 7:10–17; 9:16–17; and 10:2).[85] Indeed, the use of the same imagery in 7:13–14 and 11:2

---

[80] For a detailed discussion on the identification of his opponents, see Gerald H. Wilson, *Psalms: Volume 1*, NIVAC (Grand Rapids: Zondervan, 2002), 249.

[81] Wilson, *Psalms: Volume 1*, 250.

[82] Briggs, *Psalms*, 89.

[83] Tremper Longman III, *Psalms*, TOTC (Downers Grove: InterVarsity, 2014), 91.

[84] deClaissé-Walford, et al., *Book of Psalms*, 148.

[85] See Longman, *Psalms*, 92. The imagery lexically recalls Gen 19:24 and Yhwh's punishment of Sodom and Gomorrah.

reinforces this connection. The psalm closes with a promise to the upright that they will behold the face of Y<small>HWH</small> (v. 7). Even while society seems to be falling apart, the just judgment and protective power of Y<small>HWH</small> amid peril gives the upright a clear vision of his glory.

Looking at the whole psalm, the retrospective biographical setting of Ps 7 provides interesting food for thought. The description of societal upheaval would fit either Saul's reign or Absalom's rebellion, as early Israel was barraged by constant war and political vicissitudes. More, these were chapters in David's life when, incidentally, he *did* flee to the hill country on multiple occasions. Such settings offer much reflection for the reader: what are the righteous to do in such times of peril and violence? David's typical and didactic voice, looking back on his own trials, urges the upright to trust in the reign of Y<small>HWH</small>, whose providence and protection remain "in circumstances which make it appear that things are falling apart."[86] Following Ps 9/10, one can envision the advice of the counselors being offered as a counter to what they may have considered a faithful, but careless, naivety. Psalm 11 is a response, turning the counsel of the fainthearted on its head. The psalmist challenges them—and any who think like them—to change their course and join him in his reliance on Y<small>HWH</small> (cf. 2:12).

5.3.3.3. Psalm 12.   Much like Ps 2, Ps 12 presents readers with several different voice changes. The psalmist never uses a personal pronoun to identify whether he speaks alone or as part of a larger communal voice. Structurally, the psalm follows the voicing and audience in a chiastic fashion. In the opening section (vv. 2–5), the psalmist first prays to Y<small>HWH</small>, describing in the third person his social environment (vv. 2–3). Using jussives, his speech opens up to a wider audience in verse four, followed by a quotation of his opponents, the "smooth-talkers" (v. 5). The second section (vv. 6–8) begins with a quotation of Y<small>HWH</small> (v. 6), which in turn is followed by the psalmist—or perhaps even the poor and needy—speaking to a wider audience (v. 7), and another prayer to Y<small>HWH</small> (v. 8). The psalm closes with a general statement about the nature of evil within society, again addressed to a wider audience (v. 9).

With such distinctive voices in the psalm and markers for changes in audience, it comes as no surprise that scholars have often postulated a liturgical setting for the psalm, whether one originally concerned with an individual petitioner or with a larger community.[87] Canonically, the figure of David continues to speak, as we have seen throughout Pss 7–11. Within this literary context, Ps 12 is not referring to an individual case of slander brought before

---

[86] J. Clinton McCann, "On Reading the Psalms as Christian Scripture: Psalms 11–12 as an Illustrative Case," in *Diachronic and Synchronic: Reading the Psalms in Real Time*, ed. Joel S. Burnett, William H. Bellinger, and W. Dennis Tucker, Jr., LHBOTS 488 (London: T&T Clark, 2007), 138.

[87] See Gerstenberger, *Psalms: Part 1*, 82–83; deClaissé-Walford, et al., *Book of Psalms*, 151–52.

YHWH,[88] but the larger social setting of the wicked oppressing the upright in Pss 9–11 and the corresponding judgment requested in Pss 7–8. Indeed, the so-called oracular quotation in 12:6 rests upon the foundational commitment of YHWH to defend the helpless (e.g., 8:3; 9:10–11, 13; 10:14–18). Several scholars have pointed out such connections, especially to Ps 11.[89]

Turning to the psalm itself, in the opening section the psalmist makes two parallel requests of YHWH: that he would deliver the faithful (v. 2) and cut off all lips of flattery (v. 4). The prayer for deliverance is grounded by the knowledge that the holy and faithful have all but vanished from among humanity (v. 2), so that all without exception speak with vanity (v. 3). Similarly, the prayer for flattering lips to cease is grounded by a hypothetical quote from them, highlighting their hubris before the weak of society and implicitly before YHWH (v. 5). Concerning the first request, we should note that there is no verbal object in the MT: "Deliver, O YHWH!" (v. 2). Without the object, the psalmist is not asking YHWH for his own rescue (as in 9:13–14 or the LXX) but is concerned for the purity of God's promises and livelihood of the poor and needy. Following Ps 11, one is tempted to think that his concern lay with the very structures upholding public life.

The problem is that instead of the evil of the wicked becoming no more (גמר; 7:10), the "godly/pious" (חסיד) have ended (גמר; 12:2); the "faithful" (אמונים) have vanished from humanity (בני־אדם; cf. 8:5; 11:4).[90] For the psalmist, not only have those loyal to the covenant ceased, but none who are faithful can be found among the general population.[91] The emphasis, then, is different than in Ps 11. There, the powerful, who could uproot society, are the focus, while in Ps 12 everyone is involved, from the least to the greatest. Adapting Ps 14, one might say: "There are none who are faithful; no, not one." This is emphasized in verse three by the fronting of the term שוא (denoting emptiness), which provides a summary of the activity marking the verse: everyone speaks even to their neighbors or friends (רעה) using smooth speech (literally, "a lip of smoothnesses"). The population consists of master manipulators who use sweet

---

[88] See Seybold, *Die Psalmen*, 62.

[89] See Delitzsch, *Book of Psalms*, 192; J. Clinton McCann, Jr., "The Book of Psalms: Introduction, Commentary, and Reflections," in *New Interpreter's Bible: A Commentary in Twelve Volumes*, vol. 4 (Nashville: Abingdon, 1996), 724; McCann, "On Reading the Psalms as Christian Scripture," 138; Goldingay, *Psalms 1–41*, 196.

[90] See Kraus, *Psalms 1–59*, 208; deClaissé-Walford, et al., *Book of Psalms*, 153; McCann, "The Book of Psalms," 724.

[91] See Delitzsch, *Book of Psalms*, 194. He described the faithful as those "whose word and meaning is firm, so that one can rely upon it and be certain in relation to it." See also Craigie, *Psalms 1–50*, 138. He added that a faithful one is "a covenant member whose life was characterized by that faithfulness and loving kindness which were of the very essence of the covenant relationship and life."

but insidious words, speaking with purposeful deception and misleading. One is tempted to think that Cush the Benjaminite fits this description well (7:1).[92]

The deliverance prayed for in verse two is further nuanced in verses four and five as the psalmist asks that Yhwh bring judgment upon all smooth lips, the tongues which make great boasts. The kinds of boasts are quoted in verse five, and reveal what lies at the heart of their speech: they believe that no one rules over them, declaring themselves free from all authority and accountable to no one (cf. Ps 2:1–3). Their hubris implies that if "any authority were to assert itself over them, their mouth would put it down and their tongue would thrash it into submission."[93] The denial of Yhwh as ruler or master over them is not a denial of his existence but of his ability to do anything about their own power over others. What was once attributed only to the wicked (Ps 10:7) is can now be heard as spoken by the general populace: "You will not call us to account!" (10:13). As we saw in Ps 11, the second half of the psalm will not allow this word to be final; another voice is ready to offer better words to the people (vv. 6–7).

The second half of the psalm (vv. 6–9) moves our attention towards Yhwh, whose own words are contrasted with the words of the flatterers: "I will now arise!" (12:6; cf. 3:8; 7:7; 9:20; 10:12). In a reversal of the typical ordering, Yhwh first gives us the reason for his response, "Because of the ruin (שד) of the poor (עניים), because of the groaning (אנקת) of the needy (אביונים)." As I have emphasized throughout this chapter, it is not the great and powerful boasts of the wicked which have spurred Yhwh into action, but the sighing and groaning of the needy.[94] Above all, they have been most affected by the schemes and ruses of the smooth-talkers (9:19; 10:6–7, 11, 13). With their suffering a turning point has been reached between divine forbearance and the execution of justice. The strength behind the cries of the helpless (8:3) is ready to be revealed: "I will now place in safety (ישע) him who longs for it (יפיח לו)" (12:6). The repetition of the root ישע, used in verse two, is also the answer to the opening prayer of the psalmist: Yhwh will indeed bring deliverance. For those in ruins and groaning, longing for deliverance to come, the time is at hand. In 12:7–8, the section closes with the psalmist proclaiming his confidence in the words of Yhwh. Purged from all impurity, they are spoken without flattery and are dependable (אמן), in utter contrast to the emptiness (שוא) of the smooth talkers. While the "faithful" may have disappeared, the words of Yhwh are ever-present. The psalmist can raise

---

[92] In Pss 7–14, the verb דבר is only used in 12:3–4 and 7:1.

[93] Delitzsch, *Book of Psalms*, 195. See also Craigie, *Psalms 1–50*, 138; Wilson, *Psalms: Volume 1*, 268–69. Wilson described the situation well: "The wicked believe their mastery of deceptive language gives them power and leads to victory. That personal power comes at the cost of the truth and the exploitation of the defenseless is of no concern to them.... The wicked described here are so confident in their mastery they feel invincible—completely in control and without limits."

[94] See deClaissé-Walford, et al., *Book of Psalms*, 154.

his voice again to Yhwh, certain that Yhwh will fulfill his promise to preserve the poor and needy, protecting the one who longs for safety.[95]

It comes as a surprise, then, that the psalm ends not with these words of hope, but with the darker reality of the present situation. Just as the psalmist is sure that Yhwh will deliver the poor and needy, he also recognizes that the wicked are not easily struck down. Looking back at verse six, we must be careful how we understand the promised deliverance: Yhwh does not promise to cut down the wicked, as the psalmist has hoped; rather, he promises to place under his protection those who cry out for his help. In verse nine, the psalmist paints a vivid picture: as long as humanity (בני אדם; v. 2) considers "worthlessness" (זלות) honorable, the wicked will freely walk about, uncontested and celebrated; moreover, whenever and wherever such things are exalted, the poor and needy will undergo suffering. What is needed, then, at the end of Ps 12 is the same thing that has been needed in nearly every psalm we have encountered thus far: the turning of the human heart towards the way of Yhwh. The promise, though surrounded by "the apparent triumph of the wicked," is that faith can remain confident in the tested words of Yhwh and in the protection provided by Yhwh within trying times.[96] Hearing the voice of the figure of David in the psalm, the faithful can both follow his example in prayer and learn from his instructive words. As Athanasius instructed: "When you see the arrogance of the multitude and the evil that abounds, so that nothing is holy as far as men are concerned, flee to the Lord for refuge and say Psalm [12]."[97]

5.3.3.4. Psalm 13.

With Ps 13, the Psalter returns to familiar signals of petition like those in Pss 3–6. Thematic and lexical links to passages within Pss 7–12 are abundant. Throughout the psalm, the psalmist speaks to Yhwh using first-person singular pronouns. Different voicing can only be found in verse five, when the psalmist reports the speech of his enemy: "I have overcome him." As with previous psalms, the association with the figure of David suggests that the principal voice belongs to David, and as I have argued above, with the same literary context as the preceding Pss 7–12. We will first make our way through the psalm and comment further on this speaking persona at the end.

The psalm begins, quite unlike anything we have seen thus far, with four distressing lines of questioning addressed to Yhwh, each beginning with עד־אנה, "How long?" While there are certain parallels in these verses with Ps 6, no sins are mentioned in Ps 13, and all accusations of sin are absent. According to Craigie, this suggests the opening questions are not related to penitence but to a profound sense of anxiety.[98] The cries of "how long?" witness to afflictions or

---

[95] See Wilson, *Psalms: Volume 1*, 269.

[96] McCann, "The Book of Psalms," 724.

[97] Athanasius, *The Life of Antony and the Letter to Marcellinus*, trans. Robert C. Gregg (New York: Paulist, 1980), 115.

[98] Craigie, *Psalms 1–50*, 142.

persecution, or even illness, which has lasted for a long time.[99] They are the prayerful groans of those who need YHWH to rise up for them (cf. Ps 12:6), a means of bringing to YHWH's attention the distressing situation of his people. There are parallels here with the use of the question in Ps 10:1, to remind YHWH of his commitments to his people (9:10).

Weiser and Goldingay helpfully recognize the threefold dimension of the psalmist's questions: the religious, or relationship with YHWH (v. 2); the psychological, or inner turmoil of the psalmist (v. 3a); and the sociological, or trouble coming from his enemies (v. 3b).[100] The opening question is daring in its directness towards YHWH, "How long, O YHWH? Must you forget (שכח) me forever?" The psalmist is not referring to a forgetfulness of knowledge, but an absentmindedness; YHWH is overlooking him. The second question helps to elaborate: "How long must you hide (סתר) your face from me?" It is not simply that YHWH is refusing to act on his behalf, but that YHWH is suspiciously absent. It would be easy to hear this opening pair of questions as an accusation of unfaithfulness on YHWH's part, but when we hear them alongside the claims of the faithless or wicked throughout our group of psalms, we can sense a deep trust remaining in these words. For example, in Ps 10:11 the psalmist recalls the words of the wicked using the same terminology: "For he has said in his heart (לב), 'God has forgotten (סתר), he has hidden (סתר) his face (פנה), he will never (נצח) see it.'" When heard in this context, the psalmist is asking thoughtful questions that bring into view the very mindset of the wicked, whom he believes have gained ascendancy over him (v. 3). It is as if he were saying, "Are my enemies correct? Have you forgotten me and hidden your face? Will you ever see their wickedness? Prove them wrong! What are you waiting for?"[101] By voicing these questions aloud, he exposes them, not allowing them to take further root in his heart.

Turning inward, the psalmist then brings to YHWH's attention how his apparent forgetfulness and absence have brought about personal anguish. Without YHWH the psalmist is left only to his own counsels.[102] A clue to the substance of these counsels can be found in the final question, "How long must my enemy be exalted over me?" Seeing the present success of the enemy, the thoughts of the psalmist anxiously dwell on the schemes and machinations of what they may be up to next: "How long will YHWH allow this to continue?" Again, a contextual reading of the psalm deepens our understanding of the

---

[99] Craig C. Broyles, *The Conflict of Faith and Experience in the Psalms: A Form-Critical and Theological Study*, JSOTSup 52 (Sheffield: Sheffield Academic, 1989), 183–84.

[100] See Weiser, *Psalms*, 162; Goldingay, *Psalms 1–41*, 206. The pattern is again repeated in 13:4–6 with its focus on YHWH (v. 4), the psalmist (v. 5), and his enemies (v. 6). But see also deClaissé-Walford, et al., *Book of Psalms*, 160. Jacobson argued that all three areas are interrelated, so we should not overstress their distinctiveness.

[101] See Broyles, *Conflict of Faith*, 184.

[102] Kraus, *Psalms 1–59*, 215. He wrote: "If Yahweh now hides his countenance, then the human being is forsaken by God. He is alone with עצות."

situation in which the psalmist finds himself (10:2–11; 11:3; 12:9). Most importantly, the definitive word spoken by YHWH in 12:6, and the psalmist's confidence in that word, could provide a poignant background to the questions which open Ps 13.[103] The anxiety of the psalmist increases as the wickedness rampant in Ps 12:9 continues to be exalted in 13:3. The wicked are proving to be their own masters instead of YHWH (12:5). Samuel Terrien captured the moment eloquently: "The alienation of his celestial companion as well as his vulnerability before human hostility is so tenacious that he can no longer endure the anguish that strangles his breathing and the pain that constrains his heart."[104] How can YHWH continue to remain silent in the background?

In the next section (vv. 4–5), the psalmist continues to address YHWH. It opens with two imperatives without an intervening *waw*, which adds a sense of urgency to the prayer: "Take notice (נבט)! Answer me!" (11:4). As in the previous section, a thread of lexical terms is picked up from Ps 10: "You have seen (ראה), for you take notice (נבט) of trouble (עמל) and grief (כעס), that you might take it into your hands" (10:14). The verb נבט expresses more than a simple glance, but careful regard, as we saw in 11:4–5. The seriousness of the requests can be felt in the remainder of the section as the psalmist gives further reasons for these prayers, beginning with the final clause of verse four: "lest I sleep in death." While this might be taken as hyperbole, the fear in the expression is real. For the psalmist, his current situation is life-threatening. Unless YHWH acts, his enemies will gain the upper hand and rejoice in his own downfall (v. 5). The wordplay of מות ("to die") and מוט ("to be moved") reinforces this point. It, too, is used of the wicked in Ps 10, quoted as saying: "I will not be moved (מוט), throughout all generations I will never be in trouble" (10:6). Of paramount concern is that the wicked are not being held accountable for their actions, and that the justice that was supposed to be meted out to them seems instead to have been meted out to the upright. Unless YHWH moves to action, the enemies will prevail over them. The commitment of YHWH to the most helpless in society (8:3) will be proven false.

The final section (v. 6) begins with a firm statement of trust, "But I, in your steadfast love, have trusted; my heart shall rejoice in your salvation." Despite the anxiety of the present moment and recent past, the psalmist continues in the same posture of faith (7:2; 9:11; 11:1) and praise (7:17; 9:1–2) as in the whole cluster. Paralleling 9:15, he anticipates the deliverance of YHWH and expresses his desire to sing of YHWH's abundant care over him. The sentiment here is the opposite of the verb מוט used in verse five, denoting the turbulence of a life overwhelmed by enemies. For the psalmist, covenant faithfulness (חסד) grounds his enduring trust in the security offered him in YHWH.[105] The use of the personal pronoun (עלי) as the final word of the psalm recalls the earlier question in verse

---

[103] See Delitzsch, *Book of Psalms*, 199. He astutely noted: "The ירום of the personal cry [13:3]... harmonizes with כרם of the general lament [12:9]."

[104] Terrien, *The Psalms*, 159.

[105] See Craigie, *Psalms 1–50*, 143.

three, "How long must my enemies be exalted over me (עָלַי)?" The psalmist hopes for a complete reversal of the present circumstances.

Scholars have had a difficult time identifying what exactly the "present circumstances" are in Ps 13. Most understand the psalm as the lament of a sick person, perhaps one who is near death or mortally ill. But as Kraus noted, one cannot neglect the strong focus on the enemy in the psalm, whose very purpose is to overwhelm the psalmist and shake his confidence in Yhwh.[106] Scholars have also noted the change in tone between verses five and six, which is often attributed to the intervention of a priest or cultic leader to help the psalmist overcome his anxiety.[107] In both cases, as my analysis has shown, the lexical and thematic parallels with Pss 7–12 provide an important literary context for Ps 13.[108] For instance, rather than proposing some missing element between verses five and six, 12:6 might provide the perceived missing word of Yhwh. The psalmist continues to have confident hope in Yhwh as the one who promises to arise in defense of the poor and needy. Indeed, the whole of Ps 13 might be a response to this prophetic word. The line of questioning in verses two and three goes deeper than an emotionally charged response in a desperate situation. It is grounded in the knowledge that Yhwh has committed himself to the deliverance of the poor and needy.

5.3.3.5. Psalm 14.   Psalm 14, as one of the *Eckpsalmen* ("corner-psalms"), shares several lexical and thematic links with Ps 3, as well as other places in Pss 7–13. Very few scholars have been willing to postulate an original setting for the psalm, which perhaps highlights the difficulties in understanding the historical relationship between it and Ps 53, as well as its mixed form (wisdom, prophetic, and lament motifs are all present). That said, a majority of scholars suggest at least an exilic situation for its final form, given its apparent reference to exile in verse seven. As I will note, however, this verse need not have an overt exilic reference, and may offer a more general hope for God's work to restore Israel. In this case, its resonance with Pss 7–13 is striking.

Regarding its speaker, the superscription points again to a Davidic persona, which we have encountered throughout Pss 7–13. Speaking with a prophetic voice, the psalmist never addresses Yhwh explicitly. Nevertheless, we are left with important voicing questions. It is clear that the psalmist quotes the "Fool" in verse one, but in verses three and four scholars have been unable to determine if the psalmist is speaking in his own voice or as a prophet, quoting the verdict of Yhwh as he looks down upon humanity. The prophetic aspect of David's wider persona in the Old Testament, however, may mitigate any differences this might have for interpretation. And finally, in verse six the psalmist uses a plural second-person pronoun to address the "workers of

---

[106] Kraus, *Psalms 1–59*, 213–14.

[107] Something along the lines of Ps 12:6, but not included in Ps 13. See McCann, "The Book of Psalms," 727.

[108] See Goldingay *Psalms 1–41*, 204.

iniquity." One, then, must decide if the psalmist is addressing this group exclusively throughout the psalm, or is only singling them out for this verse.

The psalm opens with a meditative instruction regarding the "Fool" (נבל), who acts in accordance with his belief that "God is not there" (אין אלהים). As almost all commentators note, this is not likely a statement of theoretical atheism, but indicates a "practical" or "empirical" atheism.[109] When heard alongside similar statements in Pss 7–13, the words of the wicked in Ps 10 are instructive. The most direct is 10:4, in which the foundation for all the scheming of the wicked is identical to 14:1: "All of his plots are אין אלהים." Psalm 10, then, offers us the clearest insights into what it means for people to have "acted corruptly" and to have "committed abominable deeds" (14:1). They posture themselves by boasting in their immovability (10:6). Believing that God has forsaken the poor and helpless (10:11), they sit in ambush, looking for every opportunity to exploit them (10:7–10). We also find a parallel in 12:5, which focuses on the verbal abuses of the wicked, founded on the belief that they are accountable to no one (cf. 10:13). From this we see that the "Fool" assumes, whether from experience or otherwise, that Yʜᴡʜ neither interferes with nor judges his actions.[110] The disastrous consequences of Yʜᴡʜ's apparent inaction against the "Fool" and the wicked are highlighted by the verb שחת in 14:1: "They have acted corruptingly." Using the *hiphil*, the psalmist is not just saying that they have acted in a corrupt fashion, but that their actions have been deliberate, causing ruin to those around them. Again, such deeds are described in 10:7–10, and both implicitly and explicitly are the subject of the psalmist's words in Pss 11–13. In a clever turn of phrase, the psalmist points out that, rather than God not being there, in reality "the one who does well" (עשׂה־טוב) is not there.

The "Fool," then, is not a new character, but comes alongside the wicked and the general populace of smooth-talkers within Pss 7–14. Yet, they should not be conflated. Each psalm has been careful in setting up its antagonists. In Ps 11, for instance, they were not the wicked, but fainthearted counselors who had lost their trust in Yʜᴡʜ and advised David to flee to the hills for safety (11:1c–3). In Ps 12, the smooth talkers, who, while sharing characteristics with the wicked, were not always so. Indeed, the general populace seems to have fallen under their sway, such that all in society walk with an air of unaccountability (12:9). The "Fool" shares many characteristics with both groups but, as John Sailhamer has noted, it may be better to understand them as those who have "given up

---

[109] See Delitzsch, *Book of Psalms*, 203–4; Kraus, *Psalms 1–59*, 221; deClaissé-Walford, et al., *Book of Psalms*, 166; Wilson, *Psalms: Volume 1*, 287. While Delitzsch couches this in terms of denying the reality of a personal God, most commentators have said something more like Kraus: "He who denies God contests not the existence of God but the concrete activity of God." So Jacobson: "The fool's mistaken assumption is that God is not an active presence in the world." Wilson perhaps has the best summary: "The corrupt action that follows is not the result of ignorance but of a knowing commitment to a lifestyle based on the false conclusion that God has no effective place in human life."

[110] See Charry, *Psalms 1–50*, 65.

hope that God will punish the wicked and deliver the righteous."[111] The "Fool," like the smooth talkers, has heard the boasting of the wicked, but unlike the psalmist has not remained faithful to Yнwн. They have been unable to follow in David's footsteps.[112] In contrast, the wise "continue to long for the salvation of Israel out of Zion."[113] Like the psalmist, they call not for proof of God's existence, but for confidence in God's presence (14:7).

Returning to 14:2, the "Fool" is not allowed the final word. We learn that, regardless of the thoughts of the foolish and wicked, Yнwн is there and is deeply concerned with the affairs of human beings. Specifically, he looks down from heaven to see if there are any who are wise (שׂכל), seeking after God. The theme of Yнwн's examination of humanity has appeared several times (7:10; 10:14; 11:4–5) and occurs in the context of his role as Judge over the whole of creation (cf. 7:7–12; 9:4–11). Notably, in each of these occurrences, the judgment of Yнwн is introduced as the psalmist pleads for the poor and needy, who need defense from the abuses of the wicked (7:2–6, 15–17; 8:3; 9:18–20; 10:14–18; 11:6–7; 12:6–8). Yнwн's search for any who "seek" (דרשׁ) him meets a parallel in 9:11, where the psalmist states that Yнwн has not "forsaken those who seek you." Perhaps there are some, especially among the poor and needy, who continue to seek him. In an interesting turn, however, the verdict is not simply that the wicked and foolish are not seeking God (cf. 9:18; 10:3), but that no one from the whole of humanity (בני־אדם) seeks after him (14:3). If Sailhamer's insight is correct, it is because of a perceived delay in God's just judgment that they have given up hope in his commitment to them.

This verdict resembles the verdict of Ps 12: "The holy one has ceased; the faithful have vanished from humanity [בני אדם].... On every side the wicked prowl as vileness is exalted by humankind [בני אדם]" (12:2, 9). While verses five and six open up for us the question about the poor and needy, for now the gaze of Yнwн is fixed on all of humanity and leaves no exception: "All [כל] have turned aside, together [יחדו] they have been corrupted [אלח]; there are none [אין] who do well, there is not even one [גם־אחד]" (14:3). The results are disastrous. As Wilson noted, the choice of the verb אלח ("to be corrupt") creates a vivid description not merely of the actions of the wicked themselves, but their effect on society: "The corruption of the wicked has influence beyond them...the rebellion of the wicked infects for the worse the world in which they live."[114] Their actions are both corrupted and corrupting.

---

[111] John H. Sailhamer, *NIV Compact Bible Commentary* (Grand Rapids: Zondervan, 1994), 317–18.

[112] Hearing Ps 14 alongside Ps 11, with which it has numerous parallels, we may be tempted to identify the foolish with David's faint-hearted counselors.

[113] Sailhamer, *NIV Compact Bible Commentary*, 318.

[114] Wilson, *Psalms: Volume 1*, 187. Perhaps the *niphal* captures this corrupting nature. The verb itself is found only here and in Ps 53. It has etymological parallels to the souring of milk.

Before we move to the second half of the psalm, it is worth noting that Ps 14 has conceptually switched the spatial imagery of Ps 8. In Ps 8, the figure of David stares up at the night sky in awe of Yʜᴡʜ's grandeur and majesty, which causes him to reflect on the created purpose of humanity. Yʜᴡʜ has both entrusted them with the sovereign care of other creatures (8:7–9) and the protection of the most helpless and weak in human society (8:3). In 14:2, we have the opposite occurring, as Yʜᴡʜ looks down upon his creation at the state of humankind (cf. 7:10; 11:4–5). From this angle, the verdict is different: humanity has strayed far from its created purposes. Psalms 9–13 have already ruminated on the claims of Ps 8 to uncover a darker reality of humanity. Instead of ruling over God's creatures, humanity acts like them. Humanity is an unrighteous oppressor who does everything in its power to exploit the weak and helpless among them. While Ps 8 has a grand vision of creation, and while Ps 9 celebrates the vanquishing of the wicked (9:4–9), Pss 10–13 have emphasized that the wicked continue to abuse the weak, and more importantly, that God has yet to rise up and bring restoration (despite 12:6). In these psalms, the exclamations of wonder in Ps 8 are matched by the languishing groans of "how long?" in Ps 13. The verdict on humanity in 14:1–3 is another word of Yʜᴡʜ that the subjection of the world through the exploitation of the most vulnerable is utterly discordant with the vision of humanity in Ps 8 and needs desperate repair.

The opening question of verse four asks if the "workers of iniquity" (פעלי און) were ignorant of what they were doing: "Have they not known [ידע]?" As we know from the occurrence of this term in 5:6 and 6:9, "workers of iniquity" is not a general synonym for the wicked, but designates the opponents of individuals.[115] The question, of course, is rhetorical; they certainly know, but have refused to acknowledge the judgments of Yʜᴡʜ (10:5). In fact, they have renounced Yʜᴡʜ (10:3), plotting, scheming, and living in forgetfulness of Yʜᴡʜ (9:18). The point of the question is to call out the evildoers. What is in their hearts is not the reality which the psalmist knows to be true: God is there, and has judged humanity. The problem is that those who work iniquity within the community do so as if it were completely normal and casual: "they consume my people as they consume bread" (14:4).[116] As Jacobson pointed out, there is a parallel here with Micah's prophetic judgment in Mic 3:1–3 (NRSV):

> Should you not know justice?—you who hate the good and love the evil, who tear the skin off my people, and the flesh off their bones; who eat the flesh of my people, flay their skin off them, break their bones in pieces, and chop them up like meat in a kettle, like flesh in a caldron.

This "consuming of my people," as 14:4 puts it, is for Micah an image of how the powerful refuse to provide for the hungry or establish justice (Mic 3:5–9; cf. Isa

---

[115] Kraus, *Psalms 1–59*, 222.
[116] Delitzsch, *Book of Psalms*, 207.

32:6).[117] On top of this, they have also failed to call upon (קרא) YHWH. The figure of David in Pss 3–6 is our model for what this looks like (cf. 3:5; 4:2, 4), but here, in the context of Pss 7–13, the reference can be further nuanced in terms of the injustices committed throughout society. The figure of David consistently calls upon YHWH, refusing to believe the outlook of the wicked, all the while pointing the reader towards trust in the protective presence of YHWH (cf. 8:3; 9:10–13, 18–19; 10:3, 12–18; 12:2–9).

The rebuke of the "Fool" and worker of iniquity (v. 4) is followed by a warning to them concerning God's presence amongst the righteous and the afflicted (vv. 5–6). These verses recall many of the promises that YHWH has made and draw a line in the sand: YHWH is committed to the care of the righteous (cf. 7:10; 11:7).[118] Because of the commitment of God's presence among the righteous, the workers of iniquity should be afraid (14:5; cf. 12:8). Similarly, shame will come upon them for their treatment of the poor, for the poor have YHWH as their refuge (2:12; 5:12; 7:2; 11:1; 14:6; cf. 4:6; 9:11; 13:6). Again, this aligns with the basic "rule of faith" that Ps 8:3 provides for the entire cluster of psalms: "From the mouths of infants and babes you have founded strength for the sake of your adversaries, to remove the enemy and the avenger."[119]

The final verse expresses the strong desire of the psalmist for the deliverance and restoration of Israel: "O that deliverance would be given for Israel out of Zion!" (14:7). Unique to Pss 3–14, it is only in this verse that we find the appellations "Israel" (ישראל) and "Jacob" (יעקב) given to God's people. This shows, at least on one level, that the concerns of Pss 3–14 are not simply for the individual, but for the entire nation. As Hossfeld and Zenger have observed, this verse creates the "corner" or envelope that bridges the entire group together with 3:9: "Deliverance belongs to YHWH; your blessings be upon your people." They wrote: "It asks, in view of the social fracture of Israel and the threat of outside enemies, for the restitution of the people of God out of Zion—as the starting point of the (universal) rule of God."[120] This is expressed in the final two lines of the psalm: "When YHWH utterly restores his people, let Jacob rejoice! Let Israel be glad!" (14:7). The "Fool" has claimed that God is not there, but the psalmist again challenges their worldview in stark terms. As McCann has observed: "Despite what the foolish or the wicked may say (3:2; 10:14; 14:1), God is the help of God's people, individual persons or the body as a whole (3:8; 10:14; 14:5–7)."[121]

Here, then, at the end, Ps 14 brings us back to the main themes of Pss 1–2: the Two Ways (the way of the righteous exemplified by the "Blessed Man," and the way of the wicked, which perishes) and the response of YHWH, seated in heaven, to install his king upon Zion as ruler over the nations. Associated with

---

[117] deClaissé-Walford, et al., *Book of Psalms*, 167.
[118] Kraus, *Psalms 1–59*, 223.
[119] Weiser, *Psalms*, 166.
[120] Hossfeld and Zenger, *Psalmen 1–50*, 100. My own translation.
[121] McCann, "The Book of Psalms," 730.

the figure of David, the voice of Ps 14 speaks didactically to God's people, encouraging a similar hope to what we have seen throughout the group, for YHWH to deliver Israel and capture the hearts of his people.

5.4. The Role of the Figure of David in Psalms 7–14

In bringing my discussion of Pss 7–14 to a close, I want to focus on how these psalms make use of the figure of David. In my treatment of Ps 7, I argued its superscription has expanded David's biographical background to include all his dealings with the tribe of Benjamin, stretching from his encounters with Saul before David's enthronement (1 Sam 24–26) to Benjaminites associated with the rebellion of Absalom (2 Sam 15–18). Yet, we were not hearing a prayer of David in the moment of those experiences; David is retrospectively teaching us a theology of prayer. In this respect, the Biographical David has been extended in typical and didactic dimensions. Psalm 7, then, sets up a different reading experience than we had in Pss 3–6. There, I argued that the figural extension of the Biographical David into typical and typological dimensions was based on points of narrative disjuncture between the David of Pss 3–6 and the David of 2 Sam 15–18. Given the broadness of the superscription in Ps 7, however, the configuration of David cannot be based on this same strategy. Rather, in Pss 7–14 the extensions are made based on the nature of David's discourse.

On the one hand, we have the "Typical David," who prays both out of his own distress and to end the distress of others. The reader should keep the story of David in mind, and even Pss 3–6 can serve as a touch-stone through which to better understand his paradigmatic features, such as his penitent and humble posture before YHWH and his identification with the poor and needy. On the other hand, we have the "Didactic David," who speaks in a voice very similar to what we heard in Ps 1. Here, however, his voice takes on a more pronounced prophetic aspect, as he quotes forth divine speech and pronounces divine judgment concerning the nature of humanity. Moreover, the voice of David instructs his listeners with sustained didactic discourse (cf. 7:12–17; 8:3; 10:2–11; 11:4–6; 14:1–6). In these passages, the Davidic figure teaches his audience an anthropology: the commission and stewardship of humanity (Ps 8), the unimaginable evil it continues to accomplish (10:2–11), YHWH's sovereign authority and just judgment (9:4–9), and the deliverance of God's people from their enemies and oppressors (14:7). These are key themes in Pss 1–2 and, through their didactic presentation within Pss 7–14, they become anchor points for the prayers of David and others throughout the rest of the Psalter.

Moving into Ps 8, the figure of David continues to speak along these same lines as he turns toward the praise of YHWH's name, anticipated by the final verse of Ps 7. In his praise, David looks toward the heavens to take in the fullness of YHWH's grandeur, which results in his closer examination of the purpose of humanity within God's created order. Throughout this chapter I have focused on what I consider the "rule of faith" in Pss 7–14, the description of YHWH's commitment to the most vulnerable in society as they face those who oppress and exploit them (8:3). I see this call to care for the weak as part of humanity's stewardship of God's created world (8:7–9). Indeed, the remaining psalms in the group all ruminate this central issue. We might say, then, that as Ps 8 extends Ps 7's call for justice into the larger landscape of humanity—that is, beyond the concerns of David biographically and Israel collectively—Pss 9–14 prayerfully consider the extent to which the enemies of God's people seek to violently take advantage of them. Within this context, Pss 9–14 not only expose the destructive behavior of the powerful over the weak but focus attention on when YHWH appears to remain distant and unresponsive to the concerns of the poor and needy. Whether they ask, "Why do you hide yourself?" (10:1), or, "How long, O YHWH?" (13:1–3), these psalms make room for a robust faith: the patient endurance of the upright in the face of grave evil. For the editors of the Psalter, David alone could lead them in these prayers.

In this way, we see another key development in the figure of David in contrast to Pss 3–6. There, David received help from YHWH to overcome Absalom and his enemies. As we move into Ps 7 and consider the experiences of David under the pursuit of Saul and the Benjaminites, however, we recognize their consistent assault over the entirety of David's life. To use an analogy, it is like we are using a telephoto lens to view David in Pss 3–6, but a wide-angle lens in Pss 7–14. In the former, specific details emerge with the larger Davidic story blurred into the background; in the latter, the wider landscape of David's life comes into full view at the expense of detailed focus. As I argued above, Ps 7 shares a close relationship to the process of justice expounded in 1 Kgs 8:31–32, but recontextualizes its ongoing effect within David's biography. Within this canonical context, the figure of David provides the starting point for grasping the providential outworking of God's justice within his people. David has repeatedly experienced the divine aid for which the oppressed and disadvantaged hope. With David as their exemplar and teacher, they can pray alongside him for the same kind of deliverance that he experienced. At the risk of cliché, we are "with David in a school of prayer." Put in the form of a question, "How are we to pray when the justice of God has been silent concerning the weak and oppressed?" The figure of David, in patient hope, reflects on his own pursuers and deliverance, and provides a way forward in confident expectation of YHWH's deliverance.[122]

---

[122] Given this conceptual model for the Davidic figure in Pss 7–14, I am not as confident in positing a typological dimension. Rather, in my judgment, the proper place to hear the messianic elements is in the identification of the Davidic heir with or alongside those for whom David is praying. In a Christian reading, then, I would not advocate hearing Christ's voice in these psalms, but as being prayed *for* in them, as the "Typical David" intercedes on behalf of the oppressed, weak, and defenseless in society (cf. Matt 25:31–46). These Davidic prayers for the redemption and restoration of humanity can be heard as prayers for the arrival of the promised heir and the establishment of the divine kingdom. Through Ps 8's thematic connection with Ps 2, Pss 7–14 have opened up a profound

The final didactic moment in 14:7, when heard in this context, takes on a hopeful tone as the figure of David calls for YHWH to somehow intervene and deliver God's people, that they might once again praise him. The hermeneutical import of Pss 1–2 is critical at this point: the end of the story is not the rebellion of humanity against YHWH and his Anointed, but the establishing of the Davidic king upon Zion (2:7). As the Anointed of YHWH, having been attacked throughout his life from both his own people and the surrounding nations, he teaches us to pray for the actualization of the promises given him through the arrival of his heir. This adds a deeper dimension to the Psalms than we have seen thus far, but one that is important for understanding the relationship between the Davidic heir and those he has come to save (3:5, 9; 14:7).

---

environment for reflection on the human condition and the role of the Davidic heir in the deliverance of the helpless and penitent. The reader is invited to follow David's lead in praying for and helping to bring justice to the weak and helpless, as well as to look to the promised heir in hopeful expectation of the deliverance he will bring *when he joins with them.*

Nevertheless, I remain sympathetic to those who hear in David's voice typological hints of Jesus Christ. The author of Hebrews, for instance, argues that the humiliation and exaltation of Jesus are only just the beginning of his deliverance and restoration of the afflicted: "to deliver all those who through fear of death were subject to lifelong slavery" (Heb 2:15). The quotation of Ps 8 in the context of Jesus's suffering and exaltation resonates with every element of the psalm. As the promised heir, Jesus suffers alongside the afflicted (Ps 8:3), but through his defeat of the same spiritual powers that crucified him, he has been exalted into a position of authority over the whole of creation (8:5–9). Indeed, in Heb 2:10–18 the need and fittingness of the Son to join humanity under the oppression of the wicked is what enables him to serve as their high priest. He does not achieve this role as the wicked in Pss 7–14 have done, but through suffering death on behalf of both the oppressed and the oppressor. That is, he emptied and humbled himself rather than flattering himself and forgetting his place before the Creator. And now, much like David singing Ps 7 as he looks back at his experiences with the Benjaminites, Jesus, reflecting on his own deliverance from death, continues to intercede for his people, who come to his throne of grace.

6
Conclusions and Implications

In the preceding chapters I have applied a canonical approach to Pss 3–14 and have argued that the figure of David provides the best way to understand the speaking voice, a "voice without end." In this concluding chapter I will provide a summary of my findings as well as a discussion of some of the implications for other areas of psalm research. Concerning the latter, I will reflect on how my research might affect canonical and compositional readings of the Psalter, especially concerning the shape and message(s) of the book and the role of the figure of David beyond Pss 3–14. I will conclude by setting out a few lines of study which are still needed to further test my approach to psalm interpretation.

6.1. Summary of My Argument

In my introductory chapter I located my research within the larger concerns of psalm research. I identified my methodology within a canonical approach following the lead of Brevard Childs and Gerald Wilson, a line of research which has continued into contemporary studies of the Psalms. Even though there continue to be some sharp divides regarding the conclusions reached using this approach, it represents a set of concerns related to the final form of the book and its ongoing function within communities of faith. I also provided methodological grounds for reading psalms within their literary context, outlined my understanding of the structure of Pss 3–14 within Book 1 (Pss 3–41), and introduced questions related to the hermeneutical role of the biographical superscriptions and the concept of a literary persona.

This was followed in the second and third chapters with an argument for how a canonical approach to Pss 3–14 would inform the speaking persona(e). In the second chapter, I first surveyed several important premodern psalm interpreters within the history of the Christian interpretation, organized around two distinct but complementary exegetical models: prosopological exegesis and typological exegesis. The aim of this survey was to show that a handful of representative interpreters—Origen, Augustine, Aquinas, Calvin, and Athanasius—did not interpret the Psalms using a monolithic "Christian" approach. Each interpreter constructed the speaking voice in the Psalms along distinct, but complementary lines. Paired with this survey, in the second half of the chapter I surveyed psalm interpreters in the modern period, beginning with de Wette. Even though modern approaches to the Psalms have been grounded on a much different foundation than their predecessors, I showed that their own construction of the speaking voice was contingent on their identification of a historical situation, whether in the life of the author of a psalm or the cultic practices of ancient Israel.

I concluded the chapter with the observation that the construction of the speaking voice in the Psalms is largely dependent upon how an approach sets up the text's literary and historical contexts. This is true in both premodern and modern approaches. For instance, in Origen's prosopological model, the reader's own "journey of the soul" played a critical role in identifying the speaking voice as a "sinner" in Pss 37–39. In contrast, Augustine's prosopological model relied more fundamentally on the gospel narratives and Pauline exegetical principles to argue for a *totus Christus* ("whole Christ") speaking voice. In the typological models of Aquinas and Calvin, the context of the Christian canon was critically important, especially as one sought correspondences between the lives and kingdoms of David and Christ. Within the modern period, the void left by cutting off ties with David resulted in several different constructions of the speaker. While de Wette's historical approach called upon a generic "Everyman" to speak where David could no longer be historically verified, the debates within German circles at the end of the nineteenth century (the "I" versus the "we") relied upon different models of understanding the social relationship between the individual and the community in ancient Israel. In the twentieth century, cultic approaches touched on the subject along similar lines, but now sought answers in the use of psalms with the pre-exilic cult (so Mowinckel) or within a post-exilic worship environment (so Gerstenberger). Generally speaking, premodern models of the speaking voice are theologically and scripturally driven, whereas modern models relied on reconstructions of the historical, cultic, and social situations in which a psalm was composed or performed.

Having explored these interpreters for their similarities and differences, in the third chapter I undertook an analysis of the construction of the speaking persona from the context of the final form of the book. In the first part of the chapter I discussed the implications of Pss 1–2 for the speaking personae, concluding that they constructed the "figure of David" as the chief hermeneutical lens through which to understand the speaking voice. In Ps 1, David emerges as an ideal, exemplary figure (the "Blessed Man"), whom the righteous are expected to imitate in their own way of life. In Ps 2, the international concerns of Davidic kingship take center stage, within which a twofold voice emerges: the historical David and figurally, the Davidic heir of postexilic hope. Alongside the figure of David, in Pss 1–2 several other voices are introduced as important for the hearing of the book: (1) Y H W H (2:4–6, 7–9); (2) the "Blessed Congregation" of the righteous, who take refuge in Y H W H (2:12) and imitate the way of the

"Blessed Man" (1:6); and (3) the enemies of Yʜᴡʜ, the anointed king, and the righteous, who are described as sinners, scoffers, and wicked (1:1, 4–5; 2:1–3, 10–12). In the second half of the chapter I explored the hermeneutical role of the superscriptions, especially as they are found in Pss 3–14. This section was important in showing that the Davidic figure of Pss 1–2 should be identified as the principal speaker in Pss 3–14, grounded in the basic association with David (לדוד) and contextualized by the biographical superscriptions in Pss 3 and 7. Throughout this section I emphasized that the figure of David must be understood as developed within the book of Psalms itself, and not merely as a complement to the narratives in the books of Samuel. Though consonant with that "David," in the book of Psalms, "David" is a distinct figure.

To further investigate the function and voice of the figure of David, in my final two chapters I provided analyses of Pss 3–6 and Pss 7–14, respectively. From these analyses, I first argued that the biographical superscriptions in Pss 3 and 7 provided the contextual setting not only for each psalm individually, but also for those psalms following each in the group. The setting of Absalom's rebellion (Ps 3:1; 2 Sam 15–18) served an orienting function for Pss 3–6, while the more general appeal to David's trials with the Benjaminites (Ps 7:1) provided hermeneutical orientation for Pss 7–14.

Second, I argued that these biographical contexts set up the figure of David with different speaking configurations. For Pss 3–6, the initial biographical context constructed a baseline Davidic profile from 2 Sam 15–18. Within this profile, the reader is given a contextual background for the psalm that is located in the Davidic narratives (here, as he flees from Absalom during his rebellion) instead of their original cultic situation. At the same time, inconsistencies between the narrative and psalm suggest that the Psalter's own development of the figure of David speaks beyond this baseline biographical profile. The juxtaposition of Pss 1–2 with the superscription's context in Ps 3 allows the reader to probe deeper into the figure of David. In my reading, this allows the biographical profile of David to be extended in the two directions supplied by the David who emerges from Pss 1–2. First, aligning with the "Blessed Man" in Ps 1, the biographical David extends into a typical figure, which allows the reader to imitate David as she seeks to walk in the way of the righteous, under the providential gaze of Yʜᴡʜ. Second, aligning with the "David" of Ps 2, the biographical David is extended typologically. Here, the episode of Absalom's rebellion has been re-cast over the storied world of Ps 2, such that the life of David's heir is nascent within David's own biography, the heir actualizing the Davidic promises as he embodies a life paralleled by his ancestral father. Psalms 3–6, then, can be read within the storied life of David in 2 Sam 15–18, as well as with the anticipated story of his promised heir.

For Pss 7–14, the initial biographical setting again constructs a baseline Davidic profile, but this profile has been shaped differently than it was in Pss 3–6. In part, this is due to the nature of the biographical setting in Ps 7. Rather than placing David within a specific episode of his life, the superscription has a broader intertextual referent. The David of Ps 7 is not constructed by the rebellion of his son Absalom but by his lifelong trials with Benjaminites. More, we do not hear from a David who speaks in the heat of trouble (as in Ps 3), but from a David who speaks in considered reflection. As with Ps 3, I argued that this baseline biographical profile was been extended, but here in typical and didactic directions. In retrospective rumination, Ps 7 moves beyond Pss 3–6 by providing a template for prayer set within the theologically-constructed world of Pss 1–2. The David we hear in Ps 7, then, speaks as a didactic figure, instructing anyone willing to listen about the righteous and the wicked, as well as the reign of YHWH within the created world. Psalms 7–10 begin this instruction by focusing on the Two Ways, the theme of repentance, and the work of YHWH on behalf of the poor and needy. This is followed in Pss 11–14 with further reflections on the patience of the righteous and their continued dependence on YHWH, even if YHWH seems slow to act on his commitment to the weak and oppressed. Throughout, readers are also encouraged to follow David's example in how he prays for YHWH to intervene with help for the poor.

In conclusion, these two analyses demonstrate that the speaking voice in Pss 3–14 has been intimately connected to the figure of David, and that the construction of the Davidic voice is not static. In Pss 3–6, the figure of David has been constructed along biographical, typical, and typological lines, while in Pss 7–14 he speaks along biographical, didactic, and typical lines. Taken together, Pss 3–14 provide the Psalter's initial exploration of the themes presented in Pss 1–2, as well as our first introduction to the figure of David, who will remain present with the reader throughout the book.

6.2. Implications for Psalm Research

My study of Pss 3–14 serves two main purposes within the current state of the question in psalm studies. First, it fills in a gap in the canonical study of the Psalter by giving a thoroughgoing analysis of Pss 3–14. As I mentioned in my first chapter, this is an area that has received little treatment in monographs, collected volumes, and journal articles.[1] In my analysis, I have broken new ground by arguing that the biographical superscriptions have an orienting role not only for the psalm on which they have been ascribed, but also for those psalms that follow within the same psalm cluster. This has shaped the way I have understood individual psalms contextually and dialogically. For example, in Pss 3–6 this meant that the episode of David's flight from Absalom (2 Sam 15–18) has become the basic context of the entire psalm cluster, rather than an original *Sitz im Leben* for each psalm independently. Instead of arguing for a chronological reading of these psalms, I suggested that their sequence should be understood as a kind of parallelism, or as variations on a theme. They are explorations of

---

[1] Note, however, the recent publication of Philip Sumpter, "The Canonical Shape of Psalms 1–14," *OTE* 32 (2019): 514–43.

the Davidic persona which look in on David from different angles during his flight. Psalm 7 plays a similar role in its cluster, though psalms in this group have a stronger trajectory, often responding to the preceding psalm. As an approach, while more research must be done, there is promise: *the initial psalm in a small grouping of psalms orients the group towards certain themes within a particular literary context, and the psalms that follow explore those themes from different perspectives.* Such an approach might help to explain why juxtaposed psalms often share catchwords and thematic links and would provide definable limits to the use of catchwords within a set of juxtaposed psalms.

The second, and more pressing purpose of my research, was to better understand the development of the figure of David within the book of Psalms. Within the preceding chapters, my analysis proceeded by first investigating how Pss 1–2 and the superscriptions aid the reader in identifying a Davidic persona as the literary voice of the psalms, and then sought to show how the Davidic voice functioned within two psalm clusters, Pss 3–6 and Pss 7–14. In my first chapter, I broke down the current views of David within the Psalms into two broad categories. The first, following the work of Brevard Childs, begins with the biographical superscriptions. These connect thirteen psalms to various episodes within the life of David, nearly all of which come from the books of Samuel. For Childs and many other contemporary psalm interpreters, the voice of David *within psalms with biographical titles* plays a paradigmatic role for present readers of the Psalter as they reflect on a complementary portrait of David within the narrative context of 1–2 Samuel.

In practice psalm commentators have been less ambitious in hearing a Davidic voice. The commentaries by McCann, Goldingay, and Brueggemann-Bellinger, which cover a twenty-year spread (1996–2016), each discuss Childs's contribution in this regard, but when it comes to actual psalm interpretation do not apply his approach. For example, McCann wrote of Ps 3:

> The superscription is intended to encourage the reader to imagine a situation like that of David's during Absalom's revolt... Following Psalms 1–2, Psalm 3 proclaims that 'happiness'/'blessedness' consists of the good news that God's help (v. 8) is forthcoming precisely in the midst of such threats in order to make life possible (vv. 3–4) and to offer us a peace (v. 5) that the world says is not possible (v. 2).[2]

In Pss 4–6, however, he referred to the speaker as the "psalmist," and his only attempts at identifying the speaker are related to an original *Sitz im Leben*.[3] Goldingay's commentary likewise takes a very broad view of the speaker, highlighting a variety of options anywhere from a royal figure to any individual

---

[2] J. Clinton McCann, Jr., "The Book of Psalms: Introduction, Commentary, and Reflections," in *New Interpreter's Bible: A Commentary in Twelve Volumes*, vol. 4 (Nashville: Abingdon, 1996), 694.

[3] McCann, "Book of Psalms," 4:697–703. He suggests a setting of a temple court ritual for Pss 4–5, and that of a sick person praying for healing in Ps 6. David is of no concern.

within the community.[4] For Brueggemann-Bellinger, the voice we hear in Pss 3–7 is "the voice of the pious who have not received the promised prosperity" which was assured in Pss 1–2.[5] They "introduce a realism" into the Psalter, and, as psalms of David, are "somehow linked to the royal environs and assumptions of Jerusalem."[6] But note that the connection to David does not indicate a Davidic voice. For them, "Insofar as these five psalms are royal, they attest to the historical vagaries that face everyone, including kings who live under divine promise."[7] Indeed, the connection to Absalom "portrays a speaker—any speaker—whose life is deeply in jeopardy and who lacks resources to cope on his own… Like David, every person of faith may, in the midst of jeopardy, appeal through this psalm to the God of deliverance."[8] At best, then, when a superscription provides a setting for a psalm, commentators have tended to understand them as providing one of many possible contexts for reading a psalm. The Davidic voice is a voice *alongside* the reader, and not a voice in which the reader seeks to imitate or learn from; a Davidic profile only represents a *possible* voice. The approach initialized by Childs is, I think, helpful, but leaves questions unanswered: should the reader search for other episodes within the biblical narrative that could supply a literary context for a psalm? If so, are they limited to the life of David, or could other important biblical personae be investigated for a literary setting?

A second approach to the Davidic voice does not begin with the biographical superscriptions, but through a broader consideration of the shaping of the whole book. Gerald Wilson's contributions have largely shaped how scholars today portray David within this view, and Mark Smith's article, "The Theology of the Redaction of the Psalter: Some Observations," is representative of this approach.[9] Smith began by noting that the psalm superscriptions give the book a kind of chronological orientation. He wrote: "The superscriptions in Books I–III of the Psalter reflect a post-exilic idea of the Temple cult in the time of David."[10] Using Chronicles and Ezra as a guide, Smith observed that Books 1–3 have a more historical feel to them. The psalms are all attributed to pre-exilic figures, with relatively few psalms left untitled. Books 4–5, on the other hand, although containing several collections of psalms attributed to David (and a few individual psalms to Solomon), by and large leave psalms untitled. For him, this indicated

---

[4] See John Goldingay, *Psalms, Volume 1: Psalms 1–41*, BCOT (Grand Rapids: Baker Academic, 2006), 109.

[5] Walter Brueggemann and William H. Bellinger, Jr., *Psalms*, NCBC (New York: Cambridge University Press, 2014), 36–37.

[6] Brueggemann and Bellinger, *Psalms*, 37.

[7] Brueggemann and Bellinger, *Psalms*, 37.

[8] Brueggemann and Bellinger, *Psalms*, 38.

[9] Mark Smith, "The Theology of the Redaction of the Psalter: Some Observations," *ZAW* 104 (1992): 408–12.

[10] Smith, "The Theology of the Redaction of the Psalter," 409. That is, they reflect post-exilic views on the pre-exilic cult.

that Books 4–5 "shift in temporal perspective."[11] These latter psalms "represent songs for returning to Jerusalem from exile"; that is, they are not cast as pre-exilic psalms by the editors of the book.[12] In this new temporal situation, the figure of David also changes from his pre-exilic cultic function (in Books 1–3) to a new, eschatological function: "The David in Book V is not simply the historical David whose life is mentioned so frequently in the superscriptions in Books I–II. The single allusion to David's life in Book V, namely in Ps 142:1, shows that the old David is in view, but *his lament in this psalm may assume a paradigmatic character.*"[13] For Smith, the messianic milieu of post-exilic Israel helps build a characterization of David in the Psalms that is on the one hand exemplary (David as a model of piety) and on the other messianic (representing hopes of a new royal reign).[14] In Books 1–3, David is a historical figure, situated in a pre-exilic cultic environment, while in Books 4–5, David is still the historical figure, but his voice has taken on a more present and future orientation. That is, the David of Books 4–5 is more open-ended, and his voice is used paradigmatically as one who places his hope in Yhwh, who will bring about restoration from exile. As I have shown, this is simply not the case. David is not a bygone sapiential figure in Pss 3–14, but speaks along biographical, typical, and typological lines. The biographical superscriptions do not historicize David, but are tools of semantic transformation, allowing a psalm to be spoken by an ongoing, present voice in the figure of David.

Related to this concern, my reading of Pss 3–14 also challenges the notion that the so-called failure of the Davidic covenant is not in view until Books 3–4. The juxtaposition of Pss 2–3 is already bringing into focus the destiny of the sons of David. The focus on Absalom at the beginning of Book 1 (Ps 3) is paired with the focus on Solomon at the end of Book 2 (Ps 72). The sons of David, and the passing on of the Davidic promises to an heir, are presented as a central concern of the book, highlighting the failure of his sons through the person of Absalom and the hope for his sons in the person of Solomon. Here, the rebellion of Absalom opens Book 1 by type-casting Absalom and his party—in the terms of Ps 2—as rebels seeking to overthrow the sovereign rule of Yhwh and his earthly co-regent, the anointed king. In this, Absalom represents far more than the failure of David's sons, illustrating how humanity will continue to attempt to free itself from Yhwh's rule. The shocking statement made by Ps 3 is that David's own son is part of that attempt. The passing of the Davidic promises to Solomon, with their royal expectations (cf. 1 Kgs 2; Ps 1:2–3), opens up future hope for a Davidic heir who would rightly live out his faith in Yhwh before his people and rule with a righteous hand. Book 3 seems to show that any hope for this to have fruit in the history of the Davidic line has been dashed, verified by the end of the monarchy in the canonical narratives.

---

[11] Smith, "The Theology of the Redaction of the Psalter," 410.
[12] Smith, "The Theology of the Redaction of the Psalter," 410.
[13] Smith, "The Theology of the Redaction of the Psalter," 410. Emphasis added.
[14] Smith, "The Theology of the Redaction of the Psalter," 411.

The paradigmatic role of David, exemplified in Pss 3–6, is that David himself has already suffered under the failure of his sons, seen in his flight from Absalom. David's continued hope in YHWH would not only resonate throughout the pre-exilic period, when the psalm collections would have likely begun to come together, but also in the post-exilic period, when the people of God were attempting to understand how to move forward with a dashed hope. To this, the profile of David in Pss 7–14 encourages readers to pray with David for YHWH to work providentially for his people, continuing to live in hopeful expectation for the judgment of their enemies. The hope expressed in Ps 8, however, moved beyond a general trust in YHWH to act in various situations, but pairs with Ps 2 in its vision for the kingdom of God to become manifest in the world, led by the anticipated heir of David. My research, then, provides additional evidence for an eschatological orientation in the Psalter, but not one without historical and sapiential concerns. Indeed, the Psalter has constructed the figure of David by uniting the "Biographical David" with hopeful expectation in his anticipated heir, whether that is found through typological extension (Pss 3–6) or hope in the arrival of the kingdom of God (Pss 7–14).

6.3. For Further Study

My research on Pss 3–14 has relied heavily on the history of interpretation, and much in my methodology has drawn from careful readings of both premodern and modern interpreters. That said, I have ventured out into new territory with some elements of my argument, and these need further research to be better substantiated. To begin, while I have worked hard to analyze the ways in which Pss 3–14 develop the figure of David beyond Pss 1–2, this analysis must be extended not only to the end of Book 1, but also into Book 2 and later psalm clusters that are associated with David. Further, my hypothesis concerning the hermeneutical role of the superscriptions, especially the context-setting potential of biographical superscriptions, needs to be explored more thoroughly. In this regard, I want to emphasize that not enough research has been undertaken to define how a biographical superscription functions in the text. I have argued that the headings of both Pss 3 and 7 orient the reader to interpret the remaining psalms in their group, but this might not be the case for other biographical notices. This caution seems appropriate especially considering the string of biographical superscriptions in Pss 51–63.[15] In this same vein, I need to develop and further test my hypothesis concerning the other elements of the super-

---

[15] See Stefan M. Attard, *The Implications of Davidic Repentance: A Synchronic Analysis of Book 2 of the Psalter (Psalms 42–72)*, AnBib 212 (Rome: Gregorian & Biblical, 2016).

scriptions. For instance, how are the speaking personae affected by the switching of association from David to the sons of Korah or to Asaph? David Mitchell has undertaken some of this work, but more needs to be done.[16]

---

[16] See David C. Mitchell, *The Message of the Psalter: An Eschatological Programme in the Book of Psalms*, JSOTSup 252 (Sheffield: Sheffield Academic, 1997), 90–107; Mitchell, "'God Will Redeem My Soul from Sheol': The Psalms of the Sons of Korah," *JSOT* 30 (2006): 365–84.

Bibliography

Commentary

Alexander, J. A. *The Psalms*. Edinburgh: Andrew Elliot & James Thin, 1864.

Ambrose. *Commentary of Saint Ambrose on Twelve Psalms*. Translated by Ide M. Riain. Dublin: Halcyon Press, 2000.

Aquinas, Thomas. *Commentaire sur les Psaumes*. Edited by Jean-Eric Stroobant. Paris: Cerf, 1996.

———. "Commentary on the Psalms." The Aquinas Translation Project. http://hosted.desales.edu/w4/philtheo/loughlin/ATP/index.html.

———. *The Gifts of the Spirit: Selected Spiritual Writings (Chiefly from his Biblical Commentaries)*. Translated by Matthew Rzeczkowski. Edited by Benedict M. Ashley. Hyde Park, NY: New City Press, 1995.

Athanasius. *The Life of Antony and the Letter to Marcellinus*. Translated by Robert C. Gregg. CWS. New York: Paulist Press, 1980.

Athanasius (Pseudo). *Expositio in Psalmos*. Athanasiana Syriaca 4. Edited and Translated by R. W. Thomson. CSCO 386–387. Louvain: Secrétariat du Corpus, 1977.

Augustine. *Expositions of the Psalms*. Translated by Maria Boulding. Edited by John E. Rotelle. WSA 3/15–20. Hyde Park, NY: New City Press, 2000–2004.

Barnes, Albert. *Book of Psalms*. New York: Harper & Brothers, 1868.

Basil the Great. *Exegetic Homilies*. Translated by Sr. Agnes Clare Way. FC 46. Washington, DC: The Catholic University of America Press, 1963.

———. *On Christian Doctrine and Practice*. Translated by Mark DelCogliano. PPS. Yonkers, NY: St. Vladimir's Seminary Press, 2012.

———. *On Social Justice*. Translated by C. Paul Schroeder. PPS. Crestwood, NY: St. Vladimir's Seminary Press, 2009.

Braude, William G. *The Midrash on Psalms*. 2 vols. YJS 13. New Haven, CT: Yale University Press, 1959.

Briggs, C. A., and E. G. Briggs. *A Critical and Exegetical Commentary on the Book of Psalms*. ICC. Edinburgh: T&T Clark, 1906.

Brueggemann, Walter. *The Message of the Psalms: A Theological Commentary*. Minneapolis: Augsburg, 1984.

Brueggemann, Walter, and William H. Bellinger, Jr. *Psalms*. NCBC. New York: Cambridge

University Press, 2014.

Calvin, Jehan. *Commentaires de Livres des Pseaumes.* 2 vols. Paris: Librairie de Ch. Meyrueis et Compagnie, 1859.

Calvin, John. *Commentary on the Book of Psalms.* Translated by James Anderson. 5 vols. Edinburgh: Calvin Translation Society, 1845–1849.

Cassiodorus. *Explanation of the Psalms.* Translated by P. G. Walsh. 3 vols. ACW 51–53. New York: Paulist, 1990–1991.

Charry, Ellen T. *Psalms 1–50: Sighs and Songs of Israel.* Grand Rapids: Brazos, 2015.

Cheyne, T. K. *The Book of Psalms: Translated from a revised text with Notes and Introduction.* New York: Thomas Whittaker, 1904.

Chrysostom, John. *Commentary on the Psalms.* Translated by Robert C. Hill. 2 vols. Brookline, MA: Holy Cross Orthodox Press, 1998.

Craigie, Peter C. *Psalms 1–50.* 2nd ed. WBC 19. Dallas: Thomas Nelson, 2004.

deClaissé-Walford, Nancy L., Rolf A. Jacobson, and Beth LaNeel Tanner. *The Book of Psalms.* NICOT. Grand Rapids: Eerdmans, 2014.

Delitzsch, Franz. *A Commentary on the Book of Psalms.* Translated by David Eaton and James E. Duguid. New York: Funk & Wagnalls, 1883.

Diodore of Tarsus. *Commentary on Psalms 1–51.* Translated by Robert C. Hill. WGRW 9. Atlanta: SBL, 2005.

Erasmus. *Expositions of the Psalms.* Edited by Dominic Baker-Smith. CWE 63–65. Toronto: University of Toronto Press, 1998–2010.

Ewald, Heinrich A. von. *Commentary on the Psalms.* Translated by E. Johnson. 2 vols. London: Williams & Northgate, 1880–1881.

Gerstenberger, Erhard S. *Psalms: Part 1 with an Introduction to Cultic Poetry.* FOTL 14. Grand Rapids: Eerdmans, 1988.

Goldingay, John. *Psalms, Volume 1: Psalms 1–41.* BCOT. Grand Rapids: Baker Academic, 2006.

Gregory of Nyssa. *Treatise on the Inscriptions of the Psalms.* Translated by Ronald E. Heine. Oxford: Clarendon, 1995.

Grogan, Geoffrey. *Psalms.* Two Horizons. Grand Rapids: Eerdmans, 2008.

Gruber, Mayer I. *Rashi's Commentary on Psalms.* BRLJ 18. Leiden/Boston: Brill, 2004.

Ḥakham, Amos. *The Bible: Psalms with the Jerusalem Commentary. Volume One: Psalms 1–57.* Jerusalem: Mosad Harav Kook, 2003.

Heintz, Michael. "The Pedagogy of the Soul: Origen's Homilies on the Psalms." PhD diss., Notre Dame, 2008.

Hengstenberg, E. W. *Commentary on the Psalms.* Translated by P. Fairburn and J. Thomson. 3 vols. Edinburgh: T&T Clark, 1846–48.

Hippolytus. "Homily on the Psalms." Pages 175–82 in *On the Apostolic Tradition.* Translated by Alistair Stewart-Sykes. PPS 54. Crestwood, NY: St. Vladimir's Seminary Press, 2001.

Hossfeld, Frank-Lothar, and Erich Zenger. *Die Psalmen, Vol. 1: Psalmen 1–50.* NechtB. Würzburg: Echter Verlag, 1993.

———. *Psalms 2: A Commentary on Psalms 51–100.* Translated by Linda M. Maloney. Hermeneia. Minneapolis: Fortress, 2005.

———. *Psalms 3: A Commentary on Psalms 101–150.* Translated by Linda M. Maloney. Hermeneia. Minneapolis: Fortress, 2011.

Ibn Ezra, Abraham. *Commentary on the First Book of Psalms: Chapters 1–41.* Translated by H. Norman Strickman. Boston: Academic Studies, 2009.

Jerome. *The Homilies of St. Jerome, Volume 1 (1–59 on the Psalms).* Translated by Marie Ligouri Ewald. FC 48. Washington, DC: The Catholic University of America Press, 1964.

———. *The Homilies of St. Jerome, Volume 2 (Homilies 60–96)*. Translated by Marie Ligouri Ewald. FC 57. Washington, DC: The Catholic University of America Press, 1966.

Kimḥi, David. *The Longer Commentary of R. David Kimhi on the First Book of Psalms (I–X, XV–XVII, XIX, XXII, XXIV)*. Translated by R. G. Finch. London: SPCK, 1919.

Kirkpatrick, A. F. *The Book of Psalms*. Cambridge: Cambridge University Press, 1906.

Kraus, Hans-Joachim. *Psalms 1–59: A Commentary*. Translated by Hilton C. Oswald. Minneapolis: Augsburg, 1988.

Lombard, Peter. "Preface." Pages 105–12 in *Medieval Literary Theory and Criticism c. 1100–1375: The Commentary Tradition*. Edited by A. J. Minnis and A. B. Scott. Oxford: Clarendon, 1988.

Longman, Tremper, III. *Psalms*. TOTC. Downers Grove, IL: InterVarsity, 2014.

Luther, Martin. *Complete Commentary on the First Twenty-Two Psalms*. Translated by Henry Cole. 2 vols. London: Simplin & Marshall, 1826.

———. *First Lectures on the Psalms I: Psalms 1–75*. Translated by Herbert J. A. Bouman. Luther's Works 10. Saint Louis: Concordia, 1974.

Mays, James L. *Psalms*. IBC. Louisville: Westminster John Knox, 1994.

McCambley, Casimir. "On the Sixth Psalm, Concerning the Octave by Saint Gregory of Nyssa." *GOTR* 32 (1987): 39–50.

McCann, J. Clinton, Jr. "The Book of Psalms: Introduction, Commentary, and Reflections." Pages 641–1280 in *New Interpreter's Bible: A Commentary in Twelve Volumes*. Vol. 4. Nashville: Abingdon, 1996.

Oesterley, W. O. E. *The Psalms*. London: SPCK, 1962.

Olshausen, Justus. *Die Psalmen*. Leipzig: Hirzel, 1853.

Reuchlin, Johannes. *In septem psalmos poenitentiales hebraicos interpretation*. Tübingen: Thomas Anshelm, 1512.

Ross, Allen P. *A Commentary on the Psalms: Volume 1 (1–41)*. Grand Rapids: Kregel, 2011.

Sailhamer, John H. *NIV Compact Commentary*. Grand Rapids: Zondervan, 1994.

Seybold, Klaus. *Die Psalmen*. HAT 1/15. Tübingen: Mohr, 1996.

Sokolow, Moshe. "Saadiah Gaon's Prolegomenon to Psalms." *PAAJR* 51 (1984): 131–74.

Spurgeon, Charles H. *The Treasury of David*. London: Marshall Brothers, 1870.

Terrien, Samuel. *The Psalms: Strophic Structure and Theological Commentary*. Grand Rapids: Eerdmans, 2003.

Theodore of Mopsuestia. *Commentary on Psalms 1–81*. Translated by Robert C. Hill. WGRW 5. Atlanta: SBL, 2006.

Theodoret of Cyrus. *Commentary on the Psalms: Psalms 1–72*. Translated by Robert C. Hill. FC 101. Washington, DC: The Catholic University of America Press, 2000.

Wallace, Howard N. *Psalms*. Sheffield: Sheffield Phoenix, 2009.

Waltke, Bruce K., and James M. Houston. *The Psalms as Christian Worship: A Historical Commentary*. Grand Rapids: Eerdmans, 2010.

Weiser, Artur. *The Psalms: A Commentary*. Translated by Herbert Hartwell. OTL. Philadelphia: Westminster, 1962.

Wette, W. M. L. de. *Commentar über die Psalmen*. Edited by Gustav Baur. 5th ed. Heidelberg: J. C. B. Mohr, 1856. [first edition: *Commentar über die Psalmen*. Heidelberg: Mohr & Zimmer, 1811.]

———. "Introduction to the Psalms." Translated by J. Torrey. *BibRep* 3/11 (1833): 445–518.

Wilcock, Michael. *The Message of Psalms 1–72: Songs for the People of God*. Downers Grove, IL: InterVarsity, 2001.

Wilson, Gerald H. *Psalms: Volume 1*. NIVAC. Grand Rapids: Zondervan, 2002.

General Bibliography

Ackroyd, Peter R. *Doors of Perception: A Guide to Reading the Psalms*. Leighton Buzzard, England: Faith Press, 1978.

Adams, Hazard. "Titles, Titling, and Entitlement To." *The Journal of Aesthetics and Art Criticism* 46 (1987): 7–21.

Alexander, Gavin. "Prosopopoeia: The Speaking Figure." Pages 97–115 in *Renaissance Figures of Speech*. Edited by Sylvia Adamson, Gavin Alexander, and Katrin Ettenhuber. Cambridge: Cambridge University Press, 2007.

Anatolios, Khaled. *Athanasius: The Coherence of His Thought*. London: Routledge 1998.

Anderson, Gary A. "King David and the Psalms of Imprecation." *ProEccl* 15 (2006): 267–80.

Attard, Stefan M. *The Implications of Davidic Repentance: A Synchronic Analysis of Book 2 of the Psalter (Psalms 42–72)*. AnBib 212. Rome: Gregorian & Biblical, 2016.

Auffret, Pierre. "Essai sur la structure littéraire du Psaume viii." *VT* 34 (1984): 257–69.

———. "Note sur la structure littéraire du psaume 3." *ZAW* 91 (1979): 93–106.

———. *La sagesse a bati sa maison: Etudes structures litteraires dans l'Ancien Testament et specialement dans les Psaumes*. OBO 49. Gottingen: Vandenhoeck & Ruprecht, 1982.

Augustine. *Letters, Volume I (1–82)*. Translated by Sr. Wilfrid Parsons. FC 12. Washington, DC: The Catholic University of America Press, 1951.

Auwers, Jean-Marie. "Le David des Psaumes et les Psaumes de David." Pages 187–224 in *Figures de David: À Travers la Bible*. Edited by Louis Desrousseaux and Jacques Vermeylen. Paris: Cerf, 1999.

———. "Les Voies de L'Exégèse Canonique du Psautier." Pages 5–26 in *The Biblical Canons*. Edited by Jean-Marie Auwers and Henk Jan de Jonge. BETL 143. Leiden: Leiden University Press, 2003.

Auwers, Jean-Marie, and H. J. de Jonge, eds. *The Biblical Canons*. BETL 163. Leuven: Leuven University Press, 2003.

Balla, Emil. *Das Ich der Psalmen*. FRLANT 16. Göttingen: Vandenhoedt & Ruprecht, 1912.

Barbiero, Gianni. *Das erste Psalmenbuch als Einheit: Eine synchrone Analyse von Psalm 1–41*. ÖBS 16. Berlin: Peter Lang, 1999.

Barth, Christoph. "Concatenatio im ersten Buch des Psalters." Pages 30–40 in *Wort und Wirklichkeit: Studien zur Afrikanistik und Orientalistik*. Edited by Brigitta Benzing. Meisenheim am Glan: Hain, 1976.

Bates, Matthew. *The Birth of the Trinity: Jesus, God, and Spirit in New Testament and Early Christian Interpretations of the Old Testament*. Oxford: Oxford University Press, 2015.

———. *The Hermeneutics of the Apostolic Proclamation: The Center of Paul's Method of Scriptural Interpretation*. Waco, TX: Baylor University Press, 2012.

Beckwith, Roger T. *Calendar, Chronology, and Worship: Studies in Ancient Judaism and Early Christianity*. AJEC 61. Leiden/Boston: Brill, 2005.

———. "The Early History of the Psalter." *TynBul* 46 (1995): 1–27.

Bellinger, William H., Jr. "Reading from the Beginning (again): The Shape of Book I of the Psalter." Pages 114–26 in *Diachronic and Synchronic: Reading the Psalms in Real Time*. Edited by Joel S. Burnett, William H. Bellinger, Jr., and W. Dennis Tucker, Jr. LHBOTS 488. New York/London: T&T Clark, 2007.

Berger, Yitzhak. "The David-Benjaminite Conflict and the Intertextual Field of Psalm 7." *JSOT* 38 (2014): 279–96.

Bernhardt, Karl-Heinz. *Das Problem der altorientalischen Königsideologie im Alten Testament: Unter besonderer Berücksichtigung der Geschichte der Psalmenexegese dargestellt und kritisch gewürdigt.* VTSup 8. Leiden: Brill, 1961.

Birkeland, Harris. *Ānî und ānāw in den Psalmen.* Oslo: J. Dybwad, 1933.

Blaiklock, E. M. *The Psalms of the Great Rebellion: An Imaginative Exposition of Psalms 3 to 6 and 23.* London: Lakeland, 1970.

Botha, Phil J. "Interpreting 'Torah' in Psalm 1 in the Light of Psalm 119." *HTS Theological Studies* 68 (2012): 1–7. doi:10.4102/hts.v68i1.1274

———. "Intertextuality and the Interpretation of Psalm 1." *OTE* 18 (2005): 503–20.

Botha, Phil J., and Beat Weber. "'Killing Them Softly with this Song…': The Literary Structure of Psalm 3 and Its Psalmic and Davidic Contexts; Part I: An Intratextual Interpretation of Psalm 3." *OTE* 21/1 (2008): 18–37.

———. "'Killing Them Softly with this Song…': The Literary Structure of Psalm 3 and Its Psalmic and Davidic Contexts; Part II: A Contextual and Intertextual Interpretation of Psalm 3." *OTE* 21/2 (2008): 273–97.

Braulik, Georg P. "Psalter and Messiah: Towards a Christological Understanding of the Psalms in the Old Testament and the Church Fathers." Pages 15–40 in *Psalms and Liturgy.* Edited by Dirk J. Human and Cas J. A. Vos. JSOTSup 410. London/New York: T&T Clark, 2004.

Brennan, Joseph P. "Psalms 1–8: Some Hidden Harmonies." *BTB* 10 (1980): 25–29.

Brogan, T. V. F., A. W. Halsall, and J. S. Sychterz, "Prosopopoeia." Pages 1120–21 in *The Princeton Encyclopedia of Poetry and Poetics.* Edited by Stephen Cushman, Clare Cavanagh, and Paul Rouzer. 4th ed. Princeton, NJ: Princeton University Press, 2012.

Brown, Francis, S. R. Driver, and Charles A. Briggs. *The Brown-Driver-Briggs Hebrew and English Lexicon.* Boston: Houghton, Mifflin, and Co., 1906. Reprinted: Peabody, MA: Hendrickson, 2005.

Brown, William P., ed. *The Oxford Handbook of the Psalms.* Oxford/New York: Oxford University Press, 2014.

Broyles, Craig C. *The Conflict of Faith and Experience in the Psalms: A Form-Critical and Theological Study.* JSOTSup 52. Sheffield: Sheffield Academic, 1989.

Bruce, F. F. "The Earliest Old Testament Interpretation." Pages 37–52 in *The Witness of Tradition: Papers Read at the Joint British-Dutch Old Testament Conference held at Wouschoten, 1970.* Edited by A. S. Van Der Woude. OTS 17. Leiden: Brill, 1972.

Budde, Karl. "Zum Text der Psalmen." *ZAW* 35 (1915): 175–95.

Bullock, C. Hassell. *Encountering the Book of Psalms: A Literary and Theological Introduction.* 2nd ed. Grand Rapids: Baker Academic, 2018.

Byassee, Jason. *Praise Seeking Understanding: Reading the Psalms with Augustine.* Grand Rapids: Eerdmans, 2007.

Cameron, Michael. *Christ Meets Me Everywhere: Augustine's Early Figurative Exegesis.* Oxford: Oxford University Press, 2012.

———. "The Emergence of *Totus Christus* as Hermeneutical Center in Augustine's *Enarrationes in Psalmos.*" Pages 205–26 in *The Harp of Prophecy: Early Christian Interpretation of the Psalms.* Edited by Brian E. Daley and Paul R. Kolbet. Notre Dame: University of Notre Dame Press, 2015.

Carter, Craig A. *Interpreting Scripture with the Great Tradition: Recovering the Genius of Premodern Exegesis.* Grand Rapids: Baker Academic, 2018.

Childs, Brevard S. "Analysis of a Canonical Formula: 'It Shall be Recorded for a Future Generation.'" Pages 357–64 in *Die Hebräische Bible und ihre zweifache Nachgeschichte: Festschrift für Rolf Rendtorff zum 65. Geburstag.* Edited by E. Blum, C. Macholz, and E. W. Stegeman. Neukirchen-Vluyn: Neukirchener Verlag, 1990.

———. *Biblical Theology of the Old and New Testaments.* Minneapolis: Fortress, 1992.

———. *Introduction to the Old Testament as Scripture*. Philadelphia: Fortress, 1979.

———. "Psalm 8 in the Context of the Christian Canon." *Int* 23 (1969), 20–31.

———. "Psalm Titles and Midrashic Exegesis." *JSS* 16 (1971): 138–51.

———. "Reflections on the Modern Study of the Psalms." Pages 377–88 in *Magnalia Dei, the Mighty Acts of God: Essays on the Bible and Archaeology in Memory of G. Ernest Wright*. Edited by Frank Moore Cross, Werner E. Lemke, and Patrick D. Miller, Jr. Garden City, NY: Doubleday, 1976.

———. *The Struggle to Understand Isaiah as Christian Scripture*. Grand Rapids: Eerdmans, 2004.

Clements, Ronald E. *One Hundred Years of Old Testament Interpretation*. Philadelphia: Westminster, 1976.

Clines, David J. A., ed. *Dictionary of Classical Hebrew*. 8 vols. Sheffield: Sheffield Phoenix, 1993–2016.

Cole, Robert L. "An Integrated Reading of Psalms 1 and 2." *JSOT* 98 (2002): 75–88.

———. "(Mis)Translating Psalm 1." *JBMW* 10 (2005): 35–50.

———. "Psalm 1 and 2: The Psalter's Introduction." Pages 183–95 in *The Psalms: Language for All Seasons of the Soul*. Edited by Andrew J. Schmutzer and David M. Howard, Jr. Chicago: Moody, 2013.

———. "Psalm 3: Of Whom Does David Speak, of Himself or Another?" Pages 137–49 in *Text and Canon: Essays in Honor of John H. Sailhamer*. Edited by Robert L. Cole and Paul J. Kissling. Eugene, OR: Pickwick Publications, 2017.

———. *Psalms 1–2: Gateway to the Psalter*. HBM 37. Sheffield: Sheffield Phoenix, 2013.

———. *The Shape and Message of Book III (Psalms 73–89)*. JSOTSup 307. Sheffield: Sheffield Academic Press, 2000.

Cooper, Alan M. "The Life and Times of King David according to the Book of Psalms." Pages 117–31 in *The Poet and the Historian: Essays in Literary and Historical Biblical Criticism*. Edited by Richard Elliot Friedman. HSS 26. Chico, CA: Scholars, 1983.

———. "On the Typology of Jewish Psalms Interpretation." Pages 79–90 in *Biblical Interpretation in Judaism and Christianity*. Edited by Isaac Kalimi and Peter J. Haas. LHBOTS 439. New York/London: T&T Clark, 2006.

Cottrill, Amy C. *Language, Power, and Identity in the Lament Psalms of the Individual*. LHBOTS 493. New York: T&T Clark, 2008.

Creach, Jerome F. D. "Like a Tree Planted by the Temple Stream: The Portrait of the Righteous in Psalm 1:3." *CBQ* 61 (1999): 34–46.

———. *Yahweh as Refuge and the Editing of the Hebrew Psalter*. JSOTSup 217. Sheffield: Sheffield Academic, 1996.

Croft, Steven J. L. *The Identity of the Individual in the Psalms*. JSOTSup 44. Sheffield: Sheffield Academic, 1987.

Daley, Brian E., and Paul R. Kolbet, ed. *The Harp of Prophecy: Early Christian Interpretation of the Psalms*. Notre Dame, IN: University of Notre Dame Press, 2015.

deClaissé-Walford, Nancy L. *Reading from the Beginning: The Shaping of the Hebrew Psalter*. Macon, GA: Mercer University Press, 1997.

———, ed. *The Shape and Shaping of the Book of Psalms: The Current State of Scholarship*. AIL 20. Atlanta: SBL, 2014.

Devreesse, Robert. *Les Anciens Commentatuers Grecs des Psaumes*. Vatican City: Biblioteca Apostolica Vaticana, 1970.

Drobner, Hubertus R. *The Fathers of the Church: A Comprehensive Introduction*. Translated by Siegfried S. Schatzmann. Peabody, MA: Hendrickson, 2007.

Eaton, John H. *Kingship and the Psalms*. 2nd edition. Sheffield: JSOT, 1986.

Eissfeldt, Otto. *The Old Testament: An Introduction*. Translated by Peter R. Ackroyd. New York: Harper & Row, 1965.

Engnell, Ivan. "The Book of Psalms." Pages 68–122 in *A Rigid Scrutiny: Critical Essays on the Old Testament by Ivan Engnell*. Edited by John T. Willis. Nashville: Vanderbilt University Press, 1969.

Fabry, Heinz-Josef, and Klaus Scholtissek. *Der Messias*. NEB Themen 5. Würzburg: Echter-Verlag, 2002.

Firth, David, and Philip S. Johnston, eds. *Interpreting the Psalms: Issues and Approaches*. Downers Grove, IL: InterVarsity, 2005.

Fishbane, Michael. *Biblical Interpretation in Ancient Israel*. Oxford: Clarendon, 1985.

Fisher, John. "Entitling." *Critical Inquiry* 11 (1984): 286–98.

Flint, Peter W., and Patrick D. Miller, eds. *The Book of Psalms: Composition & Reception*. VTSup 99. Leiden/Boston: Brill, 2005.

Flores, Daniel E. "Thomas on the Literalness of Christ and the Interpretation of Scripture." *St. Thomas Day Lecture*. 29 Jan 2019. http://thomasaquinas.edu/print/18579.

Frei, Hans W. *The Eclipse of Biblical Narrative: A Study in Eighteenth and Nineteenth Century Hermeneutics*. New Haven, CT: Yale University Press, 1974.

Gennette, Gérard. "Structure and Functions of the Title in Literature." *Critical Inquiry* 14 (1988): 692–720.

German, Brian T. "Contexts for Hearing: Reevaluating the Superscription of Psalm 127." *JSOT* 37 (2012): 185–99.

Gerstenberger, Erhard S. "Psalms." Pages 179–223 in *Old Testament Form Criticism*. Edited by John H. Hays. San Antonio, TX: Trinity University Press, 1974.

Gillingham, Susan E. *A Journey of Two Psalms: The Reception of Psalms 1 and 2 in Jewish and Christian Tradition*. Oxford: Oxford University Press, 2013.

–––. "The Levites and the Editorial Composition of the Psalms." Pages 201–13 in *The Oxford Handbook of the Psalms*. Edited by William Brown. Oxford: Oxford University Press, 2014.

–––. *Psalms Through the Centuries: Volume One*. Malden, MA: Blackwell Publishing, 2008.

–––. "Studies of the Psalms: Retrospect and Prospect." *ET* 119 (2008): 209–16.

Gillmayr-Bucher, Susanne. "The Psalm Headings: A Canonical Relecture of the Psalms." Pages 247–54 in *The Biblical Canons*. Edited by Jean-Marie Auwers and H. J. de Jonge. Leuven: Leuven University Press, 2003.

Glueck, J. J. "Some Remarks on the Introductory Notes of the Psalms." Pages 30–39 in *Studies on the Psalms: Papers Read at the 6th Meeting Held at the Potchefstroom University for C.H.E., 29–31 January 1963*. Edited by A. H. Van Zyl. Potchefstroom: Pro Rege, 1963.

Gottwald, Norman K. "Social Drama in the Psalms of Individual Lament." Pages 143–53 in *The Bible as a Human Witness to Divine Revelation: Hearing the Word of God Through Historically Dissimilar Traditions*. LHBOTS 469. Edited by Randall Heskett and Brian Irwin. New York/ London: T&T Clark, 2010.

–––. *The Tribes of Yahweh*. Maryknoll, NY: Orbis, 1979.

Goulder, Michael. *The Prayers of David (Psalms 51–72): Studies in the Psalter II*. JSOTSup 102. Sheffield: JSOT, 1990.

Grant, Jamie A. "Determining the Indeterminate: Issues in Interpreting the Psalms." *Southeastern Theological Review* 1 (2010): 3–14.

–––. *The King as Exemplar: The Function of Deuteronomy's Kingship Law in the Shaping of the Book of Psalms*. AcBib 17. Atlanta: SBL, 2004.

–––. "The Psalms and the King." Pages 101–18 in *Interpreting the Psalms: Issues and*

Approaches. Edited by David Firth and Philip S. Johnston. Downers Grove, IL: InterVarsity, 2005.

Greef, Wulfert de. "Calvin as Commentator on the Psalms." Translated by Raymond A. Blacketer. Pages 85–106 in *Calvin and the Bible*. Edited by Donald K. McKim. Cambridge: Cambridge University Press, 2006.

Gunkel, Hermann. *The Psalms: A Form-Critical Introduction*. Translated by Thomas M. Horner. Philadelphia: Fortress, 1967.

Gunkel, Hermann, and Joachim Bergich. *An Introduction to the Psalms*. Translated by James Nogalski. Macon, GA: Mercer University Press, 1998.

Gwynn, David M. *Athanasius of Alexandria: Bishop, Theologian, Ascetic, Father*. CTC. Oxford: Oxford University Press, 2012.

Hamlin, Hannibal. "My Tongue Shall Speak: The Voices of the Psalms." *Renaissance Studies* 29 (2015): 509–30.

Harris, R. Laird, Gleason L. Archer, and Bruce K. Waltke. *Theological Wordbook of the Old Testament*. Chicago: Moody Press, 1980.

Hartenstein, Friedhelm. "'Schaffe Mir Recht, JHWH!' (Psalm 7, 9): Zum Theologischen und Anthropologischen Profil der Teilkomposition Psalm 3–14." Pages 229–58 in *The Composition of the Book of Psalms*. Edited by Erich Zenger. BETL 238. Leuven: Peeters, 2010.

Hays, Richard. *The Conversion of the Imagination: Paul as Interpreter of Israel's Scripture*. Grand Rapids: Eerdmans, 2005.

Heine, Ronald E. "Restringing Origen's Broken Harp: Some Suggestions Concerning the Prologue of the Caesarean Commentary on the Psalms." Pages 47–74 in *The Harp of Prophecy: Early Christian Interpretation of the Psalms*. Edited by Brian E. Daley and Paul R. Kolbet. Notre Dame, IN: University of Notre Dame Press, 2015.

Hensley, Adam D. *Covenant Relationships and the Editing of the Hebrew Psalter*. LHBOTS 666. London: T&T Clark, 2018.

Heskett, Randall, and Brian Irwin, eds. *The Bible as a Human Witness to Divine Revelation: Hearing the Word of God Through Historically Dissimilar Traditions*. LHBOTS 469. New York/London: T&T Clark, 2010.

Holladay, William L. "Indications of Jeremiah's Psalter." *JBL* 121 (2002): 245–61.

Holm-Nielsen, Svend. "The Importance of Late Jewish Psalmody for the Understanding of Old Testament Psalmodic Tradition." *STNJT* 14 (1960): 1–53.

Hossfeld, Frank-Lothar, and Erich Zenger. "Considerations on the 'Davidization' of the Psalter." Pages 119–30 in *The Shape of the Writings*. Edited by Julius Steinberg and Timothy J. Stone. Siphrut 16. Winona Lake, IN: Eisenbrauns, 2015.

Howard, David M., Jr. "Recent Trends in Psalms Study." Pages 329–68 in *The Face of Old Testament Studies: A Survey of Contemporary Approaches*. Edited by David W. Baker and Bill T. Arnold. Grand Rapids: Baker, 1999.

———. *The Structure of Psalms 93–100*. BJS 5. Winona Lake, IN: Eisenbrauns, 1997.

Hutton, Rodney R. "Cush the Benjaminite and Psalm Midrash." *HAR* 10 (1986): 123–37.

Irenaeus of Lyons. *On the Apostolic Preaching*. Translated by John Behr. PPS 17. Crestwood, NY: St. Vladimir's Seminary Press, 1997.

Jacobson, Rolf A. *"Many are Saying": The Function of Direct Discourse in the Hebrew Psalter*. JSOTSup 397. New York: T&T Clark, 2004.

Janse, Sam. *"You Are My Son": The Reception History of Psalm 2 in Early Judaism and the Early Church*. CBET 51. Leuven: Peeters, 2009.

Johnson, Aubrey R. "The Psalms." Pages 162–209 in *The Old Testament and Modern Study: A Generation of Discovery and Research*. Edited by H. H. Rowley. Oxford: Clarendon, 1951.

Johnson, Vivian L. *David in Distress: His Portrait through the Historical Psalms.* LHBOTS 505. New York/London: T&T Clark, 2009.

Jones, Scott. "Psalm 1 and the Hermeneutics of Torah." *Biblica* 97 (2016): 537–51.

Kannengiesser, Charles. *Handbook of Patristic Exegesis: The Bible in Ancient Christianity.* 2 vols. Leiden/Boston: Brill, 2004.

Karrer, Wolfgang. "Titles and Mottoes as Intertextual Devices." Pages 122–34 in *Intertextuality.* Edited by Heinrich F. Plett. Berlin: de Gruyter, 1991.

Kellman, Steven G. "Dropping Names: The Poetics of Titling." *Criticism* 17 (1975): 152–67.

Knoppers, Gary N. "Hierodules, Priests or Janitors? The Levites in Chronicles and the History of the Israelite Priesthood." *JBL* 118 (1999): 49–72.

Koehler, Ludwig, Walter Baumgartner, and Johann J. Stamm. *The Hebrew and Aramaic Lexicon of the Old Testament.* Translated and edited under the supervision of Mervyn E. J. Richardson. 2 vols. Leiden: Brill, 2001.

Kolbet, Paul R. "Athanasius, the Psalms, and the Reformation of the Self." *HTR* 99 (2005): 85–101.

Kraus, Hans-Joachim. *Die Königsherrschaft Gottes im Alten Testament.* BZHT 13. Tübingen: J. C. B. Mohr, 1951.

Kraut, Judah. "The Birds and the Babes: The Structure and Meaning of Psalm 8." *JQR* 100 (2010): 10–24.

Kselman, John S. "Psalm 3: A Structural and Literary Study." *CBQ* 49 (1987): 572–80.

Kuntz, J. Kenneth. "Psalm 18: A Rhetorical-Critical Analysis." *JSOT* 26 (1983): 3–31.

Labuschagne, C. J. "Significant Sub-Groups in the Book of Psalms: A New Approach to the Compositional Structure of the Psalter." Pages 623–34 in *The Composition of the Book of Psalms.* Edited by Erich Zenger. BETL 238. Leiden: Uitgeverij Peeters, 2010.

Lanahan, William F. "The Speaking Voice in the Book of Lamentations." *JBL* 93 (1974): 41–49.

Lefebvre, Michael. "'On His Law He Meditates': What is Psalm 1 Introducing?" *JSOT* 40 (2016): 439–50.

Levinson, Jerrold. "Titles." *The Journal of Aesthetics and Art Criticism* 44 (1985): 29–39.

Longman, Tremper, III. *How to Read the Psalms.* Downers Grove, IL: IVP Academic, 1988.

Ludlow, Morwenna. "Theology and Allegory: Origen and Gregory of Nyssa on the Unity and Diversity of Scripture." *IJST* 4 (2002), 45–66.

Mandalfo, Carleen. *God in the Dock: Dialogic Tension in the Psalms of Lament.* JSOTSup 357. Sheffield: Sheffield Academic, 2002.

Martin, Lee Roy. "Delighting in the Torah: The Affective Dimension of Psalm 1." *OTE* 23 (2010): 708–27.

Marttila, Marko. *Collective Reinterpretation in the Psalms: A Study of the Redaction History of the Psalter.* FAT 2/13. Tübingen: Mohr Siebeck, 2006.

Martyr, Justin. *Dialogue avec Tryphon: Édition critique, traduction, commentaire.* Edited by Philippe Bobichon. Paradosis 47/1. Fribourg, Switzerland: Academic Press Fribourg, 2003.

———. *Dialogue with Trypho.* Translated by Thomas B. Falls and Thomas P. Halton. SFC 3. Washington, DC: The Catholic University of America Press, 2003.

———. *The Writings of Justin Martyr.* Translated by Thomas B. Falls. FC 6. Washington, DC: The Catholic University of America Press, 1948.

Maxwell, Nathan Dean. "The Psalmist in the Psalm: A Persona-Critical Reading of Book IV of the Psalter." PhD diss., Baylor University, 2007.

May, Herbert Gordon. "'Al...' in the Superscriptions of the Psalms." *AJSL* 58 (1941): 70–83.

Mays, James L. "The David of the Psalms." *Int* 40 (1986): 143–55.

———. *The Lord Reigns: A Theological Handbook to the Psalms*. Louisville: Westminster John Knox, 1994.

———. "Past, Present, and Prospect in Psalm Study." Pages 147–56 in *Old Testament Interpretation: Past, Present, and Future. Essays in Honour of Gene M. Tucker*. Edited by James L. Mays, David L. Petersen, and Kent H. Richards. Edinburgh: T&T Clark, 1995.

———. "A Question of Identity: The Threefold Hermeneutic of Psalmody," *AsTJ* 46 (1991): 87–94.

McCann, J. Clinton, Jr. "On Reading the Psalms as Christian Scripture: Psalms 11–12 as an Illustrative Case." Pages 129–42 in *Diachronic and Synchronic: Reading the Psalms in Real Time*. Edited by Joel S. Burnett, William H. Bellinger, and W. Dennis Tucker, Jr. LHBOTS 488. New York/ London: T&T Clark, 2007.

———, ed. *The Shape and Shaping of the Psalter*. JSOTSup 159. Sheffield: JSOT, 1993.

———. "The Shape of Book I of the Psalter and the Shape of Human Happiness." Pages 340–48 in *The Book of Psalms: Composition & Reception*. Edited by Peter W. Flint and Patrick D. Miller. VTSup 99. Leiden/Boston: Brill, 2005.

———. *A Theological Introduction to the Book of Psalms: The Psalms as Torah*. Nashville: Abingdon Press, 1993.

McGuckin, John A. "Origen's Use of the Psalms in the Treatise *On First Principles*." Pages 97–118 in *Meditations of the Heart: The Psalms in Early Christian Thought and Practice; Essays in Honour of Andrew Louth*. Edited by Andreas Andreopoulos, Augustine Casiday, and Carol Harrison. STT 8. Turnhout: Brepols, 2011.

Millard, Matthias. *Die Komposition des Psalters: Ein formgeschichtlicher Ansatz*. FAT 9. Tübingen: Mohr, 1994.

Miller, Patrick D. "The Beginning of the Psalter." Pages 83–92 in *The Shape and Shaping of the Psalter*. Edited by J. Clinton McCann. JSOTSup 159. Sheffield: JSOT, 1993.

———. "Current Issues in Psalms Studies." *WW* 5 (1985): 132–43.

———. *Deuteronomy*. IBC. Louisville: Westminster John Knox, 1990.

———. "Gregory of Nyssa: The Superscriptions of the Psalms." Pages 215–30 in *Genesis, Isaiah, and Psalms: A Festschrift to Honour Professor John Emerton for his Eightieth Birthday*. Edited by Katharine J. Dell, Graham Davies, and Yee Von Koh. VTSup 135. Leiden/Boston: Brill, 2010.

———. *Interpreting the Psalms*. Philadelphia: Fortress, 1986.

———. "Kingship, Torah Obedience, and Prayer: The Theology of Psalms 15–24." Pages 127–42 in *Neue Wege der Psalmenforschung: Festschrift für W. Beyerlin zum 65. Geburtstag*. Edited by Klaus Seybold and Erich Zenger. HerdBS 1. Freiburg: Herder, 1994.

———. "The Ruler in Zion and the Hope of the Poor: Psalms 9–10 in the Context of the Psalter." Pages 187–97 in *David and Zion: Biblical Studies in Honor of J. J. M. Roberts*. Edited by Bernard F. Batto and Kathryn L. Roberts. Winona Lake, IN: Eisenbrauns, 2004.

Minns, Denis, and Paul Parvis, ed. *Justin, Philosopher and Martyr: Apologies*. OECT. Oxford: Oxford University Press, 2009.

Mitchell, David C. "'God Will Redeem My Soul from Sheol': The Psalms of the Sons of Korah." *JSOT* 30 (2006): 365–84.

———. "Lord, Remember David: G. H. Wilson and the Message of the Psalter." *VT* 56 (2006): 526–48.

———. *The Message of the Psalter: An Eschatological Programme in the Book of Psalms*. JSOTSup 252. Sheffield: Sheffield Academic, 1997.

Mowinckel, Sigmund. "Psalm Criticism between 1900 and 1935 (Ugarit and Psalm Exegesis)." *VT* 5 (1955): 13–33.

———. *The Psalms in Israel's Worship: Two Volumes in One*. Translated by D. R. Ap-Thomas.

Grand Rapids: Eerdmans, 2004.

———. *Psalm Studies*. Translated by Mark E. Biddle. 2 vols. SBLHBS 2–3. Atlanta: SBL, 2014.

Müller, Wolfgang G. "Interfigurality: A Study on the Interdependence of Literary Figures." Pages 101–21 in *Intertextuality*. Edited by Heinrich F. Plett. Berlin: de Gruyter, 1991.

Nassif, Bradley. "'Scriptural Exegesis' in the School of Antioch." Pages 342–77 in *New Perspectives on Historical Theology: Essays in Memory of John Meyendorff*. Edited by Bradley Nassif. Grand Rapids: Eerdmans, 1996.

Nasuti, Harry P. *Defining the Sacred Songs: Genre, Tradition, and the Post-Critical Interpretation of the Psalms*. JSOTSup 218. Sheffield: Sheffield Academic, 1999.

———. "The Interpretive Significance of Sequence and Selection in the Book of Psalms." Pages 311–39 in *The Book of Psalms: Composition & Reception*. Edited by Peter W. Flint and Patrick D. Miller. VTSup 99. Leiden/Boston: Brill, 2005.

Nogalski, James D. "From Psalm to Psalms to Psalter." Pages 37–54 in *An Introduction to Wisdom Literature and the Psalms: Festschrift for Marvin E. Tate*. Edited by Harold Wayne Ballard and W. Dennis Tucker. Macon, GA: Mercer University Press, 2000.

———. "Reading David in the Psalter: A Study in Liturgical Hermeneutics." *HBT* 23 (2001): 168–91.

Oesterley, W. O. E. *A Fresh Approach to the Psalms*. London: Ivor Nicholson & Watson, 1937.

O'Keefe, John J. "'A Letter That Killeth': Toward a Reassessment of Antiochene Exegesis, or Diodore, Theodore, and Theodoret on the Psalms." *JECS* 8 (2000): 83–103.

Oorschot, Jürgen van. "Nachkultische Psalmen und spätbiblische Rollendichtung." *ZAW* 106 (1994): 69–86.

Origen, *Commentary on the Epistle to the Romans, Books 1–5*. Translated by Thomas P. Scheck. FC 103. Washington, DC: The Catholic University of America Press, 2001.

———. *Commentary on the Epistle to the Romans, Books 6–10*. Translated by Thomas P. Scheck. FC 104. Washington, DC: The Catholic University of America Press, 2002.

———. *Homilies on Genesis and Exodus*. Translated by Ronald E. Heine. FC 71. Washington, DC: The Catholic University of America Press, 1982.

———. *On First Principles*. Translated by John Behr. OECT. Oxford: Oxford University Press, 2017.

———. *The Philocalia of Origen: A Compilation of Selected Passages from Origen's Works made by St. Gregory of Nazianzus and St. Basil of Caesarea*. Translated by George Lewis. Edinburgh: T&T Clark, 1911.

———. *The Song of Songs Commentary and Homilies*. Translated by R. P. Lawson. ACW 26. Westminster, MD: Newman, 1957.

Pak, G. Sujin. *The Judaizing Calvin: Sixteenth-Century Debates over the Messianic Psalms*. Oxford: Oxford University Press, 2010.

Patrologia Graeca. Edited by J.-P. Migne. 162 vols. Paris, 1857–1886.

Patrologia Latina. Edited by J.-P. Migne. 217 vols. Paris, 1844–1864.

Peterson, Eugene H. *Answering God: The Psalms as Tools for Prayer*. New York: HarperCollins, 1989.

Pietersma, Albert. "David in the Greek Psalms." *VT* 30 (1980): 213–26.

———. "Exegesis and Liturgy in the Superscriptions of the Greek Psalter." Pages 99–138 in *X Congress of the International Organization for Septuagint and Cognate Studies: Oslo, 1998*. Edited by B. A. Taylor. Atlanta: SBL, 2001.

———. "Septuagintal Exegesis and the Superscriptions of the Greek Psalter." Pages 443–75 in *The Book of Psalms: Composition & Reception*. Edited by Peter W. Flint and Patrick D. Miller. VTSup 99. Leiden/Boston: Brill, 2005.

Pitkin, Barbara. "Imitation of David: David as a Paradigm for Faith in Calvin's Exegesis of the Psalms." *The Sixteenth Century Journal* 24 (1993): 843–63.

Plett, Heinrich F., ed. *Intertextuality.* Berlin: de Gruyter, 1991.

Rahlfs, Alfred. *'Ani und 'Anaw in den Psalmen.* Göttingen: Dieterichsche Verlagsbuch-handlung, 1892.

Rendtorff, Rolf. *The Canonical Hebrew Bible: A Theology of the Old Testament.* Translated by David E. Orton. Leiden: Deo, 2005.

———. *The Old Testament: An Introduction.* Translated by John Bowden. Philadelphia: Fortress, 1986.

———. "The Psalms of David: David in the Psalms." Pages 53–64 in *The Book of Psalms: Composition & Reception.* Edited by Peter W. Flint and Patrick D. Miller. VTSup 99. Leiden/Boston: Brill, 2005.

Richards, Carissa M. Quinn. *The King and the Kingdom: The Message of Psalms 15–24.* PhD diss., Golden Gate Baptist Theological Seminary, 2015.

Robinson, H. Wheeler. *Corporate Personality in Ancient Israel.* 2nd ed. Philadelphia: Fortress, 1980.

———. "Inner Life of the Psalmists." Pages 45–65 in *The Psalmists.* Edited by D. C. Simpson. London: Oxford University Press, 1926.

Rondeau, Marie-Josèphe. *Les Commentaires Patristique du Psautier (IIIe-Ve siècles): Vol. II— Exegèse Prosopologique et Théologie.* OCA 220. Rome: Pontifical Institutum Studioroum Orientalium, 1985.

Russell, S. H. "Calvin and the Messianic Interpretation of the Psalms." *SJT* 21 (1968): 37–47.

Ryan, Thomas F. *Thomas Aquinas as a Reader of the Psalms.* SST 6. Notre Dame: University of Notre Dame Press, 2000.

Sarna, Nahum M. *Songs of the Heart: An Introduction to the Book of Psalms.* New York: Schocken, 1993.

Sawyer, John F. A. "An Analysis of the Context and Meaning of the Psalm-Headings." *TGUOS* 22 (1970): 26–38.

Seitz, Christopher R. *The Character of Christian Scripture: The Significance of a Two-Testament Bible.* Grand Rapids: Baker Academic, 2011.

———. "Psalm 2 in the Entry Hall of the Psalter: Extended Sense in the History of Interpretation." Pages 95–106 in *Church, Society, and the Christian Common Good: Essays in Conversation with Philip Turner.* Edited by Ephraim Radner. Eugene, OR: Cascade, 2017.

———. "Psalm 34: Redaction, Inner-biblical Exegesis and the Longer Psalm Superscriptions—'Mistake' Making and Theological Significance." Pages 279–98 in *The Bible as Christian Scripture: The Work of Brevard S. Childs.* Edited by Christopher R. Seitz and Kent Harold Richards. BSNA 25. Atlanta: SBL, 2013.

Selderhuis, Herman J. *Calvin's Theology of the Psalms.* Grand Rapids: Baker, 2007.

Sheppard, Gerald T. "'Enemies' and the Politics of Prayer." Pages 61–82 in *The Bible and the Politics of Exegesis: Essay in Honor of Norman K. Gottwald on His Sixty-fifth Birthday.* Edited by David Jobling, Peggy L. Day, and Gerald T. Sheppard. Cleveland: Pilgrim, 1991.

———. *The Future of the Bible: Beyond Liberalism and Literalism.* Toronto: United Church, 1990.

———. "Theology and the Book of Psalms." *Int* 46 (1992): 143–55.

———. *Wisdom as a Hermeneutical Construct: A Study of the Sapientializing of the Old Testament.* BZAW 151. Berlin: de Gruyter, 1980.

Simonetti, Manlio. *Biblical Interpretation in the Early Church: An Historical Introduction to Patristic Exegesis.* Translated by John A. Hughes. Edinburgh: T&T Clark, 1994.

Slomovic, Elieser. "Toward an Understanding of the Formation of Historical Titles in the

Book of Psalms." *ZAW* 91 (1979): 350–80.

Smend, Rudolf. "Über das Ich der Psalmen." *ZAW* 8 (1888): 48–147.

Smith, Kevin G., and William R. Domeris. "The Arrangement of Psalm 3–8." *OTE* 23 (2010): 367–77.

Smith, Mark. "The Theology of the Redaction of the Psalter: Some Observations." *ZAW* 104 (1992): 408–12.

Sommer, Benjamin D. "Psalm 1 and the Canonical Shaping of Jewish Scripture." Pages 199–222 in *Jewish Bible Theology: Perspectives and Case Studies*. Edited by Isaac Kalimi. Winona Lake, IN: Eisenbrauns, 2012.

Soulen, Richard N., and R. Kendall Soulen. *Handbook of Biblical Criticism*. 3rd ed. Louisville: Westminster John Knox, 2001.

Stead, G. C. "St. Athanasius on the Psalms." *VC* 39 (1985): 65–78.

Steinmetz, David C. "John Calvin as an Interpreter of the Bible." Pages 285–91 in *Calvin and the Bible*. Edited by Donald K. McKim. Cambridge: Cambridge University Press, 2006.

Suderman, W. Derek. "Are Individual Complaint Psalms Really Prayers? Recognizing Social Address as Characteristic of Individual Complaints." Pages 153–70 in *The Bible as a Human Witness to Divine Revelation: Hearing the Word of God Through Historically Dissimilar Traditions*. Edited by Randall Heskett and Brian Irwin. LHBOTS 469. New York/London: T&T Clark, 2010.

———. "The Cost of Losing Lament for the Community of Faith: On Brueggemann, Ecclesiology, and the Social Audience of Prayer." *JTI* 6 (2012): 201–18.

———. "From Dialogic Tension to Social Address: Reconsidering Mandolfo's Proposed Didactic Voice in Lament Psalms." *JHS* 17 (2017): 1–26. doi:10.5508/ jhs.2017.v17.a10.

Sumpter, Philip. "The Canonical Shape of Psalms 3–14." *OTE* 32 (2019): 514–43.

———. "The Coherence of Psalms 15–24." *Bib* 94 (2013): 186–209.

———. *The Substance of Psalm 24: An Attempt to Read Scripture after Brevard S. Childs*. LHBOTS 600. London: Bloomsbury T&T Clark, 2015.

Tanaka, Hikaru. "Athanasius as Interpreter of the Psalms: His *Letter to Marcellinus*." *ProEccl* 21 (2012): 422–48.

Tanner, Beth LaNeel. *The Book of Psalms Through the Lens of Intertextuality*. StBL 26. New York: Peter Lang, 2001.

Taylor, J. Glen. "Psalms 1 and 2: A Gateway into the Psalter and Messianic Images of Restoration for David's Dynasty." Pages 47–62 in *Interpreting the Psalms for Teaching and Preaching*. Edited by Herbert W. Bateman and D. Brent Sandy. St. Louis: Chalice, 2010.

Torjesen, Karen Jo. *Hermeneutical Procedure and Theological Method in Origen's Exegesis*. PTS 28. Berlin: de Gruyter, 1986.

Toy, C. H. "On the Asaph-Psalms." *JSBLE* 6 (1886): 73–85.

Tucker, W. Dennis, Jr. "Beyond Lament: Instruction and Theology in Book 1 of the Psalter." *Proceedings EGL & MWBS* 15 (1995): 121–32.

Tur-Sinai, N. H. "The Literary Character of the Book of Psalms." Pages 263–81 in *Oudtestamentische Studiën VIII*. Edited by P. A. H. de Boer. Leiden: Brill, 1950.

Van Fleteren, Frederick. "Principles of Augustine's Hermeneutic: An Overview." Pages 1–32 in *Augustine: Biblical Exegete*. Edited by Frederick Van Fleteren and Joseph C. Schnaubelt. Augustinian Historical Institute. New York: Peter Lang, 2004.

Wallace, Howard N. "King and Community: Joining with David in Prayer." Pages 267–77 in *Psalms and Prayers*. Edited by Bob Becking and Eric Peels. OTS 55. Leiden/Boston: Brill, 2007.

Watts, James W. *Psalm and Story: Inset Hymns in Hebrew Narrative*. JSOTSup 139. Sheffield:

Sheffield Academic, 1992.

Weber, Beat. "Die Buchouvertüre Psalm 1–3 und ihre Bedeutung für das Verständnis des Psalters." *OTE* 23 (2010): 834–45.

———. "'Herr, wie viele sind geworden meine Bedränger...' (Ps 3,2a): Psalm 1–3 als Ouvertüre des Psalters unter besonderer Berücksichtigung von Psalm 3 und seinem Präskript." Pages 231–51 in *Der Bibelkanon in der Bibelauslegung: Methodenreflexionen und Beispielexegesen*. Edited by Egbert Ballhorn and Georg Steins. Stuttgart: Kohlhammer, 2007.

———. "Psalm 1 and Its Function as a Directive into the Psalter and Towards a Biblical Theology." *OTE* 19 (2006): 237–60.

Wenham, Gordon. "Towards a Canonical Reading of the Psalms." Pages 333–51 in *Canon and Biblical Interpretation*. Edited by Craig G. Bartholomew et al. Grand Rapids: Zondervan, 2006.

Westermann, Claus. *Praise and Lament in the Psalms*. Translated by Keith R. Crim and Richard N. Soulen. Atlanta: John Knox, 1981.

Whybray, Norman. *Reading the Psalms as a Book*. JSOTSup 222. Sheffield: Sheffield Academic, 1996.

Willgren, David. *The Formation of the 'Book' of Psalms: Reconsidering the Transmission and Canonization of Psalmody in Light of Material Culture and the Poetics of Anthologies*. FAT 2/88. Tübingen: Mohr Siebeck, 2016.

———. "Why Psalms 1–2 Are Not to Be Considered a Preface to the 'Book' of Psalms." *ZAW* 130 (2018): 384–97.

Williams, Rowan. "Augustine and the Psalms." *Int* 58 (2004): 17–27.

Willis, John T. "Psalm 1—An Entity." *ZAW* 9 (1979): 382–401.

Wilson, Gerald H. *The Editing of the Hebrew Psalter*. SBLDS 76. Chico, CA: Scholars, 1985.

———. "Evidence of Editorial Divisions in the Hebrew Psalter." *VT* 34 (1984): 337–52.

———. "The Shape of the Book of Psalms." *Int* 46 (1992): 129–42.

———. "The Structure of the Psalter." Pages 229–46 in *Interpreting the Psalms: Issues and Approaches*. Edited by David Firth and Philip S. Johnston. Downers Grove, IL: InterVarsity Press, 2005.

———. "Understanding the Purposeful Arrangement of Psalms in the Psalter: Pitfalls and Promise." Pages 42–51 in *The Shape and Shaping of the Psalter*. Edited by J. Clinton McCann. JSOTSup 159. Sheffield: JSOT, 1993.

Wilson, Robert D. "The Headings of the Psalms," *PTR* 24 (1926): 353–95.

Witt, Andrew C. "David, the 'Ruler of the Sons of his Covenant' (מושל בבני בריתו): The Expansion of Psalm 151A in 11QPsª." *JESOT* 3 (2014): 77–97.

———. "Hearing Psalm 102 within the Context of the Hebrew Psalter." *VT* 62 (2012): 582–606.

Zenger, Erich, ed. *The Composition of the Book of Psalms*. BETL 238. Leuven/Paris: Peeters, 2010.

Ancient Sources Index

Old Testament

Genesis
  1 180
  1–2 181
  10:6–8 166, 170
  19:24 189
Exodus
  15 118
Numbers
  5:11–28 175
  6:24–26 138, 142
  10:35 132
Deuteronomy
  17:8–13 175
  17:14–20 145
  17:18–20 89–92
  31–32 87
  31:19–21 117, 118
Joshua
  1:6–8 90–92, 102
Judges
  5 118
1 Samuel
  1–2 Sam 1–2, 9, 10, 26, 76, 77, 80,
        108, 109, 121, 122, 124–26,
        129, 158, 160, 163, 166, 168,
        169, 170, 186, 205, 207
  1 147
  1:26–28 118
  2:1–10 117–18
  9:21 170
  15:3 180
  15:19 169

  16 129
  16:18–23 111
  18:29 168
  19:9 111
  19:17 168
  22:19 180
  23:24 168
  23:28 168
  24–26 167, 168, 170, 200
  24:5 168
  24:6 168
  24:10 167
  24:11 168
  24:12 168
  24:13 169
  24:14 169
  24:15 168
  24:16 169
  24:18 168
  24:20 168
  25:3 169
  25:29 168
  25:39 170
  26:8 168
  26:18 168
  26:18–20 168
  26:19 167
  29:6 169
2 Samuel
  1:17–27 111
  3:33–34 111
  4:8 168

226

5 151
5:12 169
6:17–18 148
7 91, 94, 100, 129, 145, 154, 161
7:12–16 99, 100, 169
7:14 100, 128
7:32 169
11 145
11–12 151
12:1 145
12:7–15 152
12:9 169
12:11 145, 169
12:13 145, 151
12:20 148
12:22 151
14:25 170
14:28–15:6 145
15 147, 159
15–18 16, 17, 26, 74, 110, 111, 120,
     122, 125–26, 133, 134, 135,
     136, 143, 152, 154, 155, 156,
     158, 159, 163, 164, 165, 170,
     200, 205, 206
15–20 167
15:1–6 148
15:1–12 147
15:12–17 125
15:14 124, 125, 168
15:25 151
15:25–26 159
15:25–32 125, 126
15:30 151
16 169
16:5–13 148
16:5–14 125
16:6 148
16:7–8 148, 151
16:8 148
16:9 169
16:11 170
16:11–12 146, 148
16:13 169
16:21–22 145
16:23–17:4 147
17:1 125, 126, 168
17:1–3 151
17:11 125
17:16 125, 126

17:22 125
18:5 126, 174
18:9 170
18:19 168, 169
18:31 169
18:31–32 125
18:32 168
18:33 174
19:1 151
19:1–2 125
19:1–8 148
20:21–22 170
21:1 148
22 111, 170
22–23 118
23:1–7 111

1 Kings
2 209
2:2–4 90–91
2:30–33 170
2:44 169
8 118
8:31–32 148, 175, 201
9:4–5 91
11:4–6 92
15:1–5 92
15:5 150
15: 9–11 92

2 Kings
11:12–14 97
14:1–3 92
16:2 92
18:1–3 92
22:1–2 92
23:8–13 147

1 Chronicles
1–2 Chr 9, 76, 113, 163, 166
1:8–10 166
15:16–24 111
15:21 113, 114, 116, 117
16:4–7 111
16:7–36 111
16:16 114
16:31–42 111
23:4 113, 115, 116
23:5 111
25:1–5 111

2 Chronicles
2:1 113

2:17 113
7:6 111
29:26-27 111
29:30 111
34:12-13 113

Ezra

3:8-9 113, 115, 116
3:10-11 111
9:6-15 107

Nehemiah

9:6-37 107
12:24 111
12:46 111

Job

21:18 92

Psalms

Book 1 2, 8, 9, 12, 13, 14, 15, 16,
      129, 158, 203, 209, 210
Book 2 12, 158, 209, 210
Book 3 1, 9, 12, 157, 209
Book 4 2, 12, 157, 158
Book 5 7, 9, 12, 157, 209
Books 1-2 9, 157, 209
Books 1-3 1, 6, 112, 129, 208-9
Books 3-4 209
Books 4-5 1, 7, 9, 112, 157, 208-9
1 6, 7, 79-80, 81, 82-94, 96, 101,
      102, 108, 111, 121, 122, 133,
      147, 177, 184, 200, 204, 205
1-2 2, 6, 8, 9, 10, 12, 16, 17, 18, 19,
      20, 27, 79, 80-103, 105, 108,
      110, 111, 118, 120, 121, 122,
      125, 127-30, 131, 133, 134,
      135, 138, 140, 141, 142, 147,
      152, 154, 158, 161, 162, 164,
      176, 177, 181, 182, 183, 185,
      199, 200, 202, 204, 205, 206,
      207, 208, 210
1-3 8
1-6 164, 177
1-10 16, 17
1-11 56
1-15 46
1-17 18, 19
1-33 42, 43
1-51 56
1-89 1
1:1 80, 82, 92, 101, 102, 127, 129,
      154, 161, 176, 181, 182, 184,

185, 205
1:1-2 82, 83-87, 88, 93
1:1-3 101, 102, 108, 154
1:2 7, 89-92, 99, 101, 143, 162, 181
1:2-3 129, 209
1:3 82, 84, 87-92, 102, 181
1:3-4 92, 93
1:4 92, 127
1:4-5 205
1:4-6 82, 84, 92-93
1:5 92-93, 127, 176, 177
1:5-6 84, 108
1:6 82, 92-93, 101, 102, 127, 176,
      205
2 6, 17, 32, 54, 56, 61-63, 79-80,
      81, 94-103, 108, 111, 121, 122,
      128, 129, 133, 154, 156-57,
      158, 159, 161, 162, 181, 182,
      189, 201, 204, 205, 209, 210
2-3 209
2-89 6
2:1 85, 101, 128, 177
2:1-2 129
2:1-3 94-96, 101, 102, 111, 161,
      162, 191, 205
2:1-6 97
2:2 127
2:3 129, 154
2:4 185
2:4-6 94-96, 160, 204
2:6 102, 129
2:6-7 129, 154
2:7 99-100, 128, 154, 161, 202
2:7-8 129
2:7-9 94-96, 97, 100, 102, 161, 204
2:7-12 182
2:8 181
2:9 127, 129, 142, 159
2:10 142, 177
2:10-12 94, 96, 101, 129, 163, 205
2:11 120, 128
2:11-12 99, 142
2:12 16, 80, 94, 101, 108, 118, 120,
      128, 129, 135, 141, 159, 176,
      181, 189, 199, 204
3 13, 14, 16, 17, 18, 19, 20, 26, 27,
      28, 45-46, 56-57, 58, 69, 74, 80,
      109, 110, 111, 112, 120, 122,
      123-34, 135, 136, 139, 140,

141, 143, 145, 146, 150, 152,
154, 158, 159, 161, 162, 164,
165, 195, 205, 206, 207, 209,
210
3–4 138, 140, 142, 145
3–5 147, 150
3–6 16, 18, 19, 20, 56, 58, 64, 121,
122, 135, 139–43, 147, 150,
152–53, 153–63, 164, 176, 177,
178, 181, 183, 186, 192, 199,
200, 201, 205, 206, 207, 210
3–7 14, 16, 17, 18, 208
3–9 17
3–14 2, 8–22, 24, 26, 28, 47, 80,
104, 105, 108, 112, 119, 122,
164, 165, 170, 171, 182, 183,
199, 203, 205, 206, 209, 210
3–41 2, 12, 203
3–89 112
3:1 123–27, 128, 164, 205
3:2 125, 127, 132, 136, 141, 145,
176, 199
3:2–3 129, 131, 132, 145
3:2–4 131, 132, 140
3:3 125, 129, 130, 131, 132, 140,
141, 159, 176, 187, 207
3:3–6 126
3:4 126, 131, 132, 140, 141, 144,
145, 159, 176
3:4–5 125, 207
3:5 129, 132, 140, 141, 199, 202
3:5–6 132
3:5–7 132, 140
3:6 125, 126, 129, 132, 143, 145,
207
3:6–7 140, 141, 159
3:7 125, 127, 128, 132, 136, 141,
177
3:8 126, 127, 129, 132, 140, 142,
145, 159, 176, 180, 191, 199
3:8–9 140, 141
3:9 13, 125, 129, 133, 140, 141, 145,
177, 199, 202, 207
4 14, 16, 19, 27, 57, 112, 118, 121,
135, 136–38, 141, 144–46
4–5 207
4–6 16, 19, 27, 28, 58, 112, 134–39,
143–52, 165, 207
4:2 136, 140, 141, 145, 176, 199

4:3 141, 144, 146, 176
4:3–6 136, 137, 140, 142, 144
4:3–7 141
4:4 140, 141, 144, 145, 199
4:5 141, 146
4:5–6 141
4:6 141, 199
4:7 137, 140, 141, 144, 145, 146
4:7–9 136, 137, 140
4:8 137, 138, 140, 142, 145
4:8–9 137, 138, 145, 146
4:9 140, 141, 143, 145
5 14, 16, 19, 47, 57–58, 112, 121,
135, 136, 138, 140, 142, 146–
48, 151, 175
5–6 140
5:2 140
5:2–3 138
5:2–4 141, 142
5:2–13 140
5:3 140
5:4 140, 143
5:4–8 138
5:5 138, 142
5:5–6 142
5:5–7 140
5:5–11 141
5:5–12 141
5:6 138, 140, 142, 176, 198
5:6–7 142
5:7 138, 147, 148
5:8 138, 140, 141, 142, 147, 148
5:9 138, 140, 141, 142, 176
5:9–11 142
5:9–13 138
5:10 142, 147
5:10–11 138
5:11 140, 142, 148, 176
5:11–12 141
5:12 141, 142, 176, 199
5:12–13 140, 141
5:13 141, 176
6 14, 16, 19, 47, 58, 112, 116, 121,
135, 136, 138–39, 142, 149–52,
192, 207
6:1–6 150
6:2 150, 151
6:2–4 138, 140, 141
6:2–6 140, 141

6:2–8 141
6:3 140, 150, 160
6:4 140, 141, 152, 176
6:5 138, 140, 141, 151, 176
6:5–6 138, 141
6:6 138, 150
6:7 143, 151
6:7–8 139, 140, 141, 150
6:8 139, 142, 150, 151, 176, 180
6:9 139, 142, 176, 198
6:9–10 140, 142
6:9–11 139, 150, 151
6:10 139, 140, 150
6:11 139, 140, 142, 176, 180
7 14, 16, 17, 18, 19, 20, 27, 28, 47,
    56, 69, 80, 112, 119, 120–21,
    122, 164–78, 179, 180, 181,
    182, 185, 186, 187, 188, 189,
    200, 201, 202, 205, 206, 207,
    210
7–8 180, 182, 183, 185, 190
7–9 16, 20
7–10 186, 187, 206
7–11 190
7–12 192, 195
7–13 195, 196, 199
7–14 16, 18, 19, 20, 64, 121, 160,
    163, 164, 165, 171, 191, 196,
    200, 201, 202, 205, 206, 207,
    210
7:1 164–71, 191, 205
7:2 168, 171, 175, 176, 194, 199
7:2–3 168, 171, 176
7:2–8 173–74
7:3 176, 184
7:3–6 171
7:4 176
7:4–6 168, 171, 175, 176, 180
7:5 169, 175, 176
7:6 176, 181
7:7 176, 177, 180, 185, 191
7:7–8 172
7:7–10 175
7:7–11 169, 171–72, 176
7:7–12 197
7:8 171
7:9 169, 172, 173, 174, 176, 177
7:9–10 174
7:9–11 174

7:10 169, 171, 172, 173, 174, 176,
    184, 190, 197, 198, 199
7:10–17 188
7:11 169, 172, 174, 176, 184, 187
7:11–12 186
7:11–17 173
7:12 176, 177
7:12–14 169
7:12–16 172
7:12–17 172, 174, 200
7:12–18 176
7:13 176
7:13–14 188, 189
7:13–17 171, 173, 186
7:14 182
7:15 169, 184
7:15–16 176
7:15–17 176
7:15–18 169
7:16 184
7:17 169, 170, 172, 175, 184, 194
7:18 16, 20, 172, 174, 175, 176, 179,
    182, 186
8 13, 14, 15, 16, 17, 19, 20, 112,
    121, 178, 179–82, 183, 186,
    188, 198, 200, 201, 202, 210
8–14 19, 28, 112, 164, 165, 177, 178
8:2 16, 20, 179, 182, 186
8:3 164, 179–80, 181, 182, 184, 185,
    190, 191, 194, 198, 199, 200,
    201, 202
8:3–4 180
8:4 179, 180
8:4–9 180, 186
8:5 180, 181, 190
8:5–9 202
8:6 181
8:7–9 181, 198, 201
8:10 16, 20, 179, 182, 186
9 16, 17, 19, 179, 182, 198
9/10 15, 58, 112, 121, 178, 179,
    182–86, 187, 188, 189
9–10 15, 105
9–11 190
9–13 198
9–14 179, 180, 182, 201
9:1–2 194
9:2–3 16, 20, 179, 184, 186
9:2–7 185

9:4 17
9:4–5 185
9:4–7 183
9:4–9 185, 198, 200
9:5 177, 183, 185
9:6–7 185
9:7 17, 184
9:8 177, 183, 185
9:8–9 183
9:8–10 185
9:8–13 185
9:9 177
9:9–10 186
9:10 183, 184, 193
9:10–11 183, 190
9:10–13 185, 199
9:11 184, 185, 194, 197, 199
9:12 183, 184, 185
9:12–13 185, 186
9:13 183, 184, 190
9:13–14 190
9:14–15 183, 185
9:15 183, 186, 194
9:16 183, 184, 185, 188
9:16–17 183, 185, 189
9:16–21 185
9:17 177, 186
9:17–18 186
9:18 183, 197, 198
9:18–19 184, 199
9:18–21 185
9:19 183, 191
9:20 177, 185, 191
9:20–21 183, 185, 186
10 16, 17, 19, 85, 182, 185, 196
10–13 198
10:1 183, 185, 193, 201
10:2 85, 183, 184, 185, 189
10:2–11 183, 185, 188, 194, 200
10:3 85, 184, 197, 198, 199
10:4 184, 196
10:5 177, 183, 198
10:6 184, 194, 196
10:6–7 191
10:7 184, 191
10:7–8 85
10:7–10 196
10:8 185
10:8–10 184

10:9 184
10:10 85
10:11 184, 191, 193, 196
10:12 183, 185, 191
10:12–15 185
10:12–18 199
10:13 183, 184, 191, 196
10:14 183, 186, 194, 197, 199
10:14–15 184
10:14–18 185, 190
10:16 183, 185
10:16–18 185, 186
10:17–18 183, 185, 186
10:18 177
11 14, 18, 19, 58, 121, 178, 186–89,
    190, 191, 196, 197
11–13 196
11–14 14, 16, 17, 183, 186, 206
11–31 16, 17
11:1 187, 194, 199
11:1–3 187, 196
11:2 187, 188, 189
11:3 188, 194
11:4 188, 190, 194
11:4–5 194, 197, 198
11:4–6 200
11:4–7 187
11:7 14, 187, 189, 199
11:8 188
11:9 188
12 14, 19, 112, 121, 178, 189–92,
    196, 197
12–21 56
12:2 190, 191, 192, 197
12:2–3 189
12:2–5 189
12:2–9 199
12:3 190
12:3–4 191
12:4 189, 190
12:5 189, 190, 194, 196
12:6 14, 189, 190, 191, 192, 193,
    194, 195, 198
12:6–7 191
12:6–8 189, 197
12:6–9 191
12:7 189
12:7–8 191
12:8 189, 199

12:9 189, 192, 194, 196, 197
12:13 14
13 14, 19, 121, 178, 192–95, 198
13:1 115
13:1–3 201
13:2 193, 195
13:3 193, 194, 195
13:4 194
13:4–5 194
13:4–6 193
13:5 192, 194, 195
13:6 194, 195, 199
14 13, 14, 18, 19, 20, 121, 178, 190, 195–200
14:1 195, 196, 199
14:1–3 14, 198
14:1–6 83, 200
14:2 197, 198
14:3 195, 197
14:4 195, 198, 199
14:5 197, 199
14:5–6 199
14:5–7 199
14:6 195, 197, 199
14:7 13, 195, 197, 199, 200, 202
15 12, 18, 19, 83, 147, 184
15–17 18, 20
15–24 8, 12, 13, 18
16 12, 18, 19, 46, 63
16–24 47
16–33 46
17 12, 18, 19, 46, 69
18 12, 46, 48, 56, 100, 170
18:1 100
18:51 100
19 12, 89
20 12, 112
21 12
22 12, 30–33, 46, 50, 53–55, 57, 58, 63, 76
22:1 31
22:16 31
22:18 31
22:19 52
23 12, 46
24 12, 46, 69, 147, 184
25 46
25–34 13
25–41 13

26 46, 69
28 46
29 46
30 43, 46, 69
31 46
32 46
32–41 16
32:11 40
33 46
33:2 120
35–41 13
35:5 92
35:28 85
37 37, 45
37–39 37, 204
37:8 40
37:30 85
38 38
38:6 38
38:13 85
39 38, 69
41 8, 63, 156
41:14 12
42–72 12
44:17 65
45 103
49:2–3 136
51 69
51–63 210
51:19 40
52–101 56
52:10 88
53 69, 195, 197
55 69
56 69
58 69
61 69
62:10 136, 137
63:7 85
71:22 120
71:24 85
72 6, 54, 63, 100, 128, 129, 156, 158, 184, 209
72:1–4 100
72:5–7 100
72:8–11 100
72:12–14 100, 181
72:15–17 100
72:18–19 12, 100

72:20 100
73–89 12
76 69
77:13 85
78 174
83:13–15 92
84 69
89 1, 6, 100, 128, 129, 134, 156–57
89:1–38 100
89:20 100
89:21 100
89:22–24 100
89:25 100
89:28 100
89:29 100
89:31–38 100
89:51–52 157–58
89:53 12
90–106 2, 12
90–150 1, 6, 112
90:9 85
92 93
92:13–15 88, 93
98:5 120
101 184
102 7
102–150 56
103:8 40
106 87, 157
106:48 12
107–145 12
108–110 12
109 63, 64
110 63
111–118 42
113–118 12
113:7 40
119 42, 89
120–134 12, 42
124 42
125 69
138–145 12

142:1 209
143:5 85
144 69
144:9 120
145 69
146–150 12
147:7 120
149:3 120
Proverbs
  1:8–33 84–85
  8:4 136
  22:20–21 36
Isaiah
  2:9 137
  11 181
  17:13 92
  32:6 199
Jeremiah
  13:24 92,
  17:1–8 87–88
  44:7 180
Lamentations
  2:11 180
  3:33 136
Ezekiel
  47:12 88–89
  48:35 89
Daniel
  9:4–19 107
Hosea
  1:3 53
Amos
  6:5 111
Jonah
  2 118
Micah
  3:1–3 198
  3:5–9 198
Habakkuk
  3:1 119, 165
  3:19 113, 114

New Testament

Matthew
    19:5 44
    25:31–46 201
Luke
    4:28–30 162
    24:44 53
Acts
    4:23–31 161
    13:32–33 161
Romans
    1:4 161
    6:6 46

    15 49
    15:3–7 48
1 Corinthians
    10:11 53
    12:12 44
Ephesians
    5:31–32 44
Hebrews
    2:10–18 202
    2:15 202
Revelation
    2:26–27 161

Deuterocanonical Books (Apocrypha)

Judith
    9:2–14 107

Sirach
    47:8–10 111

Ancient Jewish Texts

1QM 114
4QBark^c 114
4QHod^a 114
4QpPs^a (4Q171) 103

11QPs^a (11Q5) 111
11QT 114
Aramaic Targum 113

Early Christian Texts

Hippolytus
    Homily on the Psalms 103
Irenaeus
    Apostolic Preaching 32–33

Justin Martyr
    Dialogue with Trypho 30, 31
    First Apology 30, 3

Subject Index

Abishai, 169

Absalom, 16, 17, 19, 26–27, 45, 56–59, 74, 109–11, 120, 122, 125–31, 133–36, 141, 143, 145–52, 154–155, 157–58, 161–63, 164–71, 174–77, 189, 200–1, 205–10

accusation, 15, 120, 130, 133, 137, 143–44, 146–47, 170–72, 176, 178, 192–93

actualization, 6, 15, 26, 31, 34, 40, 45, 50, 69, 99, 100, 118, 123, 130, 133, 135, 153, 161, 163, 175, 193, 202, 205

adversary, 57, 136, 139, 141–42, 145, 179, 199

Ahithophel, 147, 151, 168, 174

analysis, *see* Interpretation

Anatolios, K., 68–69

anthology, *see* Psalms

Aquinas, T., 30, 50–63, 69, 71, 108, 127, 161–62, 203–4

arrangement, *see* Psalms

Athanasius, 30, 60, 64–71, 78, 192, 203

Augustine, 30, 35, 41–47, 50, 55, 57, 64, 69–70, 71, 78, 108, 162, 203–4

Bates, M., 31, 33–34, 44, 47

Bathsheba, 56, 145, 148–51

Bellarmine, R., 168

Bellinger, W., 207–8

Benjaminite, 120, 148, 165–68, 170, 174–78, 185, 190, 200–2, 205–6

Berger, Y., 170–71

Blessed Man, *see* Figure

Calvin, J., 30, 50, 59–63, 64, 69, 71, 78, 86, 108, 149, 161, 167, 203–4

Cameron, M., 43–47, 70

canon, 5, 47, 79, 111, 152, 162, 204

canonical, *see* Context, *see also* Interpretation

catchwords, 20, 207

Charry, E., 173, 177

Childs, B., 5–6, 9–10, 24, 76, 86–87, 99, 104, 109–10, 124, 126, 155, 161–62, 165–66, 175–76, 203, 207–8

Christ, Jesus

  figure of, 45, 47, 50, 54

  kingdom of, 54, 61–62

  members of, 42, 44–45, 61

  person of, 31, 33–34, 39, 43, 143, 153, 202

  prophecy of, 30–34, 43, 45, 62–63, 66, 70, 78, 114

  totus Christus, 41, 43–47, 55, 57–58, 64, 69, 76, 78, 204

  voice of, 31, 34, 48–49, 57–58, 70, 96

Christological, *see* Interpretation

Chrysostom, J., 173–74, 186

church, the, 30, 33, 38–41, 43–47, 49, 53, 55–57, 60–62, 70, 105, 108, 114, 143

cluster, *see* Psalms

Cole, R., 92, 126–27

collective voice, *see* Voice

communal voice, *see* Voice

concatenatio, see Catchwords

confession, 39, 118, 148–49

configuration, 80, 111, 122, 125, 133–34, 146–48, 152, 154, 162, 164, 177, 200, 205

congregation, 66, 75, 76, 82, 92–94

Cooper, A., 153–54

corporate voice, *see* Voice

correspondence, 30–33, 47–50, 70, 80, 90, 101–2, 105, 121, 126, 129, 146, 153–55, 158, 161, 169, 186, 187, 204

context

ancient Israel, 27, 33, 72, 79, 96, 103, 106, 113, 116–17, 142–43, 147, 204

author, 22–24, 29, 30, 53, 69, 72–74, 107, 150, 204

canonical, 2, 5, 6, 11, 23–24, 40, 79, 105, 107, 109, 118, 127, 131, 133, 135, 143, 147, 150, 152, 154–55, 158–59, 168, 176–78, 182, 189, 201, 209

cultic, 4–6, 11, 23, 26–27, 34, 76–77, 79, 82, 87, 96–98, 103–4, 106–7, 111–13, 115–18, 120, 124, 144, 147, 152, 158–59, 175, 179, 195, 204–5, 208–9

final form, 1, 3, 6, 15, 21, 23, 27, 78, 80, 96, 98, 104, 112, 117, 119–20, 135, 152, 155–57, 183, 195, 203–4

historical, 3, 15, 33, 59, 72–74, 77, 105, 109, 204

juristic, 133, 144, 147–48

life of David, *see* David

literary, 11, 21, 23, 26–28, 79–80, 97, 109–10, 121, 131, 133, 164, 189, 192, 195, 203

liturgical, 4, 6, 12, 16, 19, 23, 82–83, 97, 104–5, 118, 124, 130, 144, 149, 165–66, 178, 189

original, 15, 23–24, 27, 49, 77, 97–98, 107, 123–24, 130, 143–44, 147, 152, 158, 175, 189, 195, 205–7

ritual, 5, 76, 97, 149–50, 175, 207

secondary, 5, 27, 148, 174, 176

social, 27, 142–43, 188, 204

Craigie, P., 95, 97, 130, 147, 192

criticism, *see* Interpretation

cult(ic), *see* Context

curse, 27, 28, 85, 148, 151, 161, 169, 175, 184

Cush 19, 120, 165–67, 169–71, 178, 190

David

biographical, 122, 133, 152, 154, 156, 161–64, 177, 200, 205, 210

configuration of, 80, 111, 122, 125,

133–34, 146–48, 152, 154, 162, 164, 177, 200, 205

covenant, 1, 5, 61, 94, 100, 145, 156–58, 160, 163, 209

destiny, 128, 134, 146, 209

dynasty, 2, 6, 9, 90–91, 93, 98–99, 156–58, 160

episodes, 9, 16, 26–27, 72, 74, 76, 80, 104, 110, 121, 123–25, 134, 146, 150–51, 154, 165–68, 170–71, 174, 177, 205–8

failure of, 1–2, 9, 38, 58, 91, 128–29, 156–57, 209–10

figure of, 1–2, 7–10, 23, 26–27, 47, 55, 80, 101–2, 105, 108–12, 118, 120–25, 127, 133–37, 139–40, 144, 146–48, 150, 152–54, 156, 158, 160–65, 171, 174, 176–79, 185–87, 189, 192, 197–207, 209–10

flight of, 17, 111, 125–26, 128, 133, 148, 151–52, 161–62, 165, 168, 189, 196, 205–7, 210

heir of, 49, 64, 67, 80, 99–102, 108, 121, 128, 133–34, 154, 158, 160–63, 178, 201–2, 204–5, 209–10

historical, 1, 27, 80, 99, 129, 134, 154, 204, 209

house of, 5, 106

inner thoughts, 9–10, 109, 124, 150

king, 9, 49, 79, 83, 97, 106, 119, 121, 127–28, 130, 133, 157, 161, 179, 184, 202, 204

life of, 18, 26–27, 71–72, 104–5, 108–9, 123, 147, 149, 152, 155, 158, 167–68, 186, 205, 207–8

line of, 49, 91–92, 128

monarchy, 1, 4, 9, 98, 157, 209

narrative of, 9, 24, 26, 27, 31, 75, 80, 108–11, 121–22, 124–26, 128–29, 133, 146, 148, 150–52, 155–56, 158–59, 166–171, 174, 176, 186, 200, 205, 207–9

portrait of, 1, 27, 48, 109–10, 125, 160, 207

persona of, 101, 110, 121, 122, 133, 147, 152–54, 156, 158, 195, 207

profile of, 80, 122, 155, 205, 208

promises of, 1–2, 6, 9, 77, 91, 99, 128–30, 133–34, 156–57, 163, 205,

209
prophet, 34, 38–40, 47, 49–50, 70, 83
Psalms, of the 26, 110, 153
reign of, 26, 54, 157
Samuel, of 26, 125, 134
story of, 26, 46, 200–1
typical, 122, 134, 154, 158–61, 163–64, 177, 200–1
typological, 122, 134, 154, 161, 163–64, 177
voice of, 2, 9–10, 45, 48, 50, 57–58, 63, 100, 107, 111, 121, 123, 126, 134, 152–56, 158, 160, 163–64, 176, 182, 200, 206–8
Delitzsch, F., 147, 194, 196
deliverance, *see* Salvation
deuteronomic, 85, 91
Deuteronomistic History, 26, 125, 150
diachronic, 14, 15, 27, 177
dialogical analysis, *see* Interpretation
dignity, *see* Honor
distress, 14, 50, 75, 110, 136, 145, 148, 159–60, 176, 192, 200
Drobner, H., 33

editor(s), *see* Psalms
editorial, *see* Psalms
enemy, 15, 17, 48–49, 57–58, 63, 65, 75, 92–93, 100, 125–33, 136–39, 141–42, 145, 150–51, 157–61, 163, 168, 171, 173–74, 176, 179–80, 183, 185–86, 188, 192–94, 199–201, 205, 210
episodes, *see* David
Erasmus, 118–19
Everyman, 75–77, 92, 153, 160, 204
exceeding language, *see* Interpretation
exegetical value, 5, 24, 32, 35–36, 43, 52, 80, 108, 161, 167, 203–4
exemplary, *see* Figure
exile, 6–7, 65, 88, 134, 195, 209
extended figure, *see* Interpretation

fainthearted counselors, 187–89, 196–97
Fiedrowicz, M., 45
figural interpretation, *see* Interpretation
figuration, 48–49, 80, 133–34, 152, 154,
164, 177, 200, 205
figurative interpretation, *see* Interpretation
figure
blessed congregation, 101–2, 121–22, 135, 204
blessed man, 79–80, 87–90, 92–94, 96, 101–2, 108, 118, 121–22, 135, 154, 161, 199, 204–5
bygone, 1–2, 9, 209
David, of, *see* David
exemplar(y), 7, 9, 58–59, 61–62, 69, 76, 92–93, 102, 107, 109, 121, 126, 153–54, 156, 158, 161, 163, 201, 204, 209
function of the, *see* role
historical, 9, 108, 209
ideal, 91–93, 102, 107–8, 122, 133–34, 140, 154, 158, 160–61, 204
illustration, 126
king, of the, 54, 61, 90, 94–97, 108
literary, 1, 7
model, 1, 27, 40, 44, 48–51, 56, 59–62, 64, 66, 68–71, 78, 80, 84, 96, 103, 107–8, 153–54, 159, 161, 176, 182, 198, 201, 203–4, 209
persona(e), 2, 22–24, 26–27, 29–30, 32, 35, 37–39, 44–45, 47, 57–58, 69–72, 74–78, 79–80, 82–83, 93–95, 101–3, 106–10, 121–22, 126, 131, 133, 135, 139, 143–44, 147, 152–54, 156, 158, 160, 163–64, 171, 192, 195, 203–4, 207–8, 211
profile, 74, 80, 122, 125, 139, 150, 155–56, 162, 164, 205–6, 208, 210
role of the, 1, 121
royal, 92–93, 96, 134, 207
type, 30, 37, 47–48, 50, 61–62, 68, 70, 108, 111, 153, 161–63, 209
Fishbane, M., 154–55
frame(work), 6, 12, 14, 16, 25, 27, 37, 44, 62, 89, 125, 133, 179, 185

Gaon, S., 115–16
Gerstenberger, E., 5, 95, 99, 124, 144, 147, 149–50, 204
God, *see* YHWH
Goldingay, J., 95, 168, 177, 193, 207–8
Grant, J., 10–11, 13, 18, 90, 102, 157

Gregory of Nyssa,   40, 56
grouping,   *see* Psalms
Gunkel, H.,   4–5, 20, 75–76, 130

Hannah,   117–18
Hays, R.,   48–50
heading,   *see* Superscription
helpless, the,   40, 85, 161, 180, 184,
   190–91, 194, 196, 198, 201
hermeneutical,   *see* Exegetical
Hilary of Poitiers,   83
historical situation,   *see* Context
honor,   13–14, 119, 128, 131, 141–42,
   144–45, 176, 180–81
Hossfeld F.-L.,   12–16, 18–19, 182–83,
   186, 199
hyperbole,   63, 194

Ibn Ezra, Abraham,   167
imitation,   1–2, 24, 47, 52, 59–61, 63, 78,
   107, 109, 118, 125, 133, 135, 147, 181,
   204–5, 208
imprecation,   *see* Cursing
interpretation
   accommodation,   52–53
   adaptation,   53, 55, 148
   allegorical,   37, 45–46, 57, 62, 75, 162
   canonical,   1, 2–11, 15, 20, 76, 86,
      112, 131, 164, 203, 206
   Christological,   41, 44, 46, 56, 59, 63,
      71, 76, 119, 154, 162
   cult-functional criticism,   1, 3, 5, 23,
      76
   dialogical,   39, 94, 96, 122–23, 131,
      136–39, 144, 171–73, 185, 206
   eschatological,   6, 48–49, 79, 89, 98–
      99, 102, 153, 157, 163, 181, 209–10
   exceeding,   53–55, 98, 127
   figural extension,   2, 30, 47–54, 56–
      58, 62–64, 80, 100–2, 108, 111, 122,
      124, 129, 133–134, 146, 152, 158–59,
      161–64, 177, 200, 204–6, 210
   figurative,   55–57, 87
   form criticism,   1, 3, 4
   historical-critical,   21, 23, 29, 73–74,
      78, 130–31, 133, 147–48, 175
   history of,   2, 22–23, 29, 40–41, 47,
      50–51, 64, 72, 77, 103, 108, 112, 115,
      123, 134, 148, 153–54, 161–62, 166,
      173, 179, 210
   incarnational,   66
   inner-biblical,   76, 80, 87, 89, 94, 102,
      124–26, 134, 155–56, 158
   interfigurality,   27, 125
   intertextuality,   10, 25, 80, 108–10,
      121, 125–26, 148, 155, 206
   literal,   36, 37, 49, 51, 53–60, 62
   moral,   36–37, 46–47, 56–57, 71, 114,
      119
   mystical,   30, 36–37, 46, 55–58
   pressure,   2, 8, 26, 79, 103, 152, 154
   prosopological,   29–35, 38–40, 43–
      44, 47, 49–50, 57, 63–64, 66–67, 69–
      71, 78, 96, 153, 162, 203–4
   type,   *see* Figure, type
   typical,   55–56, 64, 69, 76–78, 90, 111,
      120, 133, 146, 148, 152–54, 158–60,
      163–64, 176–77, 182, 185, 189, 200,
      205–6, 209
   typological,   29–30, 46–51, 54–55,
      57–59, 61–64, 67–68, 70–71, 78, 80,
      96, 111, 120, 133–34, 146, 148, 152–
      54, 158, 160–64, 177, 200–6, 209–10
   typology,   68, 71, 105, 121
Irenaeus,   32–33
Israel, people of,   5–6, 83, 90, 95, 102,
   117, 128, 144, 157–58

Jacobson, R.,   144, 147, 193, 196, 198
Jerome,   41, 52–53, 62, 114
Joab,   166, 170
Johnson, V. L.,   109, 124
justice,   14, 52, 57, 59, 130, 133, 143,
   146–47, 163–64, 173, 177, 179–83,
   185–86, 188, 194, 198, 201
Justin Martyr,   30–33, 50
juxtaposition,   11, 17, 20–21, 94, 101,
   111, 133, 143, 152, 162, 164, 205, 207,
   209

Kellman, S.,   25–26
keyword,   *see* Catchwords
Kraus, H-J.,   117, 123–24, 126, 130, 144,
   146, 175, 195–96

Lefebvre, M.,   81, 87
Levinson, J.,   25
Levites,   89, 103, 113, 115–18

link(s), *see* Catchwords
Longman, T., 137, 188
Luther, M., 72, 116–17

Mandalfo, C., 172–73
man of blood, 138, 142, 148
Maxwell, N., 22–23
Mays, J., 48, 76, 97–98, 126, 145–46, 153–54, 156, 162
McCann, J. C., 98, 190, 199, 207
meditation, 1, 7, 23, 35, 66–68, 81, 84–87, 90, 124, 140, 143, 152, 165, 182, 195
Messiah, 34, 47–50, 73, 108, 134, 153, 162
messianic, *see* Interpretation
Midrash, 16–17, 115, 128, 155
Millard, M., 16–17, 19, 27
Miller, P., 90, 163, 183
Mitchell, D., 211
model, *see* Figure
modern interpretation, *see* Interpretation
Moses, 7, 83, 85–87, 90–91, 97, 104, 117–18, 166
Mowinckel, S., 4–5, 23, 34–35, 75, 106–7, 111, 120, 204

Nabal, 169–70
Nasuti, H., 159–60
nations, the, 59, 68, 79, 94, 96, 101–2, 111, 127–28, 130, 159, 161, 177, 181–86, 188, 199, 202
needy, the, 177, 181, 183–84, 189–92, 195, 197, 200–1, 206
neighboring psalms, *see* Psalms
Nogalski, J., 109–11

onlookers, 123, 139, 142–43
Oorschot, J. van, 107
opponents, 123, 136, 138–41, 145, 151, 180, 187, 189, 198
oppressors, 130, 185, 187, 198, 200, 202
Origen, 30, 35–42, 50, 64, 69, 71, 203–4

paradigmatic, 14, 49, 90, 200, 207, 209–10
penitence, *see* Repentance
period,
    exilic, 14, 72, 98, 156, 195

Hellenistic, 14–15, 186
Maccabean, 3, 72
post-exilic, 3, 7, 14–15, 72, 98–99, 107, 117, 185, 204, 208–10
pre-exilic, 1, 4–5, 14, 72, 204, 208–10
persecution, 6, 13–15, 24, 46, 56–57, 69, 74, 110, 144, 146, 155, 161–62, 168, 180, 184, 187, 192
persona, *see* Figure, *see* Voice
persona theory, 22–23
Peterson, E., 81–82
Pitkin, B., 61, 63, 161
poor, the, 13–15, 40, 85, 136, 144, 164, 177–78, 181–84, 186, 188–92, 195–97, 199–201, 206
prefiguration, 48–49
pressure, *see* Interpretation
profile, *see* David, *see* Figure
prosopological exegesis, *see* Interpretation
prosopopoeia, 32–34, 44, 63, 95–96, 105
Psalms,
    anthology, 2, 79, 87
    arrangement, 5, 11, 152
    author, 3, 8, 22–25, 27, 29–30, 33–34, 44, 52–53, 59, 69, 72–74, 79, 81, 83, 85, 91, 96, 103, 105–7, 111, 116, 127, 150, 153, 171, 202, 204
    cluster, 8, 11, 13, 16, 18–21, 26–28, 121–22, 135–36, 139, 143, 152, 159, 163–64, 178, 182, 186, 194, 199, 206–7, 210
    context, *see* Context
    democratization, 88, 118, 133, 135
    editor(s), 3, 5–6, 8, 10–11, 13, 15, 17–18, 20–21, 23–24, 49, 65, 79–80, 98, 101–3, 108, 121, 123, 134, 147, 152, 155–58, 161, 186, 201, 209
    group, 8, 11–16, 18–21, 27, 64, 96, 122, 150, 164–65, 193, 199–200, 205, 207, 210
    lament, 2, 12–14, 16, 20, 39, 48–49, 75–76, 119–20, 123, 139–40, 143, 159, 163, 173, 194–95, 209
    praise, 2, 6, 20, 35, 46, 48, 51, 56, 59, 61, 65, 100, 103, 113, 118, 120, 142, 156, 172–74, 179–80, 182, 186, 194, 200, 202

pre-scriptural, 96–97, 105, 107, 118–19, 123, 147

purpose of, 1, 6, 8, 11, 21, 26–27, 49, 51, 79, 96–98, 101, 104, 109–10, 117, 156, 158, 181

sequence, 11, 17, 21, 143, 147, 150, 152–53, 177, 206

shape of, 5–6, 8–13, 15–16, 18, 20, 40, 80–81, 93, 98, 105, 108, 110, 127, 129, 155, 176–77, 203, 208

social aspect, *see* Context

voicing of, *see* Voice

Rahlfs, A., 75

Rashi, 115

redaction, 6, 14–15, 17, 101, 104, 107, 177, 182–83

repentance, 7, 9, 38, 40, 46, 56, 58–59, 67, 102, 116, 134, 149, 156, 171, 174, 184, 187, 192, 200–1, 206

rescue, *see* Salvation

Reuchlin, J., 116–17

righteous, the, 13, 15, 40, 48–49, 79–80, 82–84, 88, 92–94, 101–3, 108, 118–19, 121, 129, 133, 135, 138, 140–42, 146–47, 151, 159, 169, 171–73, 175, 177, 179, 181, 183–84, 186, 188–89, 196, 198–99, 204–6, 209

Rule of Jerome, 52–53, 62

rumination, 82, 85–87, 89–90, 101–2, 162, 181–82, 185–86, 198, 200, 206

Russell, S. H., 62

Ryan, T., 51

Sailhamer, J., 196–97

salvation, 1, 36, 46, 48, 50, 56, 59, 66, 77, 93, 99–100, 129, 131–34, 140–41, 145, 151, 156–60, 162–63, 168, 171, 176, 183, 185–87, 190–91, 194–95, 197, 199–202, 208

Sarna, N., 81

Saul, 56, 59, 129, 166–71, 174, 176, 189, 200–1

Seitz, C., 48, 50, 62, 100–1, 126–27, 129

semantic transformation, 96–98, 100, 108, 117, 119, 131, 146–48, 150, 152, 174, 209

sense, *see* Interpretation

sequence, *see* Psalms

setting, *see* Context

Seybold, K., 130, 144

Sheba, 170

Sheppard, G., 96–98, 101, 107, 160

Shimei, 148, 151, 169–71, 175

situation, *see* Context

Sitz im Leben, 4, 11, 21, 23, 76–77, 123, 130, 144, 146, 148, 150, 158, 206–7

Smend, R., 75

Smith, M., 208–9

Solomon, 54, 73, 83, 91–92, 100, 104, 118, 148, 158, 162, 169, 208–9

Sommer, B., 86–87

soul, 36–37, 66, 74, 187

anatomy of the, 60

cure of the, 38, 40, 53

emotions of the, 67–70

journey of the, 36–38, 40, 42, 204

mirror of the, 64, 70

perfection of the, 40, 47, 70, 114

speaker, *see* Figure, *see* Voice

Steinmetz, D., 59–60

Suderman, D., 143

superscription(s), 9–10, 12, 16, 18–19, 24–27, 45, 56–57, 71, 73, 76–77, 97, 100, 103–4, 106, 108–9, 111–13, 115–16, 119–21, 123–25, 134, 139, 150, 158, 161, 165–66, 170–71, 178, 207, 210

ancient literary, 18–20, 25–26, 80, 105, 119, 134, 165–66, 178

artefact, 111, 116

ascription, 27, 73, 106, 111, 116, 122, 206

association, 12, 18–20, 26, 104–6, 108, 111–12, 115–16, 120, 127, 134, 139, 145, 150, 152, 154, 165–66, 192, 205, 211

authorship, 24, 73, 103, 106, 111, 116

biographical, 1, 6, 9–10, 16–20, 24, 26–28, 45, 56–57, 71, 74, 76–77, 80, 104–112, 119–25, 127, 129, 133–35, 143, 145–48, 150, 152–67, 170, 177–78, 188, 200–1, 203, 205–10

collection, 103, 111, 208, 210

leader, 104–6, 112–119, 134, 136, 178

liturgical, 12, 19, 104, 165–66, 178

musical, 19–20, 26, 71, 80, 104–5, 112–21, 134–35, 166, 178

orienting role, 25, 112, 122, 135, 152, 164–65, 171, 178, 182, 185–86, 205–10

performance, 5, 19–20, 104, 113, 117–18, 135

synchronic, 15, 105

temple, 4, 12, 23, 34, 72, 88–89, 92, 96, 102, 106–7, 111, 113, 115–18, 126, 130, 144, 146–49, 175, 188, 207–8

Terrien, S., 194

Theodore of Mopsuestia, 52–53, 54, 55, 149

titles, *see* Superscription

Torah, 12, 84–87, 89, 90–91, 129, 143, 162–63

  David, of 85

  Moses, of 7, 85–86, 90–91, 97

  YHWH, of 80, 82, 84–90, 92–93, 99, 101, 122, 177, 181

Torjesen, K., 36

Two Ways, the, 79, 82–83, 92, 96, 141–42, 199, 206

typical interpretation, *see* Interpretation

typological exegesis, *see* Interpretation

Uriah, 56, 145, 148, 150–51

voice,

  another person, 31, 35, 38, 44, 49

  biographical, *see* Superscription

  Body, *see* Church

  Christ, *see* Christ

  Church, *see* Church

  communal, 75–77, 138, 154, 179

  David, *see* David

  didactic, 79, 83, 93, 172–73, 189

  extended, *see* Interpretation

  historical, 23, 78, 100

  king, 95–96, 100, 163

  literary, 2, 22, 207

  prophetic, 71, 83, 94

  psalmist, 29, 83, 95–96, 103

  sinner, 38, 46

  speaking, 23, 43, 100

  typical, *see* Interpretation

  without end, 10, 129, 163, 176, 203

YHWH, *see* YHWH

vulnerable, the, 162, 179–81, 185–86, 194, 198, 200

Watts, J. W., 118

weak, the, 141, 179–81, 183, 185–86, 190, 198, 200–1, 206

Weber, B., 156

Weiser, A., 81, 193

Wenham, G., 10–11

Westermann, C., 5

Wette, W. M. L. de, 3, 29, 72–75, 77, 204

Whybray, N., 20–21

wicked, the, 79, 82–85, 92–94, 101–2, 121, 127–29, 138, 140–42, 147, 159, 162–63, 169, 171–72, 175, 177, 181–94, 196–99, 202, 205–6

Wilcock, M., 147–48, 150

Willgren, D., 81, 111–12

Williams, R., 42

Wilson, G. H., 6–7, 9, 11, 20, 21, 155–57, 191, 196–97, 203, 208

wisdom, 6, 82–85, 88, 94, 182, 195

Witt, A., 128, 157

YHWH,

  anointed of, 98, 128, 131, 145, 154, 202

  attributes of, 140, 172

  commitment of, 6, 9, 180, 183–84, 186, 188–89, 192, 194, 197, 199–200, 206

  faithfulness of, 1–2, 9, 100, 193

  house of, 88, 113, 116, 138

  judge, as, 14, 95, 140, 169, 173, 175, 183, 185, 197

  judgment of, 92, 146, 171, 179, 182–83, 185–87, 197–98

  mercy of, 141, 157

  name of, 20, 179–80, 200

  presence of, 88–89, 92, 102, 132, 142, 147–48, 181, 193, 199

  protection of, 130, 144–45, 180, 185, 188–89, 192, 198–99

  providence of, 47, 81, 89, 93, 129, 142, 145, 147, 182, 186, 188–89, 201, 205, 210

  refuge in, 94, 101–2, 108, 118, 129, 133, 135, 176, 187, 204

reign of, 4, 14, 94, 96, 99, 102, 129,
    151, 161, 183, 189, 191, 200, 206,
    209
relationship with, 15, 21, 131, 134,
    139–40, 193
salvation of, *see* Salvation
steadfast love of, 140, 156
support of, 13, 93, 133, 142, 145, 179,
    186, 206
trust in, 24, 57, 79, 81, 88–89, 108,
    120, 125, 129, 131, 141, 156–58, 160,
    168, 178, 181, 187, 189, 194, 196,
    199, 210
verdict of, 144, 146, 175, 195, 197–98
voice of, 83, 95–96, 189, 191–92, 195,
    198–99
way of, 82, 141, 164, 181–82, 192

Zenger, E., 12–16, 18–19, 182–83, 186,
    199
Zion, 7, 13, 79, 94–95, 97, 99, 102, 129–
    30, 154, 157, 159, 161, 181, 183–84,
    197, 199, 202